MEMPHIS UNDER
THE PTOLEMIES

MEMPHIS UNDER THE PTOLEMIES

DOROTHY J. THOMPSON

PRINCETON UNIVERSITY PRESS

Copyright © 1988 by Princeton University Press
Published by Princeton University Press, 41 William Street, Princeton, New Jersey 08540
In the United Kingdom: Princeton University Press,
Guildford, Surrey

LIBRARY OF CONGRESS CATALOGING-IN-PUBLICATION DATA
Thompson, Dorothy J., 1939–
Memphis under the Ptolemies / Dorothy J. Thompson.
p. cm.
Bibliography: p.
Includes index.
ISBN 0-691-03593-8 (alk. paper)
1. Memphis (Ancient city)—Civilization. 2. Ptolemaic
dynasty, 305–30 B.C.   I. Title.
DT73.M5T46 1988
932—dc19   88-12654

Publication of this book has been aided by the
Whitney Darrow Fund of Princeton University Press

This book has been composed in Linotron Bembo

Clothbound editions of Princeton University Press books are printed on
acid-free paper, and binding materials are chosen for strength
and durability. Paperbacks, although satisfactory for personal
collections, are not usually suitable for library rebinding

Printed in the United States of America by Princeton University Press,
Princeton, New Jersey

FOR JOHN

CONTENTS

LIST OF ILLUSTRATIONS AND TABLES

PLATES
(following page 154)

Please see the Acknowledgments for sources.

FIGURES

TABLES

PREFACE

This book has been long in the making. It owes its origin to a conversation at the Ramleh tram station in Alexandria on 6 January 1964, and research on it started in 1966. Much has intervened. Most importantly, over the years I have come to realize the importance of the history and culture of Egypt for an understanding of Ptolemaic history. For those, like myself, with a background in classical history, introduced to Hellenistic Egypt through the Greek papyri, a Helleno-centric viewpoint is hard to shed. In learning to appreciate the continuing importance of Egyptian traditions in that country following its conquest, I have been fortunate in my mentors, and I should like to express my gratitude. To list them all is not possible, but from Jan Quaegebeur, J. D. Ray, and H. S. Smith I have learned much. Above all I have learned from Willy Clarysse, whose knowledge of both cultures is constantly illuminating. Together with R. S. Bagnall, A. K. Bowman, John A. Thompson, and Frank W. Walbank, he has read and commented on the manuscript leading to this book; the final form owes much to improvements of all these readers, but especially those of Clarysse. The usual proviso, on my sole responsibility for what is here, of course applies.

A further result of the delay in completing this book has been an increase of interest in the ancient city of Memphis and its physical remains. How much I owe to its excavators and surveyors, to Harry Smith and David Jeffreys who started at Saqqara and have now moved on to the valley city of Memphis, should be clear from the references in my text and the maps which accompany it. What cannot appear in this way is the high degree of friendship and kindly cooperation I have constantly met from all those involved in the Memphis project. Both in my visit to the site in 1978 and since, in response to constant inquiries, they and others of the team have continued to help me. C.A.R. Andrews, Janine Bourriau, M. J. Price, and J. B. Segal should be mentioned in this context.

A stranger to the Egyptian languages, I have troubled friendly demoticists to a point where others would despair; they are a long-suffering and sympathetic group of scholars. Jan Quaegebeur and John Ray have probably suffered the most, but P. W. Pestman too has saved me from some howlers. F. de Cenival, W. J. Tait, S. P. Vleeming, and K.-Th. Zauzich have all answered my queries. R. L. Vos allowed me to use and quote his thesis on the embalming of the Apis bull, and Cary Martin has made available his transcripts of the Malcolm papyrus; it has been a pleasure to discuss related problems with him. On the Greek side, P. J. Sijpesteijn has shared with me his research on the Memphis harbor toll receipts. To all I offer my thanks.

Institutional support has also been important to the writing of this book. Girton College has employed me throughout, and supported my sabbaticals. In essence the book was written in 1982–83 when I was a visiting member at the Institute for Advanced Study at Princeton; here I found peace and quiet, together with stimulus from others there. I should like further to acknowledge grants during that year from the Fulbright Commission and Volkswagen Company. Personal support, however, is the most important of all. For that the dedication of this book to my husband is a minimal way of expressing my heartfelt thanks.

Cambridge, England
February 1988

ACKNOWLEDGMENTS

PLATES

Photographs have been provided by the following, with whose kind permission they are published here:

i   Les Musées Nationaux, Paris (Palais du Louvre)

ii   Fitzwilliam Museum, Cambridge (inv. no. 6041-11)

iii Egyptian Museum, Cairo

iv Institut Français d'Archéologie Orientale, Cairo (pl. II, *BIFAO* 25, 1925)

v   Staatliche Museen zu Berlin, Hauptstadt der DDR, Ägyptisches Museum (inv. no. 2118)

vi Egyptian Museum, Cairo

vii Forschungszentrum Griechisch-Römisches Ägypten der Universität Trier, FRG

viii Les Musées Nationaux, Paris (Palais du Louvre)

FIGURES

Figures 1–4 were kindly drawn by D. G. Jeffreys, who is currently excavating Memphis. Figure 5 is based on Quaegebeur (1980a), 64–73, and figure 6 on Otto (1956), Quaegebeur (1971b), and Wildung (1969). For figures 7–10, see chapter 5.

APPENDIXES

I should like to acknowledge the kind help of H. S. Smith and C.A.R. Andrews with the cow names in Appendix D, and of P. J. Sijpesteijn for additions to Appendix E. His full study of these and other customs house receipts should soon be available.

ABBREVIATIONS

In reference to collections of Greek papyri, I regularly use the abbreviations of John F. Oates, Roger S. Bagnall, William H. Willis, and K. A. Worp, *Checklist of Editions of Greek Papyri and Ostraca*, 3d ed. Bulletin of the American Society of Papyrologists, Supplement no. 4 (Scholars Press, 1985). For demotic papyri I have generally adopted those of P. W. Pestman, *Chronologie égyptienne*, Pap. Lugd. Bat. 15 (Leiden, 1967). For classical authors the form of *The Oxford Classical Dictionary*, ed. N.G.L. Hammond and H. H. Scullard, 2d ed. (Oxford, 1970), is employed. Other abbreviations are as follows:

ABAW	*Abhandlungen der Bayerischen Akademie der Wissenschaften.* Philos.-hist. Klasse. Munich, 1909–.
ANS	American Numismatic Society.
APAW	*Abhandlungen der Preussischen Akademie der Wissenschaften.* Philos.-hist. Klasse. Berlin, 1908–44.
APF	*Archiv für Papyrusforschung und verwandte Gebiete.* Leipzig, 1900–.
ARCE	American Research Center in Egypt. Cairo.
ASAE	*Annales du Service des Antiquités d'Egypte.* Cairo, 1900–.
BASP	*Bulletin of the American Society of Papyrologists.* New Haven, Conn., 1963–.
BICS	*Bulletin of the Institute of Classical Studies of the University of London.* London, 1954–.
BIFAO	*Bulletin de l'Institut Français d'Archéologie Orientale.* Cairo, 1901–.
BSFE	*Bulletin de la Société Français d'Egyptologie.* Paris, 1949–.
Brooklyn Inscriptions	K. Herbert, *Greek and Latin Inscriptions in the Brooklyn Museum.* Brooklyn, N. Y., 1972.
CE	*Chronique d'Egypte.* Brussels, 1925–.
EES	Egypt Exploration Society. London.
EVO	*Egitto e Vicino Oriente.* Pisa, 1978–.

GLECS	*Comptes rendus du groupe linguistique d'études chamito-sémitiques.* Paris, 1934–.
GM	*Göttinger Miszellen.* Göttingen, 1972–.
GRBS	*Greek, Roman and Byzantine Studies.* Cambridge, Mass., 1959–.
Hellenica	L. Robert, *Hellenica: Recueil d'épigraphie, de numismatique et d'antiquités grecques 1–13.* Limoges, Paris, 1940–65.
IFAO	L'Institut Français d'Archéologie Orientale. Cairo.
I. Fay.	E. Bernand, *Recueil des inscriptions grecques du Fayoum,* I, Leiden, 1975; II and III, Cairo, 1981.
IGR	*Inscriptiones Graecae ad res Romanas pertinentes.* 4 vols. Paris, 1906–27.
ILS	H. Dessau, *Inscriptiones latinae selectae,* 3d ed. 3 vols. (in 5). Berlin, 1963.
I. Philae	A. Bernand, *Les inscriptions grecques de Philae,* I, *Epoque ptolémaique.* Paris, 1969.
I. Priene	F. Hiller von Gaertringen, *Inschriften von Priene.* Königliche Museen zu Berlin. Berlin, 1906.
JARCE	*Journal of the American Research Center in Egypt.* Boston, 1962–.
JDAI	*Jahrbuch des Deutschen Archäologischen Instituts.* Berlin, 1886–.
JEA	*Journal of Egyptian Archaeology.* London, 1914–.
JHS	*Journal of Hellenic Studies.* London, 1880–.
JJP	*Journal of Juristic Papyrology.* New York, Warsaw, 1946–.
JNES	*Journal of Near Eastern Studies.* Chicago, 1942–.
JRS	*Journal of Roman Studies.* London, 1911–.
LÄ	*Lexikon der Ägyptologie,* ed. W. Helck and E. Otto. Wiesbaden, 1975–.
LCM	*Liverpool Classical Monthly.* Liverpool, 1976–.
MAS	*Münchener Ägyptologische Studien.* Munich, 1970–.
MDAIK	*Mitteilungen des Deutschen Archäologischen Instituts* (Abt. Kairo). Wiesbaden, 1956–.
OGIS	W. Dittenberger, *Orientis graeci inscriptiones selectae.* 2 vols. Leipzig, 1903–5.
OLA	*Orientalia Lovaniensia Analecta.* Louvain, 1975–.

OMRO	*Oudheidkundige Mededelingen uit het Rijksmuseum van Oudheden te Leiden.* Leiden, 1907–.
PCPhS	*Proceedings of the Cambridge Philological Society.* Cambridge, Eng., 1882–.
PP	W. Peremans and E. Van 't Dack, *Prosopographia Ptolemaica.* Studia Hellenistica 6 (1950)–.
Pestman, *Rec.*	P. W. Pestman (with J. Quaegebeur and R. L. Vos), *Receuil de textes démotiques et bilingues.* 3 vols. Leiden, 1977.
RE	*Pauly-Wissowa Realencyclopädie der klassischen Altertumswissenschaft.* Stuttgart, 1894–.
REG	*Revue des Etudes Grecques.* Paris, 1888–.
RIDA	*Revue Internationale des Droits de l'Antiquité.* Brussels, 1948–.
RPh	*Revue de Philologie de Littérature et d'Histoire Anciennes.* Paris, 1845–.
RecTrav	*Recueil de Travaux Relatifs à la Philologie et à l'Archéologie Egyptiennes et Assyriennes.* Paris, 1870–1923.
SBAW	*Sitzungsberichte der Bayerischen Akademie der Wissenschaften.* Philos.-hist. Klasse. Munich, 1860–.
TAPhA	*Transactions of the American Philological Association.* Boston, etc., 1869–.
YClS	*Yale Classical Studies.* New Haven, Conn., 1928–.
ZÄS	*Zeitschrift für Aegyptische Sprache und Altertumskunde.* Leipzig, 1863–.
ZPE	*Zeitschrift für Papyrologie und Epigraphik.* Bonn, 1967–.

A NOTE ON TRANSLITERATION

Classical historians commonly include in their preface a statement disclaiming consistency in their transliteration from Greek. I must follow this practice. I usually adopt the Greek spelling in transliteration, but when another form is better known—for example, Ptolemy—I have sometimes used that. Further, I am irregular in marking vowel lengths, aiming, however, to do this for lesser-known names. With Egyptian and Arabic transcriptions there is even less consistency. Until recently scholars employed many different forms of transcription and, in spite of the best of intentions and much help from friends, I am aware that many of these variations have persisted in my text.

MEMPHIS UNDER
THE PTOLEMIES

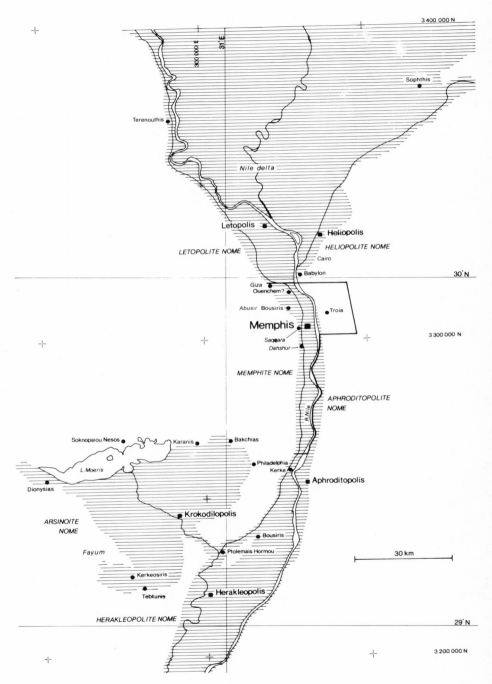

FIGURE I. Memphis and the Memphite nome.

I

THE SECOND CITY

For much of its history Memphis was the first city of Egypt. Founded shortly before 3000 B.C., it was the Old Kingdom capital of the country from the time of the union of the two lands, serving as royal residence from the early second dynasty (from *c.* 2890 to 2173 B.C.). In a nodal position some 40 kilometers south of the Delta apex, Memphis lay at a key point on the Nile, the main artery of the country (see fig. 1). It also lay on the direct route into Egypt from the northeast, down along the Pelusiac branch of the Nile, and at the eastern end of the caravan routes both from the Fayum to the southwest and, less importantly, from Siwah and the other oases of the western desert. A fresh water supply combined with its geographical position to make Memphis an obvious capital.[1] Alternating with Thebes (the home of Amon) and occasionally with northern cities in the Delta, Memphis (home of Ptah, the creator god) served regularly as the military, administrative, sacral, and economic center to the country.[2] Indeed, the Greek name for the country as a whole, *Aigyptos*, derives from one of the Egyptian names for the city, *Hekaptah* "the palace of the spirit (*ka*) of Ptah." For outside observers Memphis might be synonymous with Egypt.[3]

Differing at various periods of its history, the names of Memphis— "the Balance of the Two Lands," "the Life of the Two Lands (*'Anchtawy*)," "the White Wall (*Leukon Teichos*)"—reflect different aspects of the city, its geographic centrality, and its physical features. The name *Mnnfr*, the Greek Memphis, is in origin "the pyramid city of Pepi I,"[4] and the identity of the city as a necropolis settlement, a pyramid center, is one of its more important aspects. Memphis was a city of the dead as much as of the living. "The most favored of Egyptian cities in its position," "the

[1] Hamdan (1961), 124.

[2] For the pre-Ptolemaic history of the city, see Diod. Sic. 1.50–51 with Kees (1931), 660–64; Badawi (1948); Smith (1974), 3–5.

[3] Kees (1961), 157, for the name. Plutarch, *DIO* 66 (*Mor.* 377c), with the Nile and Buto; Lucan 3.222; Froidefond (1971), 232; Smelik and Hemelrijk (1984), 1928–29.

[4] See Smith (1974), 7–8; the etymology of Plutarch, *DIO* 20 (359b), is muddled, see Griffiths (1970), 364–65.

3

oldest and the most royal of cities," it had been "the royal citadel" for much of its past.[5] And, as residence of Pharaoh, Memphis served as a regular army base. Above all, however, this city "which gave birth to god(s)"[6] was a sacred city, the home of Ptah and of his emanation Apis, where cult encouraged culture and the *Theology of Ptah* was developed in the same environment as a flourishing native literature.[7] The treasury of Ptah served as the central treasury of the kingdom,[8] the garrison in the city as the royal bodyguard, and the dockyards as the home of the royal navy. And even when Thebes was the royal residence, Memphis remained an important administrative center for the north of Egypt. When invaders challenged the country, it was for Memphis that they aimed (Alexander, Perdiccas, or Antiochus IV), and when tourists visited Egypt the sights of Memphis were of high priority. The city was known outside Egypt, more widely in the Mediterranean. Visiting scholars were traditionally attracted to the city—Eudoxos, for instance, was instructed by the Memphite Chonouphis, as, indirectly, was Agesilaos[9]—and, when late in its history the Greeks were keen to stress its hellenic connections, they made it the home of Epaphos and of Danaos.[10] Memphis as a place of learning and inspiration is a recurrent theme of classical writers.[11]

The city therefore may be viewed in many ways, as a center of administration, a royal residence, or a garrison city, as a burial center or as a city of temples, as a port serving both as a market and as a center of production. Importantly too, it was the home of a diverse and mixed population. And when Alexander the Great conquered Egypt in 332 B.C. it was from Memphis that the city was governed. It was to this city that his general Ptolemy, son of Lagos, brought the conqueror's corpse on Alexander's death in 323 B.C. From here, too, Ptolemy ruled in his early years as satrap before becoming king. The later removal of Alexander's remains to Alexandria symbolized a change of capital for the new regime, and it was from Alexandria that Ptolemy ruled as king. Now, under these new Macedonian pharaohs, Memphis was once again the second city.[12]

---

[5] Diod. Sic. 15.43; Ath. 1.20c, for a dancer named after the city; Pliny *HN* 5.9.50 *quondam arx Aegypti regum.*

[6] *P. Oxy* 2332.531, *theotokos Memphis*; the otherwise Christian imagery is striking.

[7] Lichtheim (1973), 51–57.

[8] Bresciani (1958), 135.

[9] Plut. *DIO* 10 (*Mor.* 354e); *Mor.* 578f.

[10] Aesch. *Supp.* 311; Fraser and Maas (1955), 115.

[11] E.g., Lucan 1.639; 6.449; 8.475–79, Acoreus.

[12] On the date of this move, *c.* 320 or 312 B.C., see Fraser (1972), 2.11–12; Strabo 17.1.32, *polis . . . deutera.*

It is not possible to write a proper history of Memphis under the Ptolemies. Given the fragmentary and chance nature of surviving evidence, a coherent narrative of the city's role in the military or political events of the Ptolemaic kingdom cannot be reconstructed, nor can one provide as comprehensive an account of its social and economic life as one would wish. What is attempted here is rather a historical study of those particular aspects of the city and its population that may be illuminated from what survives. The city provides a framework for the understanding of what might otherwise seem disparate and unconnected fragments of information. Bound by the limits not only of what has survived but more particularly by the general lack of an intelligible context for much of it, the student of Ptolemaic Egypt is often reduced to mere description of what there is.[13] And without a context such description often stands alone, devoid of significance. In this study, the role of the city is to provide a unifying context for material relating to various aspects of life in Egypt under the Ptolemies. Throughout, my concerns are with the effects on the country and its population of the conquest of Alexander and of the imposition of Greco-Macedonian rule; with the effects more particularly on the city of Memphis of the foundation of a new Greek capital on the coast and all that this involved in terms of the balance of population within Egypt; and, finally, with the consequences of the introduction of new, immigrant outlooks and of the changed economic focus within the country. The context is important, for cities in Egypt were very different from those familiar to Mediterranean immigrants from the north.

The city itself is the backdrop. Both the physical makeup of the city and the economic activities of Memphis and the surrounding Memphite nome form preliminary subjects for discussion. In considering the various elements which made up the city's population, the different ethnic communities as well as the native Egyptians, and the Greeks and Macedonians who now formed the ruling class, I hope to convey some of the realities of life in the mixed community of the city and the problems which arose from the change in the country's rule. Some adaptations are quickly made while others take a longer time. Within the different groups in the city we may chart some of these, as well as the different areas of life in which they took place.

In its long history Memphis had at times served as both secular and spiritual capital of the country. The power of the temples was strong, and

[13] Cf. Finley (1985), 61–66, for an extreme expression.

religion played a central role in the life of the Egyptians. Whether or not this centrality was greater in extent or intensity than in other societies, religion and cult in Egypt were certainly different in the forms they took. In charting the changing relations of the temples of Memphis to the new Ptolemaic rulers of the land, I hope to show how it worked on the ground in one small, though important, part of the whole.

The following study of one connected group—those involved primarily in human mummification, in the transformation of man into god as the human corpse became Osiris—is possible here only because of the survival of a family archive. Through such a detailed Memphite study I hope to show not only the economic basis of this particular group within society but also the sort of changes over time which must have occurred elsewhere during the three centuries of Ptolemaic rule. Besides the mummification of men, that of animals played an important part in both the religious and economic life of the city. The organization of some of the Memphite cults is examined in an attempt to retrieve the part they played in the lives not only of the inhabitants of the city but also of tourists and pilgrims. Being central in both the city and necropolis, the cult of the Apis bull may be used as a standard for other cults. Finally comes an analysis, again made possible by the survival of a papyrological archive, of life within the "House of the deified Apis," Apis-Osiris, that temple area known to the Greeks as the Sarapieion, which was the major cult center of the necropolis for the city. This is a peculiarly Memphite study. It may, however, serve to illustrate some of the social and economic problems that arose from political weakness during the reigns (both joint and separate) of the two sons of Ptolemy V Epiphanes, together with some aspects of the Greco-Egyptian mix in society, which at certain levels and in various contexts was developing at this time. The changing relations between Hellenism and the traditions of Egypt provide a constant fascination. Yet further change, combined with some continuity, is the theme of the final epilogue, a brief overview of the fate of the city once the Romans had taken over.

EGYPTIAN CITIES

Throughout history, Egyptian cities have depended on the Nile and on its annual flood both for communications and for their economic base. Generally situated on the banks of the river, it was along the Nile that they enjoyed contact with other areas within Egypt, with Nubia to the south, and downstream with Syria to the northeast and northwards to the Aegean. Of more immediate importance was the city's agricultural base, the crops that served to feed it and which in turn depended on the flood of the Nile, that annual inundation which made Egypt by far the richest of those lands that border the Mediterranean. Given this close dependence on the river, both port facilities and irrigation works were regular features of such cities.

The annual flood, in Egyptian eyes, depended on divine approval of the state of the land and its rule. The importance of the role of the pharaoh in securing this approval was matched by his dominant position within the administration of the country. The country was governed centrally, and cities had no independent rule of their own. These basic facts of government were to be found reflected also in the physical layout of cities. As in Greek cities, temples were a regular feature of the Egyptian city, but in city centers there were no assembly points for citizens to meet on public business. Instead, in the capital and other important centers like Memphis, Thebes, or Sais, besides the offices of the central administration a palace might be found, a place where the king might stay in comfort when visiting his subjects. For the living quarters of Egyptian cities, crowded together on land not reached by the flood, were generally cramped and full of people, so that agricultural land should not be wasted.

Like oriental cities, Egyptian cities were divided into quarters, physically separated and carefully protected within the overall conglomeration they formed. These quarters might be of various types, based on the nationality of those who lived there or on their trades, and, in Memphis at least, such quarters were frequently surrounded by great walls which provided protection from both natural hazards and human assault. It was thus individual quarters which might be walled and not, as was the Greek practice, the city as a whole.

The protection of cities was the responsibility of garrison troops stationed there. In Memphis, as we shall see, the garrison point was centrally located, and this was often the case. The troops were paid by the crown and, in the Late Period, were regularly of foreign origin, for in Egypt the phenomenon of a citizen soldiery was unknown. Not only was law and order to be enforced in the city; but protection of the fields in the countryside was also a constant concern, and everywhere in Egypt the system of dykes and ditches, used to control the flood, was organized and watched over by the central government and those in their employ. The flood was also measured and Nilometers are found in most major centers. The provision of a water supply is a regular concern of government, but in Egypt drinking water would often come from the Nile. And as so often in eastern cities, private water sellers, providing fresh water to those who would pay, served to supply people's needs for this basic commodity. Wells and artesian springs were used, but the elaborate wellheads and fountain houses of the civic centers of mainland Greece are not found here. Gardens, however, were a standard feature of the Egyptian city; generally serving as orchards for dates, olives, vines, and other fruit trees, verdant areas might also be planted with garden plants or experimental crops. In Memphis such an orchard belonged to the crown and was attached to the palace; elsewhere others owned the land. The Egyptian temples, with their large enclosures, might also include green areas. In Memphis, for instance, within the 20 hectares of the temple of Ptah, Thoth's baboon lived under his own moringa tree; other trees were connected with other Egyptian deities. Amid the dust and heat there were pleasant corners of shade, as public and private land were intermingled.

There were also smells. Spice markets would scent the air, as would the purveyors of cooked food on the street corners. Different markets for differing products were found in various parts of the city. Not all smells were pleasant smells. In ancient Egyptian cities levels of sanitation were not high. In the temple enclosures, temple cleaners were employed—a lower grade of priest—to keep the area clean. Generally, however, the roads and alleyways were used to throw out all manner of excrement and waste. The scattered survival of discarded *ostraka* and papyri serves to remind us how minimal was waste disposal in these ancient cities.

With the Greeks came further public constructions to join the older temples—new buildings on a grander scale than the mud-brick homes in which the people dwelled. For following their conquest of the country the Greeks, like the Romans later, erected theaters and other scenes of popular recreation. Once introduced, we may presume that performances at the theater or the hippodrome were attended by mixed audiences. The gymnasium, however, throughout Egypt as elsewhere in the Hellenistic East, remained an exclusively Greek institution, with its membership closely controlled.

Such are the regular features of the traditional cities of Egypt. In seeing how Memphis fits the pattern, we start with a detailed topographical study of the city. It is only once the physical appearance of the city and its constituent parts has been established that we can begin to see the interrelation of these parts within the whole, in both economic and social spheres. Memphis therefore may first be viewed through the eyes of those who visited. Described by ancient travelers, its changing appearance, its natural features and man-made monuments, may be mapped and reconstructed. Through survey and excavation, archaeologists fill out the picture, and even the documents yield topographical information. Let us attempt a physical reconstruction.

PTOLEMAIC MEMPHIS

When late in the first century B.C. the geographer Strabo visited Memphis, he was following the route of many previous Greek and Roman travelers. In the fifth century B.C. Herodotus, interested in the past as much as in the present, had spent some time in the city. The priests of Ptah (Hephaistos to the Greeks) were the source of much of his information, and Ptah's temple, the "large and most remarkable" temple of Hephaistos, was featured in his account.[14] Strabo is more systematic in his description of the city, and although his picture selects only a few of the more noteworthy features and sights of the area he may serve as our preliminary guide.[15]

Memphis, records Strabo, is the royal residence of the Egyptians, near to Babylon and the apex of the Delta. It is a city of temples. There is that of Apis who is kept in a stall. (He then describes the special markings of the Apis bull, all black with white on his forehead and in patches on the flanks.) In front of this enclosure, he continues, is a courtyard which contains the stall of the mother-of-Apis. At a fixed hour, Apis is let loose in this courtyard; this show is especially for the tourists, since, although visitors may view Apis in his stall through a window, they also want to set eyes on him outside. After a short bout of exercise in the court, Apis is returned to his own stall. Next to this sanctuary and adjacent to it is the Hephaistieion. This is an extravagant structure both in the size of the central shrine (the *naos*) and in other respects. In front of it, in the avenue (the *dromos*), is a monolithic colossus. It is in this avenue that bull contests are staged, with bulls especially bred for the purpose. The bulls are let free and join in struggle together; the one judged the stronger wins the prize. Also in Memphis lies the temple of Aphrodite, considered to be a Greek goddess; but some say this is the temple of Selene, the moon goddess.

[14] 2.99.4.
[15] 17.1.31–32.

Further, there is a Sarapion[16] in a location so sandy that sand dunes are piled up there by the winds. As a result of these winds some of the sphinxes appeared buried up to their necks, while some of them were only half visible. It is not difficult to imagine the danger if a sandstorm blows up when one is walking over to the sanctuary.

The city is a large one, with a sizeable population. After Alexandria it is the second city, and its population, like that of Alexandria, is multi-racial. In front of the city and the palaces lie lakes. The palaces, now in ruins and deserted, are built on an eminence and run down to the level of the plain below the city; adjoining are a grove and a lake.

So Strabo describes the city. For him Memphis is above all a sacred city, a city of temples—those of Ptah/Hephaistos with the stalls of the Apis bull and the cow, its mother, nearby, and of Aphrodite (whom Herodotus called "the foreign Aphrodite") in the valley, and, on the desert edge of Saqqara, the great Sarapieion with its long sphinx-lined avenue, which was cleared of sand by Mariette in the mid-nineteenth century. He comments too on the population, and on the abandonment of the palaces by the early Roman period.

THE VALLEY CITY

Strabo's outline may be expanded, and the combination of the evidence of other classical writers and of the hieroglyphic, demotic, and Greek inscriptions and documents with that of archaeology begins to make possible a topographical survey of the city. This city consisted of two separate yet interrelated parts, the valley city of Memphis and the temple enclosures and necropolis of the desert edge to the west (see fig. 2). Physically distinct, the valley settlement with its dykes, temples, and different ethnic quarters was separated by a stream, the Phchēt canal, from the sharply rising, sand-covered escarpment, which, with the wadi running south from Abousir on its far, western, side, forms the bluff of North Saqqara, the city of the dead, the necropolis. The Phchēt canal, known when flooded as a lake, probably followed close to the line of the present waterway, the Bahr Libeini, serving both parts of the city alike.[17] Access to the necropolis from the valley city was by boat across this canal,

---

[16] So Strabo. In documents the usual form is Sarapieion, which I adopt here rather than the Latin Serapeum.

[17] *UPZ* 114.12; 117.9. *PP* 5352, priest of Ptah, lord of the southern lake and of the gods of the domain of Ptah, lord of the northern lake; Lichtheim (1980), 134, Setne crosses by boat; Yoyotte (1961), 95–96; Goyon (1971), 146, still in the tenth century A.D.

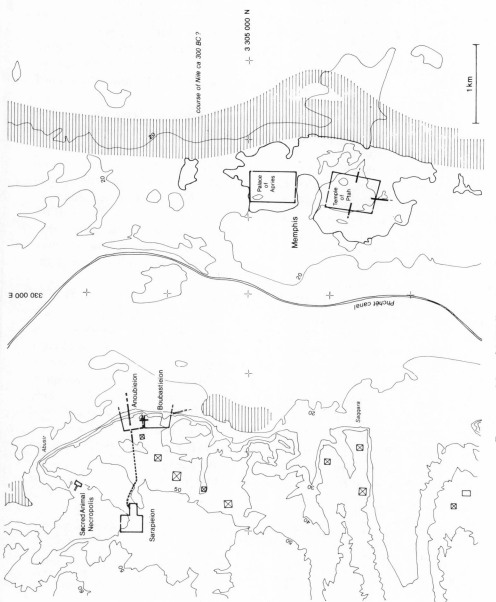

FIGURE 2. Memphis: Valley city and necropolis.

and on the eastern bank a special quay, connnected to the Ptah temple,[18] was used for ceremonial (as probably also for secular) purposes. From here Ptah will have journeyed south to visit Hathor of the Southern Sycamore, and at times the Apis bull departed on ceremonial visits;[19] from here after death the mummified Apis was transported across the Lake of Pharaoh on the first stage of its final journey up along the sphinx-lined avenue to the vaults of the Sarapieion.

To the east of the city lay the Nile with its islands. Now flowing more than 3 kilometers east of the city ruins, in the Ptolemaic period the river appears, both from a recent resistivity survey[20] and from the written record, to have flowed close up to the city along the edge of the series of *koms* or hillocks marked on the plan (see fig. 3). The tentative identification in the nineteenth century by Hekekyan of the Nilometer on this stretch of the river bank might confirm this shift, while the north-south wall of the building which he recorded certainly belonged to the (Roman) waterfront. The Memphite Nilometer was of national importance, and even after the foundation of Alexandria it remained the official measuring point for the country.[21]

The position of the main Memphite island is possibly now marked by Ez Maʿmal. Dividing the stream, this island was large enough to serve in 321 B.C. as an army camp for Perdiccas and his great invading force. Striking right at the heart of Ptolemy's new kingdom, this invasion came to grief when the disturbance in the riverbed caused by the wading troops and elephants shifted the sand and foothold of the stream; over two thousand men were consumed by the "beasts" in the river.[22] Here on the island was a temple, described by Diodorus as that of Daedalus who fashioned one of the monumental gateways to the temple of Ptah, and a wooden statue within.[23] Later in its history a Christian community was situated on the island, as so often close to an earlier pagan site.[24]

A Nile flood of 16 cubits was optimum, 14–16 good, and 12–14 the

[18] *PSI* 488.11 (257 B.C.).

[19] Harris papyrus = Breasted (1906), 4.169; Crawford (1980), 5 n. 4.

[20] In such a survey a current that is passed between copper rods inserted at intervals deep into the ground makes possible the plotting of any structures or abnormalities buried beneath the surface.

[21] Smith, Jeffreys, and Málek (1983), 40–41, confirming Butzer (1976), 35; Jeffreys (1985), 48–51, with plan 2. For the Nilometer: Hdt. 2.13.1; Diod. Sic. 1.36.11; Strabo 17.1.48; Luc. 8.477–78; Plut. *DIO* 43 (368b); P. *Oxy.* 3148 (A.D. 424) for a Nile festival; Bonneau (1971), 38, 50.

[22] Diod. Sic. 18.34.6–35; Jeffreys (1985), 47, 51–53.

[23] Diod. Sic. 1.97.6.

[24] P. *Lond.* 6.1917.9 (A.D. 330–40).

regular height reached by the Nile as measured at Memphis.[25] As the waters came over, filling the ditches and covering the fields, the city built on higher ground was protected by its dykes. For around the valley city lay 5 kilometers of dykes, and in March 257 B.C., following recent floods which reached over 10 cubits in the ditches around, these dykes were raised to 12 cubits, approximately 6 meters, by the new Greek administration. The record of these dykes, sketched in with their length on the plan (fig. 3), is crucial to many Memphite identifications.[26]

Assuming the dykes are listed from the south running northwards, they start with 600 meters of the Syro-Persikon, which must have bounded the area settled by immigrants from the Levant, those who in the third century B.C. might call themselves Phoenico-Egyptians.[27] For as we shall see, the foreign communities that settled here in separate quarters retained their identification even within the Hellenistic city. The names of stretches of the dyke reflect these quarters and perhaps facilitate their recognition on the ground. In the fifth century B.C. Herodotus recorded the Tyrian Camp in Memphis as the location of the temple of the foreign Aphrodite whom he identified as Helen, daughter of Tyndareus (and wife of Menelaos).[28] This temple was within the fine *temenos* of the Memphite king Proteus which lay south of the Ptah temple.[29] The whole area formed a Phoenician quarter. In spite of the strong Levantine connection with ships and shipping to be discussed below, the name Tyrian Camp suggests a military purpose for this settlement, at least when Herodotus visited under the Persians. Later, however, under the Ptolemies, this was a residential quarter, and if the Astarte temple is that known in the Greek papyri as the Aphrodision in Memphis, private housing, workshops, and local hotels were built up against the temple here. It was here one day in the second century B.C. that a luckless *kiki* worker fell to his

[25] Bonneau (1971), 219.

[26] *PSI* 488; the provision of gravel recorded in *P. Lond.* 7.2054.4–11 may be for this same project. Following my discussion with the Memphis survey team, my reconstruction here differs from my earlier attempt, Crawford (1983), 18–19; cf. Orrieux (1983), 99. For the results of recent survey work, see Smith, Jeffreys, and Málek (1983); Jeffreys, Málek, and Smith (1984).

[27] *PSI* 531.1; see chapter 3 below. A Syrian quarter may be recorded on Louvre stele C119 (Spiegelberg 1929a, 107–12; Munro 1973, 341), but Yoyotte (1962), 86 n. 2, doubts a Memphite location, and in any case Spiegelberg's reading is uncertain; the demotic version records rather "gods of the cool lake" (so J. D. Ray).

[28] Hdt. 2.112.

[29] This has been identified with the palace of Merenptah (Petrie 1909a, 3–4), which, however, lies to the east of the Ptah temple; see Dimick's map with Anthes (1959), 82.

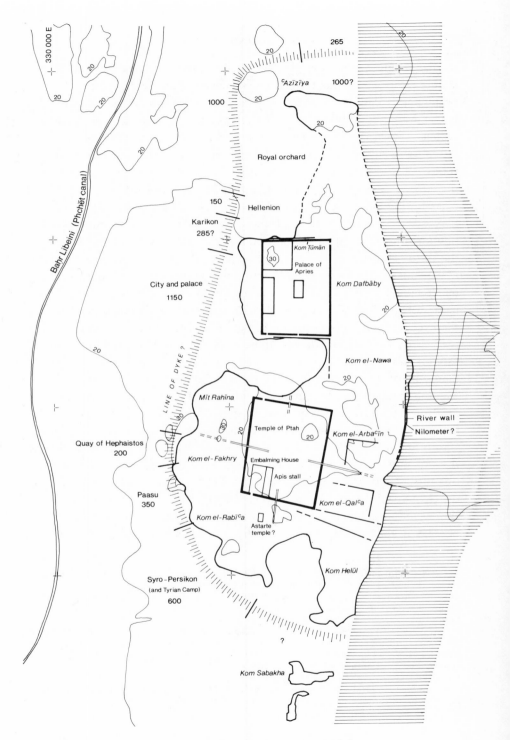

FIGURE 3. Memphis with its Ptolemaic dykes.

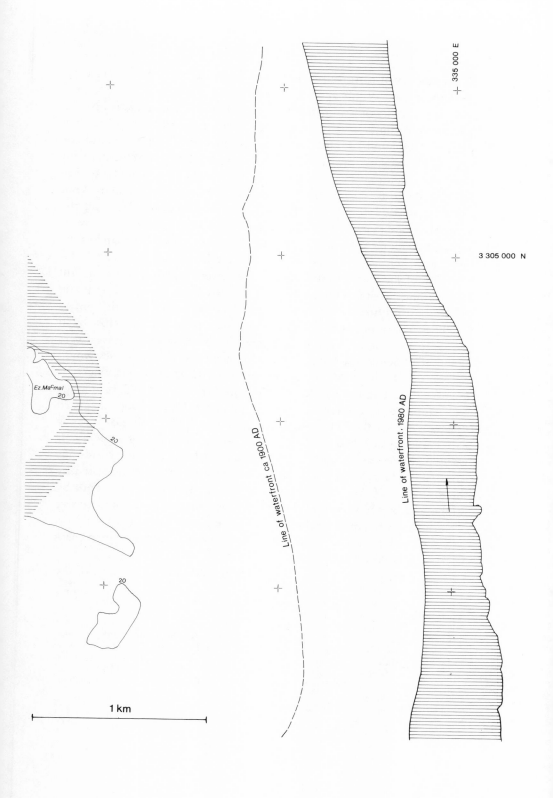

Ez.Ma^{c}mal
20

20

20

Line of waterfront ca 1900 AD

Line of waterfront, 1980 AD

335 000 E

3 305 000 N

1 km

death in a vat of castor oil.[30] Shrines and secular buildings lay close together in these city suburbs.

The next dyke of 350 meters was named Paasu. The name is obscure but the dyke must have bordered a distinct area southwest of the Ptah temple. Two hundred meters of dyke described as "above and below the quay of Hephaistos" probably bounded a more solid, stone embankment close to the temple. The largest stretch of dyke, 23 *schoinia* or 1,150 meters, lay alongside the city and the palace area. Here, centered on the kom of Mīt Rahīna, lay the city, the *polis*,[31] with the royal palace and the acropolis[32] or citadel area. Strabo described the palaces, deserted when he wrote, as built on an eminence and stretching down to the flat land of the city below, with a grove and a lake nearby. Whereas this forms a fair description of the mass of mud-brick on its towering platform which, still dominating the site to the north, was excavated and identified by Petrie as the sixth-century B.C. palace of Apries, his excavations yielded only a few Ptolemaic remains.[33] The Ptolemaic palace must have lain close by in the same area, perhaps on Kom Tūmān to the west where traces were found of Ptolemaic building. It would be here that the Ptolemies would stay on their visits to Memphis, northwest of the Ptah temple where, at least from the reign of Epiphanes in 197 B.C., the new Macedonian kings were crowned according to ancient Egyptian rites. With troops on guard nearby, whether the Idumaean saber bearers or other bodyguards,[34] the palace quarter also had its shrines. Here Arsinoe, queen of Ptolemy II, was worshipped as a goddess.[35] Besides a citadel, the presence of administrative headquarters at least during the Persian period is suggested by the discovery of Aramaic dockets and seals.[36] If, as suggested both by Strabo and by the survey of the dykes, this was also the administrative center of the Ptolemaic city, there can be no clearer sign of what a polis now signified in Egypt. It was offices of central government which characterized this Ptolemaic polis.

Beyond the palaces, tapering north for at least a kilometer towards the

---

[30] *UPZ* 120.5–8. For housing, see Petrie, Mackay, and Wainwright (1910), 44–46.

[31] *PSI* 488.11; Strabo 17.1.32.

[32] *P. Cair. Zen.* 59156.3 (256 B.C.), *akra*.

[33] Petrie (1909b), 11; Petrie, Mackay, and Wainwright (1910), 41; Kemp (1977); (1978).

[34] Thompson-Crawford (1984), and chapter 3 nn. 94–110 below. For other troops in Memphis, *P. Mich. Zen.* 32 (255 B.C.) *sitarchia* for troops; *P. Petrie* 2.20.iv.8 = 3.36.b.iv (218 B.C.) a detachment of elephants (for the Syrian war?); *UPZ* 14.23–24 (158 B.C.).

[35] Vienna stele 153.4–5; Leiden sarcophagus AMT 3.2, cf. Reymond (1981), 76, 102; Quaegebeur (1971b), 249–50.

[36] Petrie, Mackay, and Wainwright (1910), 41.

open and easily watered plains of Azīzīya, there stretched the palace gardens. A striking feature of the area, these gardens may be the same as Strabo's grove, though parks and gardens were probably a feature of Memphis, providing oases of well-watered greenery and shade amid the crowded, dusty streets and living quarters of the city.

Just north of the city proper, close to the fortress which once they must have occupied,[37] came the Carian and Greek quarters of the city. Brought from the Delta by Amasis in the sixth century B.C., the Carian and Ionian mercenaries stayed on in their new home and intermarried with the local inhabitants. And although the Caromemphites and Hellenomemphites were by now well integrated in the Ptolemaic city, they still preserved their separate quarters.[38] The location of other ethnic quarters, those of the Idumaeans, for instance, or of the Jews,[39] is not known.

If the palaces dominated the north of the city, to the south it was the temple of Ptah with its various dependencies which stood out. The large temenos of the Ptah temple was probably surrounded by a wall,[40] broken on all four sides by the ceremonial gateways listed by Herodotus.[41] To these an eastern gateway was added by Ptolemy IV from which Petrie found the red granite architrave.[42] Besides the large ceremonial hall in which the coronation ceremonies took place, there were other shrines and enclosures belonging to dependent cults. The priesthood of Ptah had many responsibilities. It was the priests of Ptah who served the Apis bull during its lifetime and its seventy-day period of mummification rites,[43]

[37] Large quantities of Persian scale armour found on Kom Tūmān may indicate a citadel, perhaps in the fourth century B.C., Petrie (1909b), 13; Jeffreys (1985), 41. If built of stone, this may have given the name of White Wall (Leukon Teichos, ỉnb ḥḏ) to the city, Hdt. 3.14; Thuc. 1.104; Quaegebeur (1971b), 251; as the color of the south, however, "white" may be used rather with reference to the origin of the city's founder Menes (so Clarysse).

[38] The Hellenion, PSI 488.12; P. Cair. Zen. 59593.7–8; P. Louvre E 3266.8.Q (197 B.C.) = App. B:2; P. Innsbruck, line 8 (75 B.C.) = App. B:18; P. Louvre 3268 (73 B.C.) = App. B:19, and the Karikon, PSI 488.11; 409.21–22 (third century B.C.).

[39] Berlin stele 2118 (Stern 1884; Schäfer 1902/3) mentions a Jewish quarter. I see no reason, with Yoyotte (1973), 34, to understand this as the Jewish Camp in the southern Delta (Joseph. AJ 14.133; BJ 1.191; Not. Dign. 28.42) since all of Chaiapis' other appointments are consistent with a Memphite career.

[40] Diod. Sic. 1.67.1, a seventh-century B.C. enclosure wall. The mud-brick wall excavated by the University of Pennsylvania dates from the first century B.C., Anthes (1965), 3, 8.

[41] North propylon of Moeris (Amenemhet III): Hdt. 2.101.1, cf. Diod. Sic. 1.51.5; south propylon of Psammetichos: Hdt. 2.153, cf. Diod. Sic. 1.67.1, placing it to the east; west propylon of Rhampsinitos (Ramses II?): Hdt. 2.121.1; east propylon of Asychis (Shoshenk I?), Hdt. 2.136.1. Diod. Sic. 1.97.6 ascribes the finest of the gateways to Daedalus. See Goossens (1945) on the Ptah temple.

[42] Petrie (1909a), 14 with plate XLV.

[43] Vercoutter (1962), 127–28; B.M. stele 375.6–7 (cf. Reymond 1981, 82), a special priest with responsibility for the food of the mother-of-Apis; see chapter 6 below.

and it was the elders of the Ptah priests who served as a governing body for other cults, like those of the Ibis or Hawk. While the ibises of Thoth were bred in the Lake of Pharaoh and along the city dyke,[44] other sacred animals were reared within the temple of Ptah itself. Here in his lifetime there dwelled the baboon of Thoth under his moringa tree,[45] in company with Apis and the mother-of-Apis who on death became the Isis cow.

The stalls of the Apis bull and the mother-of-Apis, together with their exercise court, lay opposite the southern gate of the temple which, like the Apis court, was built by Psammetichos I in the seventh century B.C. From the fifth century B.C. Herodotus describes a court with a surrounding colonnade in which statues took the place of pillars.[46] The Apis bull enjoyed a private water supply and, like its mother, had a window for public appearances.[47] Closely connected with this cult were the bullfights in the dromos of the Ptah temple which Strabo mentioned.[48] The topographical indications of classical writers are corroborated by those in the Ptolemaic *Instructions for Embalming the Apis Bull* to be discussed in chapter 6; they suggest that the Apis enclosure is to be found around the midpoint of the southern wall of the Ptah temple, where there must have been a gate close to the colossus of Ramses II. The Embalming House or *Ouabet*, originally excavated by the Egyptian Antiquities Service in 1941, lay near to the southwest corner of the temple.[49]

East of the Ptah temple and the palaces lay the Nile and the port which played such an important role in the life of the city. Presumably warehouses and loading bays lay along the Nile bank, and a royal dock is mentioned in an early Ptolemaic papyrus.[50] As well as the dockyards, which perhaps lay to the south, and the Nilometer mentioned above, there was a tollhouse here and buildings, like the guard post, connected with the control of the port. Perhaps serving as the central administrative point for other tollhouses in the nome, the Memphite port control will have played an important part in the economic life of the city. The river front was known to Herodotus as the area in front of the city, the *proasteion*. Here

---

[44] *Hor* 15 verso.4; 33.2 (157 B.C.); de Cenival (1972a), 39.

[45] Smith (1974), 41–43.

[46] Hdt. 2.153; Strabo 17.1.31.

[47] Smith (1974), 10; Plut. *DIO* 5 (353a), a well; Ael. *NA* 11.10.

[48] Lloyd (1978b), 609–26.

[49] El-Amir (1948), 51–56, wrongly identified this as the *sēkos*; cf. Dimick in Anthes (1959), 75–79, and Vercoutter (1962), 55–58. New exploration is in progress, Jones and Milward Jones (1982); (1983); (1984).

[50] See chapter 2 on "The Port" with n. 168. For shipbuilding material in the southern quarter at an earlier date, see Spiegelberg (1896), 20; Diod. Sic. 1.50.7, docks and harbors.

the Persian king Kambyses humiliated the pharaoh Psammenitos, showing him his daughter coming down to collect water from the river.[51] In
places, housing came down close to the water's edge, and in one spot an
Egyptian market is recorded in what was presumably a native quarter of
the city. It was here the Egyptian father of the Sarapieion twins (to be
discussed in chapter 7) jumped into the river to escape the knife of his
wife's Greek soldier-lover. (He swam to an island and from there took a
boat to the Herakleopolite nome, to return home only for burial.)[52] By
the first century B.C., a hippodrome in the area gave its name to a group
of Memphite ship contractors;[53] elsewhere, perhaps to the north, vineyards lay close to the river edge where they could be watered throughout
the year.[54]

The exact location of the city's theater is not yet known,[55] nor indeed
of the temple of Herakles perhaps associated with the gymnasium,[56] nor
of many other shrines which are recorded in the titles of priests. The discovery of several important inscriptions on Kom el Qalʿa[57] suggests an
important public square or building in this part of the city; statues too
could have been erected here. Faience and terracotta workshops lay here
and to the south on Kom Helūl.[58] Indeed, the workshop area of the city
would seem to have lain on this southeastern side of the city, stretching
along the river bank from Kom el Nawa in the north. (The varied production of the area will be discussed in the next chapter.)

Situated for the most part on the natural hillocks of the plain, the different quarters of the valley city of Memphis were both separate and interrelated. The actual extent to which these various areas in the valley
were enclosed with walls, like those of the necropolis, remains to be established. Eight walled enclosures have so far been identified on the
ground,[59] and it seems likely that similar quarters existed throughout the
city. Despite such thick mud-brick walls, these separate quarters all came
under the central royal administration of the city[60] and, if it existed at all

[51] Hdt. 3.14.1–3.
[52] UPZ 18.8–11 (163 B.C.); 19.9–15.
[53] BGU 1741–43; 2368 (63 B.C.). For Memphite charioteers: P. Cair. Zen. 4.59700.10–11
+ BL 5; SB 8.9930 verso (third century A.D.).
[54] P. Hib. 205.23–26 (mid-third century B.C.).
[55] P. Fouad 14.4, 9 (third century A.D.).
[56] P. Corn. 1.84–85 (256 B.C.); cf. P. Oxy. Hels. 23.4–5 (A.D. 212); SB 6.9022 inv.13 (second to third centuries A.D.), for later gymnasiarchs.
[57] Málek in Porter and Moss, (1981), 862.
[58] Petrie (1909a), 14–15.
[59] EES Report 1983/84, 4.
[60] On sḥn.w, see Reymond (1974), 192, noting a change from earlier practice (P. Fitzhugh

(see chapter 3), their autonomy was minimal. Within, to judge from demotic contracts and evidence elsewhere, the streets ran at right angles to
each other, dividing the area up in crisscross fashion.[61] In Memphis, however, the natural contours of the hillocks on which the city was built may
have caused some modifications to this pattern. As often in ancient eastern cities, the gates of these enclosures were important meeting places; so
when the priest Ḥor met with the Alexandrian minister in charge of religious affairs to inform him of the bad fortunes of the Ibis and the Hawk,
the interview was up on the necropolis at the gate of the tower of Ḥepnēbes.[62] Within the separate quarters were local markets; different trades
were practiced here, though the topographical evidence is not sufficiently
precise to allow the investigation of any correlation which might exist
between ethnic quarters and economic activities. In Oxyrhynchos, for
instance, where a number of different quarters are also recorded, besides
those known by the nationality of the inhabitants (the Jewish or the Cretan Quarter), there were others known by the trade of those who lived
there (the Shepherds', the Gooseherds', or the Shoemakers' Quarters).[63]
Such quarters formed a regular feature of Egyptian cities; they are known
also from Krokodilopolis and Hermoupolis. For Memphis only the national quarters are known by name, but the overall picture is of a diverse
and crowded city of enclosures where temples, housing, and workshops
were interspersed with groves and gardens.

The houses in which the people lived were presumably for the most
part built of mud-brick,[64] but of very differing standards. The Ptolemaic
bronze gate found by Petrie in the southern quarter of the city, south of
the pottery kilns, suggests a high degree of opulence for some.[65] As today, the flat roofs will have served as summer living quarters for men and
animals alike, and the walls of the house with courtyards within will have
enclosed the household unit of owners, family, servants, and livestock.
Outside, the bustling streets were full of life and squalor.[66]

D 4.8 [third century B.C.]); cf. Pestman, *Rec.* vol. 2.4 recto. 14 (108 B.C.) with note i (p. 46),
for a different interpretation.

[61] Appendix B for contracts from the necropolis; Orrieux (1985), 131, for comparative
material.

[62] *Ḥor* 22 recto. 3–4; 30.3–4, corner gate; Ray (1976), 148.

[63] Rink (1924), 25–44; for the possibilities of this approach, see Geertz (1979), 158–59.

[64] See Smith (1974), 11, with Petrie (1910), plate XXXVIII 6, a house rather than a fortress.

[65] Petrie, Mackay, and Wainwright (1910), 44 with plate XXXIII 15.

[66] Reflected in Ptolemaios' dreams about the twins, see chapter 7; *UPZ* 77.4–11, 21–25;
78.8–21, the school of Tothēs and insanitary uses of the streets.

THE NECROPOLIS

When, soon after his appointment in 76 B.C. of the fourteen-year-old Psenptais as high priest of Ptah, Ptolemy XII Auletes visited the high priest in his home city of Memphis, "he passed up and down in his ship that he might behold both sides of the place."[67] For to the west of the valley city, separated by the Phchēt canal, there lay the other half of Memphis, the temple suburbs of the necropolis with their native Egyptian population (see fig. 4).

As today, a number of paths led up the sandy escarpment where the temples each had their sacred avenues, or dromoi. When Setne, hero of the demotic romance of Setne Khamwas, crossed the Phchēt canal to visit the priestess of Bastet, he probably followed a route from the valley to Saqqara close to that of the modern motor road.[68] However, the main avenue leading west to the Sarapieion was the stone-paved, sphinx-lined Sarapieion way (the *ḥft-ḥr*) which Strabo took.[69] Climbing up over the escarpment from a limestone quay, the avenue passes through the more northern of the two great brick enclosures, each of which surrounds a series of temples. To the south was the Boubastieion, 350 meters by 250 meters, with walls 7–10 meters thick, and to the north an enclosure 250 meters square, the site of two or three limestone temples built on terraces up the hillside, which is almost certainly to be identified as the House of Anoubis, the Anoubieion.[70] In life, as in ceremony, the dancers of Bastet were closely connected with the men of Anoubis.[71] Close by, on the desert edge, were the catacombs where the mummified animals of the cult lay buried;[72] live cats and dogs perhaps were also reared within the enclosures. When Setne met with Tabubu in the Boubastieion and, overcome with passion, murdered his children and flung them through the window, in his fantasy he heard the dogs and cats below tearing their flesh apart as he drank with the highborn priestess of Bastet. The thick mud-brick walls of these enclosures, as well as providing some protection against the

[67] *B.M.* 886 translated by Glanville in Bevan (1927), 347–48; cf. Reymond (1981), 148–49.

[68] Lichtheim (1980), 134–35.

[69] Ray (1976), 147; *Ḥor* 8 recto.14; *UPZ* 119.10.

[70] Smith (1979), 164–66, summarizes the results of recent excavations; cf. Smith and Jeffreys (1978); (1979); (1980); (1981).

[71] Quaegebeur and Rammant-Peeters (1982), 200; Quaegebeur (1984), 159–60, together with the servants of the Ibis and the Hawk.

[72] The evidence up to that date is on map 10 of de Morgan (1897). For mummified cats, see Maspero (1882), 75, with Wilcken (1927), 10; Zivie (1984), 202. Remains are still visible below the new house of the Antiquities Service.

FIGURE 4. The necropolis of North Saqqara.

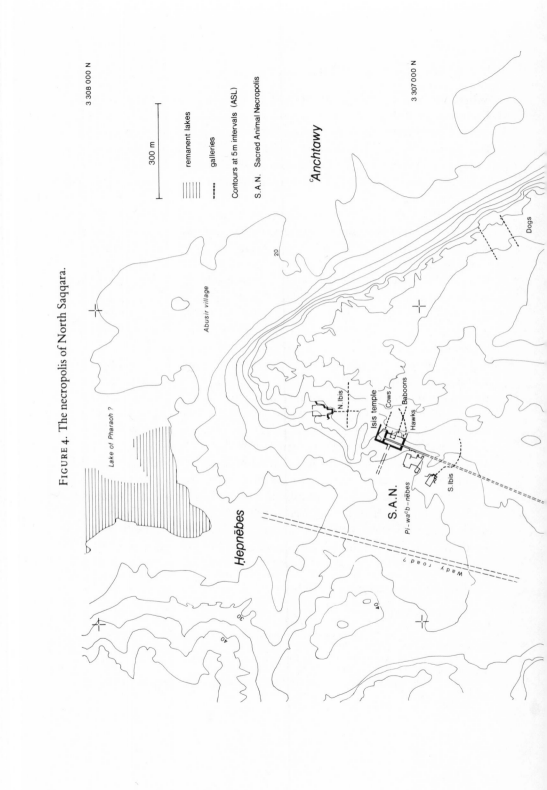

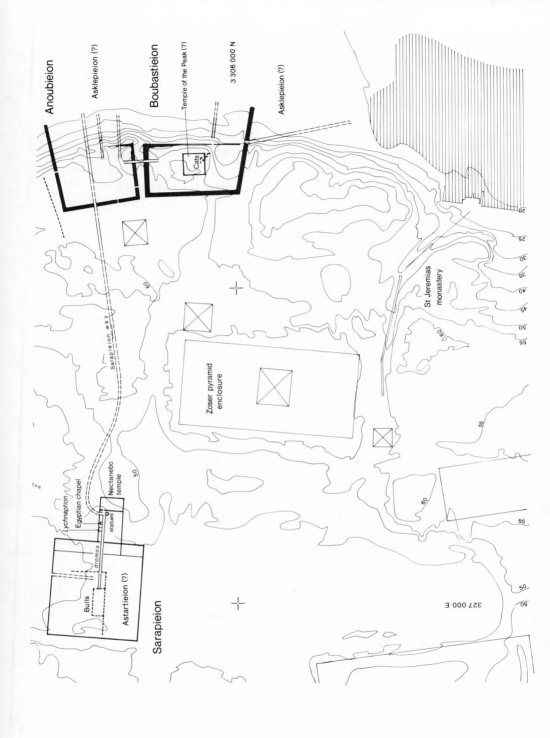

Anoubieion

Asklepieion (?)

Boubastieion

Temple of the Peak (?)

3 306 000 N

Asklepieion (?)

Cats

Sarapieion way

St Jeremias monastery

Zoser pyramid enclosure

Lychnaption

Egyptian chapel

Nectanebo temple

statues

dromos

Bulls

Astartieion (?)

Sarapieion

327 000 E

notorious sandstorms of the desert edge, served to divide off the different districts of the necropolis.

The enclosure of the Boubastieion, *Pr-B3stt*, to the south was more than simply a temple of Bastet.[73] At least two, and probably three, stone temples, now pillaged for lime, were located here, and there were subsidiary shrines, priestly dwellings, and other buildings.[74] The entry was along a brick-paved road and through a huge brick gateway from the south. And down by the Phchēt canal lay houses and courtyards with gardens and orchards interspersed among them.[75]

Either in or close to this southern enclosure lay the temple of the Peak, *Thn(yt)*, known chiefly from the record of its priests.[76] This temple had a double-roomed treasury and windows of appearances and, like other temples here, its own enclosure wall and dromos.[77] It differed from other temples in being the center of worship for several gods, for the Falcon Nekhthorheb (Nectanebo II),[78] Horos the Hawk, and Thoth the Ibis. There were scribes of the treasury of the Peak, *pastophoroi (wnw)*, and men in charge of the windows of the forecourt of the temple, with responsibilities in the cult of the Hawk and the Ibis.[79]

Close to the temple of the Peak lay the great Asklepieion, *Pr-' Ij-m-ḥtp*, the temple of Imhotep, son of Ptah, whom the Greeks saw as Asklepios.[80] Imhotep was "lord of the Peak, lord of ʿAnchtawy in Memphis,"[81] and his temple bordered the temple of the Peak to the north.[82] The Asklepios temple had its own dromos rising up from the edge of cultivation, and a

[73] *UPZ* 79.4 (159 B.C.), the location of Nektembēs' dreams. Priests of Bastet: Amasis, Berlin 14765 = De Meulenaere (1960), 104; Psenptais, *PP* 5376.
[74] Remains of buildings have been excavated and some are recorded in the papyri: *P. Louvre* E 3266.6.E = App. B:2; *UPZ* 62.34; 120.10–13 (hotels).
[75] Tabubu's house in Lichtheim (1980), 134; *UPZ* 114 I.10 (150–148 B.C.), the *paradeisos* of Zois, cf. *UPZ* 117.5. Other details occur in documents of the Undertakers' Archive discussed in chapter 5.
[76] Chonsiou, *PP* 5874; Petineftem, Brugsch (1891), 887–89; Amasis, Berlin 14765; *Hor* 23 verso. 22; *P. Louvre* E 3266.8.O = App. B:2; *P. Louvre* 2412.4 (316–304 B.C.) = App. B:29; *UPZ* 114 I.41 (150–148 B.C.). De Meulenaere (1960), 105–6 with 106 n. 1, identifies the temple with the Anoubieion; his reasons are not altogether compelling and his solution would separate the dog catacombs from the Anoubieion.
[77] Besides the description of priestly offices, see Ray (1976), 150–51.
[78] De Meulenaere (1960), 94, Chonsiou (*PP* 5874).
[79] *Hor* 23 verso.21–23. For Horos and the window of appearances, see the priesthoods for Anemhor, *PP* 5352, and Teōs, *PP* 5373.
[80] For the cult, see Wilcken (1927), 38–41; Kiessling (1953), 31–33; Wildung (1977a).
[81] *Hor* 18 verso.2–3, cf. Ray (1976), 150.
[82] North of the temple of the Peak: *UPZ* 114.11–12, 41; *UPZ* 117.4–9, the same land (for *topos* meaning "district" cf. *UPZ* 116.5); *P. Louvre* 2412 = App. B:29. For a discussion of the topography, see Wildung (1977a), 57.

cavern in the temple[83] may have been considered the tomb of Imhotep, the architect of Djoser who was heroized in the eighteenth dynasty and later deified. (The cult of this somewhat unusual god will be discussed in chapter 6.) The later legend of Joseph's Prison in the area[84] perhaps contains echoes of the earlier cult here of Imhotep/Imouthes. As elsewhere on this eastern edge of the necropolis, buildings bordered this temple both above to the west and below to the east,[85] and besides the temple personnel,[86] Egyptians of many professions lived in the enclosure.[87]

North of the Boubastieion, entry to the second enclosure was along a stone-paved causeway and through a great granite entrance gate. The first of the limestone temples in the enclosure was that of Anoubis, the necropolis god who presided over mummification. Built on terraces, this temple, which gave its name to the whole complex,[88] was probably extended by Ptolemy V Epiphanes; a surviving relief from the area shows him adoring the recumbent god.[89] A dromos with buildings alongside came up to the temple from the valley below.[90] Within the large enclosure two further temples were probably sited; their identity is uncertain.[91] The main sphinx-lined causeway came up through this enclosure from the east,[92] and inside the southern wall down towards the valley were built the strange "Bes-chambers" which Quibell found—mud-brick rooms with colored *pisé* wall decorations of Bes (the dwarf-god who protected pregnant women) flanked by male and female figures.[93] The connection of these rooms with prostitution, sacred or otherwise, cannot be proved but seems not at all unlikely. Young girls might collect for their dowry in

[83] Ray (1976), 15 and 151; Gauthier (1918), 48. For similar crypts at Hawara and Edfu, see Reymond (1973), 21, 30.
[84] Stricker (1943), 101–37.
[85] *P. Louvre* E 3266.1.O-P (App. B:2), with shops, outhouses, and funerary buildings; the distinction made by de Cenival (1972a, 14) between the temple of Asklepios and the districts of the Anoubieion, Serapieion, and Boubastieion is not supported in Greek usage, cf. *UPZ* 125.8–9.
[86] Often shared with the temple of the Peak: Amasis, Petineftem, Chonsiou (n. 76 above), Psenptais, *PP* 5376; *UPZ* 57.21, *grammateis*.
[87] E.g., *P. Louvre* E 3266.9.C (App. B:2), a barber; *UPZ* 125.8–9, *taricheutai*.
[88] Jelínková (1959), 64–65, 71; Wilcken (1927), 14–15; see chapter 5 below.
[89] Smith (1979), 164.
[90] *P. Louvre* 3264 ter. 3–4 (73 B.C.) = App. B:20; *P. Innsbruck* (75 B.C.) = App. B:18; *P. Louvre* 3268.4 (73 B.C.) = App. B:19; *P. B.M.* 10075 (64 B.C.) = Jelínková (1959), 61. In *P. Leid.* 373b and c (203 B.C.) = App. B:1 a north-south direction is implied.
[91] A likely candidate is Osiris at Rout Isout, De Meulenaere (1960), 103–5; for Rout Isout near Abousir, Yoyotte (1959a), 59; (1959b), 71 n. 2.
[92] *P. Leid.* 378 (160 B.C.) = App. B:24.
[93] Quibell (1907), 12–14.

this way.[94] Anoubis, it seems, was served in various ways. Indeed, some recently published documents recording the self-dedication of both men and women to this god through which, in return for a monthly payment, they sought protection in his service, suggest there is much still to be learned of the different groups to be found within this Egyptian temple complex.[95] He was above all the god of mummification.[96]

The evidence of the papyri shows the Anoubieion to have also been an important administrative center. Documents were registered in a *grapheion* here,[97] and the *stratēgos*, the area governor, had a representative based in this complex.[98] A detachment of police was stationed in the area, and a prison was located here, presumably for the troublesome elements of the necropolis community.[99] A secular *epistatēs* had general responsibility for the whole quarter,[100] which was made up of houses, mills, and storehouses besides the temples. The dromos of the main temple of Anoubis was, as so often in Egypt, the scene of a wide range of activities—a corn measure described as a dromos measure was, for instance, used in demotic corn loans.[101] Here, on the eastern edge of the desert bluff, lived and worked a sizeable population, for the most part native Egyptians involved in the cults of the necropolis and the business of embalming both man and animal. But besides the priests and the "men of Anoubis" others lived crowded within the enclosure walls: potters, shepherds, barbers, grain merchants, water carriers, cloth merchants, doctors, and dream interpreters.[102] It was by no means an area exclusively devoted to the dead, and the combination of the evidence of Greek and demotic papyri, the

[94] *UPZ* 2.5–23 (163 B.C.). (Hdt. II.64, sexual intercourse prohibited within the temples may apply only to the *adyton*). Kees (1961), 161, connects the Bes-rooms with the Astarte cult and a joint account for oil for the lamps of Astarte and Imhotep, *P. Louvre dem.* 2423 verso = Revillout (1882b), 78–83 + *UPZ* 143, may be evidence for an Astarte shrine in this eastern complex. See Delekat (1964), 156–76, for other possible Canaanite institutions on the necropolis.

[95] *P. Freib.* 4.72–73; add. 1 (270/69 B.C.); add. 2. In *P. Freib.* 4.72 a monthly payment of 2½ kites is recorded for the *b3k.t.* Note the early date and, in add. 1, the son of a father with both Egyptian and Greek names; the mothers' names are all Egyptian. For the type, see Scholl (1985), 488–92.

[96] See chapter 5.

[97] *UPZ* 128–42. See chapter 5 n. 107.

[98] *UPZ* 7.18.

[99] *UPZ* 5.6; 64.4, probably in the necropolis.

[100] *UPZ* 69 verso; 108.1, 28–29; Ray (1976), 141, reading Achomarres for Petimonth(?).

[101] *P. Vat.* 22 = Revillout (1885), 25–26 + *UPZ* 133; Pestman, *Rec.* 4 + *UPZ* 134; 5 + *UPZ* 132; 6 (108 B.C.).

[102] For the evidence of the Sarapieion papyri, see Guilmot (1962), 373; *P. Louvre* E 3266 = App. B:2; *P. B.M.* 10075 (64 B.C.) = Jelínková (1957) and (1959); Wilcken (1927), 13, for the Cretan dream interpreter (plate vii), cf. *UPZ* 84.79.

epigraphic record of local priests with their cult offices listed, and the careful excavation of the area is necessary in the attempt to understand the many facets of life in the "temple towns"[103] of the Memphite necropolis.

Recent excavation in these large temple enclosures to the east has finally disposed of Mariette's suggestion of a separate "Greek Serapeum," for the immigrant settlers, located in this eastern complex.[104] Of the Greek god Sarapis in this area there is no evidence,[105] and the divisive cultural tendencies implied by Mariette's designation are at odds both with the Greek statues and buildings in the western complex (Mariette's "Egyptian Serapeum") and with what is known of the Memphite cult of Osiris-Apis.[106]

To follow Strabo's route along the brick-paved, sphinx-lined avenue, up and over the sand to the Sarapieion enclosure, is to move from the unknown to the known. The western side of the Saqqara bluff, as indeed the whole of this necropolis, was dominated by the great enclosure of the Sarapieion, *Pr-Wsir.Ḥp*, within which lay the underground burial chambers of the Apis bulls and temple buildings connected with this and related cults. Here, to the west, in two main galleries tunneled deep into the rock below, were stored the huge wood and granite sarcophagi which held the mummified bulls of Apis dating from the reign of Ramses II.[107] The excavation of these chambers and of the dromos leading up to them by Mariette in the mid-nineteenth century was one of the most spectacular of all Egyptian excavations. The official hieroglyphic inscriptions recording the lives of the various bulls, the many demotic records put up by masons working in the chambers, and the votive stelae of pilgrims serve to enliven the cult of Osiris-Apis, the embalmed bull.[108] The Greek

---

[103] The term is that of Smith, cf. Smith and Jeffreys (1978), 10. On life in the area, see Ray (1977) and (1978b).

[104] Maspero (1882), 123; the view is already rejected by Wilcken (1927), 16, though his location of the Asklepieion near the Step Pyramid is not supported by the evidence of the demotic documents.

[105] Unless the "nut garden of Sarapis" in *P. Bruss.* 3.4 (Spiegelberg 1909, 11) is on this side of the necropolis. De Meulenaere (1960), 105, relying on philological arguments, still places a sanctuary of Osiris-Apis in connection with the eastern complex.

[106] See chapter 6. Mariette was constrained to suggest the statues had been moved, Wilcken (1927), 14.

[107] Strabo 17.1.31. For the excavations: Maspero (1882); Lauer and Picard (1955); Lauer (1976), 22–28, cf. Wilcken (1927), 9–18. Priests of the House of Osorapis: Louvre stele 328, De Meulenaere (1960), 94, with Osiris of Rout Isout and Anoubieion; Louvre N 2556; Paris B.N. 126; Vienna 157; B.M. 886; cf. De Meulenaere (1960), 103, all with the same three priesthoods. The Greek Osiris-Apis is normally Sarapis but Osorapis also occurs, *UPZ* II p. 130 index; cf. Poserapis for *Pr-Wsir-Ḥp*. Earlier bulls of the eighteenth and early nineteenth dynasties were buried in separate graves nearby. The granite sarcophagi start with Psammetichos I in the twenty-sixth dynasty (seventh century B.C.).

[108] See chapter 6.

graffiti along the dromos outside the chambers were not recorded in detail and have now disappeared beneath the sand.[109]

A great pylon erected by Nectanebo I (Nechtnebef) in the early fourth century B.C. and guarded by two limestone lions stood at the eastern entrance to the enclosure; only the lions survive. Through it ran a stone-paved dromos as far as the start of the sphinx-lined avenue. Outside the enclosure on the south side lay a temple to Osorapis dedicated by Nectanebo II with two larger sphinxes at the entrance to the courtyard and a hideous statue of Bes within.[110] Close to this temple at the end of the dromos on the south side, Mariette cleared an extraordinary semicircle of eleven seated Greek statues—Homer, Pindar, Pythagoras, and others. Presenting a stark contrast to the earlier Egyptian temple and the whole desert landscape, these statues are not alone in marking the adherence to this cult of the Greek immigrants of Memphis.[111] For along the dromos low walls were built which Mariette's workmen called *mastabas*, or benches. The southern wall was decorated with a motley collection of sculpture, much of it Dionysiac—the statues in Tura limestone of a panther, two strutting peacocks each ridden by a young Dionysos, a falcon with the head of a bearded man, a sphinx, a long-haired mermaid, and the simple head of a bearded man. Down on the pavement was a fine lion astride a fountain ridden by a young Dionysos with Thracian sandals. Along the northern wall stood a Kerberos statue, again ridden by Dionysos, and towards the west two chapels—one Greek (Corinthian style) in form which an inscription shows to have been the *lychnaption*, the working headquarters of those responsible for the lamps of the god,[112] and the other an Egyptian chapel which contained the painted limestone statue of the Apis bull now in the Louvre (plate i). Beneath the stone paving of the dromos lay thousands of bronze dedicatory figures, the religious souvenirs of generations of pilgrims.

Here along the dromos of the Sarapieion this amalgam of statues and buildings stands as a symbol for different aspects of the cult. The wisdom of Greece (in that semicircle of statues) has met with that of Egypt. The chthonic aspects of the god are stressed in the statuary along the dromos,

[109] Wilcken (1927), 8.
[110] Lauer (1976), 23.
[111] Wilcken (1917), 149–206, and, following their re-excavation, Lauer and Picard (1955); on their date, see chapter 4 n. 60.
[112] Wilcken (1927), 34–35 with 643; Lauer and Picard (1955), 177–80; Otto and Bengtson (1938), 155, for lamps. This may be the same building as in *UPZ* 119.11–12 (156 B.C.). For lamps in other cults, see *P. Louvre* 2423 verso + *UPZ* 143.

and the identification of the Egyptian Osiris with the Greek Dionysos so favored by the Ptolemies is clear. Portrayed, for instance, in the iconography of the Hermopolite tomb of Petosiris, this identification, endorsed in these Memphite statues, gave importance to the Sarapieion for Egyptian and Greek alike. The use of lamps in cult, an innovation of the Greeks, perhaps predates the Ptolemies, while the contiguity of Greek and native chapels for the god reflects the double appeal of the cult of Osiris-Apis known as Sarapis to the Greeks.

Within the enclosure wall[113] of the Sarapieion were other shrines. There was the temple of Astarte where, within a small shrine or *pastophorion*, Ptolemaios, son of Glaukias, lived as *enkatochos* in the troubled reign of Philometor.[114] (His status and life will be further discussed in chapter 7.) Here too was the hill sanctuary of the lioness Sachmet, whose priest is recorded in the late third century B.C.[115] Isis-in-Ḥnṭ had a hill sanctuary here,[116] and north of the dromos lay the sanctuary of the Apis calves.[117] This last was a reasonably important sanctuary with buildings attached and a revenue for several priests. The claim of the Roman writer Pliny[118] that cows which mated with the Apis bull were straightway put to death is shown by this cult to be false. To the north the sanctuary wall was broken by a pylon, marking the entrance to the great street which ran northwards along the spine of the necropolis to the Isis temple, bounding the galleries and shrines of the Sacred Animal Necropolis.[119]

When, under Ptolemy Philometor, the Delta-born priest of Thoth named Ḥor (and later Ḥarthoth) took up residence in Memphis, he described himself as "serving his days in Ḥepnēbes in the desert of the House of Osiris which is upon the mountain of the necropolis of ʿAnch-

[113] *Peribolion: UPZ* 119.15 (156 B.C.). It is unclear whether the wall which Mariette describes as "une muraille à claire–voie" ran on three or four sides of the complex; see Wilcken (1927), 11.

[114] *UPZ* 5.4, 8; 6.3–4; 7.16 (p. 648); 8.16; 12.28; 13.11, 18; 15.5; 16.4–5; 118.18, 36; 19.18–19, 36.

[115] Pestman, *Rec.* 3.3 (201 B.C.) + *PP* 6423. A papyrus found near the Sarapieion records the burial and feeding of lions, Ray (1976), 154. Sachmet is elsewhere described as "at the head of the valley," Gauthier (1919), 203, with a Hathor connection. For her cult, see further Reich (1933a), 65, 72; E. Otto (1956), 118, with a Sahure connection (Abousir); *BGU* 1216.129; *P. Bologna* 3173 verso.21–25, recto.1–8 = Botti (1941), no. 1; Cairo stelae 31099; 31103 = *PP* 5368; Quaegebeur, Clarysse, and Van Maele (1985), 32–34. For the Memphite form Shesmet, see Vercoutter (1962), 5.

[116] Pestman, *Rec.* 2.2; 3.2 (201 B.C.); 1.2 (181 B.C.).

[117] Ray (1972), 308–10; Pestman, *Rec.* 1–3 (201–181 B.C.). The reconstruction of this whole area by Guilmot (1962) must remain *exempli gratia*.

[118] *HN* 8.186. See Appendix D, no. 9, for an Apis, child of an Apis.

[119] Maspero (1882), 36, pylon; Ray (1976), 147; Pestman, *Rec.* 3.4 (201 B.C.).

tawy."[120] Ḥepnēbes, it seems, was the area between the Sarapieion and the street leading up from the north side of the Sarapieion enclosure, bounded by the *wady* with the Lake of Pharaoh to the west. Somewhere near this lake, the Ram, the lord of Mendes, probably also had his cult center.[121]

West of the great street was the Sacred Animal Necropolis with embalming houses, cult buildings, and catacombs dug deep into the rock.[122] From south to north the burial galleries cleared in excavation are those of Thoth the Ibis, Horos the Hawk, Thoth the Baboon, and Isis the mother-of-Apis. Further ibis galleries lay to the north, in the area known as Pi-waʿb-nēbes within the larger area of Ḥepnēbes.[123] The demotic ostraka of the Ḥor/Ḥarthoth archive preserve numerous details of the complex including courts and a tower. Recording trouble in the ibis cult, Ḥor mentions courts sanded over and chapels which stank.[124] The problem of sand blowing in has not changed, and the feeding and cleaning up for the live birds must have involved as many as those involved in the mass production for pilgrims of the potted ibis and hawk mummies. Baboons, rams, lionesses, and cows would have demanded even greater specialist care and attention; their mummification took place below in the valley city of Memphis or along the desert edge.

It was the Isis cows, the mothers-of-Apis, with whose catacombs the main structures of the Sacred Animal Necropolis were connected. A great temple terrace ran along the edge of the bluff overlooking the wady. The main catacomb with its fine limestone-covered vaults was entered from this terrace and was in use from 393 to 41 B.C.[125] At the south end of the terrace lay the entrance to the baboon and hawk galleries and at the northern end a large temple to Isis, mother-of-Apis. There was already a shrine to Isis, which may be the same, described as five stades (or one kilometer) beyond the palace area of Memphis, when in 664 B.C. Psammetichos I with his Carian mercenaries fought the crucial battle in his bid for the throne.[126] Herodotus later described a temple to Isis at Memphis erected

---

[120] *Ḥor* 23 recto.2–6. On Ḥepnēbes, see *Ḥor* 13.4–8; Ray (1976), 147–49; Martin (1979), pl. 2. Psenptais (*PP* 5376) is "overseer of the mysteries of Kemit and Ḥepnēbes."

[121] Psenptais (n. 120 above) was also "prophet of the god of Mendes in the Lake of Pharoah." Ram skulls and bones lie in the desert just north of the southern ibis galleries.

[122] Excavation reports: Emery (1966); (1967); (1969); (1970); (1971); Martin (1973); Smith (1976); Smith and Jeffreys (1977).

[123] Ray (1976), 148–49.

[124] Ray (1976), 136–54, for a full and lively discussion; see also chapter 6 below.

[125] Smith (1972), 176–87; (1974), 29–43, cf. Mariette (1856a).

[126] Polyaenus, *Strat.* 7.3.

in the sixth century B.C. by the Saite king Amasis, and the earliest of the cow stelae, found outside the temple terrace, also dates from this reign (533 B.C.).[127] In its present form, however, the Isis temple in the Sacred Animal Necropolis was set up in the fourth century B.C., perhaps under Nectanebo II, who built widely on the necropolis in what was a period of growing importance for the Memphite animal cults.[128]

However, the necropolis of North Saqqara was not only a necropolis for animals and birds. Originally, and throughout its history, it served as a necropolis also for the human population of the city of Memphis and the surrounding area. In a world where villages might be described by the number of prospective corpses they contained, human embalming and mummification was big business, as we shall see in chapter 5. A man's deepest desire might be to be buried as close as possible to the Apis bulls (a desire in fact achieved by Kha-em-wase, son of Ramses II who was buried in the vaults),[129] but as yet no regular human burials from the Ptolemaic period have been recorded within either the Sarapieion or any other of the temple enclosures of the necropolis. Mariette recorded priestly burials north of the Sarapieion, and other priestly tombstones come from that general area.[130] Indeed, the headland of North Saqqara must have been honeycombed with Ptolemaic graves, penetrating no doubt the chambers and vaults of earlier periods. Within the walled enclosures, Egyptians lived and worked; for the most part their burials lay without.

THE necropolis, domain of Apis, and the valley city, domain of Ptah, consisted therefore of many separate and distinct districts, which were often centered on a temple or shrine. This was the home of those to be presented in the following pages, and the scene of a variety of economic activities, some confined to the city and others dependent on the surrounding countryside. Before we can understand the dynamics of the city, and the way that different groups within it functioned, we need to investigate its economic base.

[127] Hdt. 2.176.2.
[128] E. Otto (1938), 11–34. Isis on the necropolis: *P. Leid.* 379.3 (256 B.C.) = App. B:30; Pestman, *Rec.* 2.2; 3.2 (201 B.C.); 1.2 (181 B.C.), hill residence. The Isieion of the Memphite nome with the right of asylum, *P. Cair. Zen* 59245.2 (252 B.C.), is probably different, Yoyotte (1963), 115–16.
[129] Spiegelberg (1901a), 341–42; Ḥor 8 recto.23–24; verso.6; Ray (1976), 147. For Kha-em-wase, governor of Memphis and high priest of Ptah, see Lauer (1976), 26–27.
[130] Mariette (1856a), 14; Spiegelberg (1904), 2.

2

ECONOMIC LIFE IN MEMPHIS

As the second largest city of Ptolemaic Egypt, Memphis was the scene of economic activity which was both diverse and complex. Urban and rural employments combined with the port, with its shipping and tolls, while the temples and their subsidiary interests, especially the death industry, played a prominent part in the economic life of the city and its surrounding area. The documentary evidence, stemming mainly from the Zenon and Sarapieion archives, is partial and the consequent picture incomplete; to some extent, material remains, the result of excavations and chance finds, may help to fill the gaps. Any attempt to analyze the various economic activities of Memphis and its neighborhood must depend not just on this incomplete evidence but also on inferences drawn from comparative cases.[1] The city therefore may be viewed in itself, as an urban conglomerate, or in relation to the surrounding countryside both as a market town and as a center for distribution, providing services for the population of both city and the neighboring nomes.

THE POPULATION

The Memphite nome ran for about 75 kilometers along the west bank of the Nile and varied in width from 2 to 10 kilometers (fig. 1). The city itself, in the north of the nome, is reported by Diodorus Siculus to have had a circumference of 150 stades, or 30 kilometers; if we assume a roughly rectangular shape, the city perhaps covered some 50 square kilometers, of which about 6 square kilometers (600 hectares) lay within the central dykes.[2] Of this valley area (fig. 3), approximately 126 hectares (21 percent) appear to have been occupied by temples and administrative enclosures; there may have been more of these. In addition, there were the parks, gardens, and vineyards within the central city, so that only 75 percent or 450 hectares of the valley city may have been available for reg-

[1] I have found the following discussions particularly suggestive: Wheatley (1969); Goitein (1967); Mellaart (1975); Butzer (1976), 57–80; Hopkins (1978); Geertz (1979).

[2] Diod. Sic. 1.50.4; cf. Thebes with 6,120 stades, Hdt. 2.15.3. I take a stade as 4 schoinia or 200 meters.

ular dwelling. Up on the necropolis (fig. 4), temples and human housing were found within the sacred enclosures. Of these, as known, the areas are as follows: Anoubieion, 7.5 hectares; Boubastieion, 9.3 hectares; Sacred Animal Necropolis, 0.4 hectares; Sarapieion, 9.4 hectares.[3] The Asklepieion has not yet been securely located. Allowing 8 hectares for this and other habitable parts, there may have been some 35 hectares of built-up area on the necropolis, of which maybe a quarter, perhaps 9 hectares, would serve primarily for human habitation. This, however, is only the central city, and Diodorus' circumference must have included outlying villages and settlement. All these figures are rough and ready; calculations for the size of population are even more speculative.

Nevertheless, some attempt must be made to estimate the size of Memphis' population, for this is crucial to the workings of the economic life of the city. In the absence of figures, two approaches to the problem may be adopted. The city's population may be considered as a proportion of the total population of the country, or an estimate may be made on the basis of population density in relation to the city's area. Both approaches are clearly open to criticism and neither provides anything more than a very speculative estimate.

If, on the first approach, an attempt is made to calculate the size of the population of Memphis as a proportion of the total population of Egypt, two immediate problems must be faced. How great was the total population and what proportion should be adopted? Figures preserved by ancient historians are notoriously corrupt, and textual errors abound in their transmission. This is certainly the case for Egypt, where the text of Diodorus Siculus, who discussed the subject on the basis of priestly records in the first century B.C., reads either three or seven million, depending on the manuscript.[4] Given comparable Roman figures and the scale of agricultural expansion under the early Ptolemies, the larger figure is normally adopted; however, calculations based on the agricultural potential of the country in the early nineteenth century suggest rather six million as the maximum number to be fed from home production.[5] And since in both Hellenistic and Roman times Egypt regularly exported a surplus of grain, caution seems required.

Let us look at the implications of Diodorus' alternative totals and the

---

[3] The area calculations are kindly supplied by D. G. Jeffreys; cf. Jeffreys (1985), 6–10.

[4] Diod. Sic. 1.31.8, "7 million in the past and not less [than 3 million] today"; cf. Joseph. BJ 2.3.85, 7,500,000 without Alexandria in the first century A.D.

[5] Jomard (1818), an excellent discussion; (1836), 39.

range of figures which may be calculated on their basis. If the higher figure of seven million is adopted, and if 5 percent of this total lived in Memphis, the city's population might number 350,000; if 3 percent, 210,000; if 2 percent, 140,000. If, on the other hand, a total of three million is adopted, these figures would be: 150,000 for 5 percent, 90,000 for 3 percent, or 60,000 for 2 percent. But what proportion of the total did in fact live in the second city of Ptolemaic Egypt? Fraser, accepting the 7 million total, reckons on a possible one million for Alexandria, the first city.[6] Such a figure would represent 14 percent of the total population, which is probably too high. This percentage was reached by the modern first city of Cairo only in recent years, in A.D. 1976, at which time 6 percent of the total Egyptian population lived in the second city of Alexandria.[7] Egypt, of course, is now more highly urbanized than ever before, and the different locations and economic structures of today's first and second cities (of inland Cairo and Alexandria on the coast) make comparisons of dubious value. More comparable perhaps may be the figures from the census of A.D. 1897, before the construction of the earlier Aswan dam improved the agricultural potential of the country. At that date 5.9 percent of the population lived in Cairo and 3.3 percent in Alexandria.[8] Taking 3.3 percent for the second city of Ptolemaic Egypt would, on Diodorus' higher figure, give a Memphite population of 231,000. Even in the late nineteenth century, however, modern Egypt was probably more urbanized than in the Hellenistic period. For Hellenistic Memphis 2–3 percent of the population seems a more plausible figure. On such a calculation my estimate for the city's population would be in the region of 140,000–210,000 (or 60,000–90,000 if Diodorus' lower figure is adopted).

The second approach is equally fraught with difficulty. What population density should be adopted for urban dwelling in this period? Twentieth-century Egyptian figures (54.5 per hectare in 1949 or 73.2 per hectare in 1982) are too high to be of use, and in any case there are significant differences between urban densities and those overall. For Pharaonic Egypt, Butzer has estimated a possible density of 271 per square kilometer (2.71 per hectare) for the Memphite nome, but again this overall figure, for one of the more densely populated areas of Egypt, tells us noth-

[6] Fraser (1972), I, 91; II, 171–72.
[7] *The Statesman's Year-book* 119 (1982/3), 429; if Gîza is included with Cairo, the figure rises to 17 percent. In 1798, when the total population was just below two and a half million, about 263,700 (10.6 percent) lived in Cairo.
[8] *The Statesman's Year-book* 37 (1900), 1125.

ing of the actual urban density. It also refers to an earlier period for which a total population of 2.4–3.6 million is projected. Ptolemaic figures may have been much higher.[9] In the small Ptolemaic village of Kerkeosiris in the Fayum, a total population of perhaps 1,520 lived in the 69.5 arouras of the village proper, giving a village density of 87.5 per hectare.[10] At this density throughout the 5,000 hectares, which according to Diodorus counted as city, Memphis might contain a population of 437,500, but such a total seems too high. Memphis, with much of its area in the valley within the city bounds, was subject to flooding and therefore unsuitable for dwelling; and, as we have seen, the city's circumference included parks, gardens, temples, and large areas of desert necropolis which could not support such numbers. In contrast, for the 450 hectares of habitable area within the central dykes, together with the 35 hectares of the necropolis area as reckoned above, this same density would give a population figure nearing 42,500. Urban densities, however, are likely to have been greater than those in a village, and this figure is probably too low.

We may consider a further range of possibilities. Reckoning on the greater overall area of 5,000 hectares and using a lower multiplier than the Kerkeosiris density figure, I calculate as follows. At an urban density of 50 per hectare, Memphis might have a total population of 250,000; 30 per hectare would give a total of 180,000; 20 per hectare, 100,000; and 10 per hectare, 50,000. On the basis of these combined approaches, I estimate that the total population lay somewhere in the range of 50,000–200,000, and probably at the lower end of the scale. Such an estimate remains highly speculative.[11]

Even if a total may be estimated for the population of Memphis, it is still impossible, as would be desirable, to subdivide this figure into different sectors of economic activity or different constituent groups of the population. According to the census of A.D. 1897, of the population over ten years of age 62.65 percent were engaged in agriculture. Yet whereas foreigners made up 6 percent of the population of Cairo, in agriculture foreigners formed less than 1 percent. In contrast, 47.85 percent of the foreign population at that date was involved in industries and trades,

---

[9] *The Statesman's Year-book* 119 (1982/3), 429; Kees (1955), 1; Butzer (1976), 75–76.

[10] Crawford (1971), 44, 124; the density given on p. 124 of 1.29 per hectare takes account of all village lands and not just the living area.

[11] Liebeschutz (1972), 94, suggests 150,000–300,000 for the population of later imperial Antioch. On possible approaches to calculating the population of ancient cities, see Duncan-Jones (1982), 259–77, especially 276–77, on urban densities.

compared with only 16.27 percent of the native Egyptians.[12] For ancient Memphis, what proportion of the population was involved in government service, in agriculture, or in trade is generally as unknowable as are the proportions of the different ethnic groups within the city. Any description of the economic activities of the area remains unaccompanied by any other than the most impressionistic indication of scale.

Amid all this uncertainty and lack of information, the one aspect of urban life that is well documented is its social and economic complexity. Ptolemaic Memphis was the home of a highly diversified community in which a wide range of specialized activities are recorded, in both Greek and demotic sources. In complexity it may be compared with other large pre-industrial cities of the Near East. For medieval Cairo, for instance, as known from the Geniza documents, about 450 different occupations are recorded; of these, roughly 60 percent were manual occupations, 20 percent in commerce and banking, and 20 percent professional (officials, religious functionaries, and educators). More recently, from the early nineteenth century, 288 different trades and crafts have been recorded for Cairo, whereas for nineteenth-century Damascus 435 separate occupations have been listed.[13]

Comparison from within Ptolemaic Egypt is not easy. The only details available are those not from a city but from the Zenon archive, which comes primarily from a rural community.[14] The papyri in the archive do cover the Memphite interests of the *dioikētēs* Apollonios but are concerned more especially with his large 10,000 aroura gift-estate at Philadelphia in the Fayum, together with Zenon's private interests in the same area;[15] some papers also treat Alexandria and earlier dealings overseas, in Syria and Palestine. There are therefore problems in using this material. The range of occupations which these papyri record is likely both to be wider than for one city and also different in kind. The detailed indices of *Pap. Lugd. Bat.* 21 yield the figures in table 1.

In suggesting that these figures might have some relevance to Memphis, I am assuming that the occupations recorded here but not in Memphis may be canceled out by Memphite occupations which go unrecorded, given the partial nature of our evidence. Occupations recorded for Memphis additional to those in the Zenon archives are listed in Ap-

---

[12] *The Statesman's Year-book* 37 (1900), 1126.
[13] Goitein (1967), 99, with notes.
[14] See now the interesting discussion of Orrieux (1985), 114–16, with figure 4.
[15] Orrieux (1981) convincingly establishes the distinction.

TABLE 1. OCCUPATIONS ACCORDING TO THE ZENON PAPYRI

	Number	Percentage
Officials and military men (including 11 cleruchs with land)[a]	86	30
Trades and occupations	182	64
Priests[b]	12	4
Tax-officers[c]	5	2
Total	285	100

[a] Official titles such as *grammateus* or *epistates* only count once each; in practice there were many subsidiary forms some of which are given in *Pap. Lugd. Bat.* 21, index xv.
[b] Only the Greek names are counted here.
[c] In addition to the general tax terms, details of forty individual taxes are recorded; this figure should probably be higher.

TABLE 2. ADDITIONAL MEMPHITE OCCUPATIONS

	Greek	Demotic	Total
Official and military	14		14
Trades and occupations	18	7	25
Priests and temple employees	9	10	19
Total	41	17	58

pendix A; as may be seen there, the Greek and demotic categories do not overlap. The figures are those in table 2.

Given the discrepancies in the two sets of data, some obvious points emerge. The greater range of posts held by priests and different temple workers found in the city is not surprising, and the trades and occupations of the Memphite papyri were primarily urban ones, without the rural specialisms found among the Zenon paypri. If, however, the evidence of the Zenon papyri is combined with that more specifically from the city, a total of 343 different occupations and official positions is recorded. As indicated in the notes to table 1, the figure for tax collectors and officials should probably be raised, giving an overall picture in terms of occupations similar to that found in large Near Eastern urban centers of later, pre-industrial times.

Although interesting and indicative of a high level of specialization in trades and occupations, the limitations of this information should not be forgotten. Showing diversification and specialization in the society and indicating areas of activity in which this occurred, these numbers, as already suggested, tell nothing of the actual proportion of the population involved in the different occupations listed.[16] It is, for instance, likely that well over 50 percent of the population came under the one description of "crown farmer" (*basilikos geōrgos*), but such information is entirely hidden in tables 1 and 2. Such lists also obscure what is known to have been a common feature of Ptolemaic society, the multiple occupations of individuals.[17] The specialization of the vocabulary of occupations was not matched by similar specialization among the members of the society. The ancient world was ignorant of the division of labor in the modern sense.

As we turn to consider the major fields of economic activity in Ptolemaic Memphis, we need to remember that much of the city's life was not primarily concerned with the production and distribution of tangible goods. Not only was Memphis, like most cities of the ancient world, primarily a consumer but it was also a religious center. The temples and those who worked in them were making what was taken to be a central contribution to the country's well-being, a contribution which was not to be measured primarily in economic terms.

AGRICULTURE

It is well known that the economy of Egypt was based on agriculture, and agriculture was based on the Nile. The dykes of Memphis and the great dam in the valley south of the city bear witness to the importance of the control of the Nile flood, on which this agriculture depended.[18] In contrast to the far-reaching innovation of the Fayum, Ptolemaic irrigation works seem here confined to the improvement of existing installations. The raising of the dykes around the city has already been described, and the irrigation of the fields was constantly controlled. In the main Nile valley the agricultural land, divided into carefully managed basins, was covered once a year by the flood waters of the Nile, while orchards and

---

[16] In contrast, see Hopkins' analysis (1978), 72, of the 110 trades recorded on tombstones from Rough Cilicia in the third to sixth centuries A.D.; Pompeii yields 85 known occupations and Rome 264, Hopkins (1983), xvi.

[17] Crawford (1971), 173.

[18] Dykes: *PSI* 488 (257 B.C.); *BGU* 14 iii.1, 14 (A.D. 255), western dyke. Dam: Hdt. 2.13.1; Diod. Sic. 1.36.11; Strabo 17.1.48; *BGU* 1216.28–29 (110 B.C.); *Hor* 11 verso.1; 24.A.5 (second century B.C.); Jeffreys (1985), 53–56, on dykes for both irrigation and defense.

gardens, often placed on slightly higher ground, were watered through-out the year either from canals or wells. Similarly, around the villages and city settlements intensive market gardening depended on continual irri-gation. Like other important cities, Memphis was situated in an area fed by a natural underground water supply,[19] which besides providing for the daily needs of the local population made possible perennial cultivation within the confines of the city. Whereas wheat and other staple crops were grown in the valley beyond the city, vineyards, orchards, and mar-ket gardens were all situated within the city area.

A royal garden stretched for a kilometer north of the palace quarter.[20] Shoots of royal walnut trees are mentioned in a papyrus from the Zenon archive, and besides serving the palace this garden seems also to have pro-vided a nursery for seedlings used in the development of newly reclaimed land in the nearby Fayum.[21] Apollonios, too, the dioiketes, had his or-chard and gardens within the city. Protected by special guards,[22] these also served as nurseries when, like a Persian satrap, he set out to plant his Fayum estate at Philadelphia. Here large-scale planting took place in 255 B.C. In early January of that year Apollonios wrote to his manager Zenon about setting the vines, olives, and other saplings. Zenon should send for a supply from Memphis and elsewhere, giving orders for the planting to begin, while Apollonios himself would obtain young vines and other trees from the neighborhood of Alexandria.[23] From Memphis came the local Egyptian varieties, and on 8 October 255 B.C., Zenon received a further letter from the dioiketes with instructions to take 3,000 olive shoots from his nursery and gardens in Memphis. Before the fruit was gathered Zenon should mark each tree and choose especially the wild ol-ives and laurel bushes, since the Egyptian variety was more suited to parks than to olive groves, and this presumably was what these trees were wanted for.[24] Other plants were grown from seed[25] and new varieties in-troduced, such as the stone pine grown for its edible kernel or possibly

[19] Hamdan (1961), 124; cf. *UPZ* 117.4 (89–83 B.C.) for wells in the Asklepieion, close to the Phchēt canal.

[20] *PSI* 488.12 (257 B.C.).

[21] *PSI* 430.8–9; *P. Cair. Zen.* 59156.2–3 (256 B.C.), with editor's note; Préaux (1947), 26–27; Orrieux (1983), 86–88; (1985), 84–85.

[22] *P. Cair. Zen.* 59690.22, Bargathes, a Syrian, and Asklepiades.

[23] *P. Cair. Zen.* 59195 (255 B.C.).

[24] *P. Cair. Zen.* 59185 (255 B.C.). For propagation in this way, see Theophr. *Hist. Plant.* 2.1.2 (not suitable for cultivated olives); 2.5.4–6.

[25] *PSI* 430.1–2; *P. Cair. Zen.* 59176.167 (255 B.C.), peach stones.

for wood.[26] The interest shown by Apollonios in the types and varieties of plants and trees is worthy of a cosmopolitan Greek of the generation following Theophrastus.

Other plants introduced to the area may have preceded Alexander's conquest. Memphite olives, clearly not the wild Egyptian variety, were highly regarded among the immigrant Greeks who used their friends to secure supplies.[27] It may have been the Hellenomemphites who first brought these to Memphis. The vineyards of the city and surrounding area produced a distinctive sweet wine which also enjoyed a certain reputation among the Greeks.[28] At least one of the vineyards of the city was down on the banks of the Nile[29] and others may have lain in the area west of the city, close by the Phchēt canal. Here too, perhaps, were grown the lettuces, cabbages, chickpeas, fennel, garlic, and cummin—the everyday food items listed in accounts.[30]

Property documents from the community of the necropolis mention vineyards and orchards growing in these western suburbs,[31] and, as in Alexandria, funerary gardens on the lower level of the necropolis were presumably put to more profitable use.[32] A nut garden of Sarapis is found on the necropolis within the Asklepieion,[33] and among the fruit trees gourds and other plants were probably grown. Pomegranates, figs, walnuts, and mulberries all occur in accounts from the Sarapieion.[34]

Moving outside the immediate confines of the city, where orchards, parks, and gardens were watered throughout the year, into the wider area of the Memphite nome, the patterns of landholding and agriculture are rarely clear. That part of the Zenon archive which treats Apollonios' holdings in the Memphite nome sheds some light on the situation of the mid-third century B.C., but in contrast to information surviving for the Arsinoite nome, other details that survive are scattered both in time

---

[26] *P. Cair. Zen.* 59233.4 (253 B.C.); 59106.1–4 (257 B.C.), on the problem of finding wood.
[27] *P. Cair. Zen.* 59501.7–9, black and pickled olives; *PSI*, 671.3–4; 826.12 (mid-third century B.C.).
[28] *PSI* 544.1–3; *P. Mich. Zen.* 117.13; *P. Cair. Zen.* 59149 (256 B.C.); *P. Ryl.* 564.19–21 (250 B.C.); *SB* 7182.94 (first century B.C.); cf. *P. Ross. Georg.* 2.141.19, 35, 55, 60, 68.
[29] *P. Hib.* 205.24–25 (260–250 B.C.); cf. *P. Cair. Zen.* 59593.1–4; *BGU* 2127 (A.D. 156); for vineyards on Apollonios' Memphite estate, see Wipszycka (1961), 166, 174, 180.
[30] *UPZ* 89 (160 B.C.); cf. *P. Cair. dem.* 30837.1 for mustard.
[31] *P. Leid.* 381 (October 226 B.C.) = Lüddeckens (1960), 146–49, Urk. 3Z; *P. Bibl. Nat.* 224–25 + *UPZ* 137–38 (68 B.C.) = Lüddeckens (1960), 172–77, Urk. 10.
[32] Fraser (1972), 27.
[33] *P. Bruss.* 3.4 (256 B.C.) = App. B:31.
[34] *UPZ* 89.4–16 (160 B.C.); cf. 101.12 (156 B.C.) for dried figs.

and place. The picture is impressionistic, the evidence not suitable for analysis.

Administratively, land may be divided into crown land and that conceded by the crown, to temples,[35] military settlers (cleruchs),[36] or as gift estates.[37] All these categories existed in the Memphite nome; only their proportion is unknown. On cultivated land a wide range of crops was grown: wheat, barley, *olyra* (emmer wheat, Triticum dicoccum), lentils, *arakos* (chickling), fodder crops (clover, fenugreek, grass for hay), vineyards, flax, and oil crops.[38] As elsewhere, grain land presumably predominated,[39] yet this was still insufficient to meet the exceptional demands of the large urban center of Memphis.

Wheat, olyra, and barley from the nome were regularly siphoned into the city, but this did not suffice. At the lowest possible rate of 150 kilograms (5.87 artabas) per person of unmilled grain a year, a population of 100,000 would annually consume 15 million kilograms or 587,200 artabas, the produce (after tax) of 117,440 arouras or 29,360 hectares (294 square kilometers).[40] The flood plain of the Nile from Giza to Gerza (Kerke), an area approximately 70 kilometers long with an average width of 9 kilometers, gives a cultivable area of 630 square kilometers or 63,000 hectares, of which 30–40 square kilometers lay across the river in the Heliopolite and Aphroditopolite nomes to the east.[41] For the purpose of rough calculation we may assume 600 square kilometers as possible agricultural land. At any one time, of course, cereals are unlikely to have been grown on more than half this land (300 square kilometers), and there

[35] Sacred land: *BGU* 1216.129–35, 190–93 (110 B.C.). This document shows well how relations between different areas ran along the valley; Clarysse (1980b), 97–100.

[36] See Übel (1968), 34–40; Wipszycka (1961), 156, 162; *P. Cair. Zen.* 59132 (256 B.C.); 59179 (255 B.C.); 59245 (252 B.C.); 57789.16–22; *BGU* 1216.71 (110 B.C.), 292¾ arouras catoecic land in the Memphite, compared with 1225 arouras in the Herakleopolite nome.

[37] On the *dorea* of Apollonios, see Wipszycka (1961); Orrieux (1985), 107, 109–10, 181, 205, 212; (1980), on its end, cf. *Pap. Lugd. Bat.* 20.61 (246/5 B.C.); Clarysse (1980b), 100–101.

[38] See Wipszycka (1961), 179, with references; flax: *P. Lond.* 7.2164.4 n. (not Memphite), cf. 1997.5–6 (250 B.C.); clover: *Hor* 8 recto.18–19 (second century B.C.), in a nightmare; 12A.6 (second century B.C.); vineyards on cleruchic land: *P. Cair. Zen.* 59179 (255 B.C.); arakos seed from Memphis: *P. Cair. Zen.* 59814.6 (257 B.C.).

[39] See Crawford (1971), 112–15.

[40] 150 kilograms of wheat assumes that 25 percent of the 200 kilograms minimum subsistence requirement was provided from other foods, and I allow a yield of 5 artabas an aroura, after rents and tax. For the calculation, cf. Thompson (Crawford) (1983), 72, with chapter 5 n. 93 below, for 25.545 kilograms to an artaba.

[41] Figures kindly supplied by D. G. Jeffreys. Although the Memphite nome extended somewhat south of Kerke (Yoyotte 1963), the total agricultural area was probably not significantly different. The northern boundary is also uncertain.

were others living in the nome besides the population of Memphis. But because many of the rents and taxes raised locally will have stayed in the city for distribution as temple grants,[42] as pay for troops or official allowances to crown employees, it seems that in normal years a population of 100,000 might just be fed from within the nome. If the population was larger, or in less than average years, the city then would need to be provisioned also from outside the nome.

The recently published record of a crown official charged with the distribution of grain in Memphis is a measure of the problems involved.[43] Such an appointment was previously unknown for Egypt and suggests a high level of central concern for some part, at least, of the food supply of the city. Even if he was concerned only with provisioning the army or other crown commitments, the existence of such an official does seem significant. In the early years of the second century B.C., the post was held by one Herakleides, who in one of his five-day accounts recorded the distribution of small quantities of "white wheat," sold at a price consistently 10 drachmas below the regular market rate. The grain in question was from another nome, most probably from the Hermopolite. Whatever the scale of the operation, it appears the crown was involved at least in some aspect of provisioning the city, perhaps through the compulsory purchase of grain (*sitos agorastos*) at favorable rates in other parts of the country. Otherwise the private market operated, and for shippers who could get it there Memphis provided a ready market for grain from elsewhere in Egypt; profits might be large, if only the transport could be found.[44] Private enterprise flourished here, with cleruchs and their contacts selling a cargo wherever the price was good.[45] Indeed, the variation of prices and the lack of available information on them are recurrent features in the documents. On the whole, however, the attractions of a major port and market center were, it seems, sufficient to bring in the grain required.[46]

[42] Cf. *P. Erasm.* 1.8.6–7 (153/2 B.C.), an annual *syntaxis* allowance paid directly to a *lesōnis*; 17.5–6 (mid-second century B.C.), for a queen cult.

[43] *P. Köln* 5.217 (202 or 195 B.C.). The quantities are mostly lost (one sum is 52 artabas) and at 170 drachmas, as compared with 180 drachmas, the price charged is near normal; see the editor's note on this, and on white wheat.

[44] *P. Petrie* 3.76 verso.12 (third century B.C.), where the whole account may refer to the *thesauros* of the city; *P. Col. Zen.* 8 (257 B.C.); *P. Cair. Zen.* 59253.7 (251/50 B.C.), barley; 59217 (254 B.C.), help with shipping required; *P. Mich. Zen.* 60.3–4 (248/7 B.C.), shipping proposal for wheat. Roman examples: *P. Oxy.* 1650 and 1650a (first to second century A.D.); 522 (second century A.D.). On the nature of markets, see later in this chapter.

[45] E.g., *P. Mich. Zen.* 28 (256 B.C.).

[46] See n. 44. *P. Cair. Zen.* 59141 (256 B.C.); 59132, in contrast, records grain shipped from the nome to Alexandria.

Oil formed a second basic commodity in Egypt, as elsewhere, and in oil Memphis required regular provisioning from outside the nome. On crown land in the city and the nome sufficient plants were grown for neither basic culinary nor lighting oil; both sesame for culinary use and castor oil for lighting (kiki oil extracted from *kroton*) came from the Fayum lands nearby. Annually, the city might receive from here 4,200 artabas of sesame, together with kroton (the number of artabas is lost). In addition, the Memphite nome annually brought in 2,400 artabas of sesame and 2,120 artabas of castor from the Fayum ("the Marsh").[47] Oil crops grew well on poor land under reclamation[48] and the extension of cultivation in the lands to the southwest benefited both the urban population of Memphis and others in the Memphite nome. The oil from these Fayum plants presumably was manufactured in the city. Additional supplies may have come from crops grown more locally.[49]

LIVESTOCK

The raising of livestock took place alongside the agricultural exploitation of the Nile valley. Animals consumed fodder crops and grazed on the stubble in the fields, thereby providing valuable manure for the land. In spite of the natural interdependence of the farmers and herdsmen, different interests might come into conflict here.[50] Besides cattle, mainly raised as draft animals,[51] sheep and goats were reared in significant numbers. In the Memphite nome, Apollonios' interests included a sizeable herd of goats under the overall control of one Hermias. Careful accounts were kept of additions and losses to the flock. The goats were bred for milk, cheese, hair, and hides, for sacrifice at major Greek festivals, or simply for sale as stock in the city.[52] Goats might graze alongside sheep[53] but normally the two were separately recorded.

[47] *P. Rev.* 69.1–4 = *SB/Bh.* 1, Memphis; 72.11–14, Memphite nome; Bingen (1946), especially 133–37, for extraction rates. *P. Lond.* 7.1982 (252 B.C.), kroton; *UPZ* 119.1 (156 B.C.), kiki workers, perhaps coming with the raw materials; see chapter 7 below.
[48] Crawford (1973), 248 n. 3.
[49] *PSI* 372 (250/49 B.C.), Sophthis; cf. *P. Cair. Zen.* 59160.
[50] *PSI* 380.4–7 (248 B.C.), trouble with the locals with preference given to cattle over goats. On the interdependence of arable and pastoral farming, see Power (1941), 5–7.
[51] *PSI* 380.7 (248 B.C.); 497 (257 B.C.); *P. Cair. Zen.* 59540 (257 B.C.); 59136.2 (256 B.C.). See *UPZ* 110.181–85 (164 B.C.) for communal organization.
[52] *P. Cair. Zen.* 59429 + *Pap. Lugd. Bat.* 20.35; *P. Wisc.* 2.78 (248 B.C.), with full details; *P. Cair. Zen.* 59176.54–55 (255 B.C.), 2 obols paid for two days' shearing.
[53] *PSI* 346 (2 March 254 B.C.), on lotus land; *P. Cair. Zen.* 59394, joint account.

Sheep are found in the Memphite nome at all periods.[54] In the third century B.C. Apollonios' flocks there were bred as much for wool as for any other purpose, with new strains introduced for better fleeces.[55] Many of the shepherds were non-Egyptians, for on the pattern of Jacob who, following his son Joseph into Egypt, brought his family and flocks from Canaan, immigrant and nomadic shepherds had always been a standard feature of the Egyptian countryside.[56] In the third century B.C. one of the Memphite shepherds of the Zenon archive, Nouraios, had an Aramaic name, as did Addaios, closely connected both with sheep and woollen textiles in the area. The same feature is to be found for shepherds and goatherds connected with Memphite temples.[57] The scrubland at the desert edge served as pasture land for flocks, and at least one of the Memphite shepherds lived in the Boubastieion close to the pasture where he worked.[58] Temples shared the area and temple flocks might be sizeable, though tended in smaller groups.[59]

The flocks which came under Apollonios' purview were reasonably large, though it is the Fayum flocks, around Philadelphia, for which the most detailed evidence survives. Careful tally was kept and the sheep were regularly counted. One memorandum of Zenon made for Apollonios records 6,371 sheep and 206 goats.[60] Some of these were sacred sheep, belonging to the temples; others were ascribed to crown farmers, to cavalrymen, to the peasants (*laika probata*), or to influential immigrants such as Zenon, Nikias, or Sostratos, son of Kleon. Apollonios, it seems, had some form of interest in all these animals; the memorandum may record the payment of the pasture tax, for which perhaps he undertook responsibility in the area. The list of personal names which follows the declaration of animals includes both Arabs (traditional pastoralists) and

[54] *PSI* 487 (257 B.C.); *P. Cair. Zen.* 59136 (256 B.C.); 59068 (256 B.C.); *P. Mich. Zen.* 35 (254 B.C.); *BGU* 1223 (second to first century B.C.), sheep and lambs.

[55] Wipszycka (1961), 180–81; Orrieux (1985), 260–63; *P. Cair. Zen.* 59142 (256 B.C.) and 59195 (255/4 B.C.), Milesian wool; 59145.6–7 (256 B.C.), at Sophthis; 59287 (250 B.C.), Arabian fleeces.

[56] Gen. 46–47; Vergote (1959), 175–89; cf. the Hyksos earlier.

[57] *P. Cair. Zen.* 59136.1, 7 (256 B.C.); *P. Mich. Zen.* 35.2, 7, Nouraios; *PSI* 487 (257 B.C.), Addaios acquires tar (to prevent scab). See chapter 3 n. 90 below on temple flocks.

[58] *P. Louvre* E 3266.6.D–E, F (197 B.C.) = App. B:2.

[59] *P. Cair. Zen.* 59394.6, in the Fayum; Delekat (1964) 103–4, a regular occupation for *b3k; P. Tebt.* 53.7 (110 B.C.), *probata hiera* cf. Crawford (1971), 89 n. 8. *P. Gurob* 22 provides the fullest evidence for Memphis. Sacred cattle might also be kept, *P. Louvre* E 3266.4.Q (197 B.C.) = App. B:2, perhaps for religious purposes.

[60] *P. Cair. Zen.* 59394.1–27. For the size of the flock, cf. Power (1941), 28, a "huge" nonmanorial flock of 5,500 kept in Derbyshire in the fourteenth century A.D. (30–31, other flocks were smaller).

an interpreter.[61] These were probably the local shepherds who, as the source of fleeces for the weaving sheds of Philadelphia and Memphis, came under the general control of Apollonios. For the success of these new ventures, good community relations were essential. So, when in the winter of 255 B.C. following his introduction of Milesian sheep Apollonios appointed Maron as his epistates, to supervise these shepherds and train up youngsters, he already knew the appointment would meet with the Arabs' approval.[62]

Other animals reared in the neighborhood of Memphis were transport animals—mules, donkeys, and horses.[63] Memphite dogs had a strange reputation for pooling their prey and sharing their food,[64] but perhaps these were the sacred variety rather than the guard dogs of the city.

As in all Egyptian towns and villages, pigeons were bred for manure and possibly for meat.[65] Poultry, corn-fed, was reared in the area[66] and the ubiquitous goose might provide eggs as well as meat for sacrifice.[67] Gooseherds are regularly recorded in Memphite documents and, following Apollonios' experiments in poultry breeding, in February 250 B.C. one of them (Totoēs) abducted five special coots; he claimed they came from the marsh.[68] Presumably, as shown in earlier tombs, wild birds were hunted in these marshes and, though unrecorded in the documents, the net sinkers found in Memphite excavations[69] are a sure sign of fishing in the area.

Finally came the bees, depending on the seasonal flowers for the honey that they made. For Memphis with its Carian connections, choice honey from the homeland was brought in to supplement the local brands,[70] for alongside carob, honey formed the main sweetener available at the time.[71]

[61] P. Cair. Zen. 59394.28–53; the interpreter, Limnaios, is brother to a goatherd from Aspendos.
[62] P. Cair. Zen. 59195.2 (254 B.C.); PSI 538.
[63] P. Cair. Zen. 59836, mules; 59376, horses; 59788, donkey drivers, cf. Hor 14 verso.8, obscene? Wipszycka (1961), 181, comments on the lack of evidence for pigs; this is probably due simply to chance.
[64] Ael. NA 7.19.
[65] P. Louvre E 3266.5.R, 6.G (197 B.C.) = App. B:2; see Crawford (1971), 47.
[66] Wipszycka (1961), 174; P. Cair. Zen. 59375.1, from Addaios.
[67] Petrie, Wainwright, and Gardiner (1913), 34, from the eighteenth dynasty: 1,000 egg-laying geese. On gooseherds, see chapter 7 below.
[68] P. Lond. 7.1997.2–3 (250 B.C.).
[69] Anthes (1965), 33; cf. P. Tebt. 701.197 (235 B.C.), fish imported from the Fayum.
[70] P. Cair. Zen. 59012.28–31 (259 B.C.); P. Mich. Inv. 3243.7 (third century B.C.), ed. Hanson (1972); cf. Robert (1935), 170–73 on Carian honey; for Memphite honey, see P. Cair. Zen. 59060.10; 59061.3, cf. P. Lond. 7.1941.11 (257 B.C.).
[71] Darby, Ghalioungui, and Grivetti (1977), 699–701; UPZ 89.8, 11, 16 (160 B.C.), honey and honey cakes; 104.6.

Beekeepers knew no boundaries but those of the flourishing crops they followed with their hives, and the papyri show how, frequently entangled in troublesome situations, they formed a difficult group for local officials to handle.[72]

TEXTILES

Contents of Zenon's trunk: 1 linen robe, laundered; 1 winter cloak (*chlamys*), dyed the color of earth and laundered; 1 worn cloak; 1 half-worn summer cloak; 1 winter cloak, natural shade and laundered; 1 worn winter cloak; 1 new summer cloak, the color of vetch; 1 white winter tunic (*chitōn*) with sleeves, laundered; 1 winter tunic, natural shade, with sleeves and worn; 1 worn winter tunic, natural shade; 2 white winter tunics, laundered; 1 white, half-worn tunic; 2 new summer tunics; 1 unlaundered tunic; 1 tunic half-worn; 1 white winter outer-garment (*himation*), laundered; 1 threadbare cloak (*tribōn*); 1 white, light summer garment, laundered; 1 half-worn summer garment; 1 pair of pillows from Sardis; 2 pairs of khaki shoes; 2 pairs of new white shoes; 2 new white belts.

Zenon's traveling wardrobe as listed by Peisikles in the mid-third century B.C. was no doubt more extensive than that of a regular urban Greek.[73] Nevertheless, the supply and demand for textiles was as much an aspect of ancient cities as of their medieval counterparts.[74] The Aramaic papyri from Egypt are full of references to the acquisition and transport of individual items of clothing and in this context Memphis is often the source of supply.[75] The city had long been a center for the production and sale of cloth and clothing, with the manufacture of both linen and wool based as much on the suitability of the countryside around for the primary products (sheep and flax) as on the existence of a ready market for the finished article. According to Herodotus, wool could not be worn for entry into temples nor used for burial shrouds.[76] Whereas linen was thus assured a steady demand, woollen cloaks were regularly required to cover linen tunics, warding off the desert chills.[77] From the third century B.C. the papers of Zenon offer a glimpse of various aspects of the production and retail of textiles in the city and its surrounding area. The different

[72] *P. Cair. Zen.* 59368.16 (240 B.C.), hives leased locally; 59520, a quarrel; Bingen (1978), 214.

[73] *P. Cair. Zen.* 59092.

[74] Hopkins (1978), 52–55.

[75] Porten (1968), 89–90; Grelot (1972), 130–32, no. 17; 154–57, no. 26.

[76] Hdt. 2.81, comparing Orphic and Bacchic practices.

[77] Hdt. 2.81.1.

stages of production may be seen—those involved in the cultivation of flax or the rearing of sheep, in the preparation of the raw materials and their working into finished products, as well as the scale of the operations and the impact of immigrant Greeks on the city's well-established textile production. The interrelation of the city and the surrounding area is a crucial feature in this picture.

According to Pliny, Egypt's main centers of flax production were in the Delta and around Tentyra in the south. Later, however, in the tenth to thirteenth centuries A.D., Busir (Abousir el Melekh) and the Fayum were important centers for the production of flax which then formed the country's main industrial crop.[78] In Ptolemaic Egypt both the Fayum, where the flax was grown with other oil crops in newly reclaimed areas, and the Herakleopolite nome south of Memphis figure prominently in the record of the cultivation and production of this crop. Flax woven in the sheds of Memphis came mainly from these areas. As with the Arabic *kattōn*, the Greek word *linon* denotes both the flax and linen,[79] but the context generally clarifies the meaning; the two uses correspond to two very different stages in production.

Stage one was in the countryside. In the Fayum in the third century B.C. flax was grown in smallish quantities on the gift-estate of Apollonios,[80] and elsewhere too near Memphis, especially to the south, small-scale production was, it seems, the norm. Of the early stages of preparation of the yarn not much is known. One letter to Apollonios records Zenon as his manager preparing to take on extra labor (which might be paid in cash or flax) for the flax harvest two months ahead,[81] while a detailed account of uncertain date from the same archive lists payments made at the rate of 6 *chalkoi* a day to those who plucked and stooked the flax to dry, before the linseed could be beaten out.[82] In this account a variety of payments made in connection with the plant occur which are not easily distinguished.[83] The payments for plucking and stooking were probably made

---

[78] Pliny *HN* 19.14; Goitein (1967), 104–5, 224–28.

[79] Goitein (1967), 104–5. *Stippyon* (tow) also occurs, woven (*P. Mich. Zen.* 120.3, 114½ cubits length) and unwoven (*PSI* 404).

[80] *P. Mich. Zen.* 26.4 (257 B.C.), 3 artabas seed; *P. Lond.* 7.1991.5 with tables A–C; 2164.4, 2½ drachmas for weeding.

[81] *P. Lond.* 7.1997.5–7 (mid-February 250 B.C.).

[82] *P. Cair. Zen.* 59782(b).33, 103, 119–22, 138, 158–61, perhaps from Mecheir or Phamenoth.

[83] Cols. i–vi and vii–xii seem to cover the same dates, with flax primarily, though not exclusively, listed in the earlier part of the account and tow in the second.

to employees on the land of Apollonios,[84] but the major part of the account records the purchase of green yarn of flax and tow brought in day by day from the countryside around. As with the sheep, Apollonios was actively involved with those from outside the estate. Acting as middlemen, named Egyptian peasants from the villages, chiefly in the Herakleopolite nome, brought in the bundles of flax and tow, receiving payment for their load on behalf of the producers whom they represented. Flax was bought at just over a *chalkous* a bundle, while tow came at a third of the price. So, for example, one day Hetpheus of Busiris brought in seventy-eight bundles of flax on behalf of twenty-three producers, and was paid 2 *drachmai* 2 *chalkoi* for the flax.[85] Or Harchonsis from the Herakleopolite village of Onnes brought in fifty-five bundles of flax with seven of tow on behalf of twenty-seven producers from his village.[86] It is unclear whether the central collection point was Philadelphia or Memphis, but what is clear is that the primary preparation of the yarn took place locally in the villages before the flax was sold.

Back in the village, once the flax was plucked and stooked to dry, the next stage was the extraction, by shaking, of the linseed used for oil. Then the stalks were retted, left to rot in water until the outer case was soft. Next came the scutching, as the stalks were beaten to break up the fibers they contained.[87] The process by which the flax and tow were separated out, known as hackling, is not named in the sources.[88] The carding of the separated fibers took place out of doors and sometimes in a courtyard which would provide protection from blowing sand. On one occasion workmen were paid one obol for brushing up a pile of scrap oakum when the tow was carded.[89] Finally, the carded fibers were ready to be spun.

The silence of the sources on the subject of spinning is striking, but not perhaps surprising. Ptolemaic evidence is generally sketchy—the product is found more often than its producers. Earlier tomb paintings, from the Middle Kingdom, show the task of spinning performed by women who pass the fiber through bowls of water and their mouths to keep it damp

[84] *P. Cair. Zen.* 59782(b).84, 122–31, Ephesos, 158–61, Andronikos; note the Greek names.

[85] *P. Cair. Zen.* 59782(b).53–54, 78–79, cf. 34.

[86] *P. Cair. Zen.* 59782(b).67–68, cf. 28, 45.

[87] In *PSI* 404.8, one talent of tow which has been scutched but not carded out (*stippyon errimenon*) costs 9 drachmas, the cash equivalent of 1,296 bundles.

[88] Edgar, *P. Cair. Zen.* 59782(b) introduction, thought that *tillein* referred to this process; cf. Kallerēs (1950–51), 185–86, the plucking of the plants.

[89] *PSI* 404.7, out of doors and unguarded at Pataikion's place; *P. Cair. Zen.* 59176.41–43 (255 B.C.), clearing up from the courtyard.

for handling as they spin.[90] The linen thread, linon or *linokalamē*, and coarser yarn, the *stippyon*, were now ready for disposal out of the village, and these, I suspect, were the bundles which the Herakleopolitan peasants brought up to town to be cleaned and woven up.

Eleven separate villages are named in the one Zenon flax account, ten from the Herakleopolite and one (Meia) from the Memphite nome. How, on arrival in town, the flax and tow were now handled is not clear, but some form of central storage under Zenon's control is suggested by one tow account which records 772 talents 37½ minas of tow from worked flax, 20 talents 49½ minas of old tow, 7½ minas of unusable tow and 74 talents of tow in store.[91] The quantities here are large, sufficient to keep many workers employed in making ropes, sacks, sails, and other woven products from this coarser yarn.

On arrival in town, the hanks of spun green thread passed to the linen boilers, the *linepsoi*, for cleaning.[92] Natron and castor oil (kiki) were used together for the process; since both products were subject to royal control, their provision might cause problems. In November 254 B.C., Theokles, the *oikonomos*, wrote to Zenon of his problems with the linen boilers; owed sixty *metrētai* of kiki oil, they still needed a further two hundred. The authorization for this supply must come from Apollonios in Alexandria, and seven days later the problem still rested there.[93] As Apollonios' manager in the area, Zenon is asked by the oikonomos to use his influence to get the oil released in anticipation of the dioiketes' order coming through.

On another occasion it was natron that caused the problem. This time Protarchos wrote to Zenon informing him that a local shortage was forcing the linen boilers to travel outside the nome to find supplies; Zenon should provide the natron promised so boiling might proceed and the men might work.[94] These particular linepsoi were probably on the payroll of the estate, and the problem of the supply of ingredients necessary

---

[90] E.g., Newberry (1893), 35–36 with plate XXVI, the tomb of Tehutihetep; here spinning and weaving are in close proximity. Guidotti (1984) discusses the divided bowls used for this; her figure 10 suggests that with the help of pulleys one spinner might operate two spindles.

[91] *P. Cair. Zen.* 59779.

[92] Wipszycka (1965), 23–24; Forbes (1956), 19, thinks, improbably, that boiling was part of the retting process.

[93] *PSI* 349; 566 (254 B.C.); Orrieux (1983), 105–6, arguing for Philadelphia. For a *symbolon* needed for the release of oil, see chapter 7 n. 169 below.

[94] *P. Cair. Zen.* 59304 (250 B.C.).

for their work reflects the scale of these new operations sponsored by immigrant Greeks.

Once boiled, the hanks of thread passed to the weavers. There was still some preliminary cleaning to be done before the thread was woven up and, like the spinning, this was probably women's work. Different working arrangements might be made, as envisaged in one proposal made to Zenon by a group of weavers looking for employment. The weavers proposed alternative methods of remuneration for their work. They might be paid on a piecework basis—1 drachma for cleaning and picking over a talent of linen yarn and 3 drachmas for weaving a length of cloth (*othonion*). Three men, one woman, and six days would be needed for this job, and this, they claimed, was a rock-bottom price. Alternatively, Zenon might prefer to pay a daily wage—1½ obols a day for the men and ½ obol for the women. If Zenon accepted this latter arrangement the provision of a man to service the looms would be his responsibility.[95] The arithmetic applied in the second case, with a total of 5 drachmas 2 obols, is not entirely clear; the weavers seem to have hoped their prospective employer would choose the piece-rate deal. No doubt the process might be speeded up, or fewer men employed; corner cutting was not unknown in contemporary practice. Indeed, it was the cheating of his fellow carpet weaver Nechthembes to which Pais drew Zenon's attention in an attempt to undercut Nechthembes' deal: "for the fourteen carpets he produces I shall make two more."[96] Competition was fierce; Nechthembes, claimed Pais, was such a scoundrel he deserved to have his hands chopped off.

Linen came in various qualities and weights. One talent of linen yarn might weigh up to a quarter less once boiled in natron and oil and woven up as a completed length of cloth.[97] *Byssos* was the finest quality, often made and used within the temples to clothe the statues of the gods and as mummy wrappings for sacred animals and the very rich;[98] heavier qualities of linen served as bedcovers[99] or as outer wrappings used instead of woollen cloaks.[100] The othonion remained the basic item of commerce.[101]

---

[95] *PSI* 6.599 with p. xvii; see Rostovtzeff (1922), 116–17.

[96] *P. Cair. Zen.* 59484.

[97] *Encyclopaedia Britannica* (1959), *sv* "Linen."

[98] *P. Rev.* = *SB/Bh* 1.103 (259 B.C.); *P. Cair. Zen.* 59087 (258/7 B.C.), *byssos* account; *OGIS* 90.18–19 (196 B.C.), remission of two-thirds of royal tax; *P. Tebt.* 5.62–64 (118 B.C.) for the involvement of chief priests.

[99] E.g., *P. Lond.* 7.1942.5; see chapter 7 with nn. 83–108 below.

[100] *PSI* 418.18–21.

[101] *P. Petrie* 1.30 (1).3 = 3.42 H (4) (third century B.C.); *P. Lond.* 7.1942.5 (257 B.C.); *P. Hamb.* 106.4 (254/3 B.C.); *PSI* 428.32–33; see further chapter 7 with nn. 85–86 below; Bartina (1965) discusses the terms used in biblical sources.

Many clothes were shaped on the looms,[102] but for the finishing and alteration of clothes there existed individual seamstresses who worked at home apart from the weaving sheds.[103]

Such, insofar as they may be recovered, were the basic operations in the preparation of linen. The state was interested throughout. The kiki supply was controlled, natron was taxed,[104] and government officials like Theokles were charged to inspect the washing houses, making sure sufficient supples of cleansing agents were to hand.[105] Furthermore, the state regularly required the production of a prescribed quantity of good quality linen from each area.[106] The number and use of looms were also watched. At this stage of production, control might be more effective than earlier in the fields, for schedules for crop cultivation seem marked more by contravention than by observance.[107] Yet, in spite of central supervision and control and regular government demands, the picture which emerges from the papers of both Zenon and, later, of Ptolemaios, son of Glaukias,[108] is one of private production within a market economy.[109] Taxes are levied along the way, but raw materials are freely purchased and the finished products sold on an open market; and the workers regularly bargain for their wages and a better deal.

THE Memphite manufacture of woollen textiles depended on the fleeces from the sheep raised in the countryside around.[110] These might be large flocks like those attached to the estate of Apollonios, the peasant flocks of local shepherds, or temple flocks. In this respect the early Ptolemaic period was a time of real (if limited) development. When in 279/8 B.C. Ptolemy II Philadelphos put on a celebratory procession in Alexandria, imported sheep were among the more exotic animals shown.[111] So, too, his dioiketes Apollonios, on his estates in the Fayum and the southern part of the Memphite nome, introduced new strains of sheep bred primarily

---

[102] Granger-Taylor (1982); compare the items enumerated in *P. Hib.* 67 and 68 (228 B.C.).

[103] *PSI* 854.20 (257 B.C.) with Rostovtzeff (1922), 116; *UPZ* 91.16 (159 B.C.).

[104] *P. Cair. Zen.* 59206 verso.31–33 (254 B.C.), 6 drachmas a month for Apollonios' interests.

[105] *P. Tebt.* 703.99–104 (late third century B.C.).

[106] *P. Tebt.* 703.89–99 (late third century B.C.); *P. Rev.* = *SB/Bh.* 1.103 (259 B.C.), unfortunately a very fragmentary text. Préaux (1939a), 93–116, discusses the extent and nature of control.

[107] Vidal-Naquet (1967), 33–36.

[108] See chapter 7.

[109] So Préaux (1939a), 107–9, against Rostovtzeff (1922), 117, and Edgar, *P. Cair. Zen.* 59304, introduction.

[110] Forbes (1956), 14–16; Wipszycka (1965), 27–37.

[111] Ath. 5.201 c, 130 Ethiopian sheep, 300 Arabian sheep, and 20 from Euboea; see Rice (1983), 95, with Walbank (1984a), 53, for the date.

for their wool. Teams of shepherds looked after these, and some of those in charge were perhaps imported with the sheep.

Milesian sheep grazed on the thorny desert lands, their fleeces protected beneath leather jackets. This particular breed was new to Egypt, and flocks of Milesian temple sheep are recorded in Naukratis earlier in the reign of Philadelphos.[112] Perhaps they reached the Memphite nome together with settlers from that city, or maybe, like so much else, Apollonios had them imported to the area. Some sheep, like Arabian sheep, were sheared, some even twice a year, but from Milesian sheep the wool was plucked by hand and then not rolled in mats but packed safely away in boxes for transport up to town by ship.[113] First, however, the wool was normally washed, for as with linen textiles the earlier stages of production took place locally, close to where the sheep were reared.

Sheep's wool was scoured by washing it with *stroutheion*, or soap wort. The plant was taxed and precious; its supply was closely watched.[114] Once washed, the raw wool might now be shipped as flocks,[115] or else spun locally by women in the villages. Again evidence is short, but Zenon's list of numbers of women woollen workers registered in three Fayum villages ("at Mouchi: 320; at Oxyrhyncha: 314; at Tebtunis: 150; total: 740") most probably refers to those who spun the wool.[116] This document forms one of the few surviving references to the scale of the operation; the wool these women wove came probably from local flocks. But whether Zenon employed the women or simply bought the wool they spun remains unknown; with responsibility for managing Apollonios' weaving establishments he kept a close eye on the raw materials. Skeins of wool (*kykloi*) were packed ten to a bundle (*desmion*) for transport to the weaving sheds; one quarter of a mina's weight of unwashed wool made up seven and a half bundles.[117] Thus one talent's weight of fleeces might become 1,800 bundles, but with a significant loss in weight from washing.[118]

---

[112] Spiegelberg (1928), 6, with Clarysse (1987), 32, on m*l*t.

[113] *P. Cair. Zen.* 59430. See Pliny, *HN* 8.190, for plucking; Rostovtzeff (1922), 180, for jackets; Schnebel (1925), 327, for shearing. Milesian: *P. Cair. Zen.* 59142.2, 7; 59195.3; 59430.10; Arabian: *P. Cair. Zen.* 59287.1; 59405.7; 59430.5, 8; 59825.34; *P. Lond.* 7.2077.3; *PSI* 4.377.14; 429.17; n. 111 above.

[114] *PSI* 429.13–16; *P. Cair. Zen.* 59430.15, 5½ obols tax; *P. Lond.* 7.2012.10–12 (243 B.C.), stroutheion sent with wool.

[115] *P. Cair. Zen.* 59430; 59776.6–7, *gnaphylla*, 13–14, *krokydes*; cf. *PSI* 854.19 with Rostovtzeff (1922), 116.

[116] *P. Cair. Zen.* 59295 (250 B.C.). For *ergazesthai* used for spinning wool, cf. *P. Cair. Zen.* 59776.9. For the process, cf. Crowfoot (1921).

[117] *P. Cair. Zen.* 59776.9–12.

[118] Forbes (1956), 81, up to 50 percent loss of weight.

Wool surplus to local requirements might reach the city simply scoured or else already spun. Here woollen cloth was woven, and other fabrics too were made from wool—woven carpets, cloaks and capes, mattresses, pillows, and heavy rugs for use as bedding.[119] As with linen, while private weaving still continued in the home,[120] weaving sheds on a larger scale would seem to have had a place within this urban center.

Much has been made of Apollonios' textile interests in the city.[121] The precise nature and scale of these are far from clear, yet worth consideration. What is certain is that in Memphis the dioiketes had some form of textile establishment, supervised by Addaios under Zenon and staffed mainly by girls, with some men too. The girls are called *paidiskai* and their names suggest that they were slaves.[122] The status of the men is far less clear. Zenodoros can teach the trade to Iollas, but a reference to a salary and oil allowance suggests that he at least was free.[123] Both men indeed, like Addaios himself, would seem from their names to be Semites, imported perhaps by Apollonios together with their trade.[124] The work of this establishment was twofold—both spinning and weaving took place here in close proximity.

The girls spun the wool. Several documents mention the question of supply, and Milesian wool was often the raw material which they worked. This wool was fine and soft; the cloth it made was highly prized.[125] It may thus be that Apollonios' establishment was a specialized spinning and weaving shed for luxury production, set up in close connection with his experimental flocks. Bia was spokesman for the girls, demanding rams' fleeces for making warps and causing problems with her fellow workers, as with those in charge.[126] Some girls it seems enjoyed a measure of freedom and responsibility in their work. Sphragis might

---

[119] See *Pap. Lugd. Bat.* 21, General index *sv*: *amphitropos, gynaikohuphē, himation, kaunakēs, proskephalaion, strōma, strōmation, tribōn, tribōnion, chitōn, chitōnion, chlamys, psilē, psilotapis.* Rostovtzeff (1941), 379, plate xlvi, draws attention to the evidence of painted tombs in Alexandria.

[120] E.g., *P. Cair. Zen.* 59263.2–4 (251 B.C.); 59355.89 (243 B.C.), Maiandria, wife of a colleague, weaving to Zenon's order as repayment of a loan; 59433.7–10, Theodora.

[121] Wipszycka (1961), 185–90; (1965), 87–88, cf. 81–87 for a comparable Roman concern; Bieżuńska-Małowist (1974), 66–68.

[122] *P. Cair. Zen.* 2.59142.2, 8 (256 B.C.); 59191.16, 20 (255 B.C.); *P. Ryl.* 4.556.10 (257 B.C.); *PSI* 7.854.3, 14, 15, 17, 20. For the girls' names, see notes 126–27, 129, below; Scholl (1983), 8–9, confirms this status.

[123] On the name Zēnodoros, see Toomer (1972), 180–85.

[124] *PSI* 7.854.12–13, 21 (257 B.C.); *P. Cair. Zen.* 59080.8 (257 B.C.).

[125] *P. Cair. Zen.* 59142.2, 7 (256 B.C.). The reputation of Milesian wool was high among the Romans: Verg. *G.* 3.306; Hor. *Epist.* 1.17.30.

[126] *P. Mich. Zen.* 16.1 (257 B.C.); *P. Cair. Zen.* 1.59080.8 (257 B.C.).

travel south to Sophthis to collect more wool, and, when robbed, for help she turned to Zenon.[127]

Weaving was mainly the province of the men and Iollas and Zenodoros could not afford to leave the looms. So, when Iollas clashed with Addaios and received a severe beating on the job, rather than go in person to Zenon he put his complaint in writing. Bia, he claimed, was their problem.[128] Such snippets of personal animation come through the surviving papyri, but tell little of the real importance of the project. At most only three girls[129] and two men are known by name, yet knowledge of the size and scale of the establishment are essential factors for any evaluation of its importance.

In origin, slave establishments of this type come from the world of Greece and not of Egypt; at the same time, however, they are a product of the flourishing urban life of the new world which the Greeks created in the Hellenistic East. Apollonios' Memphite establishment is often described as "large"[130] but, whereas elsewhere in Ptolemaic Egypt large textile works staffed by slave girls certainly did exist,[131] besides the workers known by name the only possible indication of the scale of this particular enterprise is the expenditure by Addaios at an early stage in the enterprise of 14 drachmas for baskets for the girls.[132] The sum is high; it might otherwise be expressed as the daily wage of fifty-six linen weavers.[133] Even half an obol would seem a high price for a wool basket; at that price 168 baskets could be bought.[134] Unknown for the calculation, however, are the number of baskets one worker might use or the rate of replacement required. Thus even such precise information sheds little light on the question of scale. Also unknown is how many others besides Apol-

[127] *P. Cair. Zen.* 2.59145.2 (256 B.C.); this Sphragis should not necessarily be identified with the slave from Palestine, 59003.5, Bieżuńska-Małowist (1974), 67–68.

[128] *P. Cair. Zen.* 1.59080.8 (257 B.C.). For female slave weaving, see *P. Oslo* 140 (second century B.C.).

[129] Bia (n. 126), Sphragis (n. 127), and just possibly Kassia, *PSI* 7.854.14, 20 (257 B.C.); *P. Cair. Zen.* 4.59699.22; 59700.5, for corn allowances.

[130] E.g., Wipszycka (1961), 190.

[131] Cf. *SB* 10209 (second to first centuries B.C.), provenance unknown, with fourteen names listed up to the eighth letter of the alphabet, perhaps forty to fifty in all; the high sickness rate—over a third—is striking; see Bieżuńska-Małowist (1974), 68. For Athens the largest known slave establishment is Lysias and Polemarchos' shield factory of nearly 120 men, Lys. 12.19; Demosthenes' father owned two establishments, 32 knife makers and 20 bed makers, Dem. 27.9–11.

[132] *P. Ryl.* 4.556.10 (April 257 B.C.).

[133] *PSI* 599.16, 1½ obols a day.

[134] In 159 B.C., when rush bundles of fuel cost 250 drachmas per 1,000 (*UPZ* 96.9), medium-sized *kistai* came at 5 drachmas and large ones at 7 drachmas (*UPZ* 96.32–35). In 257 B.C., 1,000 bundles of fuel cost 3 copper drachmas (*P. Col. Zen.* 5.38–39); extrapolating from the later prices 14 drachmas might buy 166–233 baskets.

lonios had similar establishments in Memphis or elsewhere in Egypt. The growing evidence for the investment in shipping by wealthy Alexandrians[135] might be used to suggest a similar pattern for textiles. And if Pompeii in Italy, with a population of 20,000, supported forty separate establishments manufacturing cloth and felt,[136] with its greater population Memphis should have had many more. Although the evidence is depressingly incomplete, such new slave establishments are likely to have remained exceptional within the traditional economy of Egypt.[137]

It was not only in Memphis that Apollonios and his agents started up textile production. At Philadelphia, too, in the Fayum new works were opened and the skilled workers came in from Memphis and the Memphite nome to practice their trade.[138] The techniques of carpet making were probably those of Egypt. Rugs were made reversible (*amphitapoi*) or woven to be dyed (*psilotapides* and *psilai*).[139] Yet others, in which some dealers specialized, were multicolored.[140] Besides the manufacture of new carpets, heirlooms might be reworked for use again.[141] Although in carpet making Egyptians predominated, in clothing manufacture immigrant Greeks might hope to make a living—men like the women's garment makers Demetrios and Apollophanes, whose expertise in woven goods, they claimed, ranged wide.[142]

Alongside such workshops, small-scale Egyptian artisan labor probably continued unchanged. As they did with local flocks of sheep, immigrant investors may have exercised some form of coordination between individual artisans. A Zenon account from July 255 B.C. records the following payments made:

From Harnouphis, weaver of wool,
for the months of Mecheir and
Phamenoth, for two webs   [dr. 2?]
From Stotoetis, likewise   dr. 2

[135] Thompson (Crawford) (1983), 73, with Clarysse (1981), 347–49.
[136] Hopkins (1978), 52; but this is probably an overestimate.
[137] Orrieux (1985), 216.
[138] *P. Lond.* 7.2055, Teos tries to undercut Petosarapis, perhaps a Memphite; *PSI* 341.9–10 (256 B.C.), from Moithymis. Similar movement is found with other workers, *P. Lond.* 7.2046, Peteermotis from the Sarapieion; 1936 (257 B.C.); *PSI* 515 (251/50 B.C.).
[139] See *Pap. Lugd. Bat.* 21 general index; *P. Ryl.* 4.556.3 (257 B.C.), 3 drachmas to dye a *psilotapis*, cf. 6, ten minas of wool are dyed.
[140] *P. Lond.* 7.2055.1–2, Teos, a *poikiltēs*.
[141] *P. Cair. Zen.* 59423.7–11.
[142] *PSI* 341.6–7 (256 B.C.).

Zenon, it seems, acted as central collection point for what were probably state dues.[143] Elsewhere, small orders of a single cape or chiton from a private producer imply small-scale production of a kind to leave little trace in the papyri which survive.[144]

The final stage of the manufacture of wool is the fulling of the woven cloth. For Ptolemaic Memphis, however, practically nothing is known of the organization of the fulling trade. Few fullers are named, but those that are appear to have Greek names.[145] Connected with Apollonios' estate was a group of fullers who paid a tax on natron at the rate of six drachmas a month, but nothing more is known of them.[146] Besides fulling lengths of new cloth, fullers provided a regular cleaning service, and accounts from both the Zenon and the Sarapieion archives record payments made for the cleaning of individual items of clothing.[147] In the mid-third century B.C. costs were far from standard, though generally less than an obol an item. However, when Artemidoros from the Memphite estate had the cloaks and tunics cleaned for the boys under his supervision, tunics were charged at 2 obols each and cloaks at 4.[148]

The Zenon archive from the mid-third century B.C. allows some further calculations. Wool was sold by weight with 31–36 fleeces to a talent, which might sell for 40 drachmas, or about 1 drachma 1 obol apiece;[149] rams' fleeces sold for warp were more valuable, priced at 2 drachmas each.[150] Wool flocks might fetch 48 drachmas a talent.[151] The evidence allows some rough calculations of the value added to the product in the course of manufacture. With raw wool at 40 drachmas a talent or 4 obols a mina, 1–2 minas weight of wool were used to make a tunic (chiton).[152]

---

[143] *P. Cair. Zen.* 59176.322–24 (255 B.C.).

[144] E.g., *PSI* 6.605; *P. Cair. Zen.* 59433.7–10; *P. Mich. Zen.* 58.22–26 (248 B.C.), as a sweetener.

[145] Agathon, *P. Cair. Zen.* 59539.3–5 (c. 258 B.C.); Demetrios, *P. Cair. Zen.* 59744.11; Olympios, *P. Col. Zen.* 5.40–41 (257 B.C.).

[146] *P. Cair. Zen.* 2.59208.31–33, 48–50 (254 B.C.).

[147] *P. Col. Zen.* 1.5.41 (257 B.C.); *P. Cair. Zen.* 59176.251–57; 59539.3–5 (c. 258 B.C.); 59398.7–8; *UPZ* 93.10 (159 B.C.).

[148] *P. Cair. Zen.* 59398.7–8 cf. 59176.254–57, a *himation* at ½ obol and a *chitōn* at ¼ obol. The difference may have been in the quality of the clothes (or the suspected means of the client).

[149] *P. Cair. Zen.* 59774.2–3, thirty-one fleeces; 59784.8–9 (taking ᴛ as a number), thirty-six fleeces. Kleon's imported wool appears extremely expensive at 2½ drachmas a mina (150 drachmas a talent) if the supplement is correct in *P. Cair. Zen.* 59012.62–63 (159 B.C.).

[150] *P. Cair. Zen.* 59784.10. 6 obols = 1 drachma; 100 drachmas = 1 mina; 60 minas = 1 talent.

[151] *P. Cair. Zen.* 59775.

[152] *P. Cair. Zen.* 59778.4,3 at 10 drachmas; line 13, 13½ drachmas; line 2, 20 drachmas; 59319.3, 40 drachmas for a woman's chiton; cf. 59659.15, 5 drachmas, not new; 59326.130–

In the Zenon archive six prices are recorded for tunics,[153] with a mean of 17¼ drachmas. Of such a price, therefore, the raw material appears to have constituted as little as 4–8 percent. Some outer garments used much more wool. Two felt capes which together weighed half a talent (30 minas) in 249 B.C. were listed at 37½ drachmas for the pair; of this price the raw material accounted for 53 percent.[154] The labor involved in weaving a tunic was clearly much greater than in making felt. Carpets, too, and mattresses were sold according to their weight, but although both individual weights and prices are recorded, the two do not survive together.[155] The markup in manufacture therefore cannot be known.

In considering the market in cloth and clothing, two features are immediately striking—the lack of evidence for any form of wholesale trade and the very personal nature of most of the traffic for which evidence does survive. "Trade without traders" was the rule; this trade was that among friends.[156] Somewhere large orders must have been fulfilled for army clothing, for even with individual clothing allowances in use uniformity in dress would seem likely, and perhaps for other government needs, but of these there is no trace. Nor is it known where and how the garments trade was organized, nor how the mass of Memphites found the clothes they wore. Some individual dealers are known by name, but whether such men worked from home or from a market stall is not recorded. In the second century B.C. a garment seller, one Mys, worked up in the Sarapieion, and at a later date, down in the valley close to the temple of Ptah, an Egyptian, Peteharendōtes, sold linen cloth, but also kept a boardinghouse.[157] There will have been many other such individuals

---

31, figure partially missing. The context suggests that these prices are for woollen tunics. See *Pap. Lugd. Bat.* 20.62.2 (after 254 B.C.) for a luxury embroidered (linen) chiton worth 1,270 drachmas. An army clothing allowance of 10 drachmas per annum is recorded in an unpublished Petrie papyrus (Sel. Box 137 = 2, cf. *P. Hib.* 51.3 n.); information from W. Clarysse.

[153] *Chlamys: P. Cair. Zen.* 59778.1–2, 21 drachmas and 37 drachmas; *P. Col. Zen.* 5.59 (257 B.C.), 37 drachmas, 3½ obols. *Himation: P. Cair. Zen.* 59701.4–5, 24 drachmas; 59319.4 (249 B.C.), 25 drachmas; 59776.1, 54 drachmas.

[154] *P. Cair. Zen.* 59319 (249 B.C.); cf. 59398.3, 40 drachmas, perhaps for a *gaunakēs*.

[155] Weights: *P. Cair. Zen.* 59423, two purple double-faced rugs, one of 50 and one of 40 minas; 59777, seven at 40 minas; 59486.6, 6 minas less than agreed; *P. Mich. Zen.* 13 (257 B.C.), from 2 talents of wool: three *strōmata* of 40 minas may be made, or two of 1 talent each. Prices: *P. Cair. Zen.* 59090.4 (258/7 B.C.), 10 drachmas (silver) for stromata, cf. 59327.43; 59298.3–5, 30 drachmas for a stroma; 59170 (255 B.C.), carpets to be bought from wine sale profits. The price of 68 drachmas for 30 minas of wool in Artemidoros' account, *P. Cair. Zen.* 59398.2, is likely to be for a manufactured article.

[156] The phrase is that of Orrieux (1983), 70, "un commerce sans commerçants"; cf. (1985), 264–65.

[157] *UPZ* 7.12 (163 B.C.); 8.33 (161 B.C.), *himatiopōlēs. UPZ* 109.12–13 (98 B.C.), *othonio-*

dealing in clothes, and the Sarapieion accounts illustrate the far-flung nature of such deals.[158] Whether this was traffic in new or used clothes remains unclear, but, although as yet unrecorded, such an urban community must have had a market in secondhand clothing.[159]

Aramaic papyri from Egypt of an earlier date show the widespread use of personal contacts, resulting in the shipment up and down the Nile of items of commerce, especially clothes.[160] It was, for example, through the gift of a cloak bought in Memphis that the Samian Syloson won the friendship and support of the Persian king Darius.[161] With the arrival of the Greeks, the axis for Nile shipping may have shifted but the traffic was unchanged. The main demand now came from Alexandria,[162] and the papers of Zenon well illustrate the network of friends and contacts through which Alexandrians fulfilled their needs:

> Zenon to Krotos, greetings. As soon as ever you receive this letter, collect from Pasis, the Jew, 25 minas weight of wool and give it to Artemidoros, so he may have a mattress made. It should be the length of a double seat, or slightly larger, and be finished on both sides. It is needed for Peisikles. And so this happens with all speed, send to Memphis to Artemidoros and try to have it finished in fifteen days. We have also written to Pasis to let you have the wool. Farewell. Year 33, Epeiph 28 (17 September 253 B.C.)[163]

Peisikles formed part of Apollonios' staff in Alexandria, and Artemidoros is elsewhere found involved in the latter's Memphite textile works which in this case will make the mattress. Again there is a Semitic connection. The individual nature of the requirement, from wool to finished article, is typical of transactions in the dossier, where such single items, made to order, frequently form a subject of concern. And the network used for acquiring goods spread throughout Lower Egypt.

Good clothes and fine carpets were precious items, to the acquisition of which immigrant Alexandrians were prepared to devote time, energy, and cash. As Apollonios' representative up-river, Zenon was constantly involved in expediting orders and overseeing the interests of their

---

pōlēs; with his Alexandrian connections Peteharendōtēs may (so Wilcken) be a monopoly official.

[158] See chapter 7; the sons of Glaukias exploit their Herakleopolite connections.

[159] Wilcken (1927), 378–81, "Trödelgeschäfte"; cf. Goitein (1967), 150 (cf. 101), on the used clothing market of medieval Cairo.

[160] See the documents quoted in n. 75.

[161] Hdt. 3.139.2.

[162] Hiero of Syracuse sent Ptolemy II Philadelphos 20,000 talents of Sicilian wool as cargo in the Syracosia, Ath. 5.209 a.

[163] P. Cair. Zen. 59241.

friends.[164] He also had interests of his own, using his position of authority to patronize promising young athletes. Part of this patronage involved the provision of their bedding and clothes—clothes fit for a champion to wear at the athletic competitions of the day.[165] Such costs were sometimes high, with the reward in reputation presumably worth the cost.

THE PORT

Down on the Nile to the east of the Ptah temple lay the main port of Memphis and the area known as the city frontage, the proasteion.[166] This was an active center of the city's economic life, and though the foundation of Alexandria may have affected its role, the intensification and expansion of agriculture in the North Fayum in this period will have brought new trade to the port. Overall, the port of Memphis remained important. Shipbuilding too, as earlier, commercial shipping, and the raising of tolls remained central aspects of activity in this city on the Nile.

Royal dockyards at Memphis are first recorded under Tuthmosis III in the fifteenth century,[167] but still in the Ptolemaic period royal barges were built and harbored here.[168] Boats might be made of acacia, the Egyptian *sykaminos*, of willow, or even of papyrus reeds; for substantial hulls, however, ships' timbers always came imported into Egypt, especially from the Levant.[169] With the timber came Levantines, and, as in commerce so also in the dockyards, immigrant labor might find employment in the city. In the fifth century B.C. Carian shipbuilders are found in Elephantine, whereas from contemporary Memphis fragments of records from the arsenal list workers in the dockyards with a wide range of national names: Egyptians, Persians, Babylonians, Canaanites, and Phoenicians.[170] Still in the Ptolemaic period, Naukratis the city continued as a

[164] E.g., *P. Cair. Zen.* 59048 (?257 B.C.); 59088 (258/7 B.C.); 59241 (253 B.C.); 59298.2–3 (250 B.C.); 59423; 59553 (256 B.C.); 59571 (242 B.C.); *P. Lond.* 7.1942 (257 B.C.); 1945 (257 B.C.); 2159.26–28; *P. Mich. Zen.* 72.21; 97.9–13; *PSI* 401.2; *P. Col. Zen.* 2.70.

[165] *P. Cair. Zen.* 59060.9–10 (257 B.C.), for Pyrrhos; *PSI* 364 (251/50 B.C.), for Dionysios.

[166] Hdt. 3.14.

[167] Glanville (1931) and (1932); and, later, Lloyd (1978a), 107–12, and Martin (1979), no. 413; *BGU* 1817.14–15 (60/59 B.C.).

[168] *P. Petrie* 2.20.iv.4 = 3.36.b.iv (2 December 218 B.C.); see chapter 4 nn. 40–41 below for priestly appointments connected with royal boats.

[169] Acacia: *P. Cair. Zen.* 59188.6 (255 B.C.); 59270.1 (251 B.C.); *P. Lond.* 7.1997 (250 B.C.); Casson (1971), 341. Willow: *P. Mert.* 19.5 (A.D. 173). Papyrus: *UPZ* 81.ii.6–7 (343 B.C.), called *rōps*, in a dream. "Byblos-boats" was the Egyptian term for seagoing ships built of cedar and juniper; see Meiggs (1982), 49–87, 405–9.

[170] Cowley (1923), no. 26, with Segal (1983), 42; Aimé-Giron (1931), nos. 5–73, with Bowman (1941).

center for the fitting out of ships, while in the nome there were further shipyards to the south.[171] The present high water-table level over much of the site of the city, with the consequent destruction of papyrus and building remains, is probably the reason for the lack of further evidence on what must have continued an important aspect of the city's economic activity, even after the focus switched to Alexandria.

The involvement of Memphites in Nile shipping comes as no surprise. The Nile was full of sandbanks, and knowledge of the shoals was a prerequisite for the captains of the barges on the river. In Ptolemaic Nile shipping, a three-tier system of management seems to have prevailed, with owners, contractors, and captains normally differentiated.[172] Although the owners of Nile barges who are known were prominent Alexandrians, Ptolemaic queens or others with Greek names from the capital, the contractors, the *nauklēroi*, were a different group who sometimes sailed themselves as captains on the ships. Contractors, with some exceptions, also bore Greek names in contrast to most of the captains who, from their nomenclature, appear to be Egyptian.[173] It is among these last two groups that Memphites are recorded.

The evidence is not extensive. From the city one ship's captain is half-known by name, .ḳ..uris, son of Pasis, and another Memphite writes on behalf of an illiterate captain at the port of Kerke, south of the city.[174] Only two, they are still two more than are known from elsewhere on the Nile, and they probably stand for a great many more Memphites on the river. Among the ships' contractors a group from Memphis, the naukleroi Hippodromitai,[175] which functions in the mid-first century B.C., suggests a development in shared-risk investment similar to that found elsewhere in the Mediterranean at the time. Risk sharing in a less developed form has earlier examples on the Nile.[176] This group was organized with a short-term chairman, *prostatēs* (Apollophanes in Epeiph of one year fol-

[171] *P. Mich. Zen.* 17.4 (257 B.C.); 60.7–8 (248/7 B.C.); *PSI* 382 (248/7 B.C.); 533.16 (third century B.C.); *P. Cair. Zen.* 59242 (253 B.C.); 59270 (251 B.C.); see Orrieux (1985), 109–10.

[172] Thompson (Crawford) (1983), 65–72, for this whole section; p. 67 needs modification, cf. Clarysse (1981).

[173] Nomenclature, at least Greek nomenclature, cannot be a sure guide to nationality, but the same national names held by groups of a shared profession is indicative of attitudes at least; see now Clarysse (1985).

[174] *P. Hib.* 98 = *W. Chrest.* 441.13–14 (251 B.C.), the published name is wrong (so Clarysse); *P. Tebt.* 823.18 (185 B.C.), Stotoetis, son of Gemouthes.

[175] *BGU* 8.1741–43; 14.2368 (68 B.C.); Vélissaropoulos (1980), 113–15. If *BGU* 14.2368.14 refers to the queen, this shipping may be yet another indication of such royal interests, cf. Hauben (1979).

[176] E.g., *BGU* 1933 (third century B.C.) with Hauben (1971a), 273.

lowed by Malichos in Mesore) and a recorder, or *grammateus* (Eudemos), who held office for longer periods. Two of the naukleroi are known by name—Zabdion, son of Artemidoros, and yet another Apollonios; they may also have served as captains on their ships. Among the Memphite group the names are interesting, with Malichos and Zabdion providing a clear indication of the continued involvement in Nile shipping of Levantine immigrants to the city. Other similar companies, though unrecorded, probably existed both in the city and elsewhere. The volume of Nile traffic was heavy and Memphis lay at a central point.[177]

Besides the traffic on the Nile, smaller craft will have plied the Phchēt canal which lay west of the city, with quays at the desert edge serving the temples and necropolis before continuing north.[178] On the pattern of canal traffic in the Fayum, this small-scale shipping in everyday requirements would be the preserve of Egyptians in the area. The record of tolls paid for three months on Fayum craft between the ports of Ptolemais Hormou and Krokodilopolis provides evidence for a varied freight: passengers, salt, wine, wheat, beans, fish, bags, charcoal, fleeces, tiles, private goods, sacred objects of Souchos, and measuring rope for the dykes.[179] And besides the everyday items listed here, ceremonial barges would ply the canals with sacred loads, as when Ptah visited Hathor, Lady of the Southern Sycamore, traveling south along the Phchēt canal.[180]

At the time of Napoleon's invasion in A.D. 1798 income from customs tolls amounted to 16.8 percent of the national income.[181] For the Ptolemies, too, such income was important, and tolls and local dues (sometimes official, sometimes illicit) were levied both on international freight and on internal traffic, on cargoes up and down the Nile.[182] For the barges on the Fayum canals in 226/5 B.C., 50 percent of freight charges went on harbor dues.[183] Tolls were levied on the river, too, and Memphis, placed between Upper and Lower Egypt, served as one of the main customs points on the Nile.

For the second and third centuries A.D. one of the most frequent taxes

[177] Cf. *SB* 8754 (77 B.C.).
[178] Smith (1979), 165.
[179] *P. Petrie* 3.107 (226/5 B.C.); see Hauben (1971b); Clarysse and Hauben (1976).
[180] *P. Harris* 1.49.1–3 (Ramses III).
[181] Estève (1809), 367–68.
[182] *P. Cair. Zen.* 59012 (259 B.C.); Préaux (1939a), 371–79.
[183] See n. 179. On royal barges, 75 percent went to the crown.

for which receipts survive is the tax of the Memphis harbor.[184] A Memphite toll is recorded on various products already in the Ptolemaic period and, although not in name connected with the harbor, this regularly was levied on goods that went by ship.[185] The toll point itself formed part of a guard post (*phylakē*) for the city, with the complex serving also as a public record office. There were further guardhouses along the Nile within the Memphite nome. Under the Persians a southern guard post is recorded, probably to be identified with the upper guard post of the Ptolemaic period; it lay some way south of the city on the Nile, close perhaps to the southern dyke and the border of the nome.[186] The northern guard post in the district of Ouenchem may also have served as tollhouse.[187] Regular guard posts such as these formed part of the royal control of traffic on the Nile; tolls were levied on goods that passed through, and protection was provided for ships with valuable loads.

At the main guard post the establishment included various official scribes while others no doubt, not on the staff, posted themselves on the sand nearby and offered their services for a fee. There was at least one customs officer, Sosistratos, in 258 B.C., and other officials described more generally as "those in charge of the phylakai."[188] The plural "phylakai" suggests some form of centralized control based on the city for the guardhouses of the nome. The job of these men was to levy the regular taxes on goods passing through the post and, at the same time, to prevent smuggling and illegal traffic. Like all Ptolemaic officials, they were subject to pressures which might interfere with the straightforward execution of their duty. The most common of these was certainly the bribe which formed an unquestioned part of freightage calculations; "expenditure for necessities" is how it was described.[189] A late-third-century B.C. account of expenses incurred in mounting a voyage from Memphis to Alexandria lists the following items:[190]

[184] See Appendix E with chapter 8.
[185] *P. Hib.* 1.110.24 (*c.* 270 B.C.), on grain; 2.198.126 (third century B.C.); *P. Corn.* 3.6 (mid–third century B.C.); *P. Petrie* 3.76 verso.ii.12 (third century B.C.); *P. Tebt.* 701.201–202 (235 B.C.), on fish; *P. Cair. Zen.* 59553.8–9 (256 B.C.), on wine; 59823.2 (253 B.C.), on wax.
[186] *P. Ryl. dem.* III 9.5/15; *P. Lond.* 7.1945.4 (257 B.C.), *hē phylakē hē epa[nō*; Hauben (1985); Yoyotte (1972), 7–8, places the southern guard post 60 kilometers south of the city. For my suggestion, however, that the lower guard post of *UPZ* 125.7 (89 B.C.) is lower only in relation to the Anoubieion, see chapter 5 n. 107 below.
[187] *P. Cair. Zen.* 59031.14–15, verso.4 (258 B.C.); *Pap. Lugd. Bat.* 20.61.2 (246/5 B.C.).
[188] *P. Louvre* E 3266.1.S (197 B.C.) = App. B:2; *P. Innsbruck* (75 B.C.) = App. B:18. For the position of Ouenchem in the far north of the Memphite nome, see Yoyotte (1972) in preference to Bresciani (1983).
[189] *P. Hib.* 1.110.10 (*c.* 270 B.C.).
[190] *UPZ* 149 = *W. Chrest.* 30.11–16.

	dr.	obols
For wine at the guard post and those with them, 12 *kotylai* at 2 obols	4	
For the senior officers (*presbyteroi*)	10	
Beer for them	2	1
Inspectors of the ship, 12 kotylai of wine	6	
For the *timouchoi*, 11 kotylai at 2¼ obols	4	½ ¼

Wine for the timouchoi, the officials of the Hellenion,[191] like that for the ship inspectors and (of less good quality) for the men at the guard post, or beer together with a cash payment for the presbyteroi, was probably no more than a precaution. But it was a necessary precaution and represented an outlay over and above the regular freight, clerical, and search charges.[192]

The second form of pressure which recurs regularly in the third-century B.C. papers of Zenon is the unofficial pressure exercised by those with influence in the area. The safe passage of goods through customs could be a tricky business and, on his replacement by Zenon in charge at Philadelphia in April 256 B.C., Panakestor, remaining in Apollonios' service, was appointed consignor of cargoes in Memphis, *ho pros tais apostolais*, at the high salary of 200 drachmas a month.[193] The post, in charge of consignments, was presumably an important one in easing the way for goods through the necessary clearance on the docks and in the customs-house. Even so there could be problems (see below), and in the autumn of 250 B.C., when wild boar, pigs, and kids were sent down to the king in five cages for the Arsinoeia in Alexandria, more than one of the wild boars perished en route.[194] Similarly, a letter from 12 July 250 B.C., reporting back to Zenon on a similar cargo, records a shipment to Alexandria of gazelles, 27 hares (19 dead), 62 Egyptian goose eggs (rotten), 45 turtle doves (18 dead), and 150 bunches of grapes in four crates.[195]

In July 253 B.C. a certain Kleanax wrote to Zenon about some mules destined for the Memphite gift-estate of Apollonios: "It would be desirable that you have already dealt with the matter, but if not consider send-

[191] See chapter 3 n. 83.
[192] *P. Hib.* 1.110 (*c.* 270 B.C.); *P. Cair. Zen.* 59753.36–40 and *P. Corn.* 3 (mid-third century B.C.) for *phoretra*, *grammatikon*, and *eraunetikon* charges. Memphis also charged for use of landing stages, *epibathra*, *P. Cair. Zen.* 59753.36.
[193] *P. Lond.* 7.1963; *P. Cair. Zen.* 59163; cf. *P. Lond.* 7.1940.3 for Pelops as *apostoleus*; *P. Cair. Zen.* 59299.2 (250 B.C.), *apostolai* of garlic.
[194] *P. Lond.* 7.2000 (250 B.C.).
[195] *P. Lond.* 7.1998.

ing them safely along with yours as though they were Apollonios', so they may escape trouble at the customs."[196] Apollonios, it appears, could be sure of enjoying a trouble-free passage at the customs post. Others too subscribed to this view. In late December 258 B.C. Poseidonios from Alexandria wrote to Zenon in the following terms:

> Poseidonios to Apollonios, greetings. When one of my corn ships was sailing up into the *chōra*, Sosistratos' men in Memphis boarded her and confiscated the iron which needs to be on board in case of emergency. In my view it is not possible for ships to sail without the necessary fitments. And when I wrote to them, on more than one occasion, to give the metal back, they paid no attention, but they sold it. I have written to you therefore to inform you that these are the type of men in charge of the phylakai. Farewell.
>
> Year 28, Dios 21.
>
> Docket: to Apollonios. (Letter) of Poseidonios, steward, about the customs officer Sosistratos.[197]

The lack of precision here can only sound suspicious: "necessary fitments" and "in case of emergency." Iron, of course, was a precious commodity of growing importance for new agricultural and building tools; it would probably bring in a fair price to whoever it was who sold it. Lists of ships' equipment do not normally include such fittings;[198] perhaps Sosistratos here and his team were actually doing their job.

Poseidonios, however, expected help from Apollonios, as did others of the dioiketes' friends. So too with Addaios, one of Apollonios' key men in Memphis, when the customs men had confiscated his wine. After trying personal contacts among the local officials, like so many others[199] Addaios turned for help to Zenon, Apollonios' representative and a powerful figure in the area, and asked him for an order to the customs men.[200] Men such as Zenon or his successor Eukles knew the tone to adopt in such dealings:

> Year 2, Phamenoth 2.
> To those in charge of the *phy(lakeion)*. We have dispatched from Memphis to Apollonios, Philokrates with a cargo of [. . .]. Please make sure that having registered it you let him through.
> Verso. To Asklepiades.[201]

[196] *P. Cair. Zen.* 59240 (253 B.C.).
[197] *P. Cair. Zen.* 59031 (258 B.C.).
[198] E.g., *P. Cair. Zen.* 59054 (257 B.C.).
[199] E.g., Spinther: *P. Cair. Zen.* 59343 (247/6 B.C.); Hierokles: *P.Lond.* 7.1945; 1946 (257 B.C.) cf. *P. Cair. Zen.* 59060.10–11; 59061.4–6; 59820.5–6 (253 B.C.).
[200] *P. Cair. Zen.* 59375.
[201] *Pap. Lugd. Bat.* 20.61 (246/5 B.C.).

The passage, we too may assume, was normally trouble-free for such men. Conversely, however, on occasion Apollonios might come to the help of the customs men,[202] so illustrating well the reciprocity of favors by which this system worked. Among immigrant Greeks of a certain class, social cohesion paid the greatest dividend.

No consolidated list of customs rates charged on internal trade survives from Ptolemaic Egypt. It is possible only to assert that, along with charges for protection,[203] they formed a regular part of the cost of a voyage. In individual cases details may survive, allowing some calculation of the partial costs of a particular voyage,[204] but for Ptolemaic Egypt the economic costs of shipping cannot be quantified. In medieval Egypt an outlay of 7 percent of the value of a load was to be expected in taxes and transport charges.[205] Similar calculations are impossible earlier, when one vital piece of information—the distance involved, the size of the cargo, or the figure concerned—always seems to be lacking. We therefore cannot know what profits might be made.

ARTS AND CRAFTS

Metal Work

Little is known of the arming of Hellenistic armies[206] but, not surprisingly for Hephaistos' city, Memphis seems to have been a center of the arms' industry. "I have sent you five shields, so highly prized by me that not even in Aetolia do such shields exist," wrote Zenon's friend Philinos, probably from the city, and the provision of arms in preparation for the Fourth Syrian War (219–17 B.C.) was organized from the city.[207] Besides regular army needs, the ceremonial life of the Ptolemaic court and festivals might demand military dress, and even in the chora, the Egyptian countryside outside Alexandria, a Greek resident might well go accoutred on occasion.[208] Indeed, the elaborate plaster casts made in Memphis as patterns for decorative shield bosses, sword grips, and helmet reliefs sug-

---

[202] P. Cair. Zen. 59553.6–10 (256 B.C.), to recover tax on wine.
[203] Thompson (Crawford) (1983), 70, 191 nn. 25–28. See Goitein (1967), 299.
[204] Thompson (Crawford) (1983), 69 n. 19.
[205] Goitein (1967), 343.
[206] Snodgrass (1967), 129.
[207] P. Lond. 7.2057.2–6; cf. 2065.6; P. Cair. Zen. 59035.2, purchase of a sword belt; Pol. 5.63.11, for the Syrian war.
[208] PSI 428.35–36, 61, Zenon's equipment: round shield, oblong shield, and quiver; P. Cair. Zen. 59729.10–11, payment to a bronze smith for cleaning the armor.

gest that expensive ornamental arms were made to order in the city. The discovery of a large number of limestone helmets in the same context (used either as models or as symbols of the trade) may be evidence for the manufacture of helmets here.[209] Memphis had long been an armaments center and though, with the arrival of the Greeks, new models may have been imported from abroad, Memphite manufacture continued to meet home needs.

The source of metals used is entirely unrecorded. Bronze may have come from around Dionysias and the southwestern end of Lake Moeris in the Fayum. Brought into the city by donkey train across the desert, bronze surplus to Memphite needs might then be loaded onto ships and carried to wherever else there was demand.[210] Iron ore, silver, and gold must all have been brought in from the Egyptian deserts or abroad.[211]

Besides supplying the army, workers in bronze had other markets. Small bronze figurines, featuring divinities (both animal and human in form) and sacred objects, regularly recur in an excavation of the city. From below the paving of the dromos of the Sarapieion, Mariette filled over twenty-five baskets once in a day with small bronzes of an earlier date. Their Ptolemaic counterparts are no less numerous. The market created by pilgrims must have been significant for those who made these statuettes.[212]

Such bronze workers practiced besides blacksmiths, silversmiths, and goldsmiths in the city in the production of household objects for normal and luxury use. Much of their work is known only from surviving molds and plaster casts made from metal objects. The fine plaster model of a bronze plaquette of Ptolemy Soter now in Hildesheim is simply one example of the quality of work which these artists might produce.[213] These plasters would seem to have served as models for artisans, allowing the reproduction of particular themes, patterns, and scenes; customers too might consult them as a pattern. Together with the molds they may have been produced by that mysterious workman called a *koilourgos* (literally a "hollow worker").[214] The plasters would seem to originate in a series of

[209] Rubensohn (1911), 52–55, with catalogue nos. 36–40, cf. 67; Rostovtzeff (1941), 391, plate xlviii; Reinsberg (1980), 9, 170 n. 618, 246 n. 904. For the New Kingdom industry, see Sauneron (1954).

[210] *P. Cair. Zen.* 59788.1–12, from Memphis on to Kerke, possibly for Philadelphia.

[211] Préaux (1939a), 253–56, on metal sources.

[212] Lauer and Picard (1955), 20; Smith (1974), 52–57; Himmelman (1981), 196; Quaegebeur (1980b), 70, for a second- or first-century B.C. Memphite Ptah statuette in Ephesus.

[213] Rostovtzeff (1941), 730, plate lxxxi, no. 2; Reinsberg (1980), no. 36, Abb. 49/50.

[214] *P. Athen.* I = *Pap. Lugd. Bat.* 20. 23.1 (257 B.C.); alternatively he may be a worker of

contiguous workshops in what was probably the metal workers' quarter of the city on Kom el Nawa and Kom el Arbaʿīn, close to the temple of Ptah, their patron deity.[215] They were excavated illicitly and reached the market in the first decade of the present century. Both in subject and style they generally appear to be the product of Greek artists working for a Greek clientele, though occasional Egyptian motifs do occur.[216] Dating back to the fifth century B.C. the metal workshops from which they came were possibly those of Hellenomemphites which survived and flourished on into the Ptolemaic period, producing goods for an increased market. But others too worked in the same crafts and Egyptian documents record native Memphite men and women engaged in working metal.[217] There was no Greek monopoly to this skill though the artistic tastes of the various populations of the city may have differed.

Besides plaques and medallions, reliefs and ornamental fittings, heads and busts, fine silver tableware was produced for sale in the city.[218] Such silver plate was precious and might be used to pawn. Long lists of silver objects as security on deposit illustrate the widespread practice of raising cash against collateral which occurs throughout the period.[219] Jewelry from Memphite goldsmiths has probably been found, but the nature of the antiques market tends to obscure the provenance and context of such small and precious items.

Iron, imported into the country, was probably worked in the city both for agricultural implements and other metal tools.[220] Like other metal workers, the blacksmiths probably had their quarter, but unfortunately the location of the foundry which Mariette uncovered is not recorded.[221]

Faience

Egyptian faience, a white paste of ground quartz and natron with copper oxide added to give, on firing, a lustrous bluish hue was probably a Mem-

---

repoussé metal, as suggested by D. B. Thompson, or of terracotta. See Burkhalter (1984), 336–43, on the production and use of plasters.

[215] Rubensohn (1911), 1; Rostovtzeff (1941), 374, 378, plate xlv.1, 391, plate xlviii; Thompson (1964), 50; Reinsberg (1980), 244–82, reviewed by Burkhalter (1981); the forthcoming Würzburg dissertation of W. Cheshire will discuss these further.

[216] Reinsberg (1980), 251–52, 282.

[217] *P. Louvre* E 3266.5.A–B, N, goldsmiths; 5.0, blacksmith; 7.H–I, female silversmith (197 B.C.) = App. B:2.

[218] *PSI* 348.6–7 (254 B.C.); for Apollonios' plate lent to Demetrios, see *P. Cair. Zen.* 59033; 59044 (257 B.C.).

[219] *P. Cair. Zen.* 59327 (249 B.C.); *UPZ* 5.36; 6.30 (163 B.C.); 99.6 (158 B.C.); 101.19 (156 B.C.); *SB* 7617.54, 83 (158 B.C.).

[220] *P. Cair. Zen.* 59782a; 59849; 59851; *PSI* 595.

[221] Lauer (1961), 39, reported in an undated letter.

phite product of importance.[222] The aquamarine shades of the earlier Hellenistic period gave way to a later, deeper green or peacock blue. Faience was used throughout the country as a less costly substitute for fine clay. So jugs, *oinochoai*, were made of faience, some with added portrait reliefs of Ptolemaic queens. Such oinochoai seem marked for the royal cult.[223] Medallions, too, in twisted frames are found in faience, together with free-standing portrait heads. The skillful combination of native materials and elements of design with Greek shape and content of the scenes fit well into Hellenomemphite culture, and it seems quite likely that the queen vases were made in Memphis, where three of them were found.[224] At least two types of glazing are represented in the city, and kiln sites have been recorded on Kom el Qal'a and on Kom Helūl (see fig. 3).[225]

Other faience objects from the city show the same mixture of influences, as in the Egyptian green faience altar of offerings with a decorative pattern of Greek palmettes around its edge which Petrie found.[226] From faience, too, all sizes and shapes of figurines were mass-produced by mold, often for dedication to deities of their choice by poorer pilgrims to the city. Such, perhaps, was what was later termed by an Isis priest in Latin *Memphiticu(m) sigillum*.[227] Of the organization of faience manufacture nothing at all is known.

Glass and Clay

The same is true of the Memphite industries of pottery and glass. Petrie excavated late Ptolemaic kilns by Kom Helūl at the southern end of the valley city, describing these as glazing kilns where glass was made. Later excavators of the University of Pennsylvania similarly found a glaziers' oven on their site.[228] Perhaps the area south of the Ptah temple formed an industrial sector of the city. It was certainly in this area close by the Astarte temple in the second century B.C. that kiki oil was extracted through boiling.[229] And in the Roman period the courtyard of this temple had become the site of potters' kilns.[230]

[222] D. B. Thompson (1973), 10–12, modified somewhat by the technical study of Vandiver in Kaczmarczyk, Hedges (1983), A128–30.

[223] So D. B. Thompson (1973), 119–22; see Bonneau (1971), 127, for the connection of queen cults with traditional Nile festivals.

[224] D. B. Thompson (1973), 7–18, 107; Fraser (1972), 140, claims an Alexandrian origin.

[225] Kaczmarczyk and Hedges (1983), A130; Jeffreys (1985), 19.

[226] Petrie (1909a), 14, no. 42, plate xiv.

[227] *ILS* 4368. For faience figurines, Petrie (1909a), 14, molds; Martin (1979), 40–82; Himmelmann (1981), plate x.a,b.

[228] Petrie (1911b), 34–37; Anthes (1965), plate 17.

[229] *UPZ* 120.4–8 (second century B.C.).

[230] Abdulla el-Sayed Mahmud (1978), 4; see Jeffreys (1985), 18, also on Kom Sabakha.

In a city the size of Memphis, self-sufficiency in the manufacture of glass and clay is to be expected for all but the most costly of items. Long, thin clay weights for fishing nets are found here in significant numbers.[231] The Egyptian loom, however, which was horizontal with two wooden beams, did not need the weights of its Greek equivalent. It is only with further excavation and analysis that the Memphite specialties in glass and clay may gain recognition.

Terracotta

An allied branch of manufacture well developed in the city was the making of terracotta figurines. Found in considerable numbers, often of a quality unlikely to be imported and serving as ornaments, terracottas of all kinds enjoyed a considerable vogue in Hellenistic Memphis. Ranging from the realistic to the grotesque and portraying both human and animal subjects, terracottas might be made of a rough local substance or fine imported clay.[232] The Memphite market for terracottas would be among the locals as well as the tourists.

Stone

Stone was used for building, for statues, and for making vases. It might be imported, like marble, black granite, or alabaster or, as with the limestone used in the third-century B.C. statuary on the dromos of the Sarapieion, it might be quarried locally. The Tura quarries on the east bank of the Nile just north of Memphis will have provided most of the limestone needed for the city; Trōitai from Tura (ancient Troia) occur in the Zenon archive.[233] With teams of masons on the necropolis, quarrying into the hillside, Memphites were skilled at working many types of stone.[234] Both Greek and Egyptian statuary was sculpted in the city, often, it would appear, on private commissions. Much of this work was of high quality, though there is no sign of cross influence between the two styles; it seems the sculptors worked apart.[235] A Memphite provenance

---

[231] Anthes (1965), 33.

[232] Petrie (1909a), plates xxxv–xliv; (1909b), plates xxviii–xxxiv; in Engelbach (1915), plate lxi; Scheurleer (1974), 83–99; Kyrieleis (1975), B4. For the production of both coarse and fine wares together, compare, for example, modern Turkish production at Kütahya.

[233] Pap. Lugd. Bat. 21, p. 500; cf. Strab. 17.1.34.

[234] Lauer and Picard (1955), 49. On Memphite stone, Pliny HN 36.11.56. For stone masons, P. Cair. Zen. 59172.5; cf. chapter 6 nn. 67–70 below, necropolis masons; for stone carried by water, P. Cair. Zen. 59745.16, lithēgos baris.

[235] Greek: Lawrence (1925), 181 n. 10 with plate xviii.2; 185 n. 3; 185 n. 10; 187 n. 9; cf. the fine bronze female head, 186 n. 9 with plate xxiii; Kyrieleis (1975), H6, H13, J10. Egyptian: Bothmer (1960), nos. 106 (black basalt), 108 (green schist), 132 (diorite); Quaegebeur (1980a), 59 n. 2, 60–61.

does not, however, guarantee Memphite workmanship and, just as the inscribed statues of the Memphite high priests found in Alexandria, Cherchel, and Cyrene may have been sculpted in the city,[236] so there is no certainty that statues found in Memphis were sculpted there. Besides statues, stone vessels were made in the city where several alabaster workshops were excavated by Petrie.[237]

Wood and Other Crafts

Memphite shipbuilding has already been recorded but wood, always a precious commodity, was fashioned for many other purposes. Furniture for temples and other secular use was worked locally by men skilled in carpentry.[238] Many other craftsmen practiced their trade in the city; the makers of mats and baskets may be mentioned *exempli gratia*.[239]

FOOD PRODUCTION

Domestic mills and ovens were either attached to houses or placed on wasteland between them.[240] Professional millers and bakers are also known to have lived and worked in the city.[241] Bakers probably sold the bread they made, and bakeries lay side by side with regular housing in the city.[242] A large variety of cakes was regularly produced, and the various sweet offerings were acceptable to the gods.[243]

Oil was extracted in the city[244] and, to judge from the record of tradesmen, wine and beer are likely to have been made here.[245] Although not

[236] Quaegebeur (1980a), 53–59, 61–63, 81.
[237] Petrie (1909a), 14, plate xvi, and in Engelbach (1915), 33, plate lx, for alabaster workshops.
[238] *P. Louvre* E 3266.7.F (197 B.C.) = App. B:2.
[239] *P. Ryl.* 556.10 (257 B.C.); *UPZ* 96.32–35 (159 B.C.); *P. Col. Zen.* 2.107.3.
[240] *P. Innsbruck* line 5 (75 B.C.) = Spiegelberg (1903), 103; Sethe (1920), 737–40, a mill and storehouse in the Anoubieion; *P. Louvre* 3268 (73 B.C.) = Revillout (1882a), 91–92, an oven; *P. Leid. dem.* 378 (160 B.C.) = Revillout (1880c), 113–20; (1897), 527–28, granaries above the house door; *P. B.M.* 10075.(c).1 (64 B.C.) = Jelínková (1957), 47; (1959), 61, mill and storehouses in the Anoubieion.
[241] *P. Louvre* E 3266.6.0 (197 B.C.) = App. B:2; *UPZ* 7.8 (163 B.C.); 8.32 (161 B.C.); *P. Corn.* 1.81–82 (256 B.C.). The Greek terms are *sitopoios* and *artokopos*.
[242] *UPZ* 116.10, 13 (third century B.C.), in the Hellenion in the area of Amon-Thoth; 56.15 (160 B.C.); 120.1–2 (second century B.C.), bread for the Sarapieion community came from Memphis though bakers lived in the Anoubieion, *UPZ* 7.6–7 (163 B.C.).
[243] E.g., *UPZ* 89.15 (160/59 B.C.); *PSI* 428.40, Apis bread; *P. Cair. Zen.* 59569.86 (246/5 B.C.), *popana*.
[244] *UPZ* 62.20–21 (161 B.C.); 120.7–8, 13 (second century B.C.); *PSI* 372.5–6 (250 B.C.), an oil merchant in Sophthis.
[245] *P. Louvre* E 3266.9.B (197 B.C.) = App. B:2, beer salesman; 9.C, seller of mixed wine; *P. Leid. dem.* 374.i.6 (78 B.C.) = Pestman (1963), wine with oil.

actually known until the Roman period, as in Philadelphia lentil-soup cooks and pumpkin roasters must have practiced their trade in the city.[246] Not all food was home cooked, and food stalls in the city served both regular customers and visitors to the area. For, as still today, whenever a city serves as the economic and social center for the countryside around, ready food of a cheap and basic type is always in demand.

Markets

Memphis formed a major market for the country as a whole as well as being a local center. As a port, Memphis provided a market center in which a large population, differentiated both in ethnic origin and in occupation, depended for its existence upon the city's location and historical role. Memphis lay on the Nile, but also at the end of the route which led out from the North Fayum, that fertile depression developed under the Ptolemies, for which it served as port and center of distribution. Relations with the Fayum both across the desert to the northern towns of Bakchias, Karanis, and Soknopaiou Nesos[247] and up the Nile to the port of Kerke (see fig. 1) were natural and close. Both goods and men would travel on these routes. From the Fayum came olives, dates, oil plants, vegetables, and fodder crops, while out from Memphis wine was a regular load. Under the Ptolemies men too moved around in a flourishing labor market. From Memphis to the Fayum went skilled and unskilled labor.[248] The nomenclature of the newly expanded area bears witness to the contact; Imouthes and Asklepios both appear as popular Fayum names which may derive from the Memphite god.

As the main artery of the country, the Nile was the central highway both for men and goods. Close to the apex of the Delta, between Upper and Lower Egypt, the importance of Memphis' port and market was bound up with its political history. As sometime capital of the country, the strength of its natural position was enhanced by the role it played. Before the foundation of Alexandria on the coast, Memphis probably served the country as its most important port. The effect on the city of the new capital with its Mediterranean port is not to be measured, but must be imagined. Although internal traffic that earlier came to Memphis

[246] *PSI* 402 (third century B.C.); *P. Bour.* 13 (A.D. 98).
[247] See chapter 8 and Appendix E.
[248] Clarysse (1980b) and chapter 3 below for Memphis and the Fayum; Orrieux (1985), 203–10, on labor.

now perhaps went on to Alexandria, the city still remained an important national market. The country's grain, increased now in volume, and other goods shipped north to the coast all passed through the city and its customs; imported wood and metals were carried up the Nile.[249] Memphis provided a large market for staples as well as a production center for export, and a constant flow of goods through the city brought tax for royal revenue. It was also a recognized center for the sale and purchase of slaves.[250]

The physical location of the local Memphite market areas is not known. Just one of these, an Egyptian market, is recorded close to the river. There may have been other neighborhood markets, or those for slaves or specialized goods. But whereas regular markets may be imagined for food and produce, for manufactured goods—arms, textiles, and luxury items—the picture of the papyri is rather of the small-scale production and sale from the workshop typical of the bazaar. The one exception, the larger textile establishment of Apollonios based on the labor of slaves, is significantly different. Both the scale and the work force are new to Egypt, representing the influence of the Greeks on the old economic patterns of production. Closely connected with Apollonios' estate, the workshop may have provided for the needs of estate personnel with some luxury production for the market of Alexandria. But without knowing how many similar establishments existed, the actual market for the goods produced, or the fate of this workshop on the dissolution of the estate, it is not possible to do more than simply note this innovation. Small-scale production with direct sale probably remained the norm.

Both here and elsewhere the evidence is limited. How the government supplied the army, or how the majority of the population acquired the products they needed, is rarely to be seen. In present-day Egypt regular weekly markets are an important and thriving feature of the rural landscape. They play an important role both in provisioning the peasant families of the countryside and in channeling goods produced locally out of a country area to town and city markets.[251] Whether in Ptolemaic Egypt such rural markets played a similar role in relation to the city of Memphis is unrecorded. What does survive are the papers of Zenon but, although these provide a vivid picture of the workings of the market, they do come

---

[249] The city's pivotal position is clearly illustrated in the restrictions of *C. Ord. Ptol.* 73.2–6 (50 B.C.) requiring the transport to Alexandria of all grain bought south of Memphis.

[250] *P. Hamb.* 91.13–14 (167 B.C.).

[251] Larson (1982).

from a limited class. Zenon with his friends and contacts are, in the main, immigrant urban settlers of the administrative and professional classes. Yet they are men who speedily acquired the questioning mentality needed for personal provisionment within the economy of Egypt as it functioned at the time.

Two features in the surviving evidence are particularly striking: the large number of specialized traders and the personal network of contacts through which purchases might be transacted. The traders of the area formed a recognized community and for some purposes their identity might need certification in writing.[252] Specialized salesmen are often recorded and regularly have Egyptian names—sellers, for instance, of beer, wine, oil, resin, rushes, cloth, and clothes. As was normal within this society, different functions might be held by the same individual and specialism was by no means exclusive. Some traders lived in the Anoubieion complex; their recorded dealings show them well integrated into the community of which they formed a part. As we shall see, priests were also involved in these economic activities. Mutual assistance was regular within this community and a series of contracts for short-term money loans to be repaid in kind after the harvest seems to represent a form of purchase in advance beneficial in different ways to both the parties involved.[253] These loans are very small-scale, and so perhaps were the traders.

The use made by immigrants of personal contacts in purchase may be illustrated earlier in Aramaic papyri and was not new to Ptolemaic Egypt. The question which still remains open is the extent to which this pattern was followed in other classes of the population and among the native Egyptians. The papers of the sons of Glaukias from the Sarapieion in the second century B.C. suggest the practice was more widespread. Two examples will suffice for illustration:

> Paramonos to Zenon, greetings. When you were staying I forgot to give you the details about the strigils. Purchase for me, since they are cheap in Memphis, six for men and six for boys, of the best quality Sicyonian manufacture, and one and a half artabas of dried capers, as fresh as possible. Farewell.[254]

---

[252] *PSI* 425.19–22.

[253] *P. Vat.* 22 + *UPZ* 133 = Revillout (1885), 25–26; Pestman, *Rec.* 4 + *UPZ* 134; 5 + *UPZ* 132; 6 (108 B.C.) with Pestman's legal discussion, *Rec.*, vol. 2, pp. 39–41. For other Anoubieion merchants: *P. Cair. dem.* 30602–3 + *UPZ* 130–31 (115 B.C.); *P. B.M.* 10075 + *UPZ* 142 (64 B.C.) = Jelínková (1957) and (1959). Similar short-term loans are found in the Zenon archive, Orrieux (1981), 333–34.

[254] *P. Cair. Zen.* 59488.

Paramonos was drillmaster in Alexandria, and his recognition in the mid-third century B.C. of the primacy of Memphis in the market of certain products suggests perhaps how long it might take for the new city of Alexandria to match the earlier capital. Sicyonian strigils might either have been made in the city or imported, but in either case the best value was apparently to be found in the long-established market center of Memphis. The same features are found in the second example.

In 253 B.C. Promethion, a banker of Mendes in the Delta, wrote to Zenon, on the first occasion inquiring about the price of wax and later sending his agent 500 drachmas to buy up as much of this as was possible:

> Promethion to Zenon, greetings. You have written to me about the wax to say that the cost per talent, including the toll at Memphis, comes to 44 drachmas, whereas your information is that with us it costs 40 drachmas. Now do not listen to the nonsense people are talking; for it sells here at 48 drachmas. You will therefore oblige me by sending as much as you can. Following what you wrote to me I have given your agent Aigyptos 500 drachmas of silver towards the price of the wax, and the balance, whatever it turns out, I will pay directly to whomever you tell me. And of honey too let five metretai be obtained for me. I appreciate the kindness and readiness which you have always shown to us, and if you have need of anything here do not hesitate to write. Farewell. Year 33, Pharmouthi 19.[255]

With the help of friends like Zenon, men of affairs like Promethion took advantage of the best buys to be found in Memphis.[256] Information was precious and not readily available. The network of contacts covered the whole at least of Lower Egypt.

The picture of these papyri is of a group of individuals successfully using their new position to exploit the opportunities of the society in which they now found themselves. Information was at a premium and friends were used to check on goods elsewhere. Although their networks might be wider, their methods were probably those of the country in which they now lived. For Ptolemaic Egypt provides a fine example of what has been described as the bazaar economy.[257] In such an economic system, where sellers seek to maximize their profits and consumers to find the best value for their money, information is of prime importance and often difficult to acquire. Once gained, information both on availability and on prices is highly prized and carefully guarded. Within transactions the personal reputation of those involved is of crucial importance. With the arrival of the Greeks, in the cities at least, money had now be-

---

[255] *P. Cair. Zen.* 59250; 59823 (253 B.C.).
[256] *P. Cair. Zen.* 59633.6–7, for sheepskin hats.
[257] Geertz (1979), 125, 183–85.

come the standard form of exchange. And so, in the larger cities of Ptolemaic Egypt, the bazaar economy and the mentality associated with it flourished in changed circumstances. Whereas in the villages it is possible that a barter economy still prevailed, no evidence survives for this. In contrast, the city was an active center of sale and purchase; cash passed hands, pawning was practiced when necessary, and prices were carefully watched.[258] The new royal bank at Memphis was a busy one, handling tax payments and guarantees as well as individual accounts.[259] For the city served as a center of both production and exchange for the Memphite nome, as for the whole of Lower Egypt.

THE TEMPLES

In analyzing the population of Egypt, Herodotus divided it into seven classes of occupation, and the first of these was the priests.[260] The importance of priests and temples continuing in Ptolemaic Egypt may be seen reflected in the chapters of this book. Perhaps a third of the city area was devoted to temple enclosures[261] and, because Memphis served as the religious center of the country where national priestly gatherings might take place, the temples of Memphis almost certainly represented the largest single employer within the city. Such an assertion is ultimately unverifiable, yet the vast range of temple activities that are documented with the personnel involved in them tends to give it support.[262]

First and foremost came the priests who served the gods within the sanctuary and were set apart from ordinary men.[263] In addition, a great infrastructure of temple employees and associates serviced the priesthood, the temples, and the cults of the gods: scribes, temple cleaners, bakers, catacomb builders, those who provided lodgings where pilgrims might stay, and many, many more.[264]

The temples' role within the community was not just a spiritual one.

[258] *P. Cair. Zen.* 59414, garlic; *PSI* 571.20–25 (251 B.C.), poppy seed, etc.; *P. Mich. Zen.* 46.1–12 (251 B.C.); *P. Cair. Zen.* 59053.11 (258/7 B.C.).

[259] *P. Mich. Zen.* 32.10–11 (255 B.C.); *UPZ* 114.i.1; ii.1 (150 to 148 B.C.).

[260] Hdt. 2.164. The others were soldiers, cowherds, and swineherds (note the absence of shepherds), merchants, interpreters, and ships' captains.

[261] An impressionistic guess, but see n. 3 above with Diod. Sic. 1.21.7; 73.2–3, on the strength of temples in Egypt, controlling a third of the country.

[262] W. Otto (1905), 258–405; (1908), 1–71, remains basic. See also Préaux (1939a), 47–53, 102–4, 480–91; Rostovtzeff (1941), 280–84, 322; Quaegebeur (1979); Stead (1984); J. H. Johnson (1986); chapters 4 and 7 below.

[263] Sauneron (1957).

[264] *UPZ* 7.5–6 (163 B.C.); 120.10–12 (second century B.C.). See chapter 6 below for catacomb builders and Sarapieion workers.

They also played an economic role. As elsewhere in the ancient Near East, in Egypt temples both organized their own activities and, through their weights and dromos measures, served as guarantee to those of others. "The stones of Ptah" had long been the accepted standard of weight recognized in legal contracts, and, with monetization, Ptah guaranteed the purity of silver in which payments now were made.[265] For grain, the measure of the dromos of the Anoubieion similarly served as a generally recognized measure.[266] Within the community at large, temples acted as centers for redistribution, yet their own wealth, based in land, livestock, and temple manufacture, was cumulative.[267] Temple treasuries and storehouses contained this wealth, and the priestly personnel in charge indicate, in the variety of appointments held, the wide range of temple interests. As often, the evidence is scattered in both time and place, but the sample that survives is witness to this range.

Ptah might be "lord of provisions in his temple," but it was his priestly representatives who served to guard and manage these.[268] The storeroom of the temple at Memphis in the third century B.C. came under the charge of the high priest Anemhor II;[269] the temple of Ptah is presumably the temple meant, as in other similar appointments.[270] The storeroom of the temple of Ramses was at one date in the Ptolemaic period the responsibility of Oteuris, son of Komoapis,[271] and scribes of the treasuries are recorded for the Temple of the Peak on ʿAnchtawy[272] as well as that of Ptah.[273] Other scribes of the treasury presumably belonged to the staff of this same temple, without doubt the most important in the city.[274] Priests were responsible for the clothing of the gods (high priests in two recorded cases),[275] for the food supply of the sacred cattle,[276] and for the supervi-

---

[265] Porten (1968), 63–64, 68–70.

[266] E.g., Pestman, *Rec.* 4.19 (108 B.C.).

[267] W. Otto (1905), 258–405, a still basic discussion; Stead (1984), for a model of temple economies.

[268] So Anemhor II (*PP* 5352) and Petobastis II (*PP* 5370a); Ptah here is also described as "south of his wall."

[269] *PP* 5352; figure 5.

[270] *PP* 5370a, Petobastis II; *PP* 5694a, Panouphis, son of Petosiris; *PP* 5658a, Onnophris, son of Sentaes; *PP* 5761, Petobastis, son of Horos.

[271] *PP* 5677e.

[272] *PP* 5760b, Petobastis, son of [Pete]nephtimis.

[273] *PP* 5854, Phimenis/Amasis, son of Teteimouthes.

[274] *PP* 2856, Chaiapis, son of Paneith (275–203 B.C.); *PP* 5359 and figure 6, Herieus II, son of Amasis (214–163 B.C.); *PP* 5725a, Peteharendotes, son of Tared (second century B.C.).

[275] *PP* 5352, Anemhor II, director of the wardrobe; *PP* 5372, Teōs clothes the gods with the product of his handiwork.

[276] *PP* 5874, Chonsiou, son of Esisout (d. 248 B.C.); cf. *P. Louvre* E 3266.4.Q = App. B:2, for a herd of black cattle.

sion of the lamp depository in the temple-estate of Ptah.[277] Related supervisory appointments are those of general manager in the necropolis of Apis,[278] priest in charge of craftsmen,[279] foreman of the workmen,[280] and (whatever this entailed) director of works in the golden palace.[281] In the cult titles of the Memphite priests may thus be seen the diverse economic functions and activities of a Ptolemaic temple.

Temple income was regularly divided into that from sacred land and other temple revenues, of which under the Ptolemies the most important were the *apomoira* and the *syntaxis*, a block grant from the crown.[282] The apomoira, tax income from vineyards and orchards, was specifically destined for the royal cult.[283] Collected by the state, it was transferred to the temples for this use, while the syntaxis was a more general grant to be used for the regular upkeep of temple personnel and activities. It is clear from the papyri that much of the land which earlier was sacred now came under government control;[284] the only sacred land from which the temples now gathered rent was that conceded by the crown, the land *en aphesei*. In spite of such restrictions, sacred land together with temple flocks might still form a significant source of income for the Ptolemaic temples.

In Ptolemaic Memphis how much income actually came from sacred land is unknown. At an earlier date the temples had been significant landholders, and under Ramses III the Ptah temple alone controlled 2538.5 hectares (25.4 square kilometers) of land.[285] At least some sacred land remained attached to the Ptolemaic temples in Memphis, and in 110 B.C. 420 hectares (1,680 arouras) are ascribed to Ptah and Apis on a land survey, probably from the Aphroditopolite nome;[286] there may have been other holdings outside the Memphite nome in addition to the main land of the temple, which was local. Temple livestock added to the income

---

[277] *PP* 5767, Petosiris, father of Heranch; cf. the lychnaption on the necropolis.

[278] *PP* 5540 and figure 6, Esnounouer, son of Onnophris; and the supervisors of the necropolis, chapter 5 below.

[279] *PP* 5366a, Onnophris, son of Tamounis; perhaps Onnophris I of figure 6, *PP* 5657.

[280] *PP* 6120a, Imouthes.

[281] *PP* 5364 and figure 5, Esisout II/Petobastis I.

[282] For this threefold division, see *OGIS* 90.14–15 (196 B.C.); *P. Tebt.* 5 = *C. Ord. Ptol.* 53.50–56 (118 B.C.).

[283] See the discussion of royal cult in chapter 4.

[284] *BGU* 1216 (110 B.C.) distinguishes these different forms of temple land; Quaegebeur (1979), 724, for temple land at Edfu under royal control; Crawford (1971), 100, on the evidence of *P. Tebt.* 93 (c. 112 B.C.).

[285] *P. Harris* 1 with Breasted (1906), IV.87–206 at 98.

[286] *BGU* 1216.53 (110 B.C.), cf. Quaegebeur, Clarysse, and Van Maele (1985), 27, giving a Memphite provenance. (The sacred geography of Egypt differed from its administrative geography, Yoyotte 1967/8, 106.)

used in the general upkeep of the temples and of their cults. No better indication, however, exists of the temples' loss of wealth in land than the institution itself of syntaxis. The actual dispensation of this grant might be made within the temple but the recipients of syntaxis clearly recognized its ultimate source.[287] Under the Ptolemies this is likely to have become the main income of the Memphite temples.

Further temple revenue came from the profits of the many varied temple activities, from byssos weaving, for instance, or from pressing oil.[288] Incubation (the practice of sleeping in the temple overnight in the hopes of receiving divinely inspired dreams or cures) for medicinal or for oracular purposes in the Asklepieion at Memphis would bring in gifts from prospective as from grateful patients, and temple prostitution may have brought in profit.[289] Pilgrims and tourists added to the income of the temples and those who were associated with them. A typical present from Memphis might be a potted, mummified ibis,[290] and visitors spent their drachmas on sacrifices and souvenirs.

The outlay of the temples derived from this income, and in this way royal subsidies could be redistributed at large. Alongside the upkeep of priests, cult expenditure was heavy, with imported incense to be purchased, along with oil for cult lamps and fuel for sacrifice.[291] Temple employees needed feeding, as the Sarapieion papyri show,[292] and besides the outlay on clothes for the statues and the decoration of their shrines, the cost of mounting processions for the major religious holidays may sometimes, and sometimes not, have been balanced by the gifts the participants brought.

THE DEATH INDUSTRY

Closely connected with the temples, the largest single business in the city was probably that of death. The embalming and burial of man and ani-

[287] See chapter 4 n. 19.
[288] *Byssos*: see n. 98; oil: *UPZ* 119.20–21 (156 B.C.), temple guards chasing run-away kiki workers implies a temple workshop; textiles: *UPZ* 109.13 (98 B.C.); temple workshops: Kees (1961), 163; de Cenival (1973), 217; *P. Rev.* = *SB/Bh.* 1.55.4–9, temples allowed to prepare their own sesame oil for cult purposes.
[289] Cf. chapter 1 n. 94.
[290] Lucian, *The Ship*, 15.
[291] Incense: *UPZ* 97.14,18 (158 B.C.); 99. 14, 16, 30, 36, 40 (158 B.C.); 101.7 (156 B.C.). Lamps: *UPZ* 99.7 (158 B.C.); 101.6; chapter 1 n. 112 above. Fuel: *UPZ* 97.2 (158 B.C.); 99.13, 17, 31, 41 (158 B.C.); 101.8 (156 B.C.).
[292] *UPZ* 98 (158 B.C.); 7.6 (163 B.C.), bakers.

mal, with associated sacrifices and libations, provided employment for many men and women in the western suburbs of the city. If the products were mummies, the raw materials were the corpses and the substances used in the process of embalming. The corpses came from the city of Memphis, from the immediately surrounding area, and from even further afield.[293] Herodotus lists the ingredients used for human mummification: natron and the different *pharmaka* which included ground-up spices, myrrh, cassia, and aromatic substances. All of these pharmaka would need to be imported. Cedar oil (also imported) was used for second-class products, and gum, *kommi*, was required for sticking the bandages.[294] Bandages of byssos were produced locally within the temple communities.[295] Besides those for natron and myrrh, ostraca from the excavations at Hermonthis, home of the Buchis bull, record receipts for incense used in burial ceremonies.[296] All of these substances were of course in use at Memphis too.

Natron at least was found in Egypt. The other substances were always imported and must have been among the most costly imports which passed through the port of Memphis. Some of these commodities might come from Syria, but many came from Arabia, at first through Petra and Syria, later through the Red Sea ports and Coptos.[297] Little is known of the organization of this trade, but from the second century B.C. a Minaean sarcophagus inscription commemorates a certain Zidl from South Arabia, who during his lifetime had imported myrrh and perfumes for Egyptian temples; in death he was mummified, wrapped with Egyptian byssos sent from all the temples of Egypt and buried in the Memphite necropolis.[298] He must have been a crucial individual in the supply of these necessities. When in the second century B.C. resin sellers are recorded dwelling in the city, one of these is a Syrian.[299] Foreign merchants settled in Mem-

---

[293] *P. Louvre* E 3266.7.C (197 B.C.) = App. B:2 with Quaegebeur *LA sv* "Naukratis," is, however, likely to refer to citizens from that city now living in Memphis, Yoyotte (1982/ 3), 132.

[294] Hdt. 2.86–87.

[295] *OGIS* 90.17–18, 29–30 (196 B.C.), royal remissions; *P. Tebt.* 5.245–47 (118 B.C.), for cult use.

[296] Mond and Myers (1934), 2.53–56.

[297] Préaux (1939a), 362–66; Rostovtzeff (1941), 386–92; *P. Cair. Zen.* 59089 (257 B.C.), myrrh; *UPZ* 97.14, 18 (158 B.C.), incense.

[298] Rhodokanakis (1924), 113–33; Ryckmans (1935), 151–54; Beeston (1937), 59–62, with revised translation and date. See Orrieux (1985), 97–100, on the trade of these ingredients.

[299] *P. Louvre* E 3266.5.P–Q (197 B.C.) = App. B:2: Quaegebeur (1977), 104–5, has a different interpretation.

phis might thus help to ease the trade in substances needed for embalm-
ment on the necropolis to the west.

Following mummification, funerary priests were also employed to
continue the cult after death, pouring libations for the deceased. No precise figures may be put on those involved, but, taking account of both
human and animal mummification and the continuing cult of the dead,
the numbers of priests and others involved and the overall scale of the
business were certainly significant (see chapters 5 and 6).

Memphis as a City

What kind of a city was Memphis and how did it work? A start may be
made with the "Memphite Theology" and its hymn of praise for the
creator-god, Ptah:

> He gave birth to the gods,
> He made the towns,
> He established the nomes,
> He placed the gods in their shrines,
> He settled their offerings,
> He established their shrines.[300]

The city was animated by the divine creative will, and the close connection between the god and his city is clear. In the eyes of the Egyptians
who dwelled there, their city was inextricably linked with the cults that
it housed; the city belonged to the primary order of things. Both aspects
are relevant. Memphis was a cult center, a type of holy city, and as such
was a well-established center long before the Macedonian conquest. As a
city it was very old, and the number of cults in the city was commensu-
rate with its size.

The strength of the Memphite temples and their associated activities
(and especially necropolis functions) remained of prime importance even
following the arrival of the Greeks. No longer financially independent
and in part relying on crown subsidy, the temples nevertheless were centers of production with their own workshops, storehouses, and granaries.
Indirectly, too, they had an economic role, making the city a magnet for
priests, pilgrims, and tourists who swelled the numbers while bringing
revenue to the city. In their relations with the gods, they also provided
services for the community. The afterlife of the dead was the care of

[300] Lichtheim (1973), 55.

priests, through ceremonies and through the work of the embalmers. The greatest product of all, however, was one which cannot be measured, the provision of divine order and well-being for the country and its people. For new rulers, acceptance by the old gods of Egypt was of particular importance since in Egyptian eyes, as shown in the Potter's Oracle, hostility of the Egyptian gods might be fatal to the regime. Only when man was at peace with the divine, when Ma'at, that Egyptian principle of correct conduct and right order, was seen to be strong could the country prosper. In this process the temples of Memphis, together with their priests, might play an important role. Thus, the temples were central to the city.

In straightforward economic terms it is not possible to assess the city's role. The sizeable population of Memphis will have formed an important consumer for food and goods from the Memphite nome, as from other neighboring areas. In material terms the products of the city—the metal goods, the clothes and textiles, or the ships that were built in the Memphite yards—are unlikely to have balanced what was consumed. Costly incense and spices must have been imported for cult purposes, and especially for the necropolis cults. And many of the activities of temples and priests served to redistribute the country's wealth. But the services which the city provided, both as an administrative center and in the religious sphere, gave it an importance which went beyond the economic.

3

ETHNIC MINORITIES

The city is both large and populous, it ranks second after
Alexandria and its population is a mixed one.

Strabo 17.1.32

When Strabo visited Memphis in the late first century B.C., in the early
years of the Roman occupation, like Herodotus before him he was struck
by the splendor of the city. He also commented on its population—it was
large and it was multiracial. The nationalistic prophecy of the potter-god
Chnoum had spoken of "the city, nurse of all, where all races of men have
settled,"[1] and the multiracial character of its population resulted both
from its geographical centrality and from its historical role as first city for
much of Egypt's long past. For river traffic along the Nile and down river
from Syria, it had always been an important center, and the location here
of a royal palace had brought to the city both specialist military units and
foreign visitors. From all parts of the country Egyptians would visit the
home of Ptah and of the Apis bull. Foreigners too were attracted by the
exoticism of the Egyptian cults, and with the conquest of Alexander came
a new influx of Greeks into what was already an international community.

Here I want first, briefly, to tell what is known of the story of immigration into Memphis, and then to consider how far it is possible, in the
period following Alexander's conquest, still to identify the separate ethnic groups within the city. With the limited evidence that survives, I shall
attempt to consider the roles of these different groups, and to examine
the extent and nature of their integration within the community and the
consequences for ethnic relations of changes in the political control of the
city.

As more recent experience has repeatedly shown, there may be many
reasons for immigration. In Memphis foreigners came and settled as conquerors, as merchants trading overseas, as mercenaries fighting for a for-

[1] *P. Oxy.* 2332.61-62 (late third century A.D.) with Koenen (1968); (1970) and (1974);
(1984); Lloyd (1982), 50-55.

eign power; they came as prisoners of war, as refugees escaping persecution, or simply in search of a better life. And they came both singly and in larger groups, some groups consisting only of men, others as communities on the move. The reasons for immigration were as varied over time, and the effects, not surprisingly, might differ for a variety of reasons.

The earliest foreign settlers to Memphis seem to have been of Canaanite origin. Perhaps they came first as merchants, traveling up the Pelusiac branch of the Nile and settling in the city where much later they were known as Phoenico-Egyptians. From the reign at least of Tuthmosis III, in the fifteenth century B.C., there were royal dockyards at Memphis[2] and in Egypt ships' timbers had always had to be imported. Good timber came from the Levant, as did other commodities essential to the Egyptians—resin, for instance (used in mummification), or spices from Arabia, coming up through the desert by caravan and across to the Levantine coast.[3] Later, Phoenicians may have settled in the city also as mercenaries. A certain 'Abd-Ptah fought on the expedition of Psammetichos II against the Ethiopians in 593/2 B.C., scrawling his name in Phoenician on the colossal statue of Ramses at Abu Simbel.[4] His strange, composite name suggests that he came from Memphis. As already noted, when Herodotus visited the city in the mid-fifth century B.C. the Phoenician quarter was known as the Tyrian Camp.[5] Such a name, like Stratopeda in the Delta, strongly suggests a military origin for some at least of the Phoenicians in the city.

It was certainly as mercenaries that Ionians and Carians were settled in Memphis during the sixth century B.C. Herodotus describes how Psammetichos I (664–610 B.C.) first employed these overseas troops in his struggle for the throne, settling them during his reign in two camps which faced each other across the river near Pelusium; these camps were simply called Stratopeda.[6] It was the Saite king Amasis (570–526 B.C.) who moved their descendants away from the sensitive eastern frontier to a new home in Memphis. Perhaps this move coincided with a change of capital since Herodotus speaks of Amasis providing "a guard for himself against the Egyptians"; this might well describe the position of a new

[2] Glanville (1931) and (1932).
[3] Préaux (1939a), 353-59.
[4] Sauneron and Yoyotte (1952), 188; Bernand and Masson (1957), 7; Ray (1982b), 85, for the date.
[5] Hdt. 2.112.
[6] Hdt. 2.152-54, cf. Lloyd (1975), 14-16, for another version; Diod. Sic. 1.66-67.

foreign bodyguard protecting a Saite king at the royal palace in Memphis against Egyptians of non-Delta origin.[7] The Ionians settled in Memphis had their own quarter and temple, the Hellenion. During the Persian period the community stayed on, and they were known as Hellenomemphites.[8] The Carians settled by Amasis lived in the Karikon and were known as Caromemphites.[9] These were the Memphites who in the fifth century B.C. provided Herodotus (himself from Halicarnassus, a city under strong Carian influence) with much of his Egyptian information.

When Alexander reached Memphis in 332 B.C. he was not the first foreign conqueror to take the city. Two hundred years earlier, in 525 B.C., it was the eventual surrender of Memphis which marked Kambyses' conquest of Egypt,[10] and the Persians then ruled the country until 404 and again from 341 to 332 B.C.; it was the Persian king Darius III whom Alexander replaced as pharaoh of Egypt. The effect on the city of the Persian domination, with Aramaic introduced as the new language of administration, is a fascinating, though separate, subject. The dyke around the southern part of the city became known as the Syro-Persikon, and the Persians of Memphis probably lived in this area, close to the Phoenicians or Syrians whom they perhaps used in their administration.[11] But the capital of the Persian empire lay far from Egypt and the Persian takeover was less pervasive than that of their Greek successors; if the Persians survived the Greek conquest, with few exceptions they are not to be traced in the Ptolemaic city.[12]

The arrival of the Greeks with Alexander was on a different scale and resulted in a major change in the balance of the population within the city, as in the country as a whole. As long as Ptolemy I ruled from Memphis there will have been a high concentration of Macedonians in the city, in both military and civil capacities. And many must have stayed when the

[7] Hdt. 2.154.3; the motivation is questioned by Lloyd (1975), 23; Kees (1961), 180. For Carian and Ionian troops, "foreign rascals," later involved in trouble in the city, see Segal (1983), no. 6.

[8] PSI 488.12; P. Cair. Zen. 59593.7-8. The form Hellenikon used by Aristagoras of Miletus (in Steph.Byz. s.v.) is presumably formed on the analogy of Karikon.

[9] Steph. Byz. s.v. Karikon, commenting on their intermarriage with Egyptians; PSI 488.11, dyke; 409.21-22 (third century B.C.).

[10] Hdt. 3.13-14.

[11] PSI 488.10 (257 B.C.), the dyke; for Tamōs, admiral of the fleet and then satrap of Asia Minor in the fourth century B.C., as a possible Memphite see D. M. Lewis (1977), 93 n. 48. Or might he be an Egyptianized Phoenician?

[12] Spondates, employed on Apollonios' Memphite dorea, is an exception (Pap. Lugd. Bat. 21 index ix); cf. a Persaigyptios from the nearby Herakleopolite nome, P. Hib. 1.70b.6-7 (228 B.C.). The names of Bargathes (orchard guard) and Nouraios (shepherd), also employed by Apollonios, are Aramaic.

capital moved. The study of the interaction of the new conquerors, drawn from all over the Greek-speaking world, with the native population of Egypt is one of major interest; it is not peculiar to Memphis. And though in this respect the city may serve as a microcosm for the country more generally, the phenomenon of Greek immigration is different in kind, as well as in scale, from that of other ethnic groups who formed the city's population in the period of Ptolemaic control. It is a subject which lies at the heart of this study and which will frequently recur. Here the focus is rather on the other foreign communities of Memphis.

As so often in cities where Phoenicians preceded,[13] Jews also came to Memphis, drawn both by the wealth of Egypt and the haven it afforded. The attractions of the country, of its peace and plenty, were denounced by the prophet Jeremiah in the early sixth century B.C.—"Egypt where we shall see no sign of war, never hear the sound of the trumpet and not starve for want of bread" (Jer. 42.13-14)—as he attempted to dissuade his countrymen from joining earlier Jewish immigrants in Migdol, Taphanes (Daphnae), Noph (Memphis, the city of Ptah), and the district of Pathros (perhaps Elephantine). These earlier immigrants were idolatrous, worshipping the queen of heaven and unaffected by Josiah's reforms of 622 B.C.[14] And yet in spite of his rhetoric, when Jerusalem fell to Babylon in 587 B.C., Jeremiah joined his countrymen in taking refuge in the land of Egypt.

The centers of Jewish immigration named by Jeremiah were all garrison posts. In Memphis Jews may have served as garrison troops also under the Persians, the function they certainly performed in Elephantine. But, as the prophet recognized, it was not always possible to separate Jews from other Semitic immigrants.[15] Aramaic papyri from Elephantine and Hermoupolis suggest flourishing communities of these immigrants, both Jews and non-Jews, with networks active throughout the country in the century before Alexander.[16]

The Graeco-Macedonian conquest of Egypt signaled a renewal of hostilities with Egypt's eastern neighbors, and it is possible that some of the

---

[13] Kraeling (1953), 48, for Elephantine; cf. Carthage.

[14] Jer. 44.1, cf. Isaiah 11.11. The picture is supported by the fifth-century B.C. Aramaic papyri from the Persian garrison of Jews on Elephantine; cf. Porten (1968), 173-79.

[15] E.g., C. Pap. Jud. 46.1-3 (second–first century B.C.), two Jews (potters) in the Fayum village of the Syrians.

[16] Porten (1968), 18. Hermoupolis: Bresciani and Kamil (1966); Milik (1967); Naveh (1968). Elephantine: Cowley (1923); Kraeling (1953); Driver (1957); Grelot (1972). From Memphis the one ostrakon recording the son of Yahôhanan is not sufficient evidence for a Syrian wine trade, as suggested by the editor Aimé-Giron (1931), 1–4, ostr. 1.

100,000 prisoners said to have been brought from Palestine to Egypt by Ptolemy I Soter joined the Jewish community of Memphis.[17] Apart, however, from the select 30,000 stationed in the countryside as garrison troops, the majority were probably settled in villages, to develop new lands recently reclaimed from the desert.[18]

A further Semitic group in Ptolemaic Memphis is the military detachment of Idumaeans, *machairophoroi*, who are recorded in the late second century B.C., probably as a palace guard.[19] Idumaea had been carved out of southern Judaea by the Edomites who, hard-pressed by the Nabataeans from the south, had moved in from their homeland after the sack of Jerusalem in 587 B.C. It may be that the Memphite Idumaeans were originally among those 100,000 prisoners just mentioned brought by Ptolemy Soter "from the land of the Jews."[20] An Idumaean of the *epigonē*, the son of Apollodotos, occurs in the Fayum in the third century B.C., which might support such a hypothesis.[21] It has, however, been argued that these settlers in Memphis came later, as refugees following the Jewish takeover of Idumaea by John Hyrcanus in 126 B.C. But whether they came as prisoners of war or as refugees, or indeed in part as both, the Idumaeans were a late immigrant group to the city. Separate, and independent from the Jews, in Memphis they form the only recognizable group of immigrants to postdate the Greek conquest of Egypt.

Other nationalities may be found in the city, both temporary visitors and permanent settlers, recorded as individuals rather than as members of an identifiable immigrant group. Such, it seems, were the two Arabs, Myroullas and Chalbas, who wrote to their brother Dakountis from the Sarapieion on 20 September 152 B.C.;[22] their names suggest their origin. (In the case of the Memphite priest Acoreus whom Lucan records as a member of Kleopatra VII's advisory council, a name which may once have indicated Bedouin origin has become a regular Egyptian name.)[23] "Arabs" are known from the Fayum from the Zenon archive of the third century B.C., but the designation Arab often implies only a nomadic way

---

[17] Ps.-Aristeas, *Letter to Philokrates*, 12-13, with Fraser (1972), 1.57, 696-704; for Semites settled in the Fayum, see Préaux (1939b), 387.

[18] For details, see Crawford (1971), 40-42.

[19] *OGIS* 737 (112/11 B.C.); Milne (1905), 35-37, no. 9283 = Breccia (1911), no. 142 with tav. xxv.62 = *SB* 681.

[20] See n. 17, *apo tēs tōn Ioudaiōn chōras*.

[21] *Pap. Lugd. Bat.* 20.18.3; cf. *SB* 7351 (second century B.C.).

[22] *UPZ* 72.

[23] Lucan 8.475-77, 480; 10.174, 193; the name became "royal" with the pharaoh Hakoris; cf. Posener (1969); Heinen (1966), 64 n.2, a Bedu or Arab.

of life, and such individuals probably formed part of the shifting groups who inhabited the area between the cultivation and the high desert, especially on the east bank of the Nile.[24] Whereas some Arabs may have left their tents and settled in Memphis they hardly qualify as an ethnic group within the city. The enterprising Cretan dream interpreter who practiced his trade up on the necropolis in the early Ptolemaic period[25] probably formed part of the great wave of Greek immigration which followed Alexander, whereas the group of youngsters from the Black Sea region who visited the city in the late third century B.C. were among the many temporary visitors who came to Memphis.[26]

Like most big cities, Memphis served always as a focus for internal Egyptian migration.[27] Temporary visitors traveling to the city for business and pleasure could stay with relatives, or in local hotels of the type found in much of the Near East today. The hotel of the Arsinoites was likely to be fully booked with visitors or temporary workers from the Fayum,[28] without needing custom from Upper Egypt or the Delta. In a city characterized by ethnic quarters,[29] groups would naturally stick together with a network of contacts existing for new arrivals, who might or might not settle more permanently in the city. However, the scale of migrant Egyptian labor cannot be quantified; it may be recorded simply as a factor in the overall picture of the mixed population of Ptolemaic Memphis.

Such briefly is the story of immigration. Before considering the role of the various ethnic groups within Ptolemaic Memphis, their position within the society, and their interaction with the new Greek rulers, the identity of these groups within the setting of the city must first be established. The partial and uneven nature of the evidence inevitably results in a picture which is incomplete. Yet, a detailed consideration of this evidence within the same framework of questions shows up some significant variations between the different minority groups. Several personal indi-

---

[24] *Pap. Lugd. Bat.* 21, p. 479 for refs.; *UPZ* 72.4 n. For the same practice more recently (in the Sudan), see Crowfoot (1921), 23. The east bank of the Nile was regularly known as Arabia, Hdt. 2.15.1; *P. Coll. Youtie* 121.5.

[25] Cairo stele 27567, Rostovtzeff (1941), 2.900 pl.ci.1; Grimm (1975), plate 13, no. 12.

[26] *UPZ* 149.4, *Mares*. The name Kakis from Cilicia (Zgusta 1970, 37) occurs in the same account.

[27] See Braunert (1964), 29-110.

[28] *UPZ* 120.5-13 (second century B.C.), closely connected with an oil extraction plant; cf. *P. Mich.* 8.503.3 (late second century A.D.).

[29] See Wheatley (1969), 5, for the type.

cators of ethnic identity are commonly accepted:[30] language, nomenclature, physical appearance (including dress), religion, and culture. Further, as in Memphis where the contours of the land with a series of hillocks or koms rising above the flood plain formed a natural setting for the city, ethnic identity may be physically reinforced by the existence of separate quarters where different groups live and of cemeteries where they are buried, or by separate social and political organizations. How far can these indicators be identified for the various peoples of the city of cosmopolitan Memphis?

PHOENICIANS

Egypt's close connection with the Levantine coast continued throughout its history, and the early Canaanite settlers in the city were probably reinforced both by military groups and by individual settlers. In 197 B.C. a Syrian resin seller is recorded living up on the necropolis which would provide the main market for his goods,[31] and in July 63 B.C. records of grain transport undertaken by an association of Memphite shippers name one Zabdion, son of Artemidoros, as a shipper and a certain Malichos as president of the association.[32] Here, for Phoenicians, is ethnic nomenclature surviving well into the Ptolemaic period, and these first-century B.C. shippers represent a long tradition of involvement in Nile shipping. Phoenicians and other Syrians were recorded already in the fifth century B.C. working in the Memphite dockyard, and in the late third century B.C. it was a Phoenician who devised a scheme to launch more expeditiously the monster, forty-bank ship of Ptolemy IV Philopator.[33] Zabdion and Malichos will have found other fellow countrymen working on the river.

There is some, minimal, evidence for use of the Phoenician language in Ptolemaic Memphis. A dedication to Isis-Astarte which appeals to Egyptian Horos as protector-god was set up, probably in the second century B.C., by one Fe'l'aštort son of 'Abdmilkot, a military man visiting

[30] E.g., Ware (1931) and Morris (1968), with an interesting change of emphasis, from race to status.
[31] *P. Louvre* E 3266.5.Q = de Cenival (1972a), 39; Quaegebeur (1977), 104-5, suspects "the Syrian" may be a Horos epithet but, given his trade, the straightforward interpretation seems more likely.
[32] *BGU* 1741.9; 1742.9; 1743.5 (63 B.C.), the *nauklēroi hippodromitai*.
[33] Aimé-Giron (1931), nos. 5-24, reedited by Bowman (1941), 302-13; see Parker (1941), 295-98, for the date (472/1 B.C.). Ath. 5.204c, for the launching.

the city from the garrison at Thebes. He traces his family back for five generations (to the beginning perhaps of the Ptolemaic period) and asks the goddess for blessing for himself, his wife, and his four children.[34] The four-line Phoenician inscription is on the face of a yellow limestone base on which there stands a black schist stele of superior quality portraying a Horos figure standing on crocodiles (plate iii); the black surface of the stele is covered with hieroglyphic charms and spells against snakes and scorpions.[35] The top of the base is scooped out, in front of the stele, in such a way that water poured over the stele collects in a rivulet running round the block and widening out into a basin in front. From here the water could be taken by those requiring protection through the charms. By this simple method the Phoenician dedicant, or others with access to the monument, would have no problem in "reading" the mysterious script of his adopted country, and so protecting himself against the perils of snakes and scorpions. With such magical devices to hand, literacy was unnecessary and language irrelevant as the devotees of Isis–Astarte sought protection from the gods of their adopted country.

Other Phoenicians used Greek in public contexts. In the late third century B.C., for instance, a Sidonian, Abramos, son of Abdastaratos, made an ex-voto to Astara (Astarte), whom he describes as the great goddess of his homeland; but since the dedication was made on behalf of Ptolemy and queen Arsinoe, it is likely that Abramos was at least temporarily, if not indeed permanently, resident in Memphis, the almost certain origin of this stele.[36] Once again the name is ethnic, and the use of Greek for such a dedication tells us nothing of private linguistic practice. Did the Phoenicians of Memphis continue to speak Phoenician at home and to use it in their temples, or were they sufficiently Egyptianized, and later Hellenized, to forget their native languages?

Astarte herself was Egyptianized from an early date. By the reign of Amenophis IV, in the mid-fourteenth century B.C., she had been established in the Memphite pantheon of gods, as consort of Ptah whose temple already dominated the city.[37] Hers of course was the temple in the

---

[34] Lidzbarski (1902), 152–58 = Donner and Röllig (1971), 64–65, no. 48; translated by Milik (1967), 564–65. A further Phoenician inscription on a libation table from Saqqara is reported by Chassinat (1899), 56–57.

[35] Daressy (1903), 3–11, no. 9402 with plates ii–iii; see Lacau (1921/2), 189–209, from Kom el Qal'a.

[36] Boyaval (1966), from the Michaelides collection; Bingen (1967), 236, for the date.

[37] Gardiner (1932); Ranke (1932). Baal too had his prophet in Memphis, Glanville (1932), 25–26 n. 7; for later (c. 500 B.C.), Aimé-Giron (1931), 107, with Dupont-Sommer (1956), corrected by Grelot (1972), 77; Milik (1967), 566 n.3, sees rather a citizen of Anot.

southern quarter of the city, close by the Tyrian Camp, which Herodotus called that of the foreign Aphrodite, identified by some as Helen, daughter of Tyndareus.[38] In this area close to Kom el Rabī'a lies the newly excavated New Kingdom temple of Hathor, whom the Greeks called Aphrodite.[39] Perhaps the temple of Astarte in her Memphite form? If so, it is interesting to note that by the Roman period the temple had been abandoned and its court filled with kilns; earlier ethnic indications soon disappeared under the Romans.

A further ex-voto to Astarte, a marble bas-relief from the early Ptolemaic period almost certainly from Memphis, may illustrate a scene from the Ptolemaic temple (plate iv).[40] Beneath an Egyptian portico a seated goddess, wearing the headdress of Isis-Hathor, is honored by two officiating priests, one standing before a tall bronze altar in front of the goddess and the other behind, carrying a scepter with censer in his right hand and a sprinkler in his left. The syncretism of the relief is remarkable. The ram-headed scepter to which the censer is attached, the headdress of the goddess, and the portico with winged solar disk upheld by Hathoric columns are all straight from the traditions of Egypt. The priests, however, with beards, pointed hats, and ceremonial dress are entirely Syrian, as is the device of the sun held within the moon above the goddess to the left. These Phoenician elements confirm the identification of Astarte, and the scene could be based on the local Memphite cult of the goddess. Indeed, this relief may be seen as providing the physical setting for a letter sent to Zenon, an important man in the area:

> The priests of Astarte of the Phoenico-Egyptians in Memphis, greetings. We pray for you from Astarte favor in the eyes of the king. Herostratos sent you the letter-writer on the subject of the [priest] of Astarte who presented a petition to you in the Sarapieion; he asked you to take account of the petition. If therefore it meets your approval, please grant us (sesame) and kiki oil . . . in the same way as is granted to the temples in Memphis of the Carians and the Hellenomemphites. [Details then follow.] The temple of Astarte is similar to those of the Carians and Hellenomemphites. As is done to them, let it be done to us.[41]

With a temple in the valley city and a shrine up on the necropolis, the priests of Astarte looked for fair treatment from the Ptolemaic regime.

[38] Hdt. 2.112; cf. chapter 1, above. Full references to the Ptolemaic cult of Astarte in Kiessling (1953).

[39] Abdulla el-Sayed Mahmud (1978), plates 7–8 with p. 4, for the kilns.

[40] Aimé-Giron (1925), 191–211 and plate 5; see p. 208 for a date contemporary with Alexander.

[41] *PSI* V.531 with Bingen (1946), 146.

Himself from Caria, Zenon might be expected to see the logic of their demands.

It was in the upper Astarte shrine within the Sarapieion that there resided the enkatochoi whose lives are known from the second century B.C. archive of the sons of Glaukias (chapter 7). Some of the personnel attached to this shrine would seem from their nomenclature to have retained Levantine connections. For listed in a record of the provision of oat cakes from the Sarapieion archive are two mysterious categories of *atastitai* and *taplaeitai*.[42] Although the meaning of these words, which are neither Greek nor Egyptian, is obscure,[43] some of the names of those listed here, and in particular the Egyptianized name Peteastarte ("gift of Astarte"), suggest a connection of these two groups with the shrine. And besides Petaus, son of Peteastarte, and others with straightforward Egyptian names, several of the recipients appear to bear Semitic names—Kēl, for instance, Kalatēnis or Teeklēl.[44] Without specific evidence one way or the other, the possibility remains that a Semitic dialect was in use in this cult.[45]

Whatever the linguistic practice may have been, the Astarte temple relief described above, if indeed it does record a Memphite scene, provides good evidence for traditional priestly garb within this Phoenician cult. Phoenician dress has also been identified on the fine basalt stele of Chaiapis, son of Paneith and Tanenecher (plate v). This stele comes from the Memphite necropolis, where it was found in close association with a white marble head dating from the fifth century B.C. which once formed part of a Phoenician sarcophagus.[46] The stele itself, however, is later, dating from the third century B.C. The main hieroglyphic inscription, after an offertory formula, records the career of Chaiapis who held priestly positions in various Egyptian cults of the city suburbs and, like his father before him, was a military officer with overall control of law and order in Memphis, with special responsibilities during the ceremonies which followed the death of Apis and Mnevis bulls (such major religious ceremonies were likely to be times of particular tension in the city). And among the various offices he held was "greatest of artificers in the district

---

[42] *UPZ* 98 (158 B.C.).

[43] Attempts to find a Phoenician derivation have so far been unsuccessful. For the *taplaeitai*, a connection with *tabla*, mummy ticket in Greek, might just be possible.

[44] *UPZ* 98.24, 32-3, 41; the proportion of such names is abnormally high, and there may be others hidden in this strange list.

[45] Cf. the use of Idumaean, n. 102.

[46] Berlin stele 2118, Stern (1884); Schäfer (1902/3), with plate i; Quaegebeur (1974), 62; Wildung (1977a), 55-56; for the sarcophagus (Berlin 2123): Mariette (1856b), linked to the stele by Schäfer (1902/3), 32. Mnevis was the bull of nearby Heliopolis.

of the Jews." Below are three lines of demotic which give his dates: born
11 May 273 B.C., died 13 February 203 B.C. (14 Phamenoth Year 12–4
Tybi Year 2).[47] During his long life Chaiapis had a distinguished career,
and there is nothing particularly unusual in the written record of his
tombstone. Above the hieroglyphs, however, the deceased is shown
seated, Egyptian-style, before a table of offerings, flanked by two goddesses; to his right is Nut sheltering in her sycamore tree, and behind him
stands the goddess of the west, the goddess of the necropolis. It is the
appearance of Chaiapis himself which is startling. He is bare-headed with
close-cropped, curly hair and a beard, and he wears a long-sleeved, three-
quarter-length robe with fringes. Nothing could be less Egyptian.

Chaiapis is generally identified as a Phoenician from a family which
had settled in the city and become Egyptianized before the arrival of the
Greeks. In death he was buried in a fine old marble sarcophagus suitable
to his status, either imported as an antique for the purpose or retained as
a family heirloom. The location of his tomb on the central necropolis, in
the avenue of the sphinxes close to the Apis vaults, shows a position of
privilege in Egyptian society.[48] Priest in Egyptian cults with a good, almost too good, Egyptian nomenclature, it is his physical appearance that
betrays his non-Egyptian origin.

His facial type and beard could well support the identification of him
as Phoenician. Similar types occur among the fine (undated) series of terracotta heads from Memphis which Petrie classified as Semitic Syrian.[49]
And whereas Petrie's racial typology of these heads is at times suspect,
the imagination of the artists who produced them must have been fired
by the racial mix of the community in which they lived.[50] But the robe
worn by Chaiapis is puzzling. Although the Phoenician parallels that have
been adduced are not convincing,[51] the dress is certainly un-Egyptian and
resembles rather the priestly garb of the Astarte ex-voto scene. With one
possible exception, similar dress occurs neither in the large Egyptian collection of Ptolemaic stelae in the Cairo museum[52] nor in the rural scenes
of the fourth-century painted tomb of Petosiris at Ashmunein.[53] A

[47] See Quaegebeur (1974), 62, for the dates.
[48] Vercoutter (1962), 130; cf. chapter 1 n. 129.
[49] Petrie (1909a), plate xxxvi.20, without beard; Gordon (1939) identifies the "Sumerian"
heads as Indian Buddhist priests from the first century A.D.
[50] Petrie (1909a), plates xxxv–xliii; (1909b), plates xxviii–xxxiv; Scheurleer (1974).
[51] Schäfer (1902/3), 34.
[52] Kamal (1904/5), plates lxxix–lxxxiv; the possible exception is stele no. 22210, plate
lxxiii.118, but note the longer fringes.
[53] Lefebvre (1923/4), vol. 3, plate viii.f. The dress of notables in the tomb can be paralleled from Ptolemaic stelae.

painted panel, however, dating from the fifth century B.C., which comes from the recent excavations on the Sacred Animal Necropolis in the city, shows a cow and bull in procession with attendants, their hair either shorn or close-cropped, who wear somewhat similar long, fringed robes with shorter, fringed cloaks above. This, it has been suggested, was the regular dress of the East Greeks of the city, of the Hellenomemphites (and maybe also the Caromemphites) of this period.[54] So, when Herodotus decribed the *kalasiris*, a "linen chiton with fringes round the legs," as typical Egyptian dress (worn with a woollen garment on top), he may in fact have been describing rather the distinctive dress of the immigrant urban settlers of Memphis in whose company he clearly spent so much of his visit.[55] To judge from Chaiapis, this distinctive dress continued in popularity into the Ptolemaic period and might be regularly worn in the city.[56] It was, however, Memphite rather than Phoenician garb.

Phoenicians then, in the Ptolemaic city, are found as traders, shippers, and as police officers in charge of troops. It may also have been Phoenician artists who made the silver bowls with mock Egyptian subjects for which the plaster casts survive from the early Ptolemaic period. The shapes are often foreign to both Greek and Egyptian traditions, and Memphis had developed as an important artistic center, based perhaps on the skills of its immigrant population.[57]

In traditional folklore a Phoenician (or Semitic) influence has been suggested for Herodotus' strange story of King Sethon, victorious against King Senacherib through the timely intervention of mice who ate the Assyrians' bowstrings—an aetiological explanation, perhaps current in the city when he visited, of the depiction of Horos of Letopolis who holds a mouse, an animal traditionally connected with plague.[58] If this is the case, it illustrates how well embedded in the city and its culture were these settlers from the Syrian coast.

CAROMEMPHITES

Compared with the Phoenicians, the Caromemphites have left far fewer traces in the Ptolemaic city. A distinctive cock's comb helmet painted on

[54] R. V. Nicholls in Martin (1979), 74-75, with plate i. He compares the Egyptian dress of the sixth century "Caeretan" hydria showing Heracles and Busiris, Boardman (1980), 150, figure 186. The long sleeves of Chaiapis' dress are different.

[55] Hdt. 2.81. Democritus of Epheus (Hecataeus 12.525c-d) describes the rich kalasireis worn in Ephesus of Corinthian or Persian manufacture.

[56] Cf. Philostr. *VA* 6.5, still recognized as special in the second century A.D.

[57] Petrie (1909b), 16, with plate xxvi.11; Segall (1966), 9-18.

[58] Hdt. 2.141 with Spiegelberg (1906), 93-94.

one of the ostraka from the second-century B.C. Hor archive suggests the continued presence here of Carian mercenaries,[59] and Caromemphites are to be found serving as mercenaries in garrisons overseas.[60] To judge from their grave stelae, Caromemphites living in the city had earlier used the Carian language. These tombstones, re-used in the fourth-century B.C. central buildings of the animal necropolis and in the baboon galleries, record for this earlier community a Carian nomenclature sometimes accompanied by hieroglyphic transcriptions or by translations.[61] The grave stelae also illustrate a fine funerary art in the sixth century B.C.—Carian scenes of parting, death, and mourning with an interesting mixture of Greek and Egyptian influence visible both in the scenes and in their execution.[62] The Carian cemetery from which these stones were pillaged probably lay to the northwest of the city, close both to the Carian quarter and to Abousir,[63] but by the later fourth century B.C., cemetery, script, and art would all appear to have disappeared. So too have Carian names.[64]

By the Ptolemaic period, at least some of the inhabitants of the Carian quarter of Memphis seem no longer bound by the customs of their homeland. For on death Carians might be mummified. "Carians" are listed among the family assets in a legal document from 132B.C. from the Undertakers' Archive to be discussed in chapter 5;[65] these prospective mummies may be Caromemphites or simply Egyptian inhabitants of the Carian quarter. Intermarriage and progressive Egyptianization as seen in the abandonment of their language and Carian names meant that many Carians must have lost their sense of ethnic identity.

On the other hand, there still existed the temple of the Carians mentioned in that letter of the priests of Astarte (see above) as enjoying certain privileges. This must have been the temple of Carian Zeus, Zeus of Labraunda, for whom 120 arouras of land are recorded in the neighborhood

---

[59] Ray (1976), plate xxxiii with Lloyd (1978a), 107-10, and figure 10; cf. Petrie (1909b), 17 with plate xxviii.71. For Carian mercenaries: Polyaenus, *Strat.* 7.3; Plut. *Artaxerxes* 10.3.

[60] In Thessaly *c.* 250 B.C., Launey (1949/50), vol. 2, 1252.

[61] Masson (1978), used by Ray (1981), (1982a), and (1982b) to decipher the script.

[62] R. V. Nicholls in Masson (1978), 57-87. For illustrations, see Boardman (1980), 136, figures 158-59.

[63] Smith (1974), 43-44, suggests that the Carians may have served under the Persians, and their cemetery was pillaged in revenge; it remains a suggestion. The *prothesis* stele, E. Berlin 19553, showing knives used in mourning (Hdt. 2.61.2, a Carian practice), is from Abousir, Boardman (1980), 136, figure 159.

[64] With the possible exception of Mys, a common Carian name, see Robert, *Hellenica* 8.33-34. In Memphis: *UPZ* 7.8 (163 B.C.); 8.32 (161 B.C.), a *himatiopōlēs*; 119.39 (156 B.C.), a *koproxustēs*. For Mys in the Zenon archive: *P. Mich. Zen.* 31.5 (265/5 B.C.) with Clarysse (1980b), 105.

[65] *P. B.M.* 10384.9 (Malcolm Papyrus) = App. B:7.

close to land of two other Memphite gods, Asklepios (Imhotep/Im-outhes) and Sarapis.[66] The royal subvention for oil would help to meet the cost of a cult based primarily on landed wealth. The very existence of this Carian cult will have continued to provide some ethnic focus for those of Carian origin, whether descendants of the earlier military settlers or the new arrivals who followed Alexander.

The importance of the Carians in the early Ptolemaic city seems to have been as a source of local knowledge. Well versed in the ways and customs of their adopted home, the Carians played a key role in introducing the new conquerors to the problems and possibilities of the land of Egypt. Much of the early reclamation work and agricultural innovation in the northeast Fayum came through the city of Memphis. The Zenon archive from the third century B.C. shows the city as a center of resources and personnel; it was to Memphis that the new settlement of Philadelphia often looked and, on the basis of nomenclature, it was from Memphis and the Memphite nome that much of its new population came.[67] The Carians, who figure so prominently in Zenon's circle[68] (with a Syrian and a Persian too),[69] derive both directly and indirectly from the city of Memphis. Coming from the Greek cities of Caria, new immigrants like Zenon, himself from Kaunos, or Panakestor and Iason, son of Kerkion, from nearby Kalynda, through the established Memphite community of their fellow countrymen might have access to information and expertise to supplement their individual competence and enterprise; like their compatriots back home, they Hellenized with ease. Such men did well under the early Ptolemies; their involvement and their success perhaps gave new importance to the Carians of Memphis, reflected in privileges granted their temple and opportunities to further their careers within the new administration.

HELLENOMEMPHITES

Alongside the Caromemphites, the Hellenomemphites of the city must have played a similar role. Descended from the Ionian mercenaries settled

[66] *P. Mich. Zen.* 31.5 (256/5 B.C.) with Wildung (1977a), 49–50, for a Memphite location; Wildung further suggests that Amon-Ra of the strong arm may have been identified with the Carian Zeus.

[67] Clarysse (1980b), 95–122.

[68] Edgar (1931), 16–19; Clarysse (1980b), 105–6; Wörrle (1977), 43, 63–65; Orrieux (1985), 116–20.

[69] Addaios and Spondates; Bargathes, an orchard guard, and Nouraios, a shepherd, have Aramaic names. See *Pap. Lugd. Bat* 21, chapter ix, for references.

in the city in the late sixth century B.C. they were fairly well integrated by the late fourth century B.C. The fierce East Greek curse surviving on a papyrus from this date, made by a mother against the father of her daughter, takes the reader into an Hellenomemphite world.[70] The gods here called to witness are Oserapis and the related gods who dwell in the House of Oserapis (Poserapis, *Pr-Wsir.Ḥp*). The mother is Artemisia (a good Carian name), the daughter of Amasis; her father's name Amasis suggests a descendant of those troops that pharaoh settled in the city. The popularity of the Apis cult among this immigrant group is known from other sources,[71] and the Greek these people used had a strong Ionic flavor.[72] (The demotic word for Greek is *Wjnn*, from Ionia, which well illustrates the prominence of these early settlers.) Their quarter in the city lay just north of the Karikon; their cemetery too lay near Abousir from where the fourth-century B.C. text of Timotheus comes, the papyrus buried together with its owner.[73] A demotic letter on the subject of mummies ("gods") coming from this quarter[74] and its listing among the assets of that Ptolemaic family of undertakers[75] suggest fairly extensive Egyptianization among its inhabitants. Indeed the only Hellenomemphite of the Ptolemaic period whose name is known has the fully Egyptian name of Apynchis, son of Inarous.[76] The Greek dialect of the city remained under Ionian influence, with Ionicisms in use even by those who came from elsewhere to settle in the city.[77]

Like the Caromemphites, the Hellenomemphites had their central shrine which, as at Naukratis,[78] was known as the Hellenion.[79] It was probably this original Hellenion which then gave its name to the whole Hellenomemphite quarter of the city and to its surrounding dyke.[80] Zeus

[70] *UPZ* 1, with addenda. For early Greek mercenaries (or sailors?) in the city under Ptolemy I, see Turner (1975b), on four-obols-a-day men.
[71] Jeffery (1961), 355, no. 52, for a dedicated bull with an inscription showing Doric influence.
[72] Jeffery (1961), 354-55; Edgar (1904); Masson (1977), 53-57, 61-67; *Brooklyn Inscriptions* I (570-520 B.C.); Wilcken (1927), 98, for the fourth century B.C.
[73] Turner (1968), 32; perhaps, too, the source of the Alcman roll which Mariette brought to Paris, Montevecchi (1973), 32. For the area, Wilcken (1927), 538.
[74] *P. Turner* 15.3-4 (350-275 B.C.), with an interesting consideration of the mummification of non-Egyptians on p. 79.
[75] *P. Louvre* E 3266.8.Q (197 B.C.) = App. B:2; *P. Innsbruck* line 8 = App. B:18; *P. Louvre dem.* 3268 = App. B:19.
[76] *UPZ* 116.1-2 (third century B.C.). There was a shrine of Amon-Thoth in the Hellenion, *UPZ* 116.5-6; cf. *P. Cair. Zen.* 59133.8 erased (256 B.C.).
[77] E.g., the regular use of *kithōn* for *chitōn*, *UPZ* index.
[78] Hdt. 2.178, temples of Zeus, Hera, and Apollo together with the Hellenion.
[79] *P. Cair. Zen.* 59593.7-8 (third century B.C.), Zenon visits to perform sacrifices.
[80] Świderek (1961); and chapter 1 n. 38 above.

Basileus, to whom Alexander sacrificed in the city,[81] was perhaps the main deity of this shrine.

In the Ptolemaic city, as we have already seen, the Hellenomemphites appear to have enjoyed some form of corporate organization, with representatives known as timouchoi. At Naukratis, too, there were timouchoi in the city, whereas in the *emporion* (the port) the different groups were represented by prostatai.[82] Naukratis, however, was founded as a Greek-style polis, which Memphis never was. With the exceptions of Naukratis, Ptolemais in the south, and Alexandria, no Ptolemaic city in Egypt enjoyed any form of political independence. The inclusion of all other urban centers within the overall, centralized government of the country was an important feature of Ptolemaic policy. In considering the organization of the different ethnic communities therefore, their subordination to central government, to the authority of the nome strategos stationed at Memphis, must always be remembered. Any sign of independent corporate structure is likely to be confined to the social, economic, or religious areas of life. Politically all were subject to the crown functioning through a centralized, royal bureaucracy.

The timouchoi of the Hellenomemphites occur in a third-century B.C. account, already mentioned, of expenses for a voyage down-river. Allowances are recorded for eleven kotylai of wine and of fine bread for timouchoi. One of these men, Herakleides, is named later in the account, and the context, as Wilcken convincingly argued, is that of the Hellenion, the quarter of the Hellenomemphites.[83] It was perhaps through the mediation of these representatives that the earlier Greek inhabitants of the city organized their relations with the new Ptolemaic administration. Like the epistates asked for by two Arab dekatarchs to look after their interests,[84] timouchoi might represent their people in dealings with officials of the new bureaucracy. So in changed times traditional offices were also adapted.

JEWS AND OTHER SEMITIC SETTLERS

As we have seen, the Jews of Ptolemaic Memphis are difficult to disentangle from other Semitic settlers. The precise location of the Jewish quarter

---

[81] Arrian 3.5.2.
[82] Hdt. 2.178; Hermeias in Athenaeus 4.149f; Gottlieb (1967), 28-30.
[83] *UPZ* 149.16-18, 37.
[84] *PSI* 538.

is not known; there will have been a synagogue there.[85] Nor has the Jewish cemetery been identified. The concentration of Aramaic tombstones and inscribed clay sarcophagi from the southern end of the Memphite necropolis (between Mastabat Fara'ūn and Dahshur) suggests that this may have been the cemetery for the Semitic peoples of Memphis.[86] Originating in Egypt in the Persian period, Aramaic may have continued in use into the Ptolemaic period; like the Aramaic papyri and the dockets from the palace of Apries,[87] these inscriptions are difficult to date. Many of those buried in this area have Egyptian names, but this degree of Egyptianization is not surprising. The different Semitic communities apparently observed no separatism in death, and the burial here of a priest from Syene of the Syrian god Nabû[88] provides evidence for close links between these immigrants throughout the length of Egypt. The three Persian garrison points of Memphis, Hermoupolis, and Syene/Elephantine remained key points under the Ptolemies. The fate of the Persians' Semitic mercenaries is not known; some presumably stayed on in their adopted country and were buried there. A few men with Aramaic names are still found in the city under the early Ptolemies, the descendants perhaps of these troops.[89] Indeed, the occurrence of Persian and Semitic names among a list of shepherds and goatherds, who care for the sacred flocks of various temples in the third century B.C., is interesting evidence for the continuation of these peoples, at least in pastoral activities, even after the Macedonian conquest. The papyrus, *P. Gurob 22*, is not complete; but where they may be recognized, the temples listed with their flocks sound very Memphite[90]—those of Nachbanis (perhaps Nectanebo or some Persian god?); Mithras; Aphrodite (who may be Astarte here); Hermes, the Egyptian Thoth; Sachmet, the lioness-consort of Ptah; Nephthimis or Nefertem, their son; and of Pan, the Greek form of the Egyptian Min or possibly some further Semitic god. The names of the shepherds and, in the case of Aphrodite and of Pan, the goatherds listed are certainly con-

[85] Perhaps the forerunner of the twelfth-century "synagogue of Moses" at Dammūh; Golb (1965), 255-59; (1974), 116-49.
[86] Aimé-Giron (1931), 93-109.
[87] Petrie (1910), 41; Segal (1983), 3-4.
[88] Aimé-Giron (1931), 98-100, no. 99 = Grelot (1972), 76, no. 76.
[89] For Nouraios and Bargathes, see n. 69.
[90] Identifying Sisines of *P. Gurob* 22.32 with the shepherd of *PSI* 6.626.32, Van 't Dack (1962), 341, argues for a Philadelphian origin, but the name is known from elsewhere (e.g., *P. Tebt.* 3.893.9, second century B.C., in an account with wool), and the identity of the temples with those known from Memphis is striking, Quaegebeur, Clarysse, and Van Maele (1985), 33-36. Perhaps, like *moschotrophos*, *pyrsouros* is also a cult official.

sistent with attachments to a local god. Through this list indeed we glimpse a continuing Semitic presence in the city and in the desert pastures around.

Of the organization of these various peoples little is known, though their temples, those of Astarte and of Mithras, presumably formed a focus for national identity. The enigmatic occurrence in a demotic execration text from the same period of "the commander of the Jews" may belong to a military context, or it may provide evidence in this case for some sort of corporate organization, as later with the Jews of Alexandria.[91]

The attempt to impose religious conformity was never a feature of Egypt. Egyptian religion with its built-in syncretic tendencies would normally accommodate foreign gods and goddesses within its own framework. When this was not the case, no objection was made to separate worship. Such separate worship might, however, serve to identify ethnic groups, and it may be Jews in the nearby Herakleopolite nome who are referred to in a first-century B.C. report on the subject of ethnic disturbances involving "those who do not practice the same religion."[92] The Jews in Alexandria, continually involved in the dynastic struggles of the Ptolemies, were a source of tension in the city; this Herakleopolite incident may represent a repetition of similar racial problems in the countryside.

In Memphis too, the home of Ptah and Apis, anti-Semitism is recorded in the first century B.C. A visiting Jewish priest from the Fayum town of Tebtunis might expect difficulties in the city: "I beg you, take him under your care so he may escape arrest; if he needs anything, treat him in the same way as you do Artemidoros, and especially do me the favor of putting him up in the same place; for you know that they loathe the Jews . . . ," writes one Heraklēs to Ptolemaios, described as dioiketes.[93] The language is strong and the letter takes one into a society with tensions, where those of the same nationality or faith would choose to stick together. The background to this particular letter is unknown.

IDUMAEANS

The Idumaeans are the only ethnic group whose arrival definitely postdates Alexander. Known only from two inscriptions (with possibly one

[91] Ray (1978c), 29. On Jews in Alexandria, see Fraser (1972), 1.696–704.
[92] BGU 1764.12–13 (c. 57 B.C.).
[93] Rémondon (1960), 254, improving the text of C. Pap. Jud. 141.

papyrus reference to their temple),[94] they followed many foreign mercenaries in providing a garrison force of palace guards in the city. One inscription records the dedication, probably of a sanctuary, by a *koinon* of
ktistai (a community of founders) in which the gods Apollo and Zeus are
named.[95] The brief and broken dedication is followed by a list of names.
It is clear from these names that, as in a group of similar ktistai dedications from Hermoupolis from 78 B.C.,[96] we have here a record of the local
Idumaean community. These worshippers of Apollo/Qos[97] have an interesting collection of names. Many are straightforwardly theophoric
such as Kosadaros, Kosramos, or Kosmalachos; Apollophanes, Apollonios, or Apollodoros. There are other Semitic names—Apsalamos, Zab-
das, Zabdaios, Abasmasianos, Audelos, Elmalachos—and good Greek
and Macedonian names, among which dynastic names stand out—Philippos, Alexandros, Demetrios, and Ptolemaios; there are two men with the
Roman name of Gaios.[98] The first two columns of the list are inscribed
together, and when read across they may be seen to record, with patro-
nymics, the name of a father in column i and his son in column ii. On the
broken stone there survive forty-one fathers (with patronymic) with
forty sons. Of these three generations, twenty-three of the grandfathers
(56 percent) have recognizable Semitic names but only five of the fathers
(12 percent); with one possible exception, Masyllos, none of the sons
have names which would identify them as anything but Greek. Speedy
Hellenization on this scale is likely to have taken place once these Idumaeans reached Egypt. If, as Fraser suggests,[99] the Memphite dedication
is nearly contemporary with the Hermoupolite texts, this could support
a late second-century B.C. arrival date for these particular Idumaean
troops.[100]

[94] *BGU* 1216.10 (110 B.C.), 3¼¹⁄₁₆ arouras with enclosure wall.

[95] Mariette (1872), 33; Milne (1905), 35-37, no. 9283 = Breccia (1911), no. 142 with Tav.
xxv.62 = *SB* 681. On ktistai connected with the founding of a cult, see Robert (1937), 53
n. 3, 328 n.3; *Hellenica* 4.116.

[96] *SB* 4206; 8066 (78 B.C.), with Zucker (1937) and (1938); see Rapaport (1969).

[97] On Qos, see Milik (1958), 236-41; (1960), 95-96; Teixidor (1977), 90-91, suggests that
in this text Qos may have been Zeus (Apollo would then be Reshef, a Phoenician deity,
Teixidor 1972, 419-20), but the Apollonieion in *OGIS* 737 and the equally high number of
Qos and Apollo names are against this.

[98] On Semitic names, see Wuthnow (1930); Zucker (1937), 58-62; Sala (1974); on Gaios,
see Van 't Dack (1980), 23.

[99] Fraser (1972), 2.438 n. 751, cf. 1.280-81. (The inscription was originally published as
from the early second century B.C.) A comparison with the Hermoupolis inscription shows
no significant difference in letter forms.

[100] Rapaport (1969) argues this on other grounds, *viz.*, the political events within Idumaea
(which fit well) and the occurrence of the name Demetrios, which he takes to refer to the

The second decree of the Idumaeans is an honorific decree dated to year 6, probably 112/11 B.C.[101] A meeting is recorded in the upper Apollonieion (the temple perhaps of Qos on the necropolis) at which Dorion, kinsman, strategos, and priest of the troop of sabre bearers, is thanked for his good services in plastering and whitewashing the temple. Priests, psalmists, and hymns to Dorion are all recorded in this decree. In Greek practice, hymns were normally composed only for gods or kings but Semitic paeans seem different. So too, perhaps, was the language in which they were sung; for a somewhat surprising papyrus report from the second century A.D. records a foreign tongue (*xenikē glōssa*, presumably Edomite) still in use by the related Hermoupolite community.[102] But besides giving information on the religion of the Idumaeans, the Dorion decree provides interesting evidence for the corporate organization of this group of mercenaries. The actual vote of thanks to Dorion is called a *psēphisma* and was passed in an assembly, *synagōgē*, which took place in the upper Apollonieion; this assembly consisted both of the *politeuma* and of the Idumaeans from the city. Dorion is to be awarded a (palm) branch "according to local custom," and the priests and psalmists are to remember him in their hymns; at feasts of the politeuma he is to be crowned with a special crown and the decree is to be posted in the most visible part of the temple, with a copy given to Dorion so he may appreciate the gratitude shown towards him by the community (polis).

The Idumaean mercenaries act here as a corporate group in a religious context. The unit of organization is the politeuma,[103] further defined as the troop of machairophoroi,[104] which holds meetings, synagogai, in the temple of Qos which may result in decrees, psephismata. The commu-

---

Seleucid king Demetrios (162–150 B.C.) so giving a date *post quem*; but Demetrios is too common a name to support this interpretation. His attempt to dismiss Apollonia as the home of the Hermoupolite troops (he prefers Marissa) is much weakened by an Apollōniatēs in *SB* 7351 (second century B.C.) who is connected with a priestess of Syrian gods and a shrine of Atargatis in the Fayum.

[101] *OGIS* 737; Launey (1949/50), vol. 2, 1072–77 and 1107–8, for discussion and bibliography. For the interpretation presented here, see in more detail Thompson-Crawford (1984).

[102] *P. Giss.* 99.9-13 with Zucker (1937), 13, for improved text. Sacrifices of sheep and goat recorded in the document are also not Egyptian.

[103] Launey (1949/50), vol. 2, 1074, as most other scholars (see Fraser 1972, 2.438 n. 752), takes the politeuma to be that of the Greek community in Memphis; I disagree. For the ethnic designation not used in what is clearly an ethnic politeuma, see *SB* 6664.8-9, cf. 31-33 (163–145 B.C.).

[104] *Synodoi* of machairophoroi, with prostates and grammateus, are recorded in *BGU* 1190 (80–51 B.C.), Herakleopolite, and *SB* 624 = *I. Fay* 17, from the Fayum. The distinction between synodos, koinon, and politeuma is not at all clear; see Fraser (1959/60), 151.

nity, however, is broader than just the troops, and the Idumaeans from the city join in many of its activities; in Hermoupolis and elsewhere these supporting members are called "those sharing the politeuma," the *sympoliteuomenoi*.[105] The polis of the last line of the Dorion decree probably represents the totality of this ethnic community, within the larger city of Memphis. In the Hellenistic world the vocabulary of classical Greece was often adapted and extended in meaning to cover the new social and political forms which evolved in this new world.

The corporate organization of the Idumaeans appears from this decree to have been well developed. Similar politeumata among Ptolemaic mercenary groups are found elsewhere in Egypt from the reign of Ptolemy VI Philometor; among Ptolemaic troops in Cyprus they are known as koina.[106] A parallel for their structure is perhaps to be found in the dual organization of the Semitic settlements of the earlier Persian Empire. In both the Jewish and the non-Jewish colonies of Elephantine, Syene, and Memphis, Aramaic papyri record the *degel* as the basic military unit. This was subdivided (into centuries) and distinguished from the civilian community of the city, the *qeriyah*.[107] The corporate term used for the whole colony was *ḥaylā*, the same perhaps as the polis of the Dorion decree. The limited nature of the corporate activities, confined here (and in other politeumata) to honorific decrees and religious dedications, may detract from the importance of the structure as a focus for ethnic distinctiveness. Military *esprit de corps*, however, may well have been encouraged and the religious practices of the community strengthened.

In relations with the ruling power, the support and advocacy of men like Dorion might be important. As "kinsman" (an aulic rank) and strategos, the chief administrative officer of the area, Dorion had been enrolled as priest of this military detachment.[108] Two hieroglyphic blocks from the Memphite necropolis tell us more of his family.[109] His father too was Dorion; his mother, Heranch, was also known as Herakleia, a priestess of Horos of Athribis who died late in 132 B.C. at the age of 50. (The year 112/11 B.C. seems confirmed for Year 6 of the Dorion decree.) Do-

---

[105] *SB* 4206.2-3; 8066.3 (78 B.C.), Hermoupolis; *SB* 6664.32-33 (163–145 B.C.), Xois; *OGIS* 145.4-5 (123–118 B.C.); 143.6 (*c*. 121 B.C.), Cyprus, associated with koina.

[106] References in Thompson-Crawford (1984), 1072 n. 17 (add *SB* 7270 = *I. Fay* 15, Cilician), and 1073 n. 23.

[107] Porten (1968), 35; Segal (1983), 7.

[108] *PP* 1.248; 3.5519; Mooren (1975), 106-7, no. 093/00 265. For other priests in the same cult, see *OGIS* 737.16; cf. *SB* 6664.8-9 for a priest of the politeuma of the Boeotians who is also a strategos.

[109] Cairo 22179 and 22137 = Vernus (1978), 214-18, nos. 177-78.

rion's mother would seem from her name to be a Hellenizing Egyptian from a priestly family. Her son, too, held priestly office in the cults of his homeland, in the cults of Horos, Onnophris, and Osiris. The second stone records Dorion's administrative and military career, as strategos, general, and royal scribe.[110] His priesthood of the Idumaean politeuma, an honorific post of importance to those who gave it him, is, however, nowhere mentioned in the hieroglyphic record. Successfully Hellenized in both nomenclature and appointment, this priest might prove a useful patron to the settlers in future dealings with authority. Thanked now for whitewash and plaster in the effusive language of a Greek decree, Dorion was perhaps being marked for the future as an even greater benefactor of the Idumaean community. Honorific appointments thus might play a valuable part in protecting the corporate interests of minority ethnic groups.

SUCH, insofar as they may be retrieved, were the experiences of the different immigrant groups. What conclusions, if any, may be drawn from this fragmentary picture?

First, the rate of integration. This was of course affected by many varied factors: for instance the nature and origin of the groups concerned, the way in which they reached the city (either singly or en masse on one occasion, whether as men only or as whole communities on the move), the numbers in which they came, or the length of time they had been settled. Foreign mercenary bands settled on Egyptian soil, like the Carians and the Ionians, might be expected to marry native women and perhaps to lose many of their ethnic characteristics. The transformation of such groups into Caromemphites and Hellenomemphites was a speedy one. When, as with the Phoenicians, for instance, or other Semites, a group was constantly reinforced with subsequent settlers from the homeland, the process of integration might be slower. The applicability of a group's mother tongue to their changed circumstances, and the strength of their social institutions or of their religion were important factors in the retention of ethnic identity. The language of Ionia was of more general use; Phoenician culture and religion were stronger than that of Caria. It was perhaps for those reasons that certain identifiably Ionian and Phoenician features persisted in the society of Ptolemaic Memphis. Further, in Ptolemaic Egypt, Greek was a prestige language. In this respect,

[110] Vernus (1978), no. 178; De Meulenaere (1962), 73-75, for the attribution.

too, it is not surprising to find the Hellenomemphites keeping their native tongue longer than those who came from Caria.

The syncretic tendencies of both Egyptian and Greek religion encouraged the absorption of minority cults. Astarte might become Isis or Hathor, or Aphrodite for the Greeks. For those, like the Idumaeans, who came after Alexander, identification was made with Greek gods only: Qos was called Apollo, his temple an Apollonieion. But in spite of these new names, different religious practices and cults in foreign tongues might continue unchecked in immigrant temples. And in the case of the Jews, here as elsewhere, it is likely to have been their religion above all which served to mark their separate identity. Therefore, temples, combined with separate quarters in the city, could shore up an ethnicity which otherwise appears to be eroding with changing nomenclature and, from the fourth century B.C., the progressive disappearance of ethnic cemeteries. The scene changed gradually and, while for Strabo under Augustus the city was still one of mixed peoples, following the arrival of the Romans the minority groups soon disappear from sight.[111]

Also to be considered are the varying roles within society played by the different groups. There is a problem inherent in the evidence here. Nomenclature is usually the only guide to ethnic origin, and ethnic nomenclature survives only selectively. Any conclusions on this basis therefore remain tentative. The Phoenicians, for instance, a group who, given the geographical proximity of their homeland, seem likely to have been reinforced from time to time with the arrival of new immigrants, retained their traditional connections with shipping and the spice trade. Policing and garrison duties are regularly performed by minority groups within a society, and in Egypt, following the example of the pharaohs and Persians before them,[112] the new Macedonian rulers relied on non-natives to police and control the community they now ruled. With his beard and curly hair and his Phoenician sarcophagus, Chaiapis, son of Paneith, was no Egyptian, yet his policing post in the city was surely one of importance.[113] So too with the Idumaean sabre bearers, who as garrison troops played a

[111] For Nubians in the second century A.D., see chapter 8 n. 10.
[112] The Egyptian king Busiris on the "Caeretan" hydria has a foreign bodyguard of negroes; see Boardman (1980), 150, figure 186.
[113] Elsewhere: Bithelmeinis, *PP* 2.4752, Oxyrhynchite (254/3 B.C.); Iasibis, *PP* 2.2116/2214, Diospolis Magna (158 B.C.); Persians among the desert guards in the Fayum, Crawford (1971), 59. In Memphis, Barkaios/Ammonios with police functions in the Anoubieion, *UPZ* 64.1 (156 B.C.), may be a Semite in a similar role. So more recently, in the early nineteenth century, the Turks used an Albanian force under Mohamed Ali from Kavalla; see Fraser (1981), 65.

crucial role in protecting a key city, important to whoever ruled the country. As we have seen, the Carians provided knowledge and expertise to the new rulers, and some of the new wave of Carian immigrants made successful careers in the early days of the new administration.[114] In bureaucratic careers, however, swift Hellenization was the norm, and foreign entrants (including Egyptians) thereby regularly escape detection. It is not possible, on surviving evidence, to rank the different communities in either numbers or social status; their social and economic roles may only rarely be identified.

Finally, relations with the ruling power. Ethnic representatives, the timouchoi of the Ionians or the officers of the politeuma of the Idumaeans, might act as spokesmen for the group. Informal representation, however, is well known to be often more effective. As earlier, the Phoenico-Egyptians had appealed to Zenon to act for them and protect their interests, so the Idumaeans in the late second century B.C. looked to the patronage of Dorion, a successful Egyptian with standing within the administration. In the affairs of ethnic communities, the mediation of such men could be important for access to the government of the day.

In these various ways the minority communities undeniably played a part both in the makeup and in the history of Ptolemaic Memphis, but they form only one facet of a complex picture. And within the city of Memphis, as throughout the country, it was the interaction of the two major groups of immigrant Greeks and native Egyptians which was of the greatest import. For a more complete historical evaluation of the social and political significance of the mixed population of Memphis, relations in the city between Greeks and Egyptians need further consideration. These will form a continuing theme of later chapters.

[114] See n. 68. A first-century B.C. epistrategos of the Thebaid, Boethos, is known to be Carian (though not necessarily Memphite) from his epithet Chrysaoreus; OGIS 111.4 with Strabo 14.2.25.

4

PTOLEMIES AND TEMPLES

When Alexander the Great took Egypt in 332 B.C. he visited first Heliopolis at the apex of the Delta and then Memphis, where he sacrificed to
the Apis bull and to other gods, celebrating in the city with both gym-
nastic and musical contests.[1] Arrian, unlike the later *Alexander Romance*,
makes no mention of an actual enthronement ceremony here in the temple of Ptah,[2] but it is clear that in Memphis, sacrificing to the Apis bull in
its native form, Alexander was claiming acceptance as pharaoh among the
Egyptians whom he now ruled. Aware of the tradition of the unfortunate
incident of the Persian king, Kambyses and his murder of the bull,[3] Alexander sought rather to reconcile the religious establishment of the city to
the new reality of Macedonian conquest.

After the revelations of Siwah and the foundation of Alexandria, the
conqueror left the country. It was in Memphis that his satrap, Kleomenes
of Naukratis, soon based himself, and to Memphis that Alexander's body
was brought for burial in 323 B.C. by Ptolemy, son of Lagos.[4] Protected
by such a talisman, this general seized the country as his inheritance, making Memphis his first capital. The beginning under Alexander was auspicious, as indeed were the orders issued by his general Peukestas to the
troops in Memphis and posted up somewhere in the temples area of the
Sacred Animal Necropolis:

(Orders) of Peukestas. Out of bounds. Priest's property.[5]

The conqueror and his entourage were well aware of Egyptian sensibilities.

Throughout Egyptian history the power of the temples regularly

---

[1] Arr. *Anab.* 3.1.2-3.

[2] Ps.-Callisthenes 1.34.2, accepted by Merkelbach (1954), 24; see Bergman (1968), 92-94,
for Egyptian influence on the passage.

[3] Hdt. 3.29; Plut. *DIO* 44, cf. 31. The Apis stele from Year 6 of Kambyses records the
Persian king personally providing the Apis sarcophagus which tends to discredit the traditional account; Posener (1936), 33, 171-78, rejects Herodotus. Ael. *NA* 10.28 has a similar
story about Artaxerxes Ochus; see Bosworth (1980), 262.

[4] Arist. [*Oec.*] 2.2.33.c.31 with van Groningen (1933), 187; Arr. *Anab.* 3.5.4, Kleomenes
as general of Arabia, cf. Bosworth (1980), 277. Alexander's burial at Memphis: Parian marble, *FGrH* 239.F. B.111, with 321/20 for 322/1 B.C.; Paus. 1.6.3; other sources in Fraser
(1972), 2.32 n. 79.

[5] Turner (1974).

played a key role in the success or failure of successive dynasties, and though the balance might swing between Upper and Lower Egypt, between Thebes (home of Amon) and Memphis (home of Ptah), the strength of the temples could always be measured in the land and the property they controlled. According to the Harris papyrus, under Ramses III in the twelfth century B.C. the temples owned almost one-seventh of the country's land, divided in the following proportions: Thebes, 81 percent; Heliopolis, 15 percent; Memphis, 1 percent; and the lesser temples, 3 percent.[6] Whereas the Memphite portion is far lower than that of Thebes and Heliopolis, at 10,154 arouras (2,538.5 hectares or 25.4 square kilometers), it was still a substantial holding of agricultural land, the income of which was supplemented by orchard land; in addition there were 3,079 temple workers together with livestock and geese. There is no reason to suppose that, in this conservative society, the holding had diminished by the time of Alexander's conquest. Under Kambyses the Ptah temple of Memphis was, with those of Babylon and Hermoupolis, specifically exempted from some of the financial restrictions imposed on other temples by the Persian administration;[7] this exemption may be seen as a measure of its importance. Like that of Thebes, the Memphite priesthood was powerful, holding national pretensions. Indeed, if any historical reality lies behind the stories of Kleomenes in the *Oikonomika* ascribed to Aristotle, it was the temples and priests of Egypt which formed the main target of the satrap's revenue-raising reforms.[8] Temples were rich and powerful, and they formed a potential opposition to any new regime. Like their predecessors, the Ptolemies could not ignore this power, and in Memphis are mirrored the continuing tensions between temple and state which were only to be resolved with the significant innovations of Roman rule and reform.

Ptolemy, son of Lagos, soon adopted the style of king, with the epithet of savior, Soter.[9] The capital was moved to Alexandria and with it Alexander's tomb, though for Egyptians the hope remained of a return one day to Memphis.[10] While the Greek city on the coast became the new administrative center and the focus of Greek cultural and intellectual life,

[6] Erman (1903), 469; Breasted (1906), 4.90, 161–77.

[7] Spiegelberg (1915), 29–34; the exemptions covered wood for shipbuilding, for fuel, flax, poultry, and half the revenue on livestock; Bresciani (1983), 70–71, for a Memphite origin.

[8] [Arist.] *Oec.* 2.2.33.a–f (1352.a.16–b.25).

[9] *Basileus* after 305 B.C., Diod. Sic. 20.53.3; Bresciani in Karkowski and Winnicki (1983), 103–5, in a demotic text of November 304 B.C.; Nock (1972), 720–53, on Soter.

[10] As in the potter's oracle, chapter 3 n. 1; Fraser (1972), 2.11–12 n. 28, for the change of capital probably by 320/19 B.C.

Memphis remained perhaps the chief center of native religion and sentiment until the end of the Ptolemaic period. The old palace still stood within the city, and the central cults of Ptah and Apis were in no way diminished with the arrival of new rulers. The temples were still strong in terms of the respect they enjoyed; they could offer asylum to those who took refuge there.[11]

Whereas Thebes was to reject rule from Alexandria, breaking away in revolt for long periods during the second century B.C. and finally crushed by Ptolemy IX Soter II (restored) in 88 B.C., Memphis and the Memphite hierarchy remained consistently loyal to the crown, attempting in preference to influence the system from within. It was probably thus they prevented the city's total eclipse by Alexandria. Memphite families provided guidance for the new rulers,[12] in whose dealings both within the city and with the high priesthood of Ptah there may be charted developments and modifications over the three hundred years of Ptolemaic rule. As a focus for relations between king and cult, between Ptolemy and temple, Memphis provides a more interesting case than either Alexandria or Thebes.

Kleopatra VII was the first of the Ptolemies to speak Egyptian,[13] but already by the reign of Ptolemy XII Neos Dionysos (otherwise known as the flute player, Auletes) earlier in the first century B.C., the Greek ruler was well versed in the role of pharaoh. Crowned Egyptian-style in 76 B.C. by the high priest of Ptah (the fourteen-year-old Psenptais III, son of Petobastis and Heranch), Auletes enjoyed cordial visiting terms with this supreme representative of the Memphite clergy, whom he also named his prophet.[14] The growing pharaonization of the Ptolemies is a telling stroke in the game between Ptolemy and temple played out in this period on the center court of the kingdom. On the whole the match was a friendly one; both sides shared a concern for survival.

Influence and power were the two balls served into the opposite court in a continuing encounter of varied fortune. The match was long drawn-out, displaying a variety of styles and tactics; for most of the game the

[11] Specifically recorded only in 97/6 B.C., C. Ord. Ptol. 64.8-9, cf. P. Tebt. 5 = C. Ord. Ptol. 53.83-84 (118 B.C.), the right was widely exercised; see also chapter 7 below. Orrieux (1985), 237, sees the right of asylum as a Greek import.
[12] E.g., Vienna statue 20, von Bergmann (1880), 51-52; De Meulenaere (1953), 104 (quoted by Quaegebeur 1980a, 78-79).
[13] Plut. Ant. 27.3-4.
[14] Harris stele B.M. 886; Quaegebeur (1980a), 69, no. 27; cf. Crawford (1980), 39-40, and more generally.

Ptolemies seem to have had the upper hand. The intensity and tempo of different reigns is reflected in the moves that were made. Some moves were old ones, but some were new; sometimes slow and sluggish, sometimes the game gained speed; techniques improved as each side learned the other's game; aggression alternated with circumspection, concession with interference. Depending on who might have the upper hand, so varied the flavor of the game. Finally, game, set, and match were barely called—the victor's name was barely heard amid the confusion of the times—when the arrival of the Romans canceled the validity of both game and outcome. It is the changing fortunes of the players and different tactics of their game as seen in Memphite light that form the subject of this chapter.

TEMPLES UNDER THE PTOLEMIES

The Ptolemaic takeover of Egypt involved the substitution of a Macedonian general for an absolute Persian ruler, and of Greek as the language of administration for Aramaic; Egyptian demotic survived the takeover, continuing even in official use at first, and in more general use throughout the period. The king was the main recipient of wealth and honor in the country, and the economic power of the native temples was further circumscribed. After the direct interference of Kambyses and Kleomenes, the Ptolemies practiced an indirect approach. The temples were left in control of their land (some that had been confiscated by the Persian king Xerxes was even returned by Ptolemy I),[15] and on this land they now paid an annual tax of one artaba to the aroura.[16] The priests also remained in control of cult and religion. Priestly offices might be sold and ceded as before, and the traditional organization of the native priesthood went unchanged until, in 238 B.C., Ptolemy III Euergetes added, to the existing four, an extra *phylē*, or division, of priests in honor of his daughter Berenike.[17] One innovation with potentially serious implications for the independence of the temples was the appointment within their administration of crown controllers, the epistatai. How this worked in practice may in part be seen from the Memphite evidence.

[15] According to the satrap stele, Sethe (1904–16), 11-27, translated in Bevan (1927), 28-32.
[16] Abolished by Epiphanes in 196 B.C., *OGIS* 90.30, with the abolition extended to dedicated land by Euergetes II in 118 B.C., *P. Tebt.* 5 = *C. Ord. Ptol.* 53.59; such abolitions were, however, of limited duration, Crawford (1971), 99 n. 10.
[17] In the Canopus decree, *OGIS* 56.

From the third century B.C. the high priest of Memphis, Anemhor II, who was the third in this office under the new dynasty, is recorded with the title of royal scribe for all financial matters in both temple and temple-estate of Osiris-Apis, and similarly, in the valley, in the temple of Memphis (that of Ptah) and that of Arsinoe Philadelphos.[18] The recruitment of the high priest to such a wide-ranging position of responsibility within the royal administration suggests a willingness, or even need, on the part of the crown to make use of existing personnel within the temple structures. Whether greater emphasis should be placed on crown interference, accompanied by priestly cooperation, or on royal recognition of the power of the Memphite high priest is not clear; probably both applied to some degree.

From the late third century B.C. a royal subvention, the syntaxis, already financed much of the cost of temple cult;[19] the crown clearly had an interest in the proper use of this subvention. More direct intervention by Greek financial officials in the affairs of Egyptian temples was to some extent tempered by the appointment of Egyptian priestly scribes and agents, like Anemhor just mentioned, to represent the interests of the crown. The simple position of "royal scribe" is recorded for various priests[20] and the names alone are known of several "fiscal royal scribes" or "fiscal scribes of pharaoh."[21] In greater detail the Ḥor archive of the second century B.C. records "agents of pharaoh" with both fiscal and more general cult responsibilities within the temples of the city. These were all crown nominations. One of these agents, Amasis, son of Petenephtimis, in June 172 B.C. presided over a council meeting of the elders of the Ptah priests investigating alleged abuses within the ibis cult of the Sacred Animal Necropolis,[22] and again in June 165 B.C. another, Psintaes, son of Piomis, played a similar role on the instructions of his superior who discussed the matter with him.[23] Psintaes recurs in Greek sources

[18] PP 5352, see figure 5.
[19] P. Cair. dem. 2.31219 (224 B.C.), in oil; OGIS 90.15 (196 B.C.), in both cash and kind. See Clarysse (1987), 30, for a third-century B.C. example.
[20] PP 5677e, Oteuris, son of Komoapis, royal scribe of Amon-Ra; PP 5829e, Teōs, son of T3-ḳ's; PP 5694a, Panouphis, son of Tetosiris; PP 5519, Dorion, son of Dorion; PP 5658e, Onnōphris, son of Sentaēs. Apart from Oteuris, these men may be regular administrative royal scribes who were also priests rather than priests with royal appointments within the temples.
[21] PP 5677e, Oteuris, son of Komoapis; PP 5510, Achomarres/Horos, son of Herieus, perhaps to be identified with the lesonis discussed below; PP 5829e, Teos son of T3-ḳ's; PP 5353, Anemhor/Paschinis, see figure 6.
[22] Ḥor 19 recto.16-17; PP 7376a.
[23] Ḥor 20 recto.6-7; PP 7472a/7473.

from the Sarapieion, where he is called "epistates of the temples."[24] Responsible for the payment of syntaxis to cult personnel, in this particular case a bread ration for the twins involved in ceremonies for mourning the Apis bull, he probably came under the direction of an administrative official, known in Greek by his honorific Egyptian title, *pheritob*.[25] The use of this term, like the all-Egyptian nomenclature of the epistatai or "agents of pharaoh" found in the temples of Memphis,[26] suggests a velvet glove approach towards the native temples. Egyptians represented the interests of the crown within the temples of Egypt, while the departmental superior was known by an Egyptian title.

There were others beneath the area controllers, the epistatai. When in 99 B.C. the royal couple Ptolemy X Alexander I and Kleopatra Berenike directed instructions to their representatives—military, financial, and religious—for the protection of the person and property of the *archentaphiastēs* (the embalmer-in-chief) Petesis son of Chonouphis, the temple representatives are listed as the epistatai of the temples and the chief priests (*archiereis*), together with others who represent royal interests.[27] Earlier, in the Canopus decree of 238 B.C., the Greek *archiereus* translated the demotic *mr-šn* (*lesōnis*);[28] and in second-century Memphis, besides such royal agents as Amasis son of Petenephtimis or Psintaes son of Piomis, there existed separate heads of cult for the individual temples.[29] So in June 165 B.C. the lesonis Achomarres joined Psintaes in his investigations of abuses in the ibis cult.[30] Described in Greek as epistates of the Sarapieion, an Achomarres is three years later approached by the twins on the subject of their bread supply, and receives instructions on this subject from his superior Psintaes.[31] Whereas it is possible that in calling him epistates the twins have muddled the appointments of the temple personnel, it is clear that Achomarres here is part of the royal administration

[24] *UPZ* 20.55 (163/2 B.C.); 42.23-24 (162 B.C.); 43.16 (162/1 B.C.), earlier described as *proestēkōs*; 46.8, 19; 47.12, 24; 48.10-11 (162/1 B.C.); 50.27-28 (162/1 B.C.); 52.22; 53.23 (161 B.C.).
[25] *UPZ* 51.18 (161 B.C.); cf. Skeat in *P. Lond.* 7.2188.61 (148 B.C.) and *Hor* 22.3-4 (165 B.C.), actually in Ḥepnēbes. Quaegebeur (1985), and forthcoming in the G. *Fecht Festschrift*, somewhat modifies the view of Skeat: *phritob* is an honorific title for one or more officials, not necessarily in Alexandria.
[26] See also Djedherpaïmy, *Hor* 23 recto.10-11 (September 167 B.C.), with Quaegebeur (1977), 103.
[27] *UPZ* 106.4-5; 107.5-6.
[28] *OGIS* 56.2 and Wilcken (1903), 122.
[29] *UPZ* 5.7, 13; 6.7, 12 (163 B.C.).
[30] *Hor* 22 recto.7 with Zauzich (1978a), 99; *PP* 5382b.
[31] *UPZ* 42.23-24.

sharing responsibility for the disbursement of the royal syntaxis; in a related record of loaves, he is further called oikonomos.[32] If, as seems likely, Achomarres the lesonis and Achomarres the epistates and oikonomos are the same person, then Wilcken's clear-cut distinction between crown and cult appointments cannot stand.[33] The interests of the crown were also the responsibility of heads of cult, and the Greek word epistates would thus appear to be used to translate a variety of Egyptian terms. Used regularly for the new royal controller of the temples, it might also describe the lesonis, or chief priest, a crown official with cult responsibilities rather than a priestly representative.[34] Such was Achomarres, the epistates of the Sarapieion. In contrast, the epistates of the Anoubieion would seem to be a police appointment, concerned with law and order in the area.[35] The Greek vocabulary of officialdom was simply not sufficient for the complexity of functions which existed within this society.

Royal interests, then, within the temples were represented by both area controllers and the individual chief priests. The two are never seen in conflict but rather in collusion,[36] and as already suggested the strongly Egyptian nomenclature found in this class of crown officials may be evidence that this form of royal control was moderate in nature. It was rather from outside the temple administration that royal power might more effectively be exercised, through the crown's superior authority in financial administration. So, in the affair of the twins (to be considered further in chapter 7), it was orders from the dioiketes that reduced their syntaxis rations by one-half,[37] and, while recognizing the responsibility of Psintaes for the actual payment of their loaves, it is the *hypodioikētēs*, the deputy financial representative of the crown, to whom they finally turn for positive action in their favor.[38] In practice, it seems, the appointment of royal representatives to the temples interfered little with a traditional area

[32] *UPZ* 56.2, 9-10 (160 B.C.), Achomanres; for the identification, see Zauzich (1978a), 99, and Quaegebeur (1979), 721-22, with the Egyptian term ("scribe of pharaoh who makes accounts") for *oikonomos*. The identification with Achomarres also called Horos, son of Herieus, *PP* 5510, who holds this same post remains uncertain.

[33] Wilcken (1927), 44-45; cf. Ray (1976), 141; Préaux (1939a), 480, in contrast recognizes the close relationship of area *epistates* and *archiereus*.

[34] Zauzich (1980), 1008-1009. This interpretation is not contradicted by the many examples of *mr-šn* in Bresciani (1975); indeed the complaint of *P. Ox. Griffith* 39 (156 B.C.) supports it. For a *lesōnis* during the Persian period, see *P. Ryl. dem.* 9 (p. 65); then, however, he was appointed by the priests, Pestman (1981), 101 n. j.

[35] *UPZ* 69 verso.2 (152 B.C.); 108.1, 29 (99 B.C.).

[36] *UPZ* 52.9-10; 53.10-11 (161 B.C.), accused of profiteering from their post.

[37] *UPZ* 23.21 (162 B.C.), reflected also in bread rations, *UPZ* 54.6-8, 11 (161 B.C.).

[38] *UPZ* 46.16-22 (162/1 B.C.), Sarapion should urge and require Psintaes to provide the ration.

of Egyptian influence; it was rather the subordination of the temples to the financial departments of the administration which represented the more significant diminution of a previous position of power and independence.

Alongside the detailed evidence from the Sarapieion archive, the cult titles of individual priests from Memphis and the Memphite area provide additional insight into the working of the temples within the context of the Ptolemaic state. For Egyptians, priestly appointments regularly accompanied those in administrative or financial spheres. It was so too for military men, with army commanders also holding priestly titles. Teos, son of Ouahibrêmerneith, whose stone sarcophagus has been dated to the mid-Ptolemaic period, was "scribe of the army in the district of Sebennytos," as well as holder of priestly appointments in the Memphite area.[39] Where he functioned in his lifetime is unknown, as is the case with the Sachmet priest Pichaas, son of Achoapis, described on his Memphite statue as "great commander of the army in Chenou."[40] Pichaas was also in charge of the crew of the royal barge and must have been a priest of some importance.[41] The Horos priest and army commander Dorion, son of Dorion, whose mother was the priestess Heranch/Herakleia, has already appeared in connection with the Idumaeans[42] and, as with another Memphite military priest, prophet of Bastet and army commander Apollonios/Pehernefer, the son of Peïmet,[43] the family names support the impression that such military men within the priesthood came from a group prepared to hellenize. The absorption of Egyptians who were also priests into the upper ranks of the Ptolemaic army may have proved an effective means of integrating native institutions within the new Ptolemaic state. The same phenomenon is to be seen in the later Ptolemaic period, in the south, at Edfu, where a family of senior military officers, recorded separately on both Greek and Egyptian epitaphs with both Greek and Egyptian names, are described as priests in the local cults.[44]

In spite of such marginal integration, however, in major respects the temples remained what they had always been in Egypt—strongly independent, native communities which were also important centers both of

[39] *PP* 5829d. For the Sebennytos connection with the city, compare the career of Ḥor, Ray (1976) and *PP* 5502d.

[40] *PP* 5778b.

[41] Cf. *PP* 5769, Petosiris, son of Harasuchis, Nile priest with a similar naval appointment.

[42] *PP* 5519.

[43] *PP* 5454.

[44] Yoyotte (1969).

economic activity (see chapter 2) and of learning. The sacred books contained in temple libraries formed a repository of religious learning. Librarian priests were also scribes and scholars.[45] Thoth was the god especially connected with priestly literacy,[46] and the high priests had their own library, where perhaps were stored the records of the major religious ceremonies in which they played key roles.[47] This was a literate community in which ancient wisdom was preserved in written form.

PTOLEMAIC PATRONAGE

Ptolemy Soter had not been long on the throne when the Apis bull of the cow Ta-nt-Aset died of old age. The cost of burial was high, and, in addition to the lavish allowance already made, a further 50 talents of silver were borrowed from the king.[48] The king's readiness to come forward with subvention for this sacred cult, while in good tradition,[49] was to be a sign of things to come. Through their patronage of both cult and temples, the dynasty sought to reconcile the native population to the fact of foreign rule. Cults were not only financed but supported in other ways, and the building record of the kings reflects their interests, as it does their needs. Patronage might differ in both form and intensity from reign to reign, and the record from just one city gives a picture which is incomplete. Nevertheless, the importance of the city produces a record which, though partial, may still be significant and serve perhaps as a basis for comparison.[50]

In Memphis, as seen in the first chapter, the central cults were those of Ptah and Apis—Ptah in the valley where the living Apis also had his stall,

[45] Teos, son of Ouahibrêmerneith, PP 5829d; Oteuris, son of Komoapis, PP 5677e; Nebonuchos, son of Psammetichos, PP 5643; Harimouthēs, son of Chaiapis, PP 5460b, who also wrote epitaphs (Quaegebeur 1980a, 51 n.2); Harchēbis, son of Harchēbis, PP 5502d; Herieus III, son of Herieus II, PP 5359a, figure 6; Anemhor/Paschinis, son of Pehemneter, PP 5353, with figure 6.

[46] The high priests Petobastis III (PP 5371), Psenptais III (PP 5376), and Imouthes/Petobastis (PP 5372) are "scribes of the sacred books, scholars and lector-priests at the seat of Thoth." On Thoth, see already P1. PH1b. 18.b; Quaegebeur (1980/81), 233-34, on Hermes Thoth and the House of Life as a center of learning; see chapter 7.

[47] Chaiapis, son of Paneith (PP 5856 with Wildung 1977a, 56) is "scribe of the sacred books of the storehouse of the high priests of Memphis." For such ceremonial records, see the Rosetta decree, OGIS 99.29, with Bergman (1968), 251-56.

[48] Diod. Sic. 1.84.8 with Smith (1972), table 5. For the bulls, see Appendix D.

[49] See n. 3.

[50] Málek's revision of Porter and Moss, (1981) facilitates comparison with elsewhere; Bevan (1927) makes good use of the building record of individual rulers; much remains to be done. Bingen (1984), 426-32, seems excessively negative on the importance of the clergy.

and Apis, worshipped in death as Osorapis, in the Sarapieion of the desert heights. The flood of the Nile and the greater ease of desert excavation help to explain the imbalance of the record, with far more known of necropolis cults than those of the valley below.

Soter was presumably benefiting from his Egyptian advisors[51] when, on the pharaonic model, he made donations of land to the temples of Egypt, and with his loan for an Apis burial he set the pattern for his successors.[52] The first of the Ptolemies seemed keen to learn, and the native clergy was quick to take advantage, instructing both kings and their closest representatives on the nature and needs of the gods of their adopted country.

So, on 9 January 257 B.C., the priests of Aphrodite addressed Philadelphos' dioiketes:

> The priests of Aphrodite to Apollonios, dioiketes, greetings. In accordance with what the king has written to you, to give 100 talents of myrrh for the burial [of the Hesis] please order that this is done. For you know that Hesis is not brought up to the nome unless we have in readiness everything they may require for the burial since [mummification starts] on the same day [as her death]. Know that Hesis is Isis and may she give you favor (*epaphrodisia*) in the eyes of the king. Farewell. Year 28 Hathyr 15.
>
> (PSI 4.328 = *Pap. Lugd. Bat.* 20.50)

Like bulls, cows too were often the subject of cult, and Hesis here is probably the Hathor cow of Atfih/Aphroditopolis.[53] For the Greeks Hathor might be identified with Isis, and two days after this letter was written its recipient was in Memphis celebrating the main four-day Isis festival.[54] The time of year was auspicious for the request but we know neither if the king's ruling had been a specific (for the Atfih cow only) or a general one, nor if the priests received their myrrh. In their appeal to Apollonios these priests of Aphrodite adopt the Egyptian *quid pro quo* approach which recurs throughout the period.[55] Divine protection (linked to official promotion) should be the aim of any loyal servant of the Egyptian king.

It was of course, as we saw in the last chapter, not only the native priests of Egypt who sought to benefit from a favorable regime. In Mem-

---

[51] Manetho perhaps, Plut. *DIO* 28 (= 362a); W. Otto (1908), 215-16; Quaegebeur (1980a), 78-79, for Memphite influence; Welles (1970), 509-10; Samuel (1970), 453, within the administration, cf. Pestman (1978); Clarysse (1979), 737-43.

[52] E.g., the satrap stele, n. 15, and the Harris stele, n. 151.

[53] See Crawford (1980), 16 n. 1, for an alternative suggestion.

[54] *P. Corn.* 1.30-45, an account of lamp oil for Apellaios 6-9 (January 11-14); on 27 January, Apollonios visited the Serapeum at dawn, lines 79-80.

[55] See chapter 7 with Tait, *Pap. Lugd. Bat.* 20.50.6 n.; cf. Ray (1976), 123.

phis the priests of the Phoenicians settled there addressed a similar request to Zenon, the dioiketes' manager. By granting concessionary oil allowances to their temple, like those already made to the temples of the Carians and Hellenomemphites in the city, Zenon, they claim, may expect favor from Astarte. So earlier immigrants combined with the Egyptians to instruct the new rulers in the ways and values of their adopted country. The encouragement of local cults with the protection of their priests became a hallmark of the policy of Ptolemy II Philadelphos.[56]

In Memphis the reigns of the first two Ptolemies formed a period of active temple building and of cult patronage. Royal involvement is rarely explicit, but the scale of expansion here would seem to derive from royal initiative and funding. Memphis was the Egyptian home of Osorapis, patronized by the early Ptolemies as Sarapis. At the same time as a Greek cult statue was obtained for the god, now transplanted in human form to the Sarapieion at Alexandria and developed as a binding force for the new ruling class,[57] back home in Memphis Greek statuary was lavished on the shrine. For Greeks Osiris stood for Dionysos,[58] and the symbolism of his cult, discussed by later classical writers, is strikingly expressed in the strange Dionysiac sculpture brought to adorn the dromos of the Memphite Sarapieion, described in chapter 1. As conqueror, of course, Alexander had followed the route of Dionysos in the East, and the floats of the great procession mounted in Alexandria by Ptolemy II Philadelphos are witness to the deity's power and popularity with this, as other, Ptolemaic kings.[59] The main adornment of the dromos of the Memphite Sarapieion may date from the same reign. Some have placed it earlier under Soter, and others later in the same century under Philopator.[60] Made of local stone, probably by craftsmen settled in the city, the Greek statuary associated with the Egyptian home of the immigrants' new god displays an

[56] E.g., *PSI* 4.440 = *P. Cair. Zen.* 3.59451; Crawford (1980), 17-18.

[57] Fraser (1972), 1.246-59; Świderek (1975) stresses the Hellenomemphite role in transforming Osorapis into Sarapis, cf. Engelmann (1975), 1, for a Memphite priest propagating the cult at Delos. Will (1979), 204-6, rightly emphasizes the spontaneity of the spread of the Sarapis cult. The alleged Pontic connections of the cult may originate in the Sinopion at Memphis, Griffiths (1970), 516.

[58] E.g., Plut. *DIO* 29, and *passim* for the cult.

[59] Ath. 5.198c-199a; Nock (1972), 143; Fraser (1972), 1.205-7, 211-12; Rice (1983).

[60] Wilcken (1917); Lauer and Picard (1955), 246-58, under Soter (based primarily on the statue of Demetrios of Phaleron); Matz (1957), under Philopator (based on the statues of royal children). Fraser (1972), 1.255 and 2.404 n. 512, makes the point that not all statues are necessarily of the same date; on the basis of an artist's signature found close to those on the dromos, he argues an early date for at least some of these, contemporary with the lychnaption.

arrogant confidence at this relatively early stage of the relationship between temples and Ptolemies.

A cartouche of Ptolemy I Soter found in fragments from the city site of Memphis perhaps belonged to buildings now destroyed.[61] On the east side of the Saqqara headland, in the northern of the two large enclosures with their thick brick walls, the third and most extensive phase of the central temple building dates also from these early years. A cartouche with part of the hieroglyphic name of Ptolemy II Philadelphos survives on a cavetto cornice coming from the complex.[62] It was big building time, as seen on a stele from the Sarapieion with the record of a master builder who between August 253 B.C. and December 248 B.C. worked on the vault for the Apis bull of the cow Ta-Renenutet I. Besides this building underground, he completed a temple sanctuary 132 by 69 divine cubits (2,510 square meters) and a second, slightly smaller shrine for Hathor, Lady of the Sycamore, which measured 99 by 66 divine cubits (1,801 square meters).[63]

Though barely recorded in Memphis, Ptolemy III Euergetes I continued this royal concern for the temples. The Canopus decree records the agreement of a priestly meeting held in the temple of Osiris at Canopus in 238 B.C. It is a key source for the development of the relations between temples and state and is discussed below.[64] Campaigning in the east, Euergetes I elsewhere claims he sought out sacred objects taken from Egypt by the Persians and brought them home.[65] The familiar theme is repeated by Ptolemy IV Philopator, who after his important victory at Raphia in June 217 B.C. was welcomed home by the priests and temple staff; he showed his gratitude to the gods of Egypt with generous gifts made to the temples.[66] The red granite architrave of the eastern gate of the great Ptah temple was erected by this king;[67] and it was to Memphis that he returned in triumph to celebrate the victory of his troops. Like Horos, son of Isis, the pharaoh had trampled over his enemy, and the

[61] Lepsius (1897), I, 204.
[62] Smith (1979), 164.
[63] Louvre stele 82, ed. Brugsch (1884), 114, text 3; Revillout (1891b), 124. Revillout reads the larger sanctuary (connected with the vaults) as that of Bastet. This stele, important for Memphite topography, is in need of republication.
[64] OGIS 56.
[65] OGIS 54.20-22, the Adulis stele.
[66] Gauthier and Sottas (1925), copy from Tell el-Maskoutah; SEG 8.467, Greek text; Spiegelberg (1925) and Thissen (1966), lines 19-22, 27-30. See further Spiegelberg and Otto (1926); Sottas (1927); Huss (1976), 81, with a translation in Bevan (1927), 288-92.
[67] Petrie (1909a), 14 with plate XLV.

trilingual stele which a month later records this victory and the priest's decree shows Philopator on his horse in full Macedonian battle dress, wearing the double crown of Upper and Lower Egypt (plate vi). Before him kneels the captive Syrian king, Antiochus III, and behind him, as Isis, stands his sister-wife Arsinoe. The other gods look on.[68] Never before had a Macedonian king been so portrayed by the priests of Egypt; but now the scene was set, and later priestly synods followed suit.

In later years the battle of Raphia was seen as a turning point. In arming the Egyptians Philopator opened the way to internal strife, and troubles followed.[69] The death of Philopator coincided with the loss of the south as far as Abydos in a major revolt which started in 207/6 B.C., and in 200 B.C. Koile Syria was again lost to Egypt when the mercenary general Scopas was defeated at Panion. When in 204 B.C. Ptolemy V Epiphanes, a mere child, succeeded his father, the government was in effect run by a palace clique.[70]

In the following years success against the rebels at Lykopolis in the Delta and the suppression in Alexandria of a rebellion led by Scopas broke the run of disasters. In the autumn of 197 B.C. the thirteen-year-old Epiphanes celebrated in Alexandria a premature coming-of-age, his *anaklē-tēria*;[71] and, soon after, the rebel leaders were brought to Memphis, where their punishment accompanied the celebration, on 27 November, of the royal succession according to the rites of Egypt.[72] Epiphanes' title belongs to the language of Greek dynastic cult; he was, however, the first of the Ptolemies certainly to be crowned in the old capital, crowned by the high priest of Ptah in the presence of the priestly delegates from all areas of the country. The Pschent crown, the crown of Upper and Lower Egypt, was placed on his head by the high priest Harmachis, son of Anemhor. And in his royal titulature it was Ptah (not Amon, protector

[68] Spiegelberg (1904), no. 31088 with plate II; *SEG* 8.504a, Greek text; Thissen (1966), Abb. 1-2, a Memphite copy.

[69] Pol. 5.107.2-3; see Préaux (1965); Peremans (1975) for modifications.

[70] On Epiphanes' succession, Will (1982), 108-12; Walbank (1967), 472-73, on Pol. 15.20; (1985), 38-56; on the loss of the south, Koenen (1962), 14; Pestman (1965), 157-70, with earlier bibliography; for rebel kings, Zauzich (1978b), 157-58; Clarysse (1978), 243-53.

[71] Pol. 18.53.3 with Walbank (1967), 623-25. The separation of the coming-of-age and coronation ceremonies is at odds with Dittenberger *OGIS* 1.90 n. 32 and Smith (1968), 209-14.

[72] *OGIS* 90.8, 46-47, Phaophi 17; Sethe (1904–16), 183, no. 36. On coronation rites, see Ibrahim (1975), 11-12. Barguet (1953), 36, suggests this coronation allowed Epiphanes to be identified with Zoser (founder of the third-dynasty Memphite monarchy) on the Sehêl stele of 187 B.C.

of rebel kings in the south) whose "elect" and "beloved" Epiphanes was named.[73]

One can only imagine the intensive discussion and bargaining which ensued in the course of the next four months, resulting in the package of concessions of the priestly decree (the Rosetta stone), which was published on 27 March 196 B.C. In the city of Memphis, with all its historic associations and cult apparatus and with the full body of Egyptian priests present, it seems unlikely that the young Epiphanes could dictate a policy to the priests. The titulature and language of the final decree are both Egyptian, and the first draft seems now to have been written in this language.[74] Throughout the king is god, the god Epiphanes Eucharistos,[75] who, in fulfilling his divine role in relation to his subjects and in particular to the temples and the priests, has defeated the wicked enemy and the rebels, in this way winning divine honors and recognition from the priests of Egypt.

Gifts now were made to Apis, Mnevis, and other animal gods on a grand scale. In Memphis an Apis shrine was decorated by the king.[76] In acting thus the king showed gratitude for the health, victory, power, and other benefits granted him by the gods; he freed the temples of debt and of tax arrears, abolishing dues on grain and orchard land. Cult buildings and financial support were the tangible signs of the king's gratitude in a transaction masterminded by the priests.

On the Memphite necropolis too, royal building marked the close connection of the king with the city. On the eastern edge the temple platform with its limestone wall and the Anoubieion gateway were both constructed in this reign. Identified by his cartouche, the king adores Anoubis on the gate, and the fine temple building with its colonnade stepped up the slope enhanced the pilgrims' approach to these western suburbs; the Sarapieion way was also reconstructed.[77] The Anoubieion served too as an administrative center, with registry office and prison guards. Epiphanes' endowment of the temple here might underline the close connection now made firm of the old gods of Egypt with the new Ptolemaic administration.

In 197/6 B.C. the priestly synod at Memphis had celebrated the suppres-

[73] Quaegebeur (1980a), 67 no. 16; Clarysse (1978), 251 n. 2, on the growing influence of Ptah as seen in royal titulature.
[74] Daumas (1952), 9.
[75] Nock (1972), 154. OGIS 90.37-38, 41, 46.
[76] OGIS 90.33. The Apis shrine could be that on the *dromos*; see chapter 1.
[77] Smith (1979), 164; (1981), 336; Lanciers (1986), 87-89.

sion of the followers of Seth at Lykopolis with a royal coronation and priestly decree. Ten years later, on 27 August 186 B.C., came the final defeat of Chaonnophris, the rebel king of Upper Egypt. This time the defeat was celebrated in Alexandria, and in September 186 B.C. a further decree was promulgated by the priests. The decree survives only in bilingual Egyptian form.[78] Further festivals are decreed, and in the temples the victory is to be commemorated in traditional Egyptian representations. New Year's day of the following (twentieth) year of the king (9 October 186 B.C.) was perhaps the occasion of a further decree made to mark the recent birth of a son, the future Philometor.[79] So when, on 29 October 185 B.C., the priests gathered in Memphis once more for the enthronement of the new Apis bull,[80] they reaffirmed their thanks to their rulers, raising the queen Kleopatra, now mother to an heir, to a position of equality in the ruler cult; the birthdays of both Ptolemy and his queen should now be celebrated as birthdays of the *Theoi Epiphaneis*.[81]

Three years later, on 29 May 182 B.C., the visit to Memphis of the Mnevis bull from Heliopolis was the occasion for yet a further priestly gathering in the city; a further decree was passed.[82] Rulings confirmed here are later referred to in a survey covering land in the Isieion of the Memphite nome.[83] Only priests and their nominees might enter and measure this land. The content recalls that earlier order of Alexander's general Peukestas.

What, one must ask, was the significance of this series of priestly synods, from the late third and early second centuries B.C.? From the reign of Epiphanes the cumulative nature of the evidence is striking, and with

---

[78] Sethe (1904–16), II, 214-30, no. 38, Philensis II; Winter, *LÄ* 4.1027-28, refers to a new copy. Barguet (1953), 36, for the Sehêl stele of 187 B.C. perhaps celebrating the recovery of the south; *C. Ord. Ptol. Add.* 113 with Wagner (1971), 1-21, C-D.12-14, for the trilingual stele from Karnak providing for the continuation there of the triakonteteris and traditional Pharaonic festivals referring to the recovery of Thebes.

[79] Koenen (1962), 11-16. *P. Kroll* = *C. Ord. Ptol.* 34 may also belong to this date, though it is possible that the phrase "up to Year 20" in both documents derives from *prostagmata* accompanying the priestly decree of Year 19, on which see Spiegelberg (1929b).

[80] Louvre stele 2409, Brugsch (1884), 125-26, 134; cf. (1886), 27. Thoth 22 rather than either 20 or 2 (both Brugsch) is the reading of J. D. Ray.

[81] Sethe (1904–16), 198-214, no. 37, Philensis I; *I. Philae*, vol. 1, 19.

[82] Daressy (1911), 1-8, Gorpiaios 24; (1916/17), 175-79, Apellaios 22; Sethe (1916), 284-97. The Naukratis hieroglyphic stele headed by the same date, Kamal (1904/5), no. 22188, seems copied from a fragmentary Rosetta decree, Sethe (1904–16), 294, and Spiegelberg and Otto (1926), 22 n. 1. Daressy's stelae of 182 B.C. from Nobaireh (Naukratis) and Asfoun need republication; they record the success of Aristomios/Aristonikos in Phoenicia, Holleaux (1942), 3.337-55.

[83] *BGU* 6.1216.30-40. Yoyotte (1963), 114-19, for the Isieion. For 1 Thoth of the following year as the relevant date in such *philanthrōpa*, see Spiegelberg (1929b) and n. 79 above.

the constant reaffirmation of temple rights the king fulfills a traditional role. These priestly synods and resulting decrees occur against a background of serious trouble in Egypt, with parts of the country escaping from central control. When victory is celebrated in the decrees, Horos has conquered his enemies and Ptolemy becomes the victorious pharaoh, supported by the traditional gods of Egypt. But the victories are real and the records preserve interesting details, such as the capture of Lycopolis recorded on the Rosetta stone, the success of Aristonikos in the south in 185 B.C. in the Philae decree, or in Syria in the decrees of 182 B.C. It would be naive to think that these decrees reflect simple gratitude to the ruler on the part of the priests. The relationship was a reciprocal one and in return the king confirmed temple rights. In this way priestly decrees of thanks were presumably accompanied by royal *prostagmata* which recorded these rights. Large sums were, as in the past, spent on temples and their buildings; privileges granted the priests also affected their land and must have involved some loss in royal revenue. Epiphanes would not in the first place appear to have been acting from a position of strength.

The repetition, however, of the synods and their concentration in this reign suggests a royal policy with some success in managing the relations of temples and Ptolemy. The high concentration of synods in the 180s B.C. dates from a period when Epiphanes was of an age to act for himself. In the five years from 186 to 182 B.C. at least four meetings are recorded. In September 186 B.C. Epiphanes was close to twenty-four;[84] his first son was born that year. He may personally have realized the value of continuing the priestly gatherings in Egyptian style that he first experienced at his early Memphite coronation in November 197 B.C. In Egyptian eyes the cultic honors which the priests voted the king and his consort might help redeem the unpalatable fact of foreign rule. The temples, on the other hand, relied on the king to uphold whatever rights were left them.

The death of Epiphanes in 180 B.C. marked the end of the concentrated series of priestly decrees, though not of all such decrees, nor indeed of royal involvement with the temples and their priests.[85] The two sons of Epiphanes followed their father in their patronage of Apis. Described as "twin of the living Apis upon their birth-brick," Ptolemy VI Philometor was probably born in 186 B.C. (year 19 of Epiphanes), the birth year of the Apis bull of the cow Ta-Renenutet II. Among his many gifts to the

---

[84] His birthday was 30 Mesore, 3 October, *OGIS* 90.46; see Walbank (1985), 55.

[85] Cf. *P. Tebt.* 6 (140/39 B.C.), royal protection perhaps deriving from a meeting of priests; *P. Tebt.* 5 = *C. Ord. Ptol.* 53.50–84 (118 B.C.).

cults of Memphis and its necropolis was the official hieroglyphic stele of this Apis, erected on its death in early April 164 B.C. This was the same Apis that was mourned by the twins of the Greek Sarapieion papyri, and the stele, erected in the joint names of Philometor and his brother, the future Euergetes II, together with the latter's wife Kleopatra II, shortly predates the split in the royal household later in the year.[86] Both brothers were probably in Memphis for the New Year in October 164 B.C., but disagreements followed and Philometor left for Rome.[87]

To mark his accession to power, Euergetes II perhaps attended the Memphite coronation of the next Apis bull (of the cow Ta-nt-Hor) sometime late in 164 B.C. and, like his brother, he became closely linked with the bull in his official Egyptian titulature.[88] The later provision of burial costs for Apis and for Mnevis from the royal account marks his continuing concern for the cult connected with him from an early date;[89] but by now such a provision had become almost standard.

In national affairs Rome intervened, and compromise prevailed. With his younger brother now dispatched to rule in Cyrene, Philometor and his queen returned to residence in Memphis in 163 B.C. As ruling sovereigns they visited the temples and made their sacrifice.[90] Priestly contacts were renewed and a recently redated hieroglyphic stele records yet a further synodal decree from 31 July 161 B.C.[91] Memphite cults were also patronized. The royal couple had been involved in the ibis cult at Saqqara from early in their reign[92] and now they patronized the cult with gifts. Abuses in the Memphite ibis cult, lasting throughout the previous reign, run counter to the satisfactory picture put forward in the great priestly decrees under Epiphanes; the repeated commissions of reform—"one bird one pot" should be the rule[93]—suggest that little had in practice changed. Endowments made by Philometor and his queen recorded on

[86] For Philometor and the Apis, see Gauthier (1916), 4.288 n. 2; Ray (1978a), 117-20; Brugsch (1884), 125-26 no. 6 with 135-36, commenting on the poor quality of the hieroglyphs; *UPZ* 18.20-21; 19.23-25; 21.8-9, for the twins.

[87] Diod. Sic. 31.17-18; Polyb. 31.2.14, for the Roman reaction; 39.7.6; *Hor* 4 recto.9-10.

[88] Brugsch (1886), 27, "distinguished through the start of his reign coinciding with that of the living Apis"; see Appendix D, no. 8, this bull is not recorded until its seventh year in 159/8 B.C., and the exact date of its coronation is unknown. W. Otto (1934), 6, suggests that Euergetes II was attempting to parallel his brother's claim to be an Apis twin.

[89] *P. Tebt.* 5 = *C. Ord. Ptol.* 53.77-79 (118 B.C.); the shrines listed in lines 70-71 are strikingly Memphite.

[90] *UPZ* 41.4-5; 42.4; petitions presented: *UPZ* 5; 6; 20.

[91] Cairo 22184, Spiegelberg and Otto (1926); redated by Lanciers (1987).

[92] *Hor* 21, reforms in 174 B.C.; *Hor* 19 recto.14-15, rectifying abuses, in 172 B.C.

[93] *Hor* 19 verso.8; 21 recto.18; 22 recto.14.

the gate of the upper chapel of the Thoth temple may well date from these later years of his reign, when the galleries of the south ibis complex at Saqqara were rehabilitated.[94]

The mid-second century B.C. was a troubled time for Egypt, with the two sons of Epiphanes in conflict with each other and their wives.[95] On the death in September 119 B.C. of the Apis bull of the cow Gerg(et) II, it was Euergetes II and his second wife, Kleopatra III, who provided the stele for its vault.[96] Six months later, in the spring of 118 B.C., Euergetes was reconciled with his first wife Kleopatra II, the mother of his second, and all three together marked their reconciliation with that amnesty decree already mentioned, including the traditional provision for the burial costs of the Apis and Mnevis bulls.[97]

While showing different degrees of respect for the Apis bull, the two sons of Euergetes II repeated the pattern of conflict. Ptolemy IX Soter II ruled first until ousted by his younger brother, Ptolemy X Alexander I, in October 107 B.C.; Soter II now ruled in exile in Cyprus. Described in Egyptian sources as "shining out in Egypt at the same time as the living Apis" or "distinguished in his birth together with that of the living Apis,"[98] to the Greeks Soter II was known as Chick-Pea (Lathyros). The younger brother who now ruled in Egypt, at first with his mother and then with his wife, lacked the Apis connection; his lack of respect for his brother extended to this cult. In 96 B.C. the Apis of the cow Gerg(et) Mut-iyti was near to death in its twenty-third year; work was still in progress on its vaults.[99] It must have died soon after but was not to be buried while Alexander reigned. Only in the eleventh year of the successor Apis was the bull of Gerg(et) Mut-iyti finally placed to rest, in the thirty-first year (87/6 B.C.) of the newly restored Ptolemy IX Soter II.[100] (In troubled times like these, when the lack of royal support might cause serious delays in the proper proceedings of the cult, there was more than usual need for excellent embalming.) From Armant, too, in Upper Egypt

[94] Inscribed by 158 B.C., *Hor* 3 recto. 14-16, cf. 2 recto. 13-14, for Philometor's magnanimity towards the gods. Martin (1979), 126-27, for the archaeology for the site.
[95] Discussed in more detail below.
[96] Louvre stele 4246, de Rougé (1885), 114; Brugsch (1886), 23.
[97] See n. 85.
[98] Brugsch (1886), 37. This Apis was born in the Ptah temple in Memphis in February 142 B.C., the year of Soter II's birth. See Appendix D for the bulls.
[99] Louvre stele 4156, de Rougé (1888), 5. Under the Ptolemies the average life of an Apis bull was nineteen to twenty years; for Buchis it was twenty years, Mond and Myers (1934), 1.18.
[100] Louvre stele 113, Revillout (1891b), 146. Reymond (1981), no. 17.25-26, perhaps refers to this event.

there comes a story much the same. Here the Buchis bull born in April 101 B.C. under Alexander I was not installed for almost twenty years, not until April 82 B.C. when the elder brother reigned again.[101] Soter II's regard for Apis and his home is glimpsed also in the Memphite appointment of a priest of Apis–Osiris as priest too in the royal cult for Soter II and his mother Kleopatra II, the *Theoi Philomētores kai Sōtēres*; a royal endowment for the post seems likely.[102] The Memphites perhaps reciprocated this regard. The record on a Saqqara stele in late 89 B.C. of the regnal year of the "king outside Egypt" (Soter II, that is, in Cyprus) shows a close awareness of the different spheres of the two sons of Euergetes II.[103]

It was also Soter II, that object of ridicule to the Greeks, who was the first Ptolemy to celebrate Egyptian-style his royal jubilee in Memphis, a *triakontetēris*, or thirty-year Sed festival.[104] Crowned in the city shortly after his accession in 116 B.C. and restored to power (*wḥm-ḫꜥ*) in September–October 88 B.C., he was crowned again for a second time by the high priest Petobastis III, in the thirtieth year of his rule.[105] This traditional ceremony for the renewal of royal power may have accompanied the burial of the Apis, which had died over a decade before.

During the first century B.C. Memphis enjoyed a close relationship with the royal house, though evidence does not survive for the direct patronage of cult or for royal building on the site until the reign of Kleopatra VII. This last of the Ptolemies, the first (as already noted) to learn the language of Egypt, was well aware of the importance of animal cults in the life of the country she ruled. So, when in the third year of Kleopatra and her elder brother Ptolemy XIII (50/49 B.C.) the Apis bull of the cow Ta-nt-Bastet died, the queen's personal contribution of finance for the cult is hardly a surprise. The stele of Harmachis records that the queen provided 412 silver coins to establish a table of offerings, daily allowances of one measure of wine and one of milk, with twelve loaves, for those involved in the worship and work for the bull, together with twenty-seven measures of oil for those performing the daily rite. In addition five

---

[101] Mond and Myers (1934), 2.11, 31–32, no. 12.

[102] Vienna stele 5849 = Bresciani (1967), 42, no. vi.22. Cauville and Devauchelle (1984), 48–50.

[103] Zauzich (1977), 193, "Year 26 = 29 of the king outside Egypt."

[104] Bergman (1968), 114 n. 3 (with dates based on Brugsch's earlier calculations); Hornung and Staehlin (1974); Traunecker (1979), 429–31.

[105] Brugsch (1886), 32–33, no. 50, a stele dated 24 March 86 B.C.; (1891), 871, with reference to a similar record on an Edfu stele.

hundred measures of beans, forty of another oil and the cost of meat were paid for by the queen.[106] The figures and readings may not always be exact, but the high level of involvement is clear. Similarly, a year earlier in Upper Egypt, on 22 March 51 B.C., barely a month after the death of Ptolemy XII Auletes, the queen herself took part in the installation of a Buchis bull and "all the people saw her."[107]

Starting under Ptolemy I Soter with a simple loan, by the end of the dynasty Ptolemaic kings and queens had, under the guidance of the priests, learned the role of beneficent pharaoh towards the temples and the cults of Egypt. The first of the Roman emperors was to exploit this lesson learned.

ROYAL CULT IN MEMPHIS

The assimilation of the descendants of a Macedonian general to the role of Egyptian pharaoh is one of the more remarkable phenomena of Ptolemaic rule. Persian kings earlier had been depicted on the walls of Egyptian temples, but with the Ptolemies the more general recognition of the divine aspect of the new rulers, involving actual cult, testifies as much to the desires of their subjects as to the political acumen and religious awareness of the kings themselves, and of their advisors. The progressive pharaonization of the Ptolemies, of their queens, and of their families may be seen as reinforcing the acceptance of immigrant rule among a native population.[108]

The Ptolemaic dynastic cult, as introduced for the Greek-speaking population of Egypt, is a phenomenon which has been extensively studied.[109] Less well documented is the Egyptian aspect of this cult, initiated in the early third century B.C., which combined with the Greek dynastic cult to validate the Ptolemaic line throughout the land. The study of the royal cult as found at Memphis may serve to illustrate both a general and a particular development. The extension of the cult of the Ptolemies into

[106] Louvre stele 4, Revillout (1891b), 133.

[107] Mond and Myers (1934), 2.12, no. 13; cf. Tarn (1936), 187-89; Bloedow (1963), 91-92, and Quaegebeur (1983a), 264-72, for her personal involvement. Skeat (1954), 40-41, reading Year 19, is skeptical. Heinen (1966), 28-29, uses this as evidence for the sole reign of Kleopatra, cf. De Meulenaere (1967), 300-305, the joint reign of Auletes and Kleopatra VII.

[108] On the complex role of an Egyptian pharaoh, see Posener (1960); for Persians on temples, Porter and Moss (1951), 277-90; on Hellenistic ruler cult, Préaux (1978), 238-71, with earlier bibliography; Walbank (1984b).

[109] E.g., Fraser (1972), 1.213-46. See *Pap. Lugd. Bat.* 24 for a list of eponymous priests.

the Egyptian temple is something which recurs throughout the country, but the close ties which develop at Memphis between the senior priesthoods, in particular the high priesthood of Ptah, and the ruling house based in Alexandria are peculiar to the city, in sharp contrast, for instance, to what happened at Thebes. Indeed, the age-old tensions already alluded to, between Upper and Lower Egypt, are nowhere more clearly illustrated than in the differing reactions to the ruling Ptolemies of the priesthoods of Amon in Thebes and of Ptah in Memphis. And in Memphis the cooperation (or time-serving) of the high priests of Ptah was to serve the city well.

It started with Ptolemy II Philadelphos, whose deification of his sister-wife Arsinoe II met with immediate success among Greeks and Egyptians alike. The deification of Arsinoe was a political act, and the new Greek cult, launched with top-level support, was quickly taken up by Greeks living in the capital and in the rest of the country. The queen was officially adopted into the dynastic cult of Alexander and his successors, with her own priestess, a *kanēphoros* or basket bearer, in both Alexandria and Ptolemais in the south. She was also the object of public cult with her own temples or Arsinoeia.[110] The foundation on Cape Zephyrion by the admiral Kallikrates of a temple to the queen (as Aphrodite) caught the imagination of Greek poets eager to please, and Poseidippos' epigram in her honor is preserved among the papers of Ptolemaios, son of Glaukias, from the Memphite Sarapieion.[111] The streets named after her in Alexandria, the surviving regulations for her cult as a marine goddess, with small altars set up in front of private houses, and the actual Greek dedications made to her all bear witness both to the extent of official backing and the spontaneous popularity of the new cult.[112] Indeed it may have been the popularity of this public cult, together with Arsinoe's adoption already during her lifetime as sister-god, one of the *Theoi Adelphoi*, which, as Fraser has argued, helped to reconcile the Greeks of Egypt to the unusual and somewhat unacceptable fact of brother-sister marriage.

The institution, however, of an Egyptian cult for Egyptians was a remarkable innovation, an important experiment with far-reaching consequences. It was after her death in 270 B.C. that Arsinoe entered the Egyp-

---

[110] In *P. Lond.* 7.2046 (third century B.C.) an Egyptian from the Sarapieion writes to Zenon hoping for employment in the new temple of Arsinoe at Philadelphia. For Philadelphia in the Arsinoite nome as *komē tēs Philadelphou*, see *P. Lond.* 7.1954.1; 1955.1 (257 B.C.).

[111] See chapter 7.

[112] Fraser (1972), 1.216-18; Robert (1966), 175-210; Quaegebeur (1971b), 243.

tian temples, following a decree of Ptolemy II recorded on the Mendes stele.[113] Throughout Egypt her cult statue was to be placed beside that of the local god, be he the ram of Mendes, the crocodile god Souchos of the newly named Arsinoite nome, or the mummiform Ptah of Memphis.[114] For the Egyptians, Arsinoe was to be a temple-sharing goddess, what the Greeks called a *synnaos theos*, and her status as an Egyptian goddess originated in a royal initiative. Evidence for the Egyptian cult of Arsinoe Philadelphos comes from all regions of Egypt, from more than twenty-five separate places.[115] This widespread evidence might simply reflect the efficiency of the central government in establishing the cult, but subsequent records suggest a degree of popularity for this goddess beyond that of a normal dynastic cult.

In Memphis Arsinoe became the consort of Ptah, chief deity of the city. Her cult image was introduced into his temple, and Ptah's high priest became the priest or scribe of Arsinoe, to whose cult was at first joined that of Philotera, her younger sister who died before her. The first scribe of Ptah and Arsinoe (with Philotera) was Esisout II/Petobastis I (fig. 5). This high priest was already a prophet in the temple of Ramses, while his brother Chonsiou was statue-priest of Nectanebo; earlier king cults such as these perhaps prepared the way for Ptolemaic developments in the Egyptian sphere, with members of the top priestly families holding such posts in the early Ptolemaic period (figs. 5 and 6).[116] Esisout's new appointment is listed on his grave stele, which further records special hon-

[113] Sethe (1904–16), 2.41, no. 13.

[114] On the Egyptian cult, see Sauneron (1960), 83-109; Quaegebeur (1971a), 191-217; (1971b), 239-70.

[115] Quaegebeur (1971a), 209-17, lists twenty (taking Memphis with Saqqara, and Thebes, Karnak, and Medinet Habu as one). To these may now be added: Krokodilopolis, Medinet Madi, Philadelphia, Hermonthis (1971b), 242-43, and Diospolis Parva (1978a), 250-51 with n. 32.

[116] Crawford (1980), 26-27. On these tendencies, see E. Otto (1957), 193-207; Morenz (1959), 132-207; Wildung (1969), 15-21, 100, 147-52. In the Memphite region the following king cults are recorded—Nectanebo II: Chonsiou, son of Esisout (*PP* 5844, fig. 5), prophet of the king Nectanebo II in the temple of Tadehnet; Anemhor II (*PP* 5352, fig. 5), prophet of Nectanebo II, the falcon; Esnounouer, son of Onnōphris (*PP* 5540, fig. 6), prophet of the statues of king Nectanebo in the temple of the estate of Sachmet the Great at the head of the valley; Onnōphris II, son of Esnounouer (*PP* 5657, fig. 6), prophet of the statues of the king Nectanebo II in the temple of the estate of Osiris at Rout-Isout, of the temple of Anoubis' chest, and of the temple of Osiris-Apis. See De Meulenaere (1960), 103-7, on the popularity of this cult. Ramses; Esisout II (*PP* 5361, fig. 5), prophet of the temple of Ramses in the temple of Memphis; Amasis, son of Herieus (*PP* 5351, fig. 6); Oteuris, son of Komoapis (*PP* 5677e), in charge of the storeroom of the temple of Ramses. Cult offices of the following kings are also found: Snefrou (*PP* 5356; 5354, fig. 5); Menes (*PP* 5351; 5657, fig. 6); Teti (Athothis) (*PP* 5657, fig. 6); Merenptah-men-Merenptah (*PP* 5351; 5359, fig. 6), statue priests.

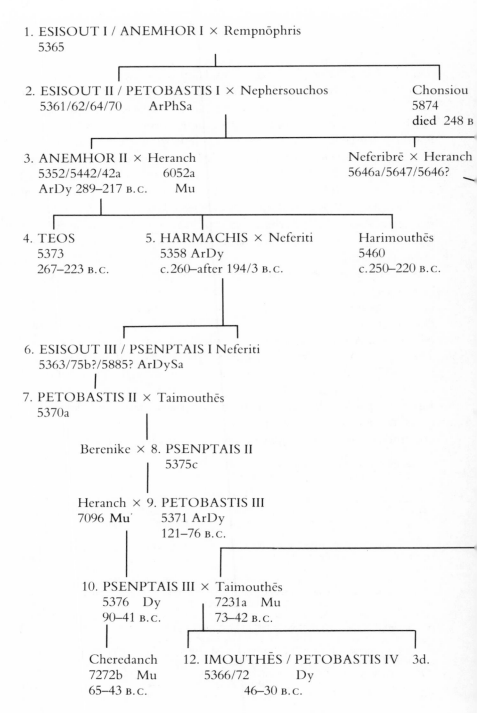

1. ESISOUT I / ANEMHOR I × Rempnōphris
   5365

2. ESISOUT II / PETOBASTIS I × Nephersouchos   Chonsiou
   5361/62/64/70   ArPhSa   5874
                                                         died 248 B

3. ANEMHOR II × Heranch   Neferibrē × Heranch
   5352/5442/42a   6052a   5646a/5647/5646?
   ArDy 289–217 B.C.   Mu

4. TEOS   5. HARMACHIS × Neferiti   Harimouthēs
   5373   5358 ArDy   5460
   267–223 B.C.   c.260–after 194/3 B.C.   c.250–220 B.C.

6. ESISOUT III / PSENPTAIS I Neferiti
   5363/75b?/5885? ArDySa

7. PETOBASTIS II × Taimouthēs
   5370a

   Berenike × 8. PSENPTAIS II
                5375c

   Heranch × 9. PETOBASTIS III
   7096 Mu   5371 ArDy
               121–76 B.C.

10. PSENPTAIS III × Taimouthēs
    5376 Dy   7231a Mu
    90–41 B.C.   73–42 B.C.

    Cheredanch   12. IMOUTHĒS / PETOBASTIS IV   3d.
    7272b Mu   5366/72   Dy
    65–43 B.C.   46–30 B.C.

FIGURE 5. The high priests of Memphis.

NOTES: High priests in capital letters. Numbers are those of PP III and IX. Ar: priest of Arsinoe;
Ph: priest(ess) of Philotera; Dy: priest(ess) in the dynastic cult; Le: high priest of Letopolis; Sa:
priest of Horus, lord of Sachebou; Mu: priestess musician; d.: daughter.

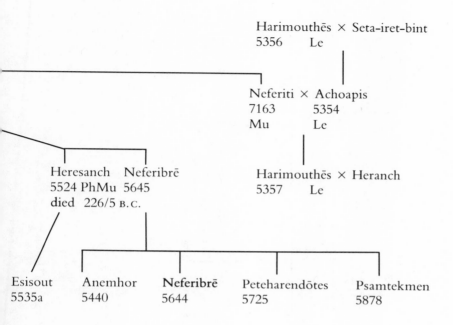

Harimouthēs × Seta-iret-bint
5356   Le

Neferiti × Achoapis
7163   5354
Mu   Le

Heresanch   Neferibrē
5524 PhMu 5645
died 226/5 B.C.

Harimouthēs × Heranch
5357   Le

Esisout   Anemhor   **Neferibrē**   Peteharendōtes   Psamtekmen
5535a   5440   5644   5725   5878

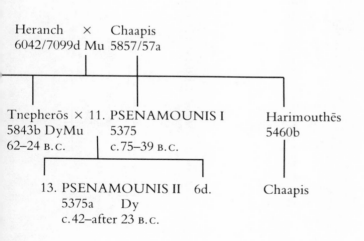

Heranch   ×   Chaapis
6042/7099d Mu 5857/57a

Tnepherōs × 11. PSENAMOUNIS I
5843b DyMu   5375
62–24 B.C.   c.75–39 B.C.

Harimouthēs
5460b

13. PSENAMOUNIS II   6d.
5375a   Dy
c.42–after 23 B.C.

Chaapis

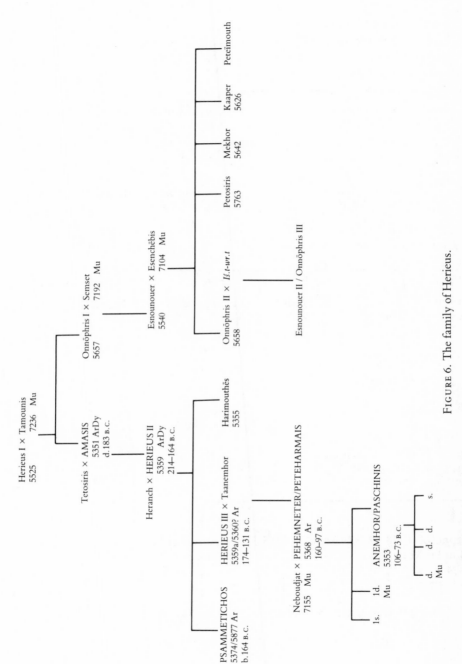

FIGURE 6. The family of Herieus.

NOTES: High priests of Letopolis in capital letters. Numbers are those of PP III and IX. Ar: priest of Arsinoe; Dy: priest in dynastic cult; Mu: priestes musician; s.: son; d.: daughter.

ors shown him by the king in year 23 of his reign (263/2 B.C.), the year, that is, when the apomoira, the tax on orchards and gardens, was transferred to the cult of Arsinoe, the goddess Philadelphos.[117] In providing such a guarantee of financial backing for the future, Philadelphos appears concerned to support his original initiative. A temple of Arsinoe stood within the royal palace at Memphis, close perhaps to the enclosure of the great temple of Ptah.[118]

The identity of the priests who were appointed provides further evidence for the importance of this cult. After the death of Esisout II, Philotera was detached from the cult of her sister and a separate priestess was named, Heresanch, daughter of Neferibre, from another important Memphite priestly family.[119] After Heresanch, however, Philotera disappears from the records, eclipsed perhaps by the growing importance of the cult of Arsinoe, which was now joined by a full dynastic cult in the Egyptian temples. The post of scribe of Ptah and Arsinoe remained in the family of high priests for four generations in all—Esisout II/Petobastis, Anemhor II, Harmachis, Esisout III/Psenptais I—and then passed to a related family, related at least in the offices they held (especially that of high priest of Letopolis) if not actually through marriage. This was the family of Herieus, of the same generation as Esisout II (see fig. 6).[120] After five holders of four generations in this family, at the end of the second century the office returned to the family of high priests, being held by Petobastis III, who died in 76 B.C. Over approximately two hundred years therefore, covering nine generations, there were at least ten holders of this office coming from only two families.[121] The office had remained a monopoly of the upper echelons of the Memphite priesthood. One further first-century scribe of Ptah and Arsinoe is recorded, Harsiesis, brother of Petobastis and son of Chaiapis and Thatres, sem-priest and prophet of

[117] B.M. 379, cf. Quaegebeur (1971b), 246. Year 23 refers to Philadelphos, not to Esisout. On apomoira, see Préaux (1939a), 171; for a similar transfer of royal income, compare the satrap stele, n. 15 above.

[118] Vienna 153 = Quaegebeur (1974), 73, no. 33.4-5; Leiden sarcophagus AMT 3 with Quaegebeur (1971b), 250; Louvre C 124 = N275 = Quaegebeur (1974), 70-71 no. 27; Cairo CG 31099.2, cf. Quaegebeur (1971b), 255, and, generally, 263.

[119] PP 2 and 9.5524; she was also a Min musician and prophetess of Isis and Nephthys in the Osiris-Apis cult of the necropolis.

[120] E. Otto (1956), 109-29; Quaegebeur (1971b), 239-70.

[121] Priests of Arsinoe: Esisout II/Petobastis (PP 5361, 5362, 5364, 5370) (with Philotera); Anemhor II (5352, 5442, 5442a); Esisout III/Psenptais I (5363, 5375b?, 5885?); Amasis (5351), Letopolite high priest; Herieus II (5359), Letopolite high priest; Pehemneter/Peteharmais (5368), Letopolite high priest; Petobastis III (5371); Harsiēsis, son of Thatrēs (5487a).

Ptah, who is recorded on a Cairo stele. During this later period, however, enough is known of the family of high priests of Ptah to suggest that Arsinoe's priesthood had left their control. By this time there was perhaps a decline in the interest in this cult of a third-century B.C. queen, corresponding to the virtual disappearance in the first century B.C. of organized royal cult within the priesthoods of the Egyptian temples.

The introduction of Arsinoe to the temples of Egypt was a bold and innovative move. And it was a popular innovation. Such a degree of direct interference in the religious life of the Egyptian temples had probably not been known since Akhenaton, and the initiative in founding this queen cult reflected the political acumen of Ptolemy II Philadelphos and his close associates. For, as at the time of Akhenaton, once established this new cult seems to have gained a spontaneous following. For in Egypt, it appears, queen cults enjoyed a particular popularity, which may date back to an earlier period.

A generation later the deification of Arsinoe was followed by that of Berenike, the daughter of Euergetes I, whose death occurred during a national gathering of priests held at Canopus in 238 B.C. Assimilated with Tefnut, daughter of the god Helios/Ra, Berenike was deified in full Egyptian style; the priests gave her father instruction in the new cult, the details of which are recorded in the Canopus decree.[122] The emphasis here on apparel and on cult procedures—the headdresses to be worn, the bread to be served, or the processions by boat—illustrates well Egyptian priestly functions.

The success of these two queen cults is striking; it may be paralleled perhaps by the contemporary popularity of the cult of Isis. In Memphis, for instance, the names Arsinoe and Berenike are the only Greek female names ever found among the Egyptian priestly community. Whereas in the administration, at least from the second century B.C., the use of both Greek and Egyptian names was fairly regular,[123] those connected with the temples, in contrast, whether high priests or humble stonecutters, generally retained an Egyptian nomenclature and one which was strikingly theophoric. The Macedonian names Arsinoe and Berenike stand as striking exceptions and are found in Memphis in the families of the high priest, other Ptah priests, and even necropolis workers of the second and first centuries B.C.[124] The success of royal initiative in introducing the cult

---

[122] OGIS 56.46-58; Sethe (1904–16), 2.142-46, no. 30; Onasch (1976), 137-55.
[123] See the important observations of Clarysse (1985).
[124] So Quaegebeur (1972), 106. Arsinoe, wife of Teos and mother of Pasy: P. Leid. dem.

of Arsinoe, and connecting it with central priestly families, is clearly shown in these names; their adoption forms part of the picture of consistent loyalty displayed by the priesthood of Memphis to Ptolemaic rule.[125]

Arsinoe was only the beginning, though in the event an auspicious beginning. It was the meeting of priests in the Osiris temple at Canopus in 238 B.C. which, besides the deification of Berenike/Tefnut, ratified the introduction of Ptolemaic ruler cult into the Egyptian temples. In all Ptolemaic synodal decrees, the reciprocal emphasis is strong; at Canopus, in return for royal benefactions, it was agreed that all priests should become priests of the *Theoi Euergetai*, of Ptolemy III Euergetes, and of his consort Berenike, and that statues of these gods be introduced as cult images into native temples. Details are given of the Egyptian ritual to be performed for them. As we have already seen, the organized priesthood was to be extended with the addition of a fifth priestly division (phyle) named after the Theoi Euergetai, and the number of priestly councillors (*bouleutai*) was to be raised from twenty to twenty-five. This synodal decree was wide-ranging in scope, with a leap year proposal included, though not susequently observed. The introduction of ruler cult was only one of a range of provisions in this concordat worked out between Ptolemy and his priests.

It was under Ptolemy IV Philopator that Greek ruler cult for the Ptolemaic dynasty was fully consolidated, now based on the Sema in Alexandria.[126] Similarly, the king's incorporation into the Egyptian temples is recorded in that synodal decree issued by the priests meeting at Memphis in 217 B.C. to celebrate the king's recent victory against Antiochus at

---

373b.1; 373c.3 (204 B.C.) + *P. Louvre* 2409 (184 B.C.); Ars(inoe), wife of Ptah priest Ioufnefer and mother of Petobastis: Drioton (1952), 253 (second century B.C.?); Arsinoe, mother of Berenike, Min sistrum player: B.M. 383 = Quaegebeur (1974), 69, no. 19 (second to first centuries B.C.). Berenike, wife of high priest Psenptais II, mother of Petobastis: Vienna 82 = Quaegebeur (1974), 72, no. 32 (late second century B.C.); Berenike, daughter of Arsinoe: as above; Berenike, mother of Haryothes, who worked on Apis vaults: Cairo CG 31110.9 (132 B.C.) = Spiegelberg (1904); Berenike, mother of Taruma, priestess of Ptah: Loebenstein (1972), 32-33 with plate xix (second sentury B.C.); Berenike, daughter of high priest Psenptais III and Taimouthes: B.M. 147 = Reymond (1981), no. 21, and 392 = no. 22; Berenike, mother of Horos/Dorion, owner of Book of the Dead: Rosati (1986), with Quaegebeur (1986), 75-76 (cf. 79-80 for a Memphite origin). I cannot agree with Drioton (1952), 261, that these priestesses are Greeks; the lack of Greek names within this community is notable.

[125] High priest Petobastis III (Quaegebeur 1980a, 69, no. 25) is scribe of Arsinoe throughout the troubled years of the first quarter of the first century B.C. For a queen cult, that of Aphrodite-Kleopatra, surviving into the third century A.D., see *W. Chrest.* 115.10, from Memphis.

[126] Fraser (1972), I, 225.

Raphia. Among other honors, the statues of the Ptolemies were to be introduced into the temples and copies of the decree set up, decorated with the scene already described of Ptolemy as pharaoh on horseback, triumphing over his enemy (plate vi). The Greek ruler here is assimilated to a degree never reached by Persian kings or their satraps.

Although according to the Canopus decree all priests were now in addition priests of the ruler gods, the Theoi Euergetai, in practice the title was given only to some individuals. In Alexandria, with its Greek dynastic cult, the priesthoods were held by prominent Greeks and Macedonians.[127] In Memphis those holding such office were regularly members of well-known Egyptian priestly families. Priests here are recorded of the Theoi Euergetai and, later, of the Theoi Philopatores and Theoi Epiphaneis.[128] (Occasionally the Theoi Adelphoi are added at the start of the list of royal gods, as a sort of optional extra.)[129] For the cult of the two sons of Epiphanes, in Memphis there is no evidence. These were troubled times when much was lost. Missing too are the stelae of the high priests of Ptah who regularly held office in the dynastic cult; perhaps this loss explains the silence. From the end of the century comes the Apis priest already noted who served for Soter II and his mother-queen Kleopatra II as Theoi Philometores and Soteres.[130]

In the first century B.C., when we again have evidence for royal cult in Memphis, a "first prophet of the lord of two lands" (that is, a priest of the king) is now recorded, and this is something new. The designation is that of Psenptais III, the high priest son of Petobastis III and of Heranch.[131] This title might simply be an archaism, a return to the language of earlier days to describe the office of high priest,[132] but more likely it

---

[127] See Mooren (1978), 53; *Pap. Lugd. Bat* 24, for the official Alexandrian priesthoods used in all official documents, both Greek and Egyptian, throughout the country.

[128] See figures 5–6. Priests of the *Theoi Euergetai* and *Philopatores*: Anemhor, *PP* 5352; Ioufnefer, father of Petobastis, *PP* 5622; Harchēbis, son of Harchēbis, *PP* 5502d. With the *Theoi Epiphaneis*: Harmachis, son of Anemhor, *PP* 5358; Esisout III, son of Harmachis, *PP* 5363; Amasis, son of Herieus (d. 183 B.C.), *PP* 5351; Herieus II, son of Amasis, *PP* 5359; Petosiris, father of Heranch, *PP* 5767; possibly Petobastis, son of Ioufnefer, *PP* 5759; Teōs, *PP* 5829a. The last three individuals together with Petobastis' father Ioufnefer probably come from the families of figures 5–6.

[129] The *Theoi Adelphoi* are recorded for Harmachis, son of Anemhor; Amasis, son of Herieus; and Teōs, cf. n. 128.

[130] See n. 102.

[131] B.M. 886 = Quaegebeur (1974), 70, no. 25 = Reymond (1981), no. 18.b.4. The office was also held by his son Imouthes/Petobastis IV, B.M. 188 = Quaegebeur (1974), 66, no. 13 = Reymond (1981), no. 26b.a.8.

[132] De Meulenaere (1960), 95–96 n. 7, on the title; E. Otto (1957), 177, on overall archaism of language. On this interpretation the title was primarily honorific and the high priest little

here represents a new and special appointment, made perhaps at the instigation of Ptolemy XII Neos Dionysos (Auletes), who in March 76 B.C. named Psenptais III as his priest. The cult of Auletes is not here attached to that of his wife, and in Greek sources this king was the first of the Ptolemies simply to incorporate *Theos* (god) into his personal titles for regular use.[133] And whereas the office of prophet in the royal cult of earlier couples might be extended throughout the priesthood, the prophet of the living pharaoh appears in contrast as a rather special, personal appointment tied to the high priest of Memphis.

It was this "prophet of pharaoh" which served as model for Augustus' appointment of a prophet and prophetess of Caesar.[134] The very personal nature of the first-century B.C. ruler cult stands epitomized in these appointments. Augustus was well aware of the importance of Egypt in his empire. Special appointments might be more effective than general incorporation, and under Roman rule, as prophet of Caesar, the high priest of Memphis played a crucial role in the extension of the Roman imperial cult.

The Egyptian aspect of ruler cult seems to have spread widely, though its importance is not easily evaluated. Combined with Greek cult it formed a focus for the hopes and prayers of all who lived in Egypt. Yet, though divine, the Ptolemies were not fully gods, and, with the exception perhaps of Arsinoe and Berenike, they were never entirely assimilated into the Egyptian pantheon. In recognition, as it were, of the special nature of their divine status, in Greek sources cult activity and sacrifices were normally offered "on behalf of the king and his family" and not directly to them, and on the walls of Egyptian temples the reigning sovereigns are regularly portrayed presenting offerings to Egyptian gods rather than as the objects of such cult themselves.[135]

Ruler cult did however pervade all areas of life, and it helped to bind together the disparate elements of the kingdom. Within the bureaucracy, predominantly Greek at least in its upper levels, the regular sacrifices made at the start of an official's day, on behalf of the king and his off-

---

more than a statue priest of pharaoh; cf. Daressy (1914), 235-36, for such a priest from Karnak.

[133] *Theos Neos Dionysos*, e.g., *OGIS* 191.2.

[134] B.M. 184 = Quaegebeur (1974), 66, no. 12 = Reymond (1981), no. 29, high priest Psenamounis II and his aunt Tnepherōs, wife of Psenamounis I held the post of *ḥm-ntr n Kysrs*.

[135] Fraser (1972), 1.226-27; Winter (1978), 158; Hornung (1982), 141-42.

spring,[136] might serve to reinforce the loyalty expressed in the written guarantee, the royal oath which, at least from the second century B.C., was made at the time of appointment.[137] This oath too was important; on a par with oaths made in the temples,[138] this solemn undertaking derived its strength in part from the divine status of its guarantors. While the written version may be a concession to Greek practices, in Egypt, as elsewhere throughout the Near East, the oath had long played a regular and accepted part in the organization of social relations. Only the king, as divine guarantor, was new.

It was not only officials for whom the dynastic cult played a role in daily life. The guarantee of the ruler-gods might also be invoked in the penalty clause of Egyptian contracts. So in 78 B.C., in a release document covering burial rights over an extended family, detailed provisions were made for corpses brought to the wrong group of undertakers.[139] Initially four days were allowed for the redirection of such corpses, and, in the event of failure to redirect within the following five days, those drawing up the contract were required to pay the rightful owners 5 deben of silver (in Greek terms, 25 staters or 100 silver drachmas) in coined money and, in addition, 5 deben of silver "for sacrifices and libations on behalf of the everlasting rulers." Similarly, a demotic loan contract for wheat and kiki oil drawn up in February 108 B.C. contains a provision of a 50 percent surcharge in the event of failure to repay on time together with 2 silver deben for "royal sacrifices and libations."[140] In similar Greek documents the charge was known as "drachmas sacred to the king and queen," and a Greek receipt issued on 28 December 162 B.C. by Ptolemaios, son of Glaukias, to his friend the Cretan Demetrios, son of Sosos, for the oil allowance of the Sarapieion twins, displays in its use of this penalty clause a familiarity with the Egyptian world of contracts.[141] Indeed, the royal

[136] *BGU* 8.1767.1-2; 1768.9 (first century B.C.); cf. Crawford (1978), 197.

[137] E.g., *P. Tebt.* 27.53-54 (113 B.C.); see Préaux (1939a), 449; Wilcken (1927), 84, for the inclusion of Sarapis and Isis.

[138] E.g., *UPZ* 110.38-40 (164 B.C.); *PSI* 361.6-7 (251/50 B.C.), an oath by the *daimon* of the king and by Arsinoe, is the earliest private example.

[139] *P. Leid.* 374 i.10-12 (78 B.C.) = App. B:17; see Johnson (1986), 79–80, and chapter 5 below.

[140] *P. Vatican* 22 + *UPZ* 133 = Revillout (1885), 25-26; cf. Pestman, *Recueil* 4.21-22 (108 B.C.), without the royal levy. On the nature of the contract, see Pestman, *Recueil*, vol. 2, nos. 4-6, with pp. 39-41.

[141] *UPZ* 31.13-14 (162 B.C.). See further *P. Ox. Griffith* 58.15-17 (153 or 142 B.C.); *UPZ* 195.15 (119/17 B.C.); 196.36-37 (116 B.C.); 125.24-25 (89 B.C.); *P. Tor. Amenothes* 8.36-37 (116 B.C.) and *P. Ryl.* 65.11-12 (67 B.C.), to be paid *eis to basilikon*. There appears to be no connection with the Alexandrian sales tax deducted for Alexander, *P. Hal.* 242-45 (third century B.C.).

dimension of such day-to-day contractual arrangements among the Egyptian population—undertakers, tradesmen, and temple workers alike—testifies to the importance of ruler cult in the mental outlook of both rulers and ruled. The additional levy of "sacred drachmas" besides the regular fine in penalty clauses may add weight to the operation of a contract. Further, while on the one hand benefiting from such clauses, the crown might also be approached in an appeal for justice in case of dispute. Revenue levied from such fines was fed back into the system, in a process of reaffirmation of the ruler's divinity.

The recognition of this royal role is nowhere more clearly seen than in the case of recipients of syntaxis, the block grant made to the temples by the crown for the payment of cult and cult personnel.[142] Through syntaxis, as through the apomoira grant for the cult of Arsinoe, the Ptolemies ensured the continuation of their own royal cult. Within the temples, recipients reacted favorably, recognizing the ultimate origin of their support. So the twins Taous and Thaues, playing their part in the mourning for the Apis bull in 164 B.C., also served for Mnevis, making additional sacrifices to the god Asklepios/Imouthes. They describe this complex service as performed "on behalf of the king."[143] Similar claims were expressed by Petesis, embalmer-in-chief of the deified Apis and Mnevis when, in 99 B.C., he wrote to Ptolemy X Alexander and queen Berenike about the problems he suffered. Although his may be special pleading at a time when Apis lacked royal support, Petesis clearly hoped for the success of his appeal, assuring the king and queen, as great and victorious gods, that besides his cult activity for the bulls he made prayers and sacrifices to bring them "health, victory, power, strength, and overlordship of the land beneath heaven."[144] Others had similar expectations,[145] and so the concept of kings and queens as gods became well embedded in the outlook of at least the priestly sector of the native population.

The appeal, however, was wider. The general popularity of the ruler-gods may perhaps be indicated in the large number of small terracotta busts of Ptolemies that survive.[146] Their cheap quality suggests a mass production for popular consumption in contrast to those small plaster heads of rulers which may represent the prototypes of bronze and silver

[142] See *Hor* 33.10-11 (157 B.C.) with discussion p. 139.
[143] *UPZ* 17.5-6 (163 B.C.); 20.41 (163 B.C.); see chapter 7 below.
[144] *UPZ* 106.9-14 (99 B.C.); see chapter 5 below.
[145] *UPZ* 14.28-30 (158 B.C.) Ptolemaios, son of Glaukias; *Hor* 7.11-12.
[146] E.g., Scheurleer (1978), 1-7; Martin (1979), nos. 338-39; D. B. Thompson (1973), 78-101, for a wide discussion of the evidence.

portraits.[147] Unlike life-size, public statuary, these smaller Ptolemaic kings and queens were made for private ownership on a wider scale. Possession of a royal bust of course need not in itself involve recognition of a ruler's divinity, but when kings are gods then royalists tend also to worship. Such portraits may indicate the success of the Ptolemies, with their extensive ruler cult, in capturing the imagination of their subjects.

THE HIGH PRIESTS OF PTAH

On 29 August 168 B.C. a meeting took place in the Great Sarapieion in Alexandria between one Hor, a priest from the ibis shrine on the Memphite necropolis, and the ruling sovereigns, Ptolemy VI Philometor, his wife Kleopatra II, and his brother Ptolemy VIII Euergetes II.[148] The year had been an exceptionally difficult one, with Antiochus Epiphanes of Syria occupying Egypt until shortly before this date. (On the same day as this meeting in the capital, the wife together with the brother of one Hephaistion, in writing to urge his speedy return from the Memphite Sarapieion, referred both to the particular strain and to the general hardship of "times like these.")[149] So, when Hor regaled his rulers with the account of his successful prophecy in which he had rightly foretold the departure date from Egypt of the invader king and the salvation of Alexandria with all its people, he might expect royal gratitude for his now proven talents. In the event, however, his main personal gain was perhaps the audience itself, which remained the high point of his career, a source of authority and guarantee of credibility for future dealings with his colleagues in the priesthood.[150]

Hor was not alone among Memphite priests in visiting the capital, and a much grander encounter between king and Memphite priest is recorded on the grave stele of Psenptais III, high priest of Ptah in Memphis during the reign of Ptolemy XII Neos Dionysos (Auletes):

> I betook me to the residence of the kings of the Ionians which is on the shore of the Greek sea to the west of Rakotis. The king of Upper and Lower Egypt, the master of two lands, the father-loving and sister-loving god (Philopator Philadelphos), the new Osiris, was crowned in his royal palace. He proceeded to the temple of Isis, the lady of Yatudjat. He offered unto her sacri-

[147] E.g., Rubensohn (1911), no. 12, 5 cm high; Reinsberg (1980), 81-88.
[148] *Hor* 2 recto.12; verso.4-12. For Hor's background and earlier career, see Ray (1976), 117-20.
[149] *UPZ* 59.13-16; 60.11-14 (159 B.C.).
[150] Ray (1976), 121-23.

fices, many and costly. Riding in his chariot forth from the temple of Isis, the king himself caused his chariot to stand still. He wreathed my head with a beautiful wreath of gold and all manner of gems, except only the royal pectoral which was on his own breast. I was nominated Prophet and he sent out a royal rescript saying: "I have appointed the high priest of Memphis Psenptais to be my prophet." And there was delivered to me from the temples of Upper and Lower Egypt a yearly revenue for my maintenance.[151]

A return visit was made by Auletes to Memphis, where he visited the Sarapieion with his entourage and inspected the city by boat.

In these reciprocal visits of king and high priest of Ptah may be seen the close relations by then existing between the Greek rulers and one of the oldest Egyptian priestly families. The growth and development of this relationship reflect the changes in strength and influence of both parties while illustrating, in microcosm, adjustments which followed the imposition of Ptolemaic rule.

Psenptais III was, as we have already seen, "prophet of pharaoh," priest therefore in the Egyptian dynastic cult; but he was also high priest of Ptah, and it was in this role that he performed the royal coronation. According to Ps.-Callisthenes, Alexander the Great had been crowned pharaoh at Memphis,[152] and at least from the reign of Epiphanes the Ptolemies regularly underwent the traditional ceremony, crowned by the high priest of Ptah.[153] Ptah, Hellenized as Hephaistos already by the fifth century B.C. when Herodotus acquired much of his Egyptian material from Ptah's Memphite priests, was a suitable associate for any ruler of Egypt. "Ptah south of his wall" or "Ptah of the white wall," with his impressive temple and extensive landed property, was lord of the Sed festivals as Ptah-Tatenen, celebrating the unification of Upper and Lower Egypt, and in this role he became associated with the jubilee festivals of the Ptolemies.[154] As with Ptolemy, the post of high priest remained within one family, and the career of Psenptais illustrates how the relationship between king and high priest might develop from political necessity.

The Memphite family of the high priest of Ptah is unusually well

---

[151] Harris stele, B.M. 886.8-10. The translation is based on that of Glanville in Bevan (1927), 347-48. Reymond (1981), 148, no. 18, gives a somewhat different translation.

[152] I.34.2, accepted by Merkelbach (1954), 24; see Bergman (1968), 92-94, for Egyptian influence.

[153] *OGIS* 90.29; Sethe (1904-16), 2.183, no. 36, Epiphanes' Memphite coronation. The phrase "customary rites of coronation" has been taken as evidence for earlier royal coronations, e.g., *W. Grund.* 21 n. 7, but such rites may have been preserved in the records of the House of Life, Bergman (1968), 251-56.

[154] Holmberg (1946), 12-17, 58, 81, 203.

known from a variety of sources. Although their funeral stelae provide the fullest documentation, several statues and sarcophagi also survive, and Books of the Dead which belonged to their family.[155] A series of stone funeral stelae, both hieroglyphic and demotic, of the high priests themselves and of their family associates, apart from a break of almost ninety years in the second century B.C., covers the whole of the Ptolemaic period. On the assumption of one high priest in office at a time, it is thus possible to reconstruct a complete stemma of high priests throughout the period.[156] In their simplest form these stelae record only basic genealogical information about the recipient, together with dates of birth, death, and burial following mummification. In their more developed form, especially in the first century B.C. (as seen already in the record of Psenptais III), more personal information may be recorded. The stele, for instance, of this high priest's wife Taimouthes is one of the more intimate documents to survive from antiquity. The high priest's wife had given birth to three daughters, but the couple had no son. They said their prayers to her patron god Imhotep (Imouthes)/Asklepios whose demand came, in a dream, for construction work in the hall of his temple on the necropolis; in return he promised a son. So finally, on 13 July 46 B.C., a son was born to them, the future high priest Imouthes/Petobastis IV, whose name recalls the god whose gift he was. His mother lived just four years more.[157] Such prayers of parents communicating with the god in dreams find parallels in fourth-century B.C. Greek material from Epidauros,[158] but Taimouthes' final address from the grave to her high priest husband is striking in the sentiments it records:

> . . . cease not to drink, to eat, to get drunk, to enjoy love, to make the day joyful, to follow your inclination both night and day; allow no grief to enter

[155] Full references in Quaegebeur (1980a), 64-71; see Crawford (1980); D. J. Thompson (1989).

[156] Figure 5, based on the work of Quaegebeur (1974); (1980a), now included in *PP* 3² = 9, whose transcriptions I have adopted. Reymond (1977) and (1981) comes to different conclusions on the basis of the same material; see Quaegebeur (1980a), 48-49; Devauchelle (1983), 135-45, with the same number of priests but one fewer generation. The most doubtful link in the stemma is that of Neferibre (*PP* 5647/5646a), brother of high priest Anemhor II; his identification with the father of Heresanch and husband of Heranch (*PP* 5646) is nowhere explicit but seems likely, given Heresanch's appointment in the cult of Philotera. I would date Heresanch's death to 226/5 B.C., in Year 22 of Euergetes I, contra De Meulenaere (1959a), 246, on Louvre statue N2556. The names of the high priests between Harmachis (d. after 194/3 B.C.) and Petobastis III, who took office in 104 B.C., are known from Vienna stele 82 = Reymond (1981), 118, no. 17.

[157] B.M. 147 = Quaegebeur (1974), 65, no. 11; (1980), 70, no. 28; Reymond (1981), 165, no. 20. Further translations by Maspero (1879), 1.185-90; E. Otto (1954), 190-94.

[158] *IG* 4².1.121-27. On the Egyptian tradition of such dreams, Posener (1960), 85-86; Sauneron (1959), 40-53.

your heart. . . . The West Land is a land of sleep and of deep darkness, a place whose inhabitants lie still. Sleeping in the form of mummies they do not wake to see their brothers; they are conscious neither of their father nor of their mother; their hearts forget their wives and their children.[159]

The *carpe diem* theme is an old one in Egypt, found already in the songs to the dead known as the Harpers' Songs from the Middle Kingdom.[160] It is thus, with a combination of hedonism and despair, that Taimouthes' surviving spouse appears to have commemorated his wife.

The first recorded Ptolemaic high priest of Ptah from Memphis is Esisout, otherwise known as Anemhor, whose wife was Rempnōphris. Nothing is known of either the family or the office in the immediately preceding period, but Esisout/Anemhor heads a stemma of ten generations with thirteen holders of the office (fig. 5). The most striking feature of this stemma is the closed family group within which the post is held. Once the office devolves on a brother (to Harmachis from Teōs in the fourth generation), and once, in the ninth generation with the accession of Psenamounis I, on the half-brother (and brother-in-law) of a high priest's wife. Psenamounis I, who succeeded Psenptais III in 41 B.C., is known as high priest from the funerary stele of his wife and half-sister Tnepherōs, the sister of his predecessor's wife.[161] In marrying his (half-)sister, Psenamounis stands alone in this practice, more common among the Ptolemies. This high priest had only two years in office, and on his death the office reverted to the young son of Psenptais III, Imouthes/Petobastis IV, who was in turn succeeded by his cousin Psenamounis II, the son of Psenamounis I and Tnepheros. The case of Anemhor II in the third generation shows that retirement was an available option for high priests; the fourth high priest Teōs in fact predeceased his father Anemhor to whose position he had earlier succeeded.[162] More often, however, holders died in office and their sons regularly inherited the priesthood. As was the case within the royal house, these sons were often very young. Psenptais III was fourteen when in 76 B.C. he became high priest of Ptah, and his son Imouthes/Petobastis IV was only seven years and ten days old when named high priest on 23 July 39 B.C.[163] It seems indeed that a hered-

---

[159] Adapted from the translation of Glanville in Bevan (1927), 349.

[160] E.g., Lichtheim (1973), 194-97; for elsewhere in the Near East, cf. Walbank (1967), 84-85, on Polyb. 8.10.3, the tombstone of Sardanapallos; Brandon (1965), 79-82.

[161] B.M. stele 184 = Reymond (1981), 223, no. 29.

[162] Since Teos carries the title *wr ḥrp ḥmw*, "chief of artificers," it is strange that Reymond (1977), 8, does not consider him a high priest.

[163] Full references for these various priests may best be found in *PP* 3 and 9 to which the numbers on figure 5 refer.

itary claim to the office counted for more than did the personal capacities of the individual who filled the post.

High priests were related not only by blood but also in the offices they held. Many of the key priesthoods of the area would appear to have been monopolized by a group of interrelated families. The high priest of Ptah has already been found serving as scribe in the cult of Arsinoe and as priest in the dynastic cult. Indeed, an enumeration of the many varied appointments of the high priests of Ptah adds up to a listing of the major cults of Memphis and the surrounding countryside.[164] Without taking account of the priesthoods of associated members of their families, and in addition to the cult of Ptah in which all in some capacity served, these high priests held office also in the valley cults of the living Apis (fig. 5, nos. 2, 3, 4, 9, 10, 12), Nefertem (3), Renenet (3), and Banebded (the ram of Mendes) in the Lake of Pharaoh (9, 10). On the necropolis they served in the cults of Osiris-Apis (3, 9, 10), Anoubis on his mountain (9, 10), Imouthes son of Ptah (9, 10), Bastet lady of ʿAnchtawy (2, 9, 10), Thoth (9, 10), Horos (2, 3, 4, 5, 6), and Sokaris (2, 7); just as Horos (the falcon) is regularly associated with a window of appearances, so such a window, with all the gods who might appear there, is listed among the cults held by several of these high priests (nos. 1-6).[165] In the surrounding area, priestly appointments are recorded in the cults of Osiris at Rout-Isout (9, 10), Osiris lord of Rosetau (9, 10, 12), Osiris-Apis at Bousiris (7), Horos lord of Letopolis (13), Horos lord of Sachebou (2, 6),[166] Sachmet at Sat (3), Min lord of Senout (11), Hathor lady of the southern sycamore (2), Chnoum lord of Semehor (7), and Chnoum-Chentiouaref (3). In addition, two high priests served in the cult of earlier kings, in the temple of Ramses (2) and in the cult of Nectanebo II the falcon (3). In such multiplicity of offices lay both their spiritual and their economic preeminence.

The central family of high priests was thus linked to other important families from the upper ranks of the Memphite clergy through offices held. In particular, the position of high priest (*wnr*) of Letopolis, which in the generation of Anemhor II was held by his brother-in-law Achoapis (see fig. 5), was for much of the period under the control of another

[164] See *PP* 3 and 9 for these priesthoods; the association of offices may be of topographical interest.

[165] Cf. Ray (1976), 151, the window of appearances in the temple of the Peak.

[166] So too in the second-century Teos (*PP* 5829a) and Petosiris, father of Heranch (*PP* 5759), also priests in the dynastic cult and probably part of the family. Anemhor II, figure 5, no. 3, is prophet-nurse of Horos the child, who dwells in Sachebou, and Petobastis II, no. 7, prophet of Horos-Ra, lord of Sachebou. For Sachebou, between Letopolis and Terenouthis, see Sauneron (1950), 63-72; Yoyotte (1959c), 75-79; De Meulenaere (1963), 5-7.

priestly family which also later held posts in the cult of Arsinoe and in the dynastic cult.[167] This is the family of Herieus tabulated in figure 6;[168] they were perhaps related through some missing link to Achoapis son of Harimouthes. It was after the fifth generation of high priests of Ptah (Esisout III/Psenptais I), in the reign of Epiphanes, that the positions of scribe of Ptah and Arsinoe and of priest in the dynastic cult switched to this family, where they remained, as far as the evidence goes, for close to one hundred years.[169] The high priesthood of Letopolis stayed in the family even longer. It is striking how these cult connections ran north and south along the west bank of the Nile, rather than across the river to the east.[170] It seems that in the geography of cult the river formed a significant barrier, though it also served to link the temples up and down the Nile.

The wives of the high priests were priestesses, often priestess-musicians,[171] and in 44/3 B.C. Tnepherōs, wife of Psenamounis I, already a sistrum player of Ptah, was appointed "wife of Ptah." This was a new

[167] *Wn-r* of Letopolis: Harimouthes (*PP* 5356); Achoapis (*PP* 5354); Harimouthes (*PP* 5357); Amasis (*PP* 5351); Herieus II (*PP* 5359); Herieus III (*PP* 5359a/5360?); Psammetichos (*PP* 5374/5877); Pehemneter/Peteharmais (*PP* 5368); Anemhor/Paschinis (*PP* 5353); Onnōphris, son of Tamounis (*PP* 5366a), perhaps the same as the father of Esnounouer (*PP* 5677) on figure 6. Imouthes, son of Esoēris (*PP* 5365a), and [Herieus], son of *Nfr-iw* (*PP* 5360a), must fit somewhere in the family. Younger brothers carry the simple title of *wn-r3*: Onnōphris I (*PP* 5657) and Harimouthēs (*PP* 5355). See figures 5, 6. Reymond (1981) in her tables, with different reconstruction of the evidence, speaks of the Letopolitan line. The connection of Memphis with Letopolis, capital of the second nome of Lower Egypt, is pre-Ptolemaic, Limme (1972), 92; for location of the temple (perhaps at Ouenchem), see Smith and Tait (1983), 55–56; on *wn-r3* ("mouth opener") of Letopolis, see Vercoutter (1962), 84, line 1 n. A; Kaplony (1966), 137–63.

[168] Figure 6 is based on E. Otto (1956); Quaegebeur (1971b) and *PP* 9. If (see previous note) Onnōphris *PP* 5366a and Onnōphris *PP* 5657 may be identified, a further Letopolite high priest may be added. Some of the texts are used by Wildung (1969). Although the precise connection is unknown, this family appears linked to earlier high priests of Letopolis.

[169] The record for Arsinoe priests is probably complete; in the dynastic cult at least two holders must be missing between Herieus II (fig. 6) and Psenptais III (fig. 5).

[170] Yoyotte (1980/81), 74 n. 245.

[171] Normally described as sistrum players, the following are recorded—Ptah musicians: Heranch, mother of Psenptais III (*PP* 7096); Heranch, mother of Taimouthēs (*PP* 7099d); Esenchēbis, mother of Onnōphris (*PP* 7104); Thatrēs, mother of Petobastis and Harsiēsis (*PP*7120); Taimouthēs, daughter of Taimouthēs (*PP* 7231); Tnepherōs, daughter of Chaiapis and Heranch (*PP* 5843b); Taruma, daughter of Berenike (*PP* 7245e); Heranch, wife of Anemhor II (*PP* 6052a), also a Sachmet musician. Min musicians: Heresanch, daughter of Neferibre (*PP* 5524); Berenike, daughter of Meriptah and Arsinoe (*PP* 7098a). Sachmet musician: Heranch, wife of Anemhor II (*PP* 6052a), also for Ptah. Anoubis musicians: Ithoros, mother of Irerna (*PP* 7126); Irerna, daughter of Petobastis and Ithoros (*PP* 7134); Semset, mother of Esnounouer (*PP* 7192). Heka musician: Neferiti, daughter of Esisout II/Petobastis I (*PP* 7163). Sokaris musician: Tamounis, mother of Amasis (*PP* 7236). Other musicians: Neboudjat, mother of Anemhor/Paschinis (*PP* 7155); Taimouthēs, daughter of Chaiapis and Heranch (*PP* 7231a); Cheredanch, daughter of Psenptais III (*PP* 7272b). See figures 5, 6.

appointment, though it may echo the earlier Theban "wife of Amon."[172] And in this innovation there stands symbolized Memphis' current ascendancy in the age-old rivalry with Thebes. Whereas for the later years of Ptolemaic rule the home of Amon was a center of trouble and secession, the consistent loyalty of Memphis and its priesthood was here being recognized by Kleopatra VII in the creation of this honorific post for the wife of the high priest of Ptah. The importance of the high priest's wives is marked also in their elaborate funeral stelae. From these almost as much is known of the women of this family as of their high priest husbands.[173]

A small number of families linked by marriage would seem therefore, in their monopoly of key offices, to form an elite among the numerous priestly families of Memphis. Each new Memphite stele published adds to the growing prosopographical picture, though what proportion of the city's population were priests cannot be known.[174] Not surprisingly, in such a privileged group the ranks were closed; the priesthood remained hereditary and exclusive, rarely penetrated by the Greek settlers of Egypt.

A further striking feature of the family of high priests of Ptah is their use of double names as found for four out of thirteen holders of the office: Esisout/Anemhor, Esisout/Petobastis, Esisout/Psenptais, and Imouthes/Petobastis. Double names, with one native name and one Greek name, are not infrequent in Ptolemaic Egypt; they are normally understood as representing a stage in the process of Hellenization for Egyptian members of society.[175] Most commonly found within the administration, occasionally this practice is to be seen among the priesthood too. Horos/Dorion, whose surviving Book of the Dead has already been mentioned, was a member of the priestly community prepared to compromise and even Hellenize in taking a name (Dorion) with particular attractions for such men.[176] Among the high priests, however, the double names are both Egyptian, never Greek. The same feature is found among the names of the cow-mothers of the Apis bull and for the later generations of the family of high priests of Letopolis, who perhaps followed Memphite suit. The significance of this practice is unclear, but the unusual use of double

---

[172] B.M. 184 = Reymond (1981), no. 29.10. For Arsinoe granted honors similar to those of the sacred wife of Amon of Thebes, see Quaegebeur (1971a), 208; Sauneron (1960), 103.

[173] For such stelae, see Reymond (1981), nos. 12, 20, 22-24a, 28-29.

[174] Quaegebeur (1974); Málek in Porter and Moss (1981).

[175] Crawford (1971), 134-35. They may, however, as among the military settlers of Upper Egypt, suggest the reverse, Pap. Lugd. Bat. 14, pp. 47-105; 19, pp. 30-37.

[176] Cf. chapter 3 nn. 108-9. The practice occurs more widely in the first century B.C., e.g., Apollonios/Perhernefer (PP 5454) and Thaues/Asklepias in chapter 5.

Egyptian names clearly represents some measure of the importance of these particular priestly families. Perhaps echoing royal usage where multiple Egyptian names were regularly employed,[177] their nomenclature may have served to set the high priests of Memphis apart from the rest of the population.

The high priest of Memphis bore the title *wr ḥrp ḥmw*, "chief of artificers,"[178] and combined with the proliferation of cult offices already referred to, this appointment forms a further indication of his primacy among Memphite priests. Chief in the cult of Ptah, the high priest's authority also (as already noted) embraced the cult of Apis, lord of the necropolis; for Apis was Ptah, as well as his son and emanation, and the living Apis dwelled in Ptah's temple in the valley below.[179] As the high priest of Ptah performed the burial of the bull and later, when it was found, crowned the new Apis,[180] so too he crowned the king, for Ptolemy was now Ptah's chosen ruler.[181] At least from the reign of Ptolemy V Epiphanes this coronation took place in the temple of Ptah, and in this ceremonial role the high priest came face to face with the Greek ruler of the country. With Upper Egypt in decline and often in revolt, Ptah had eclipsed Amon, the protector of earlier kings.[182] So, when he crowned the king, Ptah's high priest stood as chief representative of all the priests of Egypt. It was in virtue of this position that under Auletes Psenptais III was by royal command assigned "from the temples of Upper and Lower Egypt a yearly revenue for maintenance."[183] With this grant proclaimed as an honor by its recipient, in fact all temples were now being taxed by the king to help support the favored priesthood of the age.

The ceremonial dress of these high priests is illustrated on their grave stelae: a long linen gown with panther's skin across the shoulders and wig of Ptah on the head.[184] High priests too, like kings, were invested with

---

[177] The royal parallel should not be pressed since the practice is found elsewhere, sometimes in less important families: Phimenis/Amasis, prophet of Ptah (*PP* 5854); Achomarres/Horos, prophet of Ptah (*PP* 5510); Harendotes/Peteharmachis, Apis worker (Bresciani 1967, 30, stele ii. 16); Hetephor/Peteharendotes, Apis worker (35-36, stele iv.8); Hartos *Gbr*, merchant (*P. Cair. dem.* 30602-3 [116/15 B.C.]).

[178] De Meulenaere (1974), 183-84, suggests rather a title of *ḥmww-wr-sḥm*, "the craftsman of the most powerful."

[179] In detail, Bergman (1968), 251-56.

[180] Reymond (1981), no. 17.25-26, for Petobastis III involved in an Apis burial; Nigidius Figulus, n. 189 below, on Apis and the coronation.

[181] Ptah names were taken by Ptolemies III, IV, V, VI, X, and XIII, Holmberg (1946), 257, based on Gauthier (1916); Thissen (1966), 35-36.

[182] Clarysse (1978), 251 n. 2, including Alexander (naturally) and Ptolemies I and II.

[183] See n. 151.

[184] Reymond (1981), plate x.

the symbols of their office, and at least from the late second century B.C. the king, in turn, would perform the ceremony. "He [sc. Ptolemy] handed out the golden crook, mace, robe of linen from the southern house [and] the leather garment according to [the ritual of] Ptah's festivals and solemn processions. He placed the golden ornaments on my head, according to the age-old custom, in my seventeenth year of age," is how Petobastis III described his investiture at the hand of Ptolemy X Alexander I.[185] Thus, while in actual power they differed fundamentally, in the ceremonial bestowal of authority king and high priest were closely joined. The king came to Memphis for his coronation and in turn the high priest might, like Psenptais III, travel to Alexandria for his investiture.[186] The third century B.C. statues of Petobastis I (under Ptolemy II Philadelphos) and Psenptais I (under Euergetes I) erected in the Alexandrian Sarapieion show the connection between the two cities already at an earlier date.[187]

PTOLEMY AS PHARAOH

According to the Rosetta stone, when the high priest crowned the king at Memphis "rites customary to the accession" were performed.[188] Whereas in normal conversation Greek was probably the language of communication between Ptolemy and his priest, in temple ceremonies Egyptian would have been used, incomprehensible as it was to most of the Ptolemies who underwent these rites. It is a Roman commentator from the late Republic, Nigidius Figulus, who somewhat surprisingly gives further detail of this ceremony, which came unchanged from the Egypt of the pharaohs.[189] The temple of Memphis, he writes in an attempt to explain to a Roman audience the mysteries of Egypt, is the spot where Typhon (that is, Seth) was buried. (The place of royal enthronement in this account was thus linked to the mystery of Osiris, that mystery central to Egyptian religion.) Here, he continues, the kings are first initiated in sacred matters in the temple. Next comes the rite in which, dressed in special ceremonial garb, the king must yoke the Apis bull, held by the Egyptians as a most important god. Leading the bull through a

---

[185] Vienna stele 82 = Reymond (1981), no. 17.10-11, with modified translation.
[186] B.M. 886 = Reymond (1981), no. 18.8-10; cf. Glanville in Bevan (1927), 348.
[187] Quaegebeur (1980a), 53-59. The Cherchel statue of Petobastis II (c. 180 B.C.) may also originate from Alexandria; see Quaegebeur (1980a), 61-63.
[188] OGIS 90.29 (196 B.C.).
[189] De sphaera graecanica et barbarica (ed. Schanze), 421.

district of the city, so he may be seen to have experience of human physical exertion, he is required to refrain from any form of cruel dealing with
all beneath his sway. Led by a priest of Isis[190] to the inner sanctuary (called
the *adytos*), kings are bound by oath to refrain from interference with the
calendar, intercalating neither month nor day, nor changing any feast day,
but completing the 365 days as instituted of old.[191] Then a further oath is
added, that they will always care for the protection and provision of both
land and water. Finally, the diadem is put in place, and the king controls
the land of Egypt.

Much here is obscure; a diadem has replaced the double crown of the
Rosetta decree, a priest of Isis the high priest of Ptah. Nevertheless, it is
clear that this covenant of the king with his people, a covenant mediated
through his priests, in which calendar and control both of the flood and
of agricultural land are guaranteed by the king's physical prowess and by
his oath, dates from an Egypt long before the Greeks arrived. In continuing the age-old ceremony, Ptolemy recognized the important role such
ceremonies might fulfill in a land where ceremony was always strong. In
the eyes of the Egyptians this was no less true of the period of the Ptolemies; the importance of such ceremonies must not be underestimated. In
the rites of coronation, king and country were closely bound. And the
high priest of Ptah in Memphis played a focal role in mediating between
his king, his people, and the gods in an effort to ensure the well-being of
the land of Egypt—the annual flood and the crops it brought.

Further questions arise. What were the means by which the new rulers
came to appreciate the role they must fulfill, and how did this role translate from the ceremonial sphere to that of politics and the realities of rule?

The first question can never be fully answered. Some of the possible
modes of communication between immigrant Greek rulers and their native Egyptian subjects have already been suggested, and the process seems
likely to go back at least to the satrapy of Kleomenes. Egyptians versed
in the lore of ancient Egypt played some part in the counsels and administration of the early Ptolemies. The effect of their influence perhaps built
up, and soon was reinforced as Greek officials learned the ways expected
of them in the land in which they lived. When Apollonios, the dioiketes,
visited the Sarapieion or gave land nearby to Egyptian gods, he was ful-

[190] A Ptah priest was rather to be expected. Isis, however, was far better known to the
Romans.
[191] In this context it is not surprising that the rationalization of the calendar, so optimis-
tically adopted in the Canopus decree, *OGIS* 56.33-47, was not put into effect.

filling certain expectations of the native Memphites, though personal concerns may have also played a part.[192] Others followed suit, and the growing adoption of Egyptian cults by the primarily Greek-speaking sector of the population[193] will have increased for these people, too, the importance of Egyptian ceremonies. What started tentatively grew, until by the time the Romans came Ptolemy was also pharaoh, with Hellenized Egyptians fully involved both at his court and within his administration.[194]

The translation of ceremonial authority into political power is likely to be a complex process. For these priests of Ptah the process was further complicated by the fact that the political capital of the country was now geographically separate from the religious center. The early foundation of a Sarapieion in Alexandria did little to modify the preeminence of the Memphite temples;[195] it was this preeminence which Epiphanes recognized when he returned to Memphis for his Egyptian coronation in 197 B.C. To overcome this problem of distance and the gap between old and new, with increasing frequency the Ptolemies made royal visitations to the city, or took up residence there. The Greek verb used to designate royal residence in the city is *epidēmein*; the noun *parousia* is also found, with both words testifying to the fact that Memphis no longer enjoyed the role of capital it held in the early years of the new regime.[196] When Ptolemies visited Memphis they acted as pharaoh, making the proper sacrifices to the gods, and making themselves available to their subjects. However incomplete, a catalogue of known royal visits to the city reveals an interesting correlation between these visits and times of political significance for the kingdom as a whole.

The apparent concentration of royal visits to the city in the second century B.C. may be a feature more of the evidence that survives—the priestly decrees, the Sarapieion archive together with that of Hor—than of historical reality; similarly, the paucity of early evidence from the city does much to obscure the real situation of the third century B.C. The apparent growth of contact between the king and Memphis, between

---

[192] *P. Corn.* 1.30-45, 79-80, visits to the Sarapieion on 6-9 and 27 January 257 B.C.; *P. Mich. Zen.* 31.4-6 (256/5 B.C.) with Wildung (1977a), 49-50, para. 25, for land; *P. Cair. Zen.* 59034 (257 B.C.), request for a Sarapis temple.

[193] Brady (1935), especially 34-41.

[194] Quaegebeur (1980a), 78-79, quoting the high priests and Vienna stele 172; De Meulenaere (1959b), within the administration.

[195] Fraser (1972), 1.267-68.

[196] *UPZ* 42.4, 18 (162 B.C.), both words; *UPZ* 109.11-12 (98 B.C.), a parousia the year before.

Ptolemy and priests, may therefore be an illusion. And yet that evidence which does survive to cover the three hundred years of Ptolemaic rule—the funerary stelae, for instance, of the high priests or of the Apis bulls—seems to confirm the picture of a growth of closer awareness between these two parties, reflected in more frequent royal visits to the city. With Rome in the wings, at home some solidarity might seem required.

Recorded royal visits may be roughly divided into those primarily undertaken for religious or ceremonial purposes and those in which a political or strategic aim was uppermost. Often, of course, the reasons for visits overlapped, with visits serving various ends. For, given its strategic position at the apex of the Delta, Memphis served as a key point between Alexandria and Syria to the east. It might similarly form a stopping place when the ultimate destination lay further up the Nile to the south.

Once Ptolemy I Soter left the city for Alexandria, Memphite visits of the early Ptolemies are rarely mentioned. Crown officials might travel on their circuits, but whereas under Ptolemy II Philadelphos the Zenon archive is full of information on both men and goods traveling north to Alexandria on the coast, a royal visit south is only once found here on record. Following the second Syrian war, in mid-July in 253 B.C., it seems the king was in the city; his presence there at such an unattractive time of year, during the rising of the flood, has plausibly been linked to the land settlements then being made for his soldiers in the nearby villages of the north east Fayum.[197] From the comparative comfort of the city with its palace, the aging king might be seen in person as the benefactor of his troops.

The next recorded occasion a Ptolemy spent time in the city was on the eve of Raphia, when again the Egyptian state faced the hostility of a Syrian king. War was in the air and, when in 219 B.C. Antiochus III seized Tyre and Ptolemais, Ptolemy IV Philopator set out for Memphis, which stood in the direct line of invasion.[198] This time the Syrian king withdrew but Ptolemaic arms were weak, and, gaining time to build up strength, the king's advisors Sosibios and Agathokles urged diplomatic openings with the foe. While, therefore, troops were gathered and drilled in Alexandria, the capital moved to Memphis, where envoys on both sides might remain in ignorance of preparations on the coast.[199] The deception worked, and on 22 June 217 B.C., in spite of losses, the Ptolemaic troops prevailed at Raphia. Returning home to Egypt in October, the king came down to Memphis; here, as already mentioned, on 15 November the synod of priests which gathered in the city passed in his honor that trilingual decree which recorded his victory (plate vi).

Perhaps the memories of this occasion were still alive when in 197 B.C., after his Alexandrian anakleteria, the young Ptolemy V Epiphanes was brought to Memphis to celebrate military success over the rebels as well as to undertake the Egyptian ceremonies for his succession to the throne. The presence of the priests from all of Egypt will have lent solemnity to the occasion, and the following four months of negotiations defined the reciprocal honors to be recorded on the Rosetta decree.[200] As seen already, in this visit of 197/6 B.C. politics and religion both were served.

The pattern was now set and, though unrest continued in the country, in 192/1 B.C. there was sufficient peace in Memphis for work finally to start on the vault of the Apis bull, which had already reached the advanced age of eighteen years.[201] The priests, now freed from the need to travel to Alexandria for their annual synod, came instead to Memphis, home of Ptah. It was here in late October 185 B.C. that the priests, gathered for the enthronement of the new Apis bull, raised the queen Kleopatra to a position of equality in the ruler cult. Others of that series of priestly decrees already noted as marking the reign of Ptolemy V Epiphanes may also emanate from synods in the city, with Ptolemy and his queen sometimes in attendance.

In 180 B.C. Ptolemy VI Philometor inherited the throne; ten years later a Syrian king again seized on internal weakness to invade. Conflict between the two sons of Epiphanes, Ptolemy VI Philometor and Ptolemy VIII Euergetes II, was to be a continuing refrain for the next twenty-five years. During the two invasions of Antiochus IV Epiphanes, Memphis again was a key center. Antiochus had reached some form of agreement with Philometor, and during his first invasion in 169 B.C. he had the elder Ptolemy with him; the younger brother, Euergetes II, ruled as king in Alexandria. Antiochus left the country and both sides appealed to Rome. In Egypt, however, events began to go against the Syrian king, for Philometor left Memphis for the capital, where he and his brother with haste patched up their differences, eventually showing solidarity against foreign invasion.[202] It was probably during his second invasion of 168 B.C.

[200] Note 72.
[201] Brugsch (1884), 130; see Appendix D.
[202] Polyb. 28.22-23; 29.23.4, with Walbank (1979), 357-60, on the invasions, and 396, for the reconciliation; Will (1982), 316-25, on both invasions.

that Antiochus had himself proclaimed king of Egypt, with a regular coronation at Memphis, where he now installed his military governor
Kleon.[203] The Syrian king's departure from the land in late July on Roman intervention was swiftly followed by a joint visit of state to Memphis
from the two brothers, with the aim of restoring confidence in the city
now that Antiochus' governor had gone.[204]

The joint reign of the two sons of Ptolemy V Epiphanes together with
Kleopatra II, wife of Philometor, was not an easy one. The retreat of the
Syrian king was soon followed by internal dissension and revolt. The effect of these troubles on the community of the Memphite Sarapieion will
be discussed in chapter 7;[205] here our concern is with the royal dimension
to the unrest. When in 164 B.C. the three rulers made a show of solidarity
in visiting Memphis together, their visit was, it seems, timed to coincide
with celebrations of 1 Thoth (3 October), the New Egyptian Year.[206]
Soon the two brothers were in conflict once more, and as the younger,
Euergetes II, began to prevail, Philometor followed the example of so
many Hellenistic kings and voyaged to Rome to beg for his kingdom.
With Roman help a compromise was established whereby Euergetes II
ruled in Cyrene. So, in Thoth 163 B.C., the elder brother Philometor and
his queen marked their return to power at home by taking up Memphite
residence.[207] New Year royal residences like these seem by now to be established and future visits to the city may frequently be seen to fall in
early Thoth.[208] In marking an important date in the religious calendar of
the country with a visit to the city and temples of Memphis, the king was
enjoying his freedom after the flood to sail again upon the Nile.[209] He was
also celebrating an Egyptian festival in an Egyptian center, which presumably gratified his Egyptian subjects and their priests.

The struggle with his younger brother continued, but Philometor remained king until his death in Syria in 145 B.C. When Euergetes II at last

[203] *Hor* 2 recto.9; verso.7-8; 3 verso.11 with Ray (1976), 125-29, for a lucid discussion of
the sources. *P. Köln* 4.186 may now be added to the military dossier.
[204] *Hor* 3 verso.20-23 written later with all references to the Brother (Euergetes II) suppressed, cf. *Hor* 3 recto.12; verso.10.
[205] See also Will (1982), 360-61.
[206] Wilcken (1927), 249-50.
[207] *UPZ* 41.4-5; 42.4; 5; 6; 20; *Hor* 3 recto, donatives to the ibis shrine perhaps at this date;
UPZ 111, amnesty up to 17 August 163 B.C.
[208] Thoth, 158 B.C.: *UPZ* 14; *Hor* 3, see introduction. Thoth 99 B.C.: *UPZ* 106 = *C. Ord.
Ptol.* 62 (15 October 99 B.C.); 109.11-12, visit of Ptolemy X Alexander, and Kleopatra Berenike puts everyone on their toes, *UPZ*, p. 467 n. 3. Many similar visits are probably
unrecorded.
[209] Pliny *HN* 5.10.57 with Bonneau (1961); Pliny may of course again be wrong; cf. chapter 1 with n. 118.

inherited the throne and shortly after married his brother's widow, Kleopatra II, he traveled to Memphis for his coronation, timing the occasion to coincide with the birth of Kleopatra's child, to be named Memphites.[210] The king, whose main support once came from the Alexandrian mob, now made a bid for a more widespread following in his kingdom. But all was not well and when, in 140/39 B.C., the roving ambassadors of Rome headed by Scipio Aemilianus visited Egypt at the start of their eastern tour, they were escorted up-river to Memphis. Here they admired the natural resources of a kingdom which could be so great if only rulers worthy of it could be found.[211]

It was clear the present rulers were not worthy when once again the land was torn apart by royal strife. Euergetes' marital problems and the different areas of support for his two wives, the mother Kleopatra II and her daughter Kleopatra III, kept the country in a state of tension. Memphite documents help to date the varying royal fortunes. As early as November 132 B.C. the split was public knowledge, with Kleopatra II dropped from the dating formula.[212] On 30 October 131 B.C. Euergetes II and Kleopatra III were still named in the dating of the Memphite marriage contract of the archentaphiast Petesis,[213] but eventually they fled to Cyprus, that haven of refugee Ptolemies. Here the king had summoned and murdered the young Memphites, his son by Kleopatra II. This exile did not last. Kleopatra II was holding on to Alexandria when Euergetes II returned to Egypt with his younger wife and took up residence in Memphis. It was from this city that the king, entrusting the command of his troops to the Egyptian general Paos, now planned an attack on the south, where a rebel native king, Harsiesis, had seized the opportunity to establish partial control in the Thebaid.[214] Launched from the home of Ptah, the attack on Thebes and Upper Egypt was eventually successful, and from late in 130 B.C. Euergetes II again controlled the south. Once more a Memphite base proved valuable and on the winning side,[215] and

---

[210] Diod. Sic. 33.13.

[211] Diod. Sic. 33.28b.3; Will (1982), 427-28.

[212] P. B.M. 10384 (3 November 132 B.C.) = App. B:7, Year 39 Phaophi 10.

[213] P. Leid. 373a + UPZ 128 = App. B:8, Year 40 Phaophi 6. Otto and Bengtson (1938), 70, connect this date with royal Memphite residence. Mørkholm (1975), 10-11, points to Euergetes II minting in Alexandria into Year 40. Will (1982), 429-32.

[214] Harsiesis: Koenen (1959); Pestman (1967), 58-61, for references and dates. Paos: W. Chrest. 10.8, against Hermonthis on 15 January 130 B.C.; OGIS 132 (130 B.C.); PP 197 = 132.

[215] The suggestion, Koenen (1968), 192, that the Potter's Oracle was put together around 130 B.C. is attractive in many ways; the primacy of Memphis over Alexandria fits well with

by the time of his death in June 116 B.C. an uneasy reconciliation between the king and his two wives had finally been reached.

In 88 B.C. the scenario was to be repeated. In 116 B.C. Ptolemy VIII Euergetes II had been succeeded by two sons and, like the two sons of Epiphanes, these sons could not agree on who should rule. For a brief period the two Kleopatras, mother and daughter, ruled with the elder son, Ptolemy IX Soter II. The king's younger brother Alexander was meanwhile based in Cyprus, while the queen who continued to rule with Soter II was probably Kleopatra III.[216] By the end of October 107 B.C. Ptolemy X Alexander had supplanted his elder brother on the throne. Soter II now, in turn, sought refuge in Cyprus, while in Egypt, until her death (allegedly at the hand of her son) in 101 B.C., Kleopatra III exercised an uneasy rule together with Alexander, who disregarded the Apis bull. Thus, Soter II now ruled in Cyprus, Alexander I in Alexandria (from 101 B.C. with Kleopatra Berenike), while a half-brother, Ptolemy Apion, held the kingdom of Cyrene; the political weakness of the Ptolemaic kingdom at the time stands symbolized in this tripartite division of territory. In 88 B.C. family tensions surfaced again when Soter made a final and successful bid to oust his brother and regain control of Egypt.[217] Thebes was again in revolt and Soter returned from Cyprus to find the country in distress and split in loyalties. Reacting swiftly to a need for confidence in the countryside, he made for Memphis, where he called on all the religious strength and support from Lower Egypt which that city might provide. Hierax, his general, was dispatched south to the home of Amon.[218] In Memphis, as already recorded, early in 86 B.C. Soter II was crowned a second time, celebrating here a traditional Egyptian jubilee festival, a tria-konteteris. In the south the final defeat of Thebes and of the rebels, in which the Pathyrite priests of Hathor no doubt rejoiced together with their lord, the king, was devastating.[219] In the third year of the revolt, Pausanias records, Ptolemy wrought such destruction that the Thebans retained nothing that might remind them of their earlier prosperity and success.[220]

---

contemporary events. But the material and maybe the form are much older; see chapter 3 n. 1.

[216] This is the traditional view of the classical authors (see Will 1982, 440-45), recently challenged by Cauville and Devauchelle (1984), 47-50, whose revision I cannot fully accept.

[217] Préaux (1936), 547-50; Samuel (1965), with the modifications of Mørkholm (1975), 14-15.

[218] W. Chrest. 12.8-16 (1 November 88 B.C.).

[219] SB 6300; 6644; W. Chrest. 12 (88 B.C.).

[220] Paus. 1.9.3.

Memphis and Lower Egypt had once more triumphed over the south, but this apparent triumph marks the weakness of the final Ptolemies. In spite of a large-scale building program in the south, undertaken in an attempt to regain support in the area, Upper Egypt was now effectively lost to central control, with power, as it were, delegated to a dynasty of native nomarchs.[221] Auletes might favor Memphis with his visits but control over the countryside was weak. Meanwhile, Rome grew strong in Egypt and finally, on 3 August 30 B.C., Octavian seized Alexandria. Imouthes/Petobastis IV, the sixteen-year-old high priest of Memphis, had died two days before.[222] There was a new power in Egypt.

For the Ptolemies, however, with their growing patronage of its cults and temples, their contacts, both ceremonial and personal, with the high priests, and their visits and residence in the city, Memphis had proved a city second only to Alexandria in importance. And by gradually assuming the role of pharaoh, this Macedonian dynasty had come to be identified with the country it ruled.

[221] For temple building at Edfu, Dendera, Kom Ombo, Philae, Athribis, and elsewhere, especially under Soter II and Auletes, see the indices in Porter and Moss (1937) and (1939). De Meulenaere (1959b); Shore (1979); the appointment of these strategoi to priesthoods in the dynastic cult is some measure of their incorporation in the Ptolemaic state.

[222] Skeat (1953), 98-100; B.M. stele 188 = Quaegebeur (1974), 66, no. 13 = Reymond (1981), no. 27.10-11.

PLATE i. The Apis bull.

PLATE ii. Apis on the move.

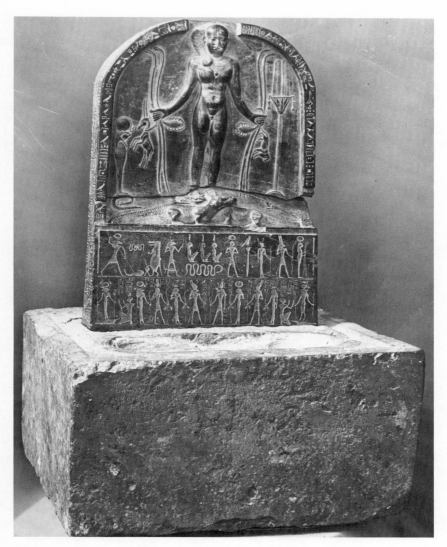

PLATE iii. Against snakes and scorpions.

PLATE iv. Drawing of an Astarte stele indicating the lost portion.

PLATE V. Chaiapis stele.

PLATE vi. Raphia stele.

PLATE vii. The Cretan dream interpreter.

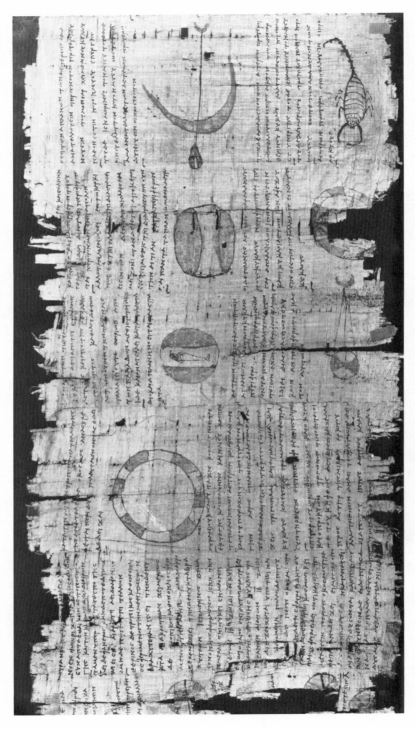

PLATE viii. "The Art of Eudoxos."

5

THE UNDERTAKERS

In charge of the necropolis was a supervisor, with many groups under his purview. Alongside the Memphite concern with the mummification and cult of the animal deities (see chapter 6) came the regular human embalming and undertaking business, in which Memphis probably differed little from other urban centres. As with all industries the quality of workmanship might vary and different payments bought different products. Both Herodotus and Diodorus Siculus give accounts of the possible costs and qualities of mummification, listing the tools and the ingredients used in the process. One raw material however, the human corpse, was in constant supply. The embalming industry was a steady one as long as religious beliefs demanded the preservation in death of the lifetime form of the individual.

There were many involved in this business, in many different capacities. Their status is not easy to disentangle through the philological uncertainties of the terminology used. For since embalming was an Egyptian practice, Egyptian terms will lie behind the Greek descriptive names and the looser usage of the imported language appears to cover a range of technical descriptions specified only in their Egyptian form. And within Egypt regional differences in terminology also occur. Herodotus already writes of skilled craftsmen involved in the trade, and Diodorus records that the *taricheutai* or embalmers were held in honor and high esteem; they mixed with the priests, had free entry to temples and were ritually pure.[1] Such were the men who form the subject of this chapter, important and substantial individuals within a society where they played a crucial role. Not all involved in the trade however enjoyed such respectability.

In Greek, when describing the process of mummification, Diodorus records a grammateus or scribe who marked up the cadaver before work was started on it. The *paraschistēs* did the preliminary work on the corpse; his role was necessary but violatory, and after cutting open the corpse he was subjected both to verbal abuse and physical violence.[2] Only after

[1] Hdt. 2.86, cf. 89.1, on necrophiliac tendencies; Diod. Sic. 1.91.1, *technitai*.
[2] Diod. Sic. 1.91; see *UPZ* 194-96 (119-116 B.C.) for disputes among the Theban *paraschistai*.

such a violation could the work of restoration go ahead. The men of An-oubis, the *rmt.w n Inp*, known from the demotic documents, whose trade this was, were one of the recognizable groups of the area, listed among the typical inhabitants of a Memphite settlement.[3]

These "men of Anoubis" or morticians might perform specialized functions. First, at least in the Memphite area, there were the undertak-ers, the "god's sealers" (*ḥtmw-ntr*) as they were known in Egyptian, prob-ably *entaphiastai* in Greek though the name does not actually occur in Memphis.[4] These may be the same as the *nekrotaphoi* for whom in the first century B.C. there survives the record of a trade association.[5] Indeed, the organization of these undertakers into trade associations is a regular feature. A professional oath from Hawara of a similar group in the first century B.C. shows two families grouped together to form a single professional association with eleven members.[6] The members promised to refrain from collecting corpses over which they had no rights, to per-form their undertakers' duties, to anoint with unguents, and to take re-sponsibility for mummification within specified localities. Provision was made for the payment of taxes, and penalties were laid down for noncom-pliance. Next, concerned with the provision of ritual objects, with liba-tions and the cult of the dead after burial, were the *choachytai* (*w3ḥ-mw*).[7] Rules for their trade associations are again known from elsewhere,[8] and in Memphis as at Thebes both men and women choachytai are recorded. These two groups of undertakers and libation pourers were closely asso-ciated; their families both worked together and intermarried.[9] The Greek

[3] *P. Louvre* E 3266.2.D and *passim* (197 B.C.) = App. B:2.
[4] Sauneron (1952); Pestman (1963); Reymond (1973), 140. *UPZ* 190.6 (98 B.C.), an *enta-phiastēs* from Thebes. The common but incorrect translation of *ḥtmw-ntr* as archentaphiast, e.g., Sethe (1920), 724, seems to derive from the title of Petesis, son of Chonouphis, *UPZ* 106-9 (99/8 B.C.); see n. 103 below.
[5] *P. Ryl.* 65 (67 B.C.), probably from Oxyrhynchos; *SB* 25; 5766; 5774, Panechates from Panopolis is called both entaphiastes and nekrotaphos.
[6] *P. Ash. dem.* 18 (70-60 B.C.), Reymond (1973).
[7] See Bataille (1952), 245-71.
[8] *P. Berlin dem.* 3115 (110-107 B.C.), the association of Amon of Opet at Djeme, see de Cenival (1972b), 103-35. All who had practiced as choachytai for ten years should join, and at sixteen years nonmembers were to be frozen out of practice; members and their families were protected in both life and death and regular meetings were held for communal, but strictly limited, drinking.
[9] Thebes: *UPZ* 190 (98 B.C.). Memphis: *P. Louvre* E 3266 (197 B.C.) = App. B:2, Taues, daughter of choachyte Peteimouthes married Samōus as her second undertaker husband. In *P. Louvre* 2409 (184 B.C.) = App. B:4 Aphynchis (fig. 7, level 7) has a choachytes, Tai-mouthes, as mother, but his father was presumably an undertaker. Perhaps daughters could inherit the position from their father but not their children in turn. For the close connection between these two groups, see Revillout (1880d).

term "taricheutai" (ḫrj-ḥb or reader-priests) seems to have been used in other contexts for those involved in the death industry; it might be applied to any of the more specialized groups concerned with the preservation of the human cadaver.[10]

Besides their names and cult associations, little is known of these specialized groups of necropolis workers. Since their trade was essentially Egyptian, they have left behind only a small trace in the Greek documentation, and the publication of demotic material still lags behind. An archive of demotic contracts from Memphis does, however, offer some possibility of glimpsing the social organization and working conditions of both the undertakers and choachytai who worked on the necropolis during the three centuries of Ptolemaic rule. Most of the contracts which form the basis of this chapter belong to a single archive shipped to Europe and sold there by Anastasi, an Armenian merchant from Alexandria, in the first half of the nineteenth century.[11] A first shipment of papyri and antiquities to Europe in 1828 formed the nucleus of the Egyptian collection in Leiden, and from a shipment ten years later, auctioned in London in 1839, the British Museum acquired various documents. Other parts of the archive may come from the Paris auction which followed Anastasi's death in 1857. This Undertakers' Archive is now scattered among European museums in Leningrad, Leiden, Paris, London, Innsbruck, Turin, and possibly elsewhere. The full publication of the archive, which runs from 203 to at least 65 B.C.,[12] will make possible further study, and the following comments and conclusions must remain tentative pending such a publication.

In the archive survive the papers of individuals from only five generations (fig. 7, levels 5–10) covering 130 years, but the information preserved in the contracts themselves, and especially in those involving Imouthēs and Shemti (level 6), the children of Tauēs by her two marriages, makes possible the reconstruction of a family tree which spans eleven generations and therefore goes back to the very beginning of the Ptolemaic period. It is striking that the earlier generations recorded in this Un-

---

[10] See *UPZ* 125.8-9 (89 B.C.), with an undertaker father; *P. Innsbruck*, lines 2–3, 8 (75 B.C.) = App. B:18 and *P. Louvre* 3268 (73 B.C.) = App. B:19, for Ptahmaacherou (fig. 7, level 7) as ḫrj-ḥb; *P. Leid.* 374 i.15; ii.12 (78 B.C.) = App. B:17. For the organization of these reader-priests/god's sealer-embalmers at Hawara, see *P. Ash. dem.* 18 (70-60 B.C.) with Reymond (1973), 25. In discussing a demarcation agreement, Shore and Smith (1960), 277–94, comment on the specialization of different workers. On necropolis workers and functions generally, see Bataille (1952), 181–283.

[11] Dawson (1949), 158–60.

[12] See Appendix B with figures 7-11.

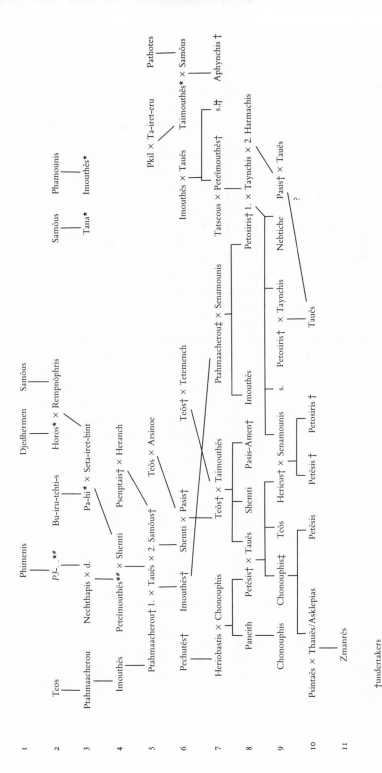

FIGURE 7. The undertakers.

dertakers' Archive were choachytai rather than undertakers; they seem to have belonged to the important family which, for at least two generations, provided the supervisor of the necropolis—an important post, to judge from its name.[13] In the latter half of the period choachytai appear to give way to undertakers. This change of course is simply the consequence of the succession to this particular set of family deeds[14] rather than the reflection of any general phenomenon. Work for both undertakers and choachytai continued throughout the period.

Other documents concerning Memphite choachytai provide information on families which span the period of conquest and early Macedonian Memphis, before the king moved to Alexandria. One papyrus for the reign of Alexander IV (316–304 B.C.), at present the earliest known demotic document from Ptolemaic Memphis, records a family with three earlier generations, a family which may therefore be traced back to the early years of the fourth century B.C.;[15] and two further, interrelated documents from the mid-third century B.C. contain genealogies going back for four generations, to the mid-fourth century B.C., well before Alexander's conquest (figs. 8–10).[16] Although on the present evidence it is not possible to attach these families of choachytai to those recorded in the main Undertakers' Archive, they perhaps formed part of the same original cache and do, in any case, provide evidence for at least some continuity on the necropolis from the period before the arrival of the Greeks. It is the more extensive Undertakers' Archive together with these earlier documents of choachytai which forms the basis for the following discussion.

THE DOCUMENTS

The undertakers' papers consist mainly of legal documents—marriage and property contracts and papers used in legal proceedings. In Egyptian law the ability to produce the relevant deed was essential to uphold a claim. The written document was a precious possession and might be named in bequests alongside other family heirlooms.[17] "Do not disdain

[13] See Bataille (1952), 271-73, on this post in Thebes.
[14] The composition of the archive is discussed below.
[15] *P. Louvre* 2412 = App. B:29.
[16] *P. Leid.* 379 + *UPZ* 126 (2 March 256 B.C.) = App. B:30; *P. Bruss.* 3 (256 B.C.) = App. B:31.
[17] For example, *P. B.M.* 10229.11 (78 B.C.) = App. B:16, for title; *P. Leid.* 381.3 (226 B.C.) = App. B:23; *P. Bibl. Nat.* 225.3 (68 B.C.) = App. B:21, for inheritance; Pestman (1983), 293-94.

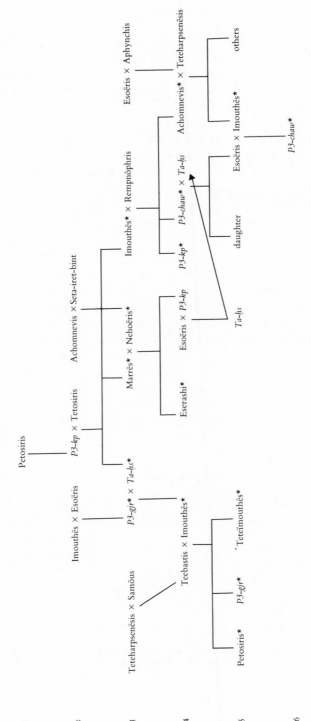

FIGURE 8. Choachytai in *P. Leid.* 379 + *P. Bruss.* 3.

your papyrus documents, (even) when to have force they are too old," was the wisdom taught.[18] Any change in ownership or control of family interests was recorded in writing; contracts were exchanged between all relevant parties, duly witnessed, and guaranteed by other interested members of the family.

Within this archive the two main groups of contracts preserved are those recording a division of property and those accompanying a formalization of marriage. There are other documents, too—a loan contract and a lease and documents relating to legal disputes. In property contracts, two different forms of documents were required to establish title, neither being fully effective without the other. The first took the form of a receipt issued by the first party to the second for payment in respect of the object concerned; this document of sale had to be accompanied by a formal renunciation of interest in the object also drawn up by the "vendor," a renunciation or release which was in effect a recognition of the rights of the second party over the object which had been "sold."[19] In any division of family property or change in family circumstance, all interested parties would make and receive such pairs of contracts in an attempt to safeguard their separate rights. When several children or other relatives were involved, this resulted in contracts full of cross-reference to other such documents (both receipts and release declarations) recording the same agreement. That the receipts issued in these transactions often mark what is only a fictitious sale is suggested both by the total absence from the record of sums actually paid and by the close relationships existing between the individuals who "sell" each other property and then recognize the other's rights, thereby confirming a division.[20]

The result of the legal forms is a staggering proliferation of paperwork and a mass of documentation. A family archive might be very bulky indeed. So, for instance, in Pharmouthi (May–June) 197 B.C. the two children of Tauēs—Imouthēs, her son by Ptahmaacherou, and Shemti, her daughter by Samōus—together with their mother (fig. 7, levels 5–6), drew up a series of documents to govern their holding of family property. Tauēs herself came from a family of choachytai, but both of her husbands were undertakers and Imouthēs also succeeded to this profession. The

---

[18] P. Louvre 2414.5a-6 in Hughes (1982), 53; Vleeming (1983) gives a somewhat different translation.
[19] M. Grund. 167; Seidl (1962), 51; Pestman (1969), 62. The Greek terms were (1) either ōnē or prasis and (2) (syngraphē) apostasiou.
[20] So already Revillout (1897), 503.

property concerned came variously from Tauēs herself, from her family going back to the generation of her great-grandparents, and from each of her husbands. This particular set of contracts was not the first in which her children had taken an active part. Already in Mecheir (March–April) 199 B.C. Imouthēs had issued both a receipt and recognition of rights to his half-sister Shemti over her one-quarter share of property—a funerary chapel and attached revenues—from his father, which had perhaps come to Shemti though her husband Pasis.[21] From 197 B.C., however, two of the documents drawn up have actually survived. In *P. Louvre* E 3266 (App. B:2), with Tauēs acting as guarantor, Imouthēs recognizes Shemti's rights over slightly varying proportions (from one-third to one-half) of a series of individual pieces of property which came from their mother's family of choachytai, while in *P. Louvre* 2408 (App. B:3), again with Tauēs as guarantor, Imouthēs recognizes Shemti's right to half of the inheritance of her father Samōus, Tauēs' second husband,[22] and to half of the property from Tauēs herself. In the second case the receipt of "sale" accompanies the release document, and in the course of the contracts many related documents are mentioned. From these references it is possible to reconstruct the complete set of twenty separate contracts drawn up at this time, thereby illustrating the immense legal activity in which Egyptians of substance regularly engaged.[23] For this is but one of many similar settlements.

The two documents which have survived for the children of Tauēs were probably preserved among the family papers of Shemti, whose husband's papers were merged in the archive inherited by her son. Two out of twenty contracts represents a survival rate of 10 percent. But in fact the rate is rather 3.3 percent of the total number of documents, since each of these contracts must have been written out in triplicate—one for each of the two parties and one for official deposition. So in recording this agreement between half-brother and half-sister, on this particular occasion a total of at least sixty documents must have been prepared.[24] We

---

[21] *P. Louvre* 2408 (197 B.C.) = App. B:3, refers to both receipt and release contracts; the documents referred to in *P. Louvre* E 3266.12.C–D may be connected with this earlier transaction. For one-fourth of this property belonging to Pasis in 204/3 B.C., see *P. Leid* 373b–c = App. B:1.

[22] There may have been a second child by this marriage not mentioned in either of the surviving contracts or maybe Samōus retained half of his income for his wife (Pestman 1961, 124).

[23] Appendix C.

[24] Cf. *P. Cairo dem.* 30602-3 (115 B.C.), representing two out of twenty-four property contracts or 8.3 percent of those drawn up between the descendants of the tradesman

unfortunately have no idea how many other families were living (and drawing up contracts) on the necropolis at this time, nor do we know the normal scribal production rate for such documents. It does, however, appear that the single official scribe of the Anoubieion, the *monographos*, did not go short of work.[25]

A further, less common, form of document recording property transfer is the gift or endowment form of contract.[26] There are only two examples of this among the Memphite contracts published or described to date. In *P. Vienna* 3874 in 149/8 B.C. the undertaker Teōs, son of Pasis and Shemti (fig. 7, level 7), endowed his daughter Tauēs with half of his property; his second daughter, Shemti, receives the other half and his wife Taimouthēs guarantees the gift.[27] Earlier, from among the choachytai documents, is *P. Leid.* 379 (256 B.C.), in which Petosiris (fig. 8, level 5), the eldest son of Imouthēs and Teebastis, uses this form of contract to divide property from his father's side of the family between himself (one-third plus one-twelfth) and his sister Teteïmouthēs (one-fourth); his brother *P3-gjr* received the other one-third (see fig. 9).[28] There is nothing in the Memphite documents to refute the view of Revillout that this was a form of contract used only by fathers and eldest sons acting as head of the family.

More temporary transfers of property within the family might be governed by lease agreements. Such, it appears, was the Malcolm papyrus of 3 November 132 B.C. recording a renewal for three years of an earlier lease for ten years drawn up in September 144 B.C. between the present lessor's father and the same lessees.[29] A block of family property which came to the undertaker Imouthēs, son of Ptahmaacherou (fig. 7, level 8), and from him to the parties of the present lease is thus temporarily reassigned. Such leases might, however, be constantly renewed, thus making for the easier administration of property split by partible inheritance.

It is marriage contracts, in the widest sense of the term, which form the second most common type of document within the Undertakers' Ar-

---

Horma, son of Teos and Taapis; of actual written documents (seventy-two) this is 2.8 percent. The composition of archives is the crucial factor in determining the rate.

[25] See Wilcken (1927), 602–3; Zauzich (1968).

[26] Revillout (1897), 512; Seidl (1962), 51.

[27] App. B:5. Reymond (1973), 37, draws attention to the fact that the son, known from *P. B.M.* 10398 = App. B:9 (120/19 B.C.), is omitted from the division; it is possible he was not yet born.

[28] App. B:30. On this unequal division, see n. 62.

[29] *P. B.M.* 10384 = App. B:7 to be published by C. J. Martin. Revillout's interpretation of this as a loan contract is not supported by the full transcript.

chive. Marriage in itself needed no contract, and legal enactments were made only when there was property or children involved. Under this heading therefore come deeds which regulate the legal and economic relations between husband and wife and provide for their children. Such agreements were regularly addressed by the husband either to the wife or, in one case, possibly her father,[30] and it was through these that provisions were made for the transfer and inheritance of the family property. Only six marriages with deeds are recorded in the Memphite material, but the legal forms are known from other parts of the country.[31]

In Middle and Lower Egypt of the Ptolemaic period the marriage contract between husband and wife regularly involved a dowry payment by the wife, while on his side the husband made certain undertakings. From Memphis come two main forms of contract. First there is the deed, probably made at the time of marriage, in which in return for a dowry payment the husband accepts the woman as wife; the eventuality of divorce is then provided for with details of maintenance payments in the event of the nonreturn of the dowry. This contract was normally guaranteed by the husband's father or mother and retained in the possession of the wife.[32] For the sake of convenience I shall term this the alimony type of contract. Next comes the agreement which was regularly made at a later stage of the relationship, often when a child or children had been born to the couple. This agreement consisted of two separate documents: first a receipt issued by the husband to his wife for a payment specified in silver deben in return for which he endows her with all his property,[33] and second an agreement he makes concerning her daily maintenance as his wife, sometimes with provisions also made for the inheritance of their sons, or future male children.[34] (This last clause is surprising since it is clear from

[30] *UPZ* 118 (83 b.c.), in the record of Greek legal proceedings, preserves the essence of a maintenance contract made between Psintaes and Chonouphis, son of Petesis, the father of Thaues/Asklepias,; see below. Contrary to Pestman (1961), 45-46, I would identify Thaues/Asklepias (who together with her son Zmanres guarantees the agreement) with Psintaes' wife (*UPZ* 118.10-11); cf. *P. Leid.* 381. 4 (226 b.c.) = App. B:23. The original contract may have been in demotic, with Chonouphis acting for his daughter only in the Greek legal proceedings.

[31] Lüddeckens (1960); Pestman (1961), with earlier bibliography. The deed between Setne and Tabubu in the Setne Romance, Lichtheim (1980), 135, records a seventh (Pestman 1961, C4).

[32] Pestman (1961), type B.

[33] Pestman (1961), type C. Since, however, no deed of release is made, this only represents a provisional conveyance of property, a *proprasis,* cf. Pestman (1961), 41.

[34] *Syngraphē trophitis* in Greek. Memphite examples of this type: *P. Leid.* 381 (226 b.c.) = App. B:23, receipt only; *P. Louvre* 2149, receipt + 3265 (102 b.c.), support (App. B:10); *UPZ* 118 (83 b.c.), support; *P. Bibl. Nat.* 224, receipt + 225 (68 b.c.), support (App. B:21).

the records of property divisions that daughters, too, regularly inherited; perhaps "sons" included "daughters"). I term this the support type of marriage agreement, and in the strict sense it is not a marriage contract. It may, however, be considered here as regulating the legal and economic relations between husband and wife.

From Memphis there are no examples of both alimony and support contracts being made by the same couple, but evidence from Siut in one case records both forms of contract made at an interval of six months.[35] The two sorts of deeds must have served different purposes. Their detailed provisions will be discussed below.

Such then are the major forms of demotic contract found in the Undertakers' Archive. Many of the later deeds also have a Greek docket recording their registration at the office of the Anoubieion in Memphis. It was in the autumn of 146 B.C., in what was to be the last year of Ptolemy Philometor's life, that an order was issued that demotic documents prepared by the monographos were to be copied, docketed in Greek, and registered in the official archives.[36] Theban evidence records a 5 percent *enkyklion* tax on property transfers dating from before this new order; later evidence is for a 10 percent tax.[37] It may well be that, hard-pressed by the continuing struggle with his younger brother, Philometor (or his advisors) saw the possibility of raising increased revenue from this new procedure of registration. Whatever the purpose, the effect was to extend governmental control over the lives of the Egyptian-speaking inhabitants of the country. To be valid, contracts now had to be deposited and filed. Officially annotated second copies were returned to the contracting parties, and it is these which have survived in family archives. Greek translations of properly registered demotic documents now began to be used by their owners in Greek lawsuits,[38] and in yet one more respect the Egyptians found themselves in contact with and subject to the Greek-speaking administration.

The grapheion or registry of the Anoubieion on the Memphite necro-

For further details of the contract form, see Pestman (1961), table C. Sons are named in all Memphite examples, with two sons in *P. Bibl. Nat.* 224 (68 B.C.).

[35] *P. B.M.* 10593 (19 January 172 B.C.) with a dowry of 110 deben; 10594 (18 July 172 B.C.) with a wife's payment of 21 silver deben, Pestman (1961), B5 and C10.

[36] *P. Par.* 65 = Wilcken (1927), 596-603.

[37] *UPZ* 163-66 (182-152 B.C.), *eikostē; UPZ* 168.3 (121 B.C.), *dekatē.* In *UPZ* 129 (124 B.C.) from Memphis Timotheios and his associates may be the tax officials.

[38] *UPZ* 118 (83 B.C.); *UPZ* 160-62 (119-117 B.C.), quoting documents back to 182 B.C. (*UPZ* 163-69). *UPZ* 114 (86 B.C.), the Zois papyri, preserves Greek documents which must have come into the family papers when they moved house.

polis may actually date from the period of this reform, though in other respects the temple already served as an administrative center. There was a further registry office down in Memphis where both Greek and demotic contracts were filed,[39] but, given the nature of the necropolis community, most depositions in the office of the Anoubieion would be in demotic. The organization of this grapheion is not known in detail, but several individuals, all with Greek names (though not necessarily of Greek nationality), are recorded as docketing contracts there in the period 131–64 B.C.[40] The main appointment was probably that of *antigrapheus*, and the surviving sample suggests that only one official at a time normally held this post, with at least one subordinate representative. The office was not a large one. But in using a temple complex for an official government office, the Ptolemaic authorities exploited a well-established practice; temple registration was used to validate a contract.

Duly docketed and registered, these demotic contracts were preserved among the undertakers' family papers and buried by sand until their rediscovery in the nineteenth century A.D. What is to be learned from these contracts and the few related Greek papyri? They do, of course, provide a rich source of evidence for Egyptian law, and the forms and vocabulary of many of these contracts have been much studied by demotic legal scholars. In other respects, the evidence of legal documents is limited, limited both in scope and in quality. They do, however, enable us to begin to investigate the economic base of this specialized necropolis community, their family structure and patterns of inheritance, and to inquire into living standards and glimpse changes there and the reasons for them. These are the concerns of this chapter.

THE ECONOMIC BASE

The livelihood and assets of the "men of Anoubis" were of a somewhat peculiar nature. "House, land, courtyard, real estate, wall, building plot,

---

[39] *UPZ* 125.7 (89 B.C.); 127 (135 B.C.) may be the docket to a demotic contract from this office.

[40] From the Anoubieion: *P. Hermitage* with *P. Ross. Georg.*, vol 2. 5 (6 August 135 B.C.), Iason; *P. B.M.* 10384 (11 November 132 B.C.), Philotas with Hermaiskos, his representative; *UPZ* 128 (30 October 131 B.C.), Theon with Herakleides, his representative; 129 (13 October 124 B.C.), Herakleides; *P. Pavese* 1120 = App. B:26 (22 August 118 B.C.), Herakleides with Apollonios, his representative; *UPZ* 130-31 (6 April 115 B.C.), Diphilos; *UPZ* 132-34, Pestman, *Recueil* 6 and *P. Louvre* 2419 = App. B:10 (6 February 108–13 February 102 B.C.), Herakleides; *UPZ* 135 (15 January 78 B.C.), Tauron (see *PP* 7892a); 136 (23 November 75 B.C.), Areios; 137-38 (2 September 68 B.C.), Theon (perhaps the representative of Areios); 139-42 (5 November 65–8 December 64 B.C.), Areios.

orchard, vineyard, servant, maidservant, all household effects, possessions, deeds, contracts, agreements with any free person" was how on 2 September 68 B.C. the undertaker Herieus, son of Petēsis and Thauēs (fig. 7, level 9), baldly described his worldly goods (both moveable and immoveable) to his wife Senamounis in what was probably a standard form of contract.[41] The emoluments and possessions of an undertaker were those connected with his trade; they consisted of embalming sheds on the necropolis, funeral chapels where ceremonies were performed for the dead, and rights to funerary functions—above all mummification—over specified households, villages, or sections of the population, with all the profits attached to this employment. A family's wealth might be calculated in the number of prospective mummies it controlled; these were the assets inherited and divided among members of the family. In Greek they were *leitourgiai*, *karpeiai*, and *logeiai*—priestly functions, emoluments, and perquisites.[42]

The headland of North Saqqara (fig. 4) is of limited size, measuring about 3 kilometers north to south and 1.5 kilometers east to west; distances were not great, and different branches of the family of the Undertakers' Archive seem to have lived in different areas of the necropolis. Although the identity between ownership and actual residence is nowhere made explicit, houses belonging to earlier generations of the family appear to have been located in the Anoubieion, that large temple enclosure on the eastern edge of the headland.[43] One branch of a later generation probably moved, and when Chonouphis, son of Petēsis (fig. 7, level 9), is described as "one of the embalmers from the Asklepieion near Memphis," the natural assumption is that the temple enclosure of Imouthēs/ Asklepios nearer to the cultivation had now become his home.[44] The great enclosure walls of these various temple areas of the headland, which are featured in property descriptions,[45] will have provided protection against the fierce sandstorms which blow in the area. The communities of these temple towns were always very mixed, and just as it was not only "men of Anoubis" who lived in the Anoubieion,[46] so too these undertak-

---

[41] *P. Bibl. Nat.* 225.2-3 (App. B:21); cf. Pestman (1961), 120, for the formula.
[42] Wilcken (1957), 130.
[43] *P. Leid.* 378 (160 B.C.) = App. B:24; *P. Vienna* 3874 (149/8 B.C.) = App. B:5; *P. Innsbruck* (75 B.C.) = App. B:18; *P. Louvre* 3268 and 3264 ter (73 B.C.) = App. B:19-20, two houses east of the sanctuary wall, near the *dromos*.
[44] *UPZ* 125.8-9 (89 B.C.); Wilcken argues he was merely on the temple staff; see below.
[45] *P. Louvre* 2412.4 (316–304 B.C.) = App. B:29; *P. Leid.* 378 (160 B.C.) = App. B:24.
[46] See chapter 1 n. 102.

ers and choachytai might make their home elsewhere on the necropolis. The actual premises used for mummification seem to have lain outside the temple enclosures, separate and away from the living quarters of its practitioners.[47] The funerary chapels of the choachytai were up on the main spine of the necropolis, close to the Isis temple,[48] with embalming sheds and other related structures scattered over the area.[49]

The houses where the embalmers lived huddled together in close proximity were normally made of mud-brick, with doors and windows specified in descriptions. In one case where a brother and sister are recorded as owners of adjacent houses in the Anoubieion, the brother, in the smaller house to the south, is expressly forbidden the construction of a window in the north wall of his house which might penetrate his sister's property.[50] For measurement the divine cubit (0.525 meters) was used, and recorded house sizes range from 14.2 square meters to 138.9 square meters.[51] The most common size is in the range of 19–22 square meters, and might include storehouses or granaries placed above the door.[52] In the case of the two houses in the Anoubieion inherited by the children of Petosiris and Taynchis (fig. 7, levels 8-9) there were shops, storage rooms, and a mill to the west, while to the east an empty building plot contained an oven where bread might be baked for the family, or for wider use.[53] As today in the villages of Egypt, houses might have large courtyards in front of them.[54]

The greatest assets of the choachytai and undertakers remained the inhabitants of the area whom they viewed as prospective mummies. The funerary interests of the family of the archive stretched over most of the

---

[47] So too at Kusis; see Dunand (1985), 121-23.

[48] *P. Leid.* 379 (256 B.C.) = App. B:30, two chapels in an area close to the Isis temple described as in the south necropolis (perhaps the Giza necropolis was considered the north necropolis). They might live elsewhere, *P. Louvre* 2412 (316–304 B.C.) = App. B:29, in the temple of the Peak.

[49] *P. Bruss.* 3 (238 B.C.) = App. B:31, near the necropolis road; *P. Leid.* 373b–c (203 B.C.) = App. B:1, shrine with burial chamber and garden dug out of the mountain west of the dromos of Anoubis; *P. Louvre* E 3266.1.H–L (197 B.C.) = App. B:2, 3 funerary buildings with enclosure, three shops and adjacent sheds, on the necropolis; *P. B.M.* 10384.4–5, 10-12 (132 B.C.) = App. B:7; *P. Leid.* 380a–b (64 B.C.) = App. B:28.

[50] *P. Leid.* 378.7 (160 B.C.) = App. B:24.

[51] *P. Louvre* 3268 (73 B.C.) = App. B:19, 5 by 10.33 divine cubits; *P. Leid.* 378 (160 B.C.) = App. B:24, 24 by 21 divine cubits.

[52] *P. Leid.* 378 (160 B.C.) = App. B:24.

[53] *P. Innsbruck* (75 B.C.) and *P. Louvre* 3268 (73 B.C.) = App. B:18–19. The slightly different measurements of the houses here probably reflect the inclusion of storerooms in the earlier case.

[54] *P. Louvre* 2412 (316–304 B.C.) = App. B:29, a courtyard of 930.2 square meters.

Memphite nome, for the Memphite necropolis clearly provided a funerary center for the area. Listed in detail were the villages, families, and dependents over whom they possessed exclusive rights. In 197 B.C. these included the inhabitants of two villages of Ouenchem to the north of the nome, of two villages on the New Land of Ptah in the central district of Memphis (the Akhi-of-Heriatoum and the Arsenal), of the Quarter of the Greeks to the northwest of Memphis, and of the Naukratite settlement there.[55] Another document records rights over the Carians.[56] Such funerary interests continued to be inherited, ceded, divided, and leased throughout the period of the archive.

FAMILY AND INHERITANCE

The undertakers themselves appear through their legal documents as a close and endogamous group, in which profession and property were inherited vertically, with marriage used as a means of reinforcing the family control of both. But whereas property passed to both sons and daughters, the profession went only through the male line.

In contrast, in the case of the choachytai both profession and property were inherited by sons and daughters alike, and among this group property inheritance assumes a more complex form, with some evidence for lateral inheritance which is not found among the undertakers. Partible inheritance was the rule for both groups (and presumably in the society as a whole), and many individuals might have stakes in the same funerary chapels, buildings, or mortuary interests.

Two features of the property documents that cause problems of interpretation require preliminary comment. First, the lack of information on the actual occasion of the property divisions recorded means that the stage at which children regularly inherited from their parents is unknown. Property divisions may often have followed on the death of a father or mother, or they may be connected with the marriage of a sister, the death of a brother, or some other event of significance for the family. And although the name of the guarantor, who is always an interested party, occasionally gives a clue as to the reason for the division, the reason

---

[55] *P. Louvre* E 3266 (197 B.C.) = App. B:2. On Ouenchem, see chapter 2 n. 188 above; on the Naukratite settlement, Yoyotte (1982/83), 132. For the Greeks, *P. Louvre* E 3266.8.Q (197 B.C.), see also *P.B.M.* 10384.8-10 (132 B.C.) = App. B:7 and *P. Innsbruck* line 8 (75 B.C.) = App. B:18 with Yoyotte (1972), 4. *P. Pavese* 1120 (118 B.C.) = App. B:26 records interests in the eastern part of the nome.

[56] *P. B.M.* 10384.9 (132 B.C.) = App. B:7.

for any particular contract generally remains obscure. Arrangements made at an earlier date may be reaffirmed on a later occasion, following a change in family circumstances.[57]

Second, there is the paucity of vocabulary for family terms. Demotic has words only for mother, father, brothers, sister, son, and daughter, which, combined with the practice of tracing property back, regularly to grandparents and in one case to great-great-grandparents ("the father of the mother of the father of the mother"), serves to bemuse the modern interpreter.[58] It is not surprising generations are sometimes omitted.[59]

A typical property division is *P. Leid.* 379 from 2 March 256 B.C., already mentioned as preserved among the papers of the choachytai.[60] The family stemma is reconstructed in figure 9, and both the contracting parties are choachytai. Petosiris, the eldest son of Imouthēs and Teebastis, confirms his sister Teteïmouthēs in her quarter portion of their inheritance, which comes from their relatives as specified A–L. Such a division might suppose the recent death of their father. *P3-gjr*, the other brother, receives ⅓ of the inheritance while Petosiris himself keeps ⅓ + ¹⁄₁₂. The guarantors are their mother Teebastis and, in this case, *P3-gjr*, with whom separate contracts were made at the same time. The actual property in which A–L previously had interests is described first in general terms as "houses, buildings plots, tombs dug out of the mountain, built tombs, burials, emoluments and priestly functions." And these are then specified as

> Two tombs dug out of the mountain (with neighbors given), near the temple of Isis
> A built tomb provided with a roof in the southern part of the necropolis (with neighbors given), on the dromos of the Anoubieion
> A built tomb provided with a roof in the southern part of the Memphite necropolis (with neighbors listed), on the avenue of [king] Shabaka
> A further built tomb workshop known as the Workshop of *Ta-[.]j* situated on the necropolis (with neighbors)
> The built tomb of Atum
> The enclosure known as that of *Pa-mn*
> The burials performed by *Pa-wtn* son of Paapis

[57] *P. B.M.* 10398 (120/19 B.C.) = App. B:9 reaffirms a division between the two daughters of Teos and Taimouthes (fig. 7, levels 7–8) made at an earlier date, *P. Vienna* 3874 (149/8 B.C.) = App. B:5, Reymond (1973), 37; *P. B.M.* 10384 (132 B.C.), which reaffirms a lease made thirteen years before, may have been occasioned by the death of Petosiris' father. See Pestman (1969) on how the laws of succession worked.
[58] Willems (1983), 153; cf. *P. Louvre* E 3266.1.H (197 B.C.) = App. B:2.
[59] E.g., *P. Louvre* E 3266.8.D, 10.D (197 B.C.).
[60] App. B:30 (with *UPZ* 126). I am grateful to P. W. Pestman for the translation.

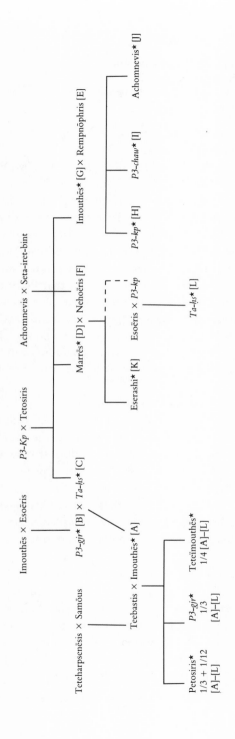

FIGURE 9. The property division of *P. Leid.* 379.

The liturgy village[61] *T3mnj* in the Memphite nome
All from the temples in the same liturgy village
The people of the Memphite nome and all the people who come [under their control]

The description again becomes very general with the repetition of priestly offices, emoluments, and other interests.

The relatives from whom these interests come are, by modern Western standards, fairly extended. The inheritance from *Ta-ḥs* (L), of the same generation as the contracting parties but related only through great grandparents suggests that her father *P3-kp* (known as the son of Marres only from *P. Bruss.* 3 = App. B:31) is already deceased. However, the names of the grandparents and the other related owners of that generation seem to have remained attached to the property. The natural assumption from such a pattern of inheritance would seem to be that Petosiris, *P3-gjr*, and Teteïmouthēs were the only survivors of their generation. That this was not the case becomes clear from *P. Bruss.* 3 (November–December 238 B.C.), a later property document from the same family. The inheritance patterns among these choachytai were far from simple, and somehow in 256 B.C. *Ta-ḥs'* inheritance went to the three children of Imouthēs and Teebastis.

The property division recorded in *P. Bruss.* 3 is illustrated in figure 10. The contracting parties are the two daughters of *P3-chaw*, himself the elder son of Imouthēs and Rempnōphris, and of his wife, the daughter of *P3-kp*, who is probably to be identified with the *Ta-ḥs* just met. Esoëris confirms her sister (name unknown) in ½ + ⅒ (= ⅗) of property coming from various relatives (A–F on fig. 10); she herself has ⅓ + 1/15 (⅖) of the same inheritance. Her husband Imouthēs and son *P3-chaw* act as guarantors. The smaller portion for Esoëris may be explained on the hypothesis that she had already received a dowry from the family on marriage.

The daughters of *P3-chaw* are themselves of the same generation as the contracting parties of *P. Leid.* 379 (fig. 9), and several of the relatives from whom they received their inheritance are the same as those in the earlier document. Unfortunately, the specification of the property in the Brussels papyrus is only very general: "all animals, all emoluments, all contracts, all title deeds, all burial chambers, funerary chapels, priestly functions, sources of income" (line 3), and the only detailed description of

---

[61] A village where the choachytai had sole rights for their priestly functions.

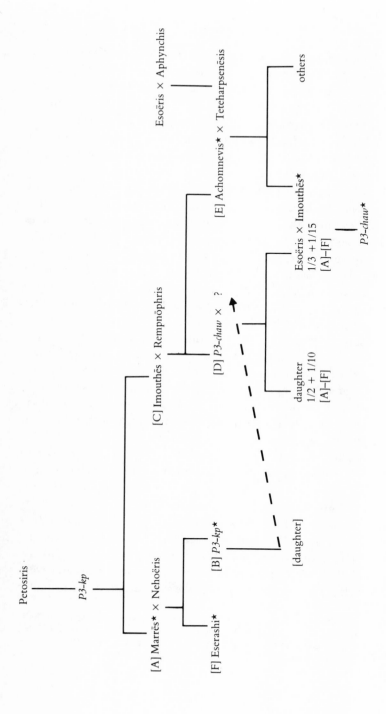

Petosiris

P3-kp

[A] Marrēs ★ × Nehoēris

[F] Eserashi ★

[B] P3-kp ★

[daughter]

[C] Imouthēs × Rempnōphris

[D] P3-chaw × ?

daughter
1/2 + 1/10
[A]–[F]

Esoēris × Imouthēs
1/3 + 1/15
[A]–[F]

P3-chaw ★

[E] Achomnevis ★ × Teteharpsenēsis

Esoēris × Aphynchis

others

★ choachytai (others may have held this rank)
[A]–[F] property divided

FIGURE 10. The property division of P. Bruss. 3.

property, that of Marrēs, son of *P3-kp*, in line 4, does not allow identification with any part of the property specified in *P. Leid.* 379. In both cases the neighbors were all choachytai, but the actual properties cannot be identified. Whoever may actually have worked in the embalming houses or practiced their offices in the burial chambers and funerary chapels, the profits must have been divided among many different members of the family. Inheritance involved division, and division is potentially contentious. Legally valid records were essential.

The different proportions into which an inheritance was divided raise further questions. In the division illustrated in figure 9, Petosiris, as elder brother, receives more than either his brother or sister; other examples exist for such preferential treatment for eldest sons.[62] The fact that Teteïmouthēs, the daughter, receives less than either of her brothers may suggest that, like Esoëris in figure 10, she had already received part of her inheritance as a dowry, for normally sons and daughters inherited in equal parts. The family property thus might pass to the next generation either during the parents' lifetime or on their death.

Other reasons may lie behind the unequal division of inheritance between children which is sometimes recorded; they can rarely be known for sure. There are, for instance, two cases from the Undertakers' Archive where sons seem voluntarily excluded from a family inheritance. *P. Vienna* 3874 (149/8 B.C.),[63] as mentioned earlier, records the equal division of their father's property (both moveable and immoveable) between Tauēs and Shemti (fig. 7, level 8), the two daughters of Teōs and Taimouthēs. A papyrus from thirty years later, *P. B.M.* 10398 (120/19 B.C.),[64] is the recognition by the girls' brother of this same division in which he makes no personal claim to the property; their mother Taimouthēs is the guarantor in both cases. Similarly, in *P. Innsbruck* (75 B.C.)[65] Taynchis (fig. 7, level 8) "sells" her daughter Senamounis one-fourth of the property which comes to her from her husband Petosiris, from her father Peteimouthēs, and from her uncle who is her father's brother. Her other two daughters guarantee the arrangement and were themselves each the recipient of $\frac{1}{4}$ + $\frac{1}{8}$ of the same property. The smaller

---

[62] In *P. Louvre* E 3266 (197 B.C.) = App. B:2 Imouthes receives $1/3$ + $1/24$ and his half-sister Shemti only $1/3$. In *P. Hermitage* 1122.6 (135 B.C.) = App. B:6 the property is divided $2/3$ to $1/3$ between the elder and younger brother. A reference to this Egyptian practice is found in *P. Enteux.* 18.4 (223/2 B.C.); see Seidl (1965); Pestman (1969), 66.

[63] App. B:5.

[64] App. B:9.

[65] App. B:18.

portion of Senamounis cannot this time be explained on the assumption that she is the only married daughter since her sister Taynchis is recorded as married, herself with a married daughter, two years later.[66] Twenty-seven years before the Innsbruck property division, when the elder Taynchis received a marriage settlement from her first husband Petosiris, the couple already had a son.[67] It is, however, quite possible that the son was no longer alive in 75 B.C., or perhaps, like the son of Teōs and Taimouthēs, in this case also the son was excluded from his mother's inheritance. In both cases one may assume that alternative arrangements were made for the sons and that only part of the picture survives.

In the documents of the Undertakers' Archive no distinction is generally made between moveable and immoveable property.[68] Sometimes the two are listed separately,[69] but normally the two are run together and included in the one division. This was not necessarily always the case, and a property division from a family of tradesmen in the Anoubieion from the late second century B.C. shows different treatment.[70] The tradesman in question had, in the course of his life, been married twice. His immoveable property—a house, a storehouse, and a shed on the necropolis—went equally to all his children (or their descendants) by both his marriages, whereas his moveable property—precious metals, materials, jewelry, house contents, and livestock (the description is standard)—was divided only between the two surviving sons of his second marriage. So within broadly accepted outlines the individual might make different dispositions of his property.

Property, then, was normally divided among children in varying proportions in a system primarily of partible ownership, rather than with divisions on geographical lines. But infinite subdivision of a fixed asset is never viable and ways must be found to recombine holdings into manageable units. The problem may be examined in considering the property which became known as the inheritance of Ptahmaacherou. This is the description given the property in two separate contracts from 75 B.C. and 73 B.C., yet many of the same elements of this inheritance are

---

[66] *P. Louvre* 3268 (73 B.C.) = App. B:19.

[67] *P. Louvre* 2419 + 3265 (102 B.C.) = App. B:10.

[68] E.g., *P. Bruss.* 3.3 (238 B.C.) = App. B:31; *P. Innsbruck*, lines 11–12 (75 B.C.) = App. B:18.

[69] *P. Louvre* 2412 (316–304 B.C.) = App. B:29.

[70] *P. Cair. dem.* 30602-3 (115 B.C.); two documents survive of the twelve drawn up to cover this division.

found in an earlier property division from 197 B.C.[71] The inheritance takes its name from the reader-priest Ptahmaacherou (fig. 7, level 7), who was the grandfather of the Senamounis who on 23 November 75 B.C. received her $\frac{1}{4}$ share of the inheritance from her mother Taynchis. The individuals with interest in this property are shown on figure 7 and the different elements of the inheritance are tabulated in table 3. The inheritance of Ptahmaacherou was presumably that part of the property listed in *P. Innsbruck* (75 B.C.) which Taynchis (level 8) received from her first husband Petosiris (rather that is than from her father or from her uncle), and it seems to have formed a major part of the whole inheritance described in that division. The same inheritance is listed again eighteen months later when a further series of contracts was drawn up, possibly following the marriage of Senamounis' half-brother Pasis (level 9), the son of Taynchis and her second husband Harmachis, to her niece Tauēs (level 10), the daughter of her sister.

The frequency of these contractual arrangements is typical of property practices on the necropolis, and from this later series survive two of the relevant contracts from 23 February 73 B.C. In *P. Louvre* 3268 Senamounis recognizes the rights of Pasis to $\frac{1}{4}$ + $\frac{1}{8}$ of the family property,[72] and in *P. Louvre* 3264 ter Pasis recognizes the rights of Senamounis to her $\frac{1}{4}$ share. These are the latest of the contracts which have survived from the archive and, coming from the top of the collection, they are likely to have worn the worst. In spite of this, the property described in the fragmentary *P. Louvre* 3268 clearly bears a close resemblance to part of that inherited over a hundred years earlier by the children of Tauēs (levels 5–6) from her extended family of choachytai as recorded in *P. Louvre* E 3266 (197 B.C.).[73] That Ptahmaacherou was the grandson of Tauēs is now known from the Malcolm papyrus,[74] and the inheritance from Tauēs came down through her son Imouthēs. In 75 B.C. this same property, which had been preserved intact in its present form for two generations as one third of the earlier interest, was (as we have seen) again divided, among the three granddaughters of Ptahmaacherou. For in this year Senamounis received $\frac{1}{4}$ and her two sisters received $\frac{1}{4}$ + $\frac{1}{8}$ each from their mother Taynchis

---

[71] *P. Innsbruck* (75 B.C.), *P. Louvre* 3268 with 3264 ter (73 B.C.) and E 3266 (197 B.C.) = App. B:18-20 and 2.

[72] The property perhaps came to Pasis from his wife; cf. *P. Louvre* 3264 + 2411 (65 B.C.) = App. B:22 in which one-eighth of the inheritance is transferred to Senamounis by her niece, the wife of Pasis.

[73] On this division, see above with Appendix C.

[74] *P. B.M.* 10384 (11 November 132 B.C.) = App. B:7.

TABLE 3. THE INHERITANCE OF PTAHMAACHEROU

P. Louvre E 3266 (May–June 197 B.C.)	lines	P. Innsbruck (23 November 75 B.C.)	lines	P. Louvre 3268 (23 February 73 B.C.)	lines
Imouthēs to Shemti		*Taynchis to Senamounis*		*Senamounis to Pasis*	
Funerary rights over:		Funerary rights over:		Funerary rights over 1/4 + 1/8:	
1/3 of 2 villages in Ouenchem Crocodile's Tail North Guard Post	1 S–T	1/3 of 1 village in Ouenchem Crocodile's Tail called the North Guard Post		[1/3] of village in [Ouenchem]	
with all inhabitants		with all inhabitants	8	with all inhabitants	8
1/3 of 2 villages in New Lands of Ptah Achi-of-Heriatoum Arsenal		1/3 of 2 villages of New Lands of Ptah		[1/3] of 2 villages in [New Lands of Ptah] Achi-[of-Heriatoum] Arsenal	
with all inhabitants	2 N–O	with all inhabitants	8	with all inhabitants	8
1/3 of Quarter of the Greeks under the administration of Memphis	8 P–Q	1/3 of the Quarter of the Greeks under the administration of Memphis	8	[1/3] of the Greeks	8
1/2? of 3 funerary chapels	1 H	1/3 of 3 funerary chapels on the necropolis	11		
		1/3 of further chapels	11		
In addition many other chapels and funerary interests over individual families		1/3 of pastophoroi of Osiris-Apis and Osiris-Mnevis	7	[1/3] of those of the sanctuary of Osiris-Apis and of [Osiris–Mnevis]	
		1/3 of the grape growers	7		
		In addition (probably not as part of this inheritance):			
		2 houses on the dromos of Anoubis with outbuildings	4–5	2 houses on the dromos of Anoubis with outbuildings (cf. *P. Louvre* 3264 ter)	

of the property which had come from her first husband Petosiris, son of Ptahmaacherou (levels 8–9). This division highlights a problem inherent in a system of partible inheritance. In this case, however, one of the factors countering the effects of subdivision may also be illustrated, for at the same time there came added interests from Taynchis' own family, from her father and her father's brother, in the form of two houses on the dromos of Anoubis. These added interests would supplement the divided inheritance of her children, resulting in a more viable inheritance for each, though one which was still fragmented and significantly smaller than earlier. There were only two ways in which this process of subdivision, occurring whenever there was more than one child to a marriage, might be reversed—by cession or exchange of interests, or by marriage within the family. In marrying the daughter of his half sister, Pasis (level 9), the son of Taynchis' second marriage, would be marrying into part of his mother's inheritance.

In such a system of diverging devolution and partible inheritance one would expect that the sale or exchange of discrete and fragmented holdings occasionally took place among members of the family. The apparent absence from the latest of the records of the inheritance of Ptahmaacherou (table 3) of some of the items recorded earlier may be the result of such a process; or they may simply be illegible or missing from what is a very poorly preserved papyrus. In other cases where surviving contracts do not mark actual division of property, one suspects the result of tidying-up operations.[75] The one lease preserved in the archive may have been occasioned by similar needs.[76]

It was, however, marriage which served as the principal means of preserving property in viable units and of reuniting divided interests. As in other, comparable, societies, in small groups with a system of partible patrimony, marriage was regularly arranged within the family. Such a general assertion is possible on the basis both of names and of documented cases, and the actual composition of the Undertakers' Archive itself provides evidence for the system in practice.

As preserved, the Undertakers' Archive consists of the collected papers of two branches of the family which must have been reunited in the second half of the first century B.C. Presumably the most recent papers were at the top of the deposit and have not survived the centuries. As is regular with such unofficial discoveries, the circumstances of find are nowhere recorded; the papyri were divided and scattered when sold. The docu-

---

[75] The addition of new elements between 197 and 75 B.C. may be similarly explained.
[76] *P. B.M.* 10384 (132 B.C.) = App. B:7.

ments which form the basis of figure 7 start in the sixth recorded generation of the family and appear to represent the papers of Shemti, daughter
of Taues and Samous, including some from her husband Pasis; then those
of her son Teos and of his daughter Taues (level 8), to whose collection
were added papers from the latter's husband Petesis, son of Heriobastis
and Chonouphis. These papers then passed to the eldest son of Taues and
Petesis, Chonouphis, and, finally, to his son Petesis. From level 8 there
also survive the papers of Taynchis, daughter of the undertaker Peteimouthes,[77] which passed to Senamounis, her eldest daughter by her first
husband Petosiris. Senamounis in turn married Herieus, a younger son
of Taues and Petesis and brother of Chonouphis of level 9. Their two
undertaker sons, Petesis and Petosiris, are recorded in *P. Bibl. Nat.* 224–
225 of 68 B.C.[78] To explain the composition of the archive as it stands, it
is necessary to assume that these two branches of the family came together in marriage in the tenth or subsequent generation, at the end of the
Ptolemaic period.

The accumulation of these papers itself serves to indicate patterns of
marriage and family composition within this endogamous group. The
role of women in the transmission of property was clearly important and,
although in marriage settlements provision was made only for the inheritance of male children, it is clear from the actual records of property
divisions and transfers that daughters inherited in the same way as sons.
When women married, their dowry was always specified in monetary
terms.[79] Property remained legally separate on marriage, and no common fund was established. It is noteworthy that two of the women whose
papers have survived married twice, and in all four marriages their husbands were undertakers. In level 5 Taues, the mother of Shemti and Imouthes, has already been mentioned. She was the well-endowed heiress to
a family of choachytai, though both her husbands—Ptahmaacherou, son
of Imouthes, and Samous, son of Psenptais and Heranch—were undertakers. In the second branch of the family Taynchis (level 8), daughter of
Peteimouthes and Tatseous, also had two husbands, first Petosiris, son of
Ptahmaacherou and Senamounis, by whom she had four children, and
later Harmachis, son of Horma and Heranch, by whom she had at least
one son. It is unknown whether these second marriages followed on death
or divorce. The second alternative is possible and is regularly provided

---

[77] Son, perhaps, of Imouthes who was half-brother of Shemti in level 6.
[78] App. B:21.
[79] See below on living standards.

for in the marriage contract,[80] but the first is perhaps more likely and in the case of Taynchis almost certain. Nor is it known what the age differential may have been on marriage, though younger women probably married older husbands. Such multiple marriages will, however, have tended to increase the number of interrelated children in each generation.

There is no evidence here for brother-sister marriage and little for the cross-cousin marriage which might have been expected in such a close family group. In one classic case of marriage of first cousins[81] from within the choachytai of the third century B.C., Imouthēs (fig. 8, level 5), son of Achomnevis, marries his father's brother's daughter Esoëris, the daughter of *P3-chaw* and *Ta-ḥs*.[82] Such a marriage would help to consolidate the family property and prevent its dissipation. It is with similar aims, presumably, that uncles marry their nieces. So, among the undertakers, Pasis (fig. 7, level 9), the son by her second husband of Taynchis, married a Tauēs, who was probably a granddaughter of the same Taynchis through her first marriage.[83] A somewhat similar case of endogamous marriage may be seen among the choachytai (fig. 8) when *P3-chaw* (level 4), son of Imouthēs and Rempnōphris, marries *Ta-ḥs* (level 5), the daughter of Esoëris and *P3-kp*, who shared a grandfather with her husband.[84] Such examples are scattered in the archive but may be significant in illustrating how property might be retained within the family group.

LIVING STANDARDS

Rarely in the ancient world is it possible to investigate the living standards of its inhabitants, and when, just occasionally, details do survive for any aspect of this subject, the information they provide tends to be very partial. Thus, while food allowances for a particular individual may be recorded, nutritional requirements are simply one aspect, albeit a crucial aspect, of life, and clothing, heating, or housing requirements and costs, for example, are unlikely to be recorded in the same context. In this respect therefore, the information preserved in documents of the Undertakers' Archive is particularly welcome in the details it preserves; and al-

---

[80] *UPZ* 118 (83 B.C.) records legal action following the breakup of a marriage.

[81] See Goody (1976), 15.

[82] *P. Bruss.* 3 = App. B:31.

[83] *P. Louvre* 3268 (73 B.C.) = App. B:19 with 2411 (65 B.C.) = App. B:22. In my view, *P. Leid.* 373a (131 B.C.) = App. B:8 does not record such a marriage as implied by Lüddeckens' reading of lines 6–7, cf. Revillout (1897), 525-27, with Pasis and Shemti as the parents of Teos.

[84] *P. Leid.* 379 (256 B.C.) with *P. Bruss.* 3 (238 B.C.) = App. B:30-31; such a marriage is necessary to explain the inheritance pattern of the earlier document. See figures 9–10.

though, as we shall find, it is full of problems, with many questions still unresolved, it may be used to tell us something of the basic economic expectations of this particular group in society.

An approach to the question of the standard of living of the necropolis workers may perhaps be made through a study of the two forms of marriage contracts, those with provisions for either alimony or regular maintenance discussed above.[85] The details contained within such Memphite contracts can be most clearly expressed in tabular form, as in tables 4 and 5.

In the first of these forms of contract (table 4), the husband makes arrangements, in the event of the marriage ending in divorce (on either side), for alimony payments to be made should he fail to return the dowry. The second form of contract (table 5) is concerned rather with regular support within marriage. The wife provides a silver dowry and in return her husband endows her with all his property. He then, in a separate contract, makes regular provision for her day-to-day support within the marriage. In both types of contract, maintenance appears provided for in both cash and kind. The cash payments are more problematic.

The monetary provisions of the two forms of contract are very differ-

TABLE 4. ALIMONY MARRIAGE CONTRACTS

Reference	Date	Wife's payment	Alimony arrangement
P. Leid. 373a (App. B:7)	131 B.C.	750 deben (3,750 staters)	Daily allowance: 4 cooked loaves Monthly allowance: ? + 1/2 hin kiki oil 7.5 deben Annual clothing allowance: 200 deben (1,000 staters)
P. B.M. 10229 (App. B:16)	78 B.C.	660 deben (3,300 staters)	Daily allowance: 4 cooked loaves Monthly allowance: 1 hin sesame oil 1 hin kiki oil 7.5 deben Annual clothing allowance: 300 deben (1,500 staters)

[85] See the section above on "The Documents."

TABLE 5. SUPPORT CONTRACTS

Reference	Date	Wife's payment	Provisions for support
P. Leid. 381 (App. B:23)	226 B.C.	21 deben in silver	nil
P. Louvre 2149 + 3265 (App. B:10)	102 B.C.	50 deben in silver	3.8 deben in silver 60 artabas olyra
UPZ 118	83 B.C.	(25 deben) 500 dr. silver	(3.6 deben) 72 drachmas silver 60 artabas olyra
P. Bibl. Nat. 224–25 (App. B:21)	68 B.C.	21 deben in silver	2.4 deben in silver 36 (40 hin) artabas olyra

ent, though in both they are expressed in Egyptian monetary terms. In the alimony type of contract, both maintenance and dowry payments are expressed in deben (made up of ten kites), in staters (or tetradrachms, which were the actual coins in circulation), and in copper talents made up of 300 deben. The rate of 24 obols to 2 kites (or one tetradrachm) is regularly recorded; in Greek terms two drachmas made a kite and 20 drachmas a deben. In the second form of contract, however, where the wives' payments appear much lower, the deben recorded are expressly silver deben—silver of the treasury of Ptah (in Memphis) which signifies real silver. For these silver deben, *argyriou drachmai* in Greek, no further monetary equivalent is given and the regular (annual) payments that the husband contracts to make are also specified in silver. Both types of payment present problems of interpretation. In the case of payments with the alimony type of contract, the problem is that of knowing what the deben was actually worth at any given date.[86] What is striking here is the occurrence of the same figure (7 deben and 5 kites) specified for monthly maintenance in the two documents which are more than fifty years apart in time. Was this, as it appears to be, a standard figure? What the wives' dowry payments of 750 and 660 deben, respectively, may have meant in real terms remains uncertain.[87]

[86] This is especially problematic if, as Gara has recently argued (1984), 122–34, the use of bronze units for expressing payments is simply a method of accounting in a system based ultimately on fluctuating grain values.

[87] Wife's payments from the Ptolemaic period, recorded by Pestman (1961), table B, chronologically stand at 90, 100, 110, 750, 500, and 660 debens.

In the second type of contract, those with provisions for regular support within marriage, the problem is somewhat different. To what extent
were the sums of silver specified in these contracts actually paid, or were
the documents simply traditional in form? The reason for suspecting that
the latter may be the case is the regular recurrence of the sum of 21 silver
deben for the wife's payment in documents spanning the whole of the
Ptolemaic period. Of the sixteen contracts of this type tabulated by Pestman, ten have the figure of 21 deben, three of 50, and one each of 6, 25,
and 51; 21 silver deben does seem to be a standard figure throughout the
period.[88] Whether a standard figure is also a fictional figure is unknowable, but it is at least possible that the figures specified in the contract had
no base in reality. And if the wife's payment is understood as fictional, is
the same true of the husband's cash allowance to his wife? In these contracts there is no regular relationship apparent between the rate recorded
for the wife's payment and the level of her allowance. It is only rarely that
anything useful can be said about the level of support. When, however,
sometime before 83 B.C. Psintaēs made a support contract in favor of his
wife Thauēs/Asklepias and undertook to provide an annual allowance of
72 drachmas in addition to 60 artabas of olyra, he was in effect making an
allowance which, on figures given later in the penalty clause, would have
been sufficient to purchase annually a further 36 artabas.[89] The same sort
of sum may be envisaged in other support contracts. Otherwise in the
Memphite documents the only striking feature in respect of the cash allowances is the progressive erosion of the level of the husband's support.
And in the possible presence of units of account, and of fictional payments, interpretation of the monetary side of these contracts appears
problematic in the extreme.

To move from cash to kind is to move from quicksand to somewhat
firmer ground. Provisions for food are made in both types of marriage
contracts. In the alimony type of contract, the provision was in terms of
both bread and oil, while in the support contracts olyra wheat alone is
specified. In alimony contracts bread came in the form of "cooked
loaves," the *artoi peptoi* of the Sarapieion papyri, which were coarse, country, *kyllestis* loaves made of olyra, the husked emmer wheat (*Triticum dicoccum*) of pre-Ptolemaic Egypt[90] which continued in use in native circles
on into the Ptolemaic period. The same allowance of four loaves a day

[88] Pestman (1961), 105-6 and table C.
[89] *UPZ* 118. 14; this penalty price may be on the high side (so Wilcken).
[90] Hdt. 2.77.4. *UPZ* 20.12, 38; 57. 2. On Egyptian loaves, see Darby, Ghalioungui, and
Grivetti (1977), 515-26.

CHAPTER 5

found in the alimony provisions is recorded in the Sarapieion papyri as the daily ration for the twins engaged in mourning ceremonies for the Apis bull, which died in 164 B.C.[91] From the Sarapieion papyri it is known that thirty (or fifteen pairs of) loaves were reckoned as the equivalent of one 40-*choinix* artaba of olyra. The monthly ration allowed for as alimony (as for the twins) was therefore four artabas of olyra, hence 48⅔ artabas a year (taking account of the extra five days at the end of Mesore). Emmer wheat was of neither the quality nor the nutritive value of naked durum wheat and was regularly valued against this at a ratio of 5:2.[92] On this basis these provisions and rations may be seen as the annual equivalent of 19.46 artabas or 497 kilograms of unmilled durum wheat a year.[93] With 250–300 kilograms annually now recognized as adequate for subsistence,[94] the alimony provisions of these contracts are not ungenerous. And if, as earlier, a 150 kilogram minimum is adopted, the provisions appear quite lavish.

The 60 artabas of olyra allowed for in two of the support contracts is the equivalent of 24 artabas or 613 kilograms unmilled durum wheat a year. In the absence of separate allowances, this relatively high rate may have included an element for oil and other daily necessities. In the latest of the support contracts, that from 68 B.C., the smaller provision of 36 artabas—artabas, moreover, which are specified as of 40 *hin* or 24 *choinikes* (the Egyptian *oipē*)[95]—is the equivalent of only 8.64 artabas or 221 kilograms of unmilled wheat a year. Whereas by itself this allowance falls somewhat below the regular subsistence level, the cash allowance will have increased the overall provision.

In addition to olyra loaves in the alimony contracts, reasonable provision was further made for oil, with sesame oil for cooking and kiki oil for lighting.[96] The level of allowance here is below that made for the twins, who were provided with one metretes each a year of both cooking and lighting oil to share between them. A metretes was made up of 80 Egyp-

[91] *UPZ* 42–54; in practice less was paid; see chapter 7 below.
[92] Skeat (1974), 99.
[93] The weight equivalence of 25.545 kilograms for a 40-*choinix* artaba (or 3.75 *modii*, Duncan-Jones 1976, 50) depends on the weight given by Pliny, *HN* 18.66, of 20% Roman pounds (or 6.812 kilograms) for a modius of Alexandrian corn; in earlier calculations, Crawford (1979), 143–44, I failed to take account of the wheat:olyra ratio.
[94] Clark and Haswell (1970), 62.
[95] It is just possible that *hin* here stands for *choinix*, Pestman (1961), 148, on archaizing tendencies; in this case the allowance would be the equivalent of 368 kilograms of unmilled durum wheat. Identical provision is made in a non-Memphite document from the reign of Epiphanes, *P. Louvre* 2347 (Revillout 1903, 1009), corrected by Pestman (1961), C7.
[96] *UPZ* 17–41.

184

tian hin,[97] so the twins' allowance stood at 4 hin apiece of each oil a month, four times the allowance provided by Teōs for his wife in 78 B.C.

In all these cases, however, as already seen, the cash allowance made a significant difference to the overall level of support. So in 131 B.C., if olyra prices were anything near the 300 bronze drachmas of thirty years earlier,[98] the 7.5 deben monthly alimony provision made by Petēsis for his wife was the equivalent of a further 5 artabas of olyra a month, more than doubling the 4 artabas provided as loaves. Similarly, in a support contract recorded in 83 B.C., the total provision of 72 drachmas and 60 artabas of olyra may be otherwise expressed as 981 kilograms of unmilled wheat a year. This is more than three times the level of subsistence. These were not families close to the poverty line, but men and women whose functions on the necropolis made them individuals of substance and economic standing in the community.

By 68 B.C., however, when the undertaker Herieus drew up a contract to support his wife Senamounis, things were changing for the family. Senamounis had come into only one quarter of the inheritance of Ptahmaacherou (table 3); and while in this contract the wife's payment recorded was standard, her maintenance, compared with earlier levels, was low.[99] In both cash and kind she was to be supported at a lower level than either the wife of Petosiris in 102 B.C. or Thauēs, wife of Psintaēs, in 83 B.C. In this ninth generation of undertakers, Herieus and Senamounis, both descendants of the heiress Tauēs, daughter of Shemti and the choachytes Peteimouthēs who was supervisor of the necropolis, were perhaps beginning to feel the pinch of partible patrimony. Whether it was now or, more probably, as a result of a later marriage that the papers of the descendants of Tauēs' daughter Shemti were reunited with those of her half-brother Imouthēs, the property and resources of these later generations had diminished. This is reflected both in the maintenance contract just mentioned that Herieus made for Senamounis in 68 B.C. and in the diminished scale of the divided family property recorded only a few years before.[100]

A further source of economic information might be the penalty clauses and the fines laid down in contracts in the Undertakers' Archive. Fines were specified in cases of nonobservance of the terms of a contract, for

---

[97] Viedebantt (1913), 1645.

[98] *UPZ* 52.16-19; 53.18-20 (161 B.C.); cf. 91.7 n. (159 B.C.) for prices ranging 250–360 drachmas. Changing prices makes this calculation of dubious value.

[99] *P. Bibl. Nat.* 224-25 = App. B:21.

[100] *P. Innsbruck* (75 B.C.) = App. B:18 and *P. Louvre* 3268 (73 B.C.) = App. B:19 with table 3.

failure to hand over corpses which rightfully belonged to others, for mummifying even the most insignificant of corpses which was not theirs to mummify, for opening windows where no windows were allowed, or for failing to prevent challenges in contravention of the terms of an agreement. In these and other cases, monetary fines were laid down and expressed in deben and staters.[101] There are, however, two problems in the use of such evidence. The uncertainty of the figures in many of these documents, read and published in the infancy of demotic studies, combines with the rapid changes in the value of the units of bronze to demand caution in interpretation. At present this evidence is unusable.

UPWARD MOBILITY

The choachytai and undertakers of Memphis formed part of the essentially native community which lived and worked on the necropolis. Their births, marriages, and deaths, recorded within a native legal system, belong in a context which is primarily Egyptian: mummification and the cult of the dead.

One group of papers, however, is in Greek. These documents come from Petēsis, the husband of Tauēs in level 8, and from his son Chonouphis. Petēsis was the son of Chonouphis and Heriobastis, and the demotic contract with alimony provisions recording his marriage to the daughter of Teōs and Taimouthēs is dated to 30 October 131 B.C.[102] At the time of this marriage Petēsis was a regular undertaker (ḥtmw-ntr), but he was later appointed to the rather unusual priestly post of "undertaker-in-chief for the most great and everlasting gods, the deified [which means mummified] Apis and Mnevis."[103] It may have been as a result of this appointment that the family moved house, from the Anoubieion down towards the Phchēt canal to the Asklepieion. Certainly Petēsis' horizons broadened as he came into contact with a wider society of both Greeks and Egyptians. So when, at the turn of the century, he was the subject of assault and his property was attacked, it was to the king, Ptolemy X Alexander I and his

---

[101] As read, fines in penalty clauses are specified as follows: *P. Louvre* E 3266.11.E–12.F (197 B.C.), 100 deben; *P. Louvre* 2409 (184 B.C.), 2,000 deben; *P. Leid.* 378 (160 B.C.), 5,000 and 3,000 deben; *P. B.M.* 10398 (120–119 B.C.), 30,000 deben; *P. Louvre* 3268 (73 B.C.), 30,000 deben (App. B:2, 4, 24, 9, 19); cf. Pestman, *Rec.* I.8 (181 B.C.), 200 deben.

[102] *P. Leid.* 373a (App. B:8). He and his brother Paneith are receiving parties in *P. Hermitage* 1122 (135 B.C.) = App. B:6.

[103] *UPZ* 106.10-11; 107.11-12; 108.10; 109.1-2 (99/8 B.C.); perhaps his Egyptian title was *mr ḥtmw-ntr* (so Clarysse).

niece-queen Kleopatra Berenike, then on a visit to the Sarapieion, that he complained in Greek, on 15 October 99 B.C.[104]

Petēsis first gives the reason why, in his view, the royal rulers should pay attention. As archentaphiast he fulfills the many needs and demands of the deified Apis and Mnevis, in his worship of them; but he is also involved in prayers and sacrifices to the ruler gods for whom, in good Egyptian style, he prays for health, victory, strength, and mighty power over all the lands below heaven. He has been set upon and attacked by certain individuals up on the necropolis; these attacks have been random and without reason. The complaint is unspecific in the extreme, and if there were good reasons for Petēsis' unpopularity they are kept well hidden. He now throws himself on the mercy of the king and queen, requesting that they order Philokratēs, kinsman and *epistolographos*, to put out an order covering both Petēsis and his property. This order, to be written up on a whitewashed board and countersigned by the royal scribe, is to contain instructions that no one may attack the house nor lay hands on its owner, for any reason whatsoever. Petēsis' appeal seems to have carried weight. A native embalmer, with responsibilities in the important cults of the Apis and Mnevis bulls as well as the royal cult, was in a sensitive position, and six days later, on 21 October, a sealed copy of the petition was forwarded by royal command to Apollodoros, the strategos. His subordinate Timonikos sent it on to the epistates, the crown appointee in the Anoubieion. Action was taken and the whitewashed board, with instructions written in both Greek and demotic, was set up as requested.

The attacks, however, continued. Petēsis drafted a second petition to the king complaining that Noumenios, from the office of the strategos, had entered his house (probably in July–August 98 B.C.), wrecked it, and removed the furniture and fittings in defiance of the royal instructions; the new strategos, Ariston, should be instructed to conform with the existing rulings covering Petēsis and his property. The final document in the dossier is a very fragmentary official copy of a letter of Petēsis, dated 5 November 98 B.C., to one Axion, whom he addresses as brother. Although the content is far from clear, he seems to speak of connections in Alexandria who may be expected to have influence at court. The connections were made through one Peteharendotēs, a linen seller down in the temple of Ptah, and the god Sarapis, the Alexandrian form of the deified Apis, is called on for additional help.

[104] *UPZ* 106-9 (99/8 B.C.), for the whole affair.

Petēsis, it seems, was more than a humble Egyptian necropolis worker. With responsibilities in the major cult of the necropolis and with property worth stealing, he was prepared to exploit connections in the capital, however remote, or to petition his sovereigns in an attempt to gain protection for himself and his family. The identity of his earlier attackers is unknown, but the man accused of ignoring official orders on the second occasion was from a central administrative office. It was at this stage that Petēsis may have gone to law. In editing this dossier, Wilcken suggested that the papers preserved may have been used in a lawsuit;[105] this seems very plausible and would explain their survival in the archive. Given his adversary, it was naturally a Greek action in which Petēsis engaged. For in spite of the existence of native courts, in actions involving Greek officials use of the Greek courts was required. Indeed, for many Egyptian families increasing familiarity with Greek legal processes is likely to have aided the process of Hellenization.[106]

Once the family had become familiar with Greek procedures and the Greek language, it was not likely to discontinue the process of Hellenization. It comes therefore as no surprise that when Petēsis' son Chonouphis made an interest-free loan to Peteimouthēs, son of Horos, on 27 September 89 B.C. it was covered by a Greek contract registered down below in Memphis, at the phylake and not in the Anoubieion.[107] Such a loan (12 silver staters or tetradrachms [48 drachmas] for ten months, free of interest) was often made within a family.[108] It is Egyptian in form if not in language, and in it Chonouphis describes himself as one of the embalmers from the great Asklepieion near Memphis.[109] He was probably an undertaker like his father, though without the appointment of archentaphiast, and his son Petēsis was a recipient, with others in the family, of funerary revenues in a demotic contract drawn up on 22 May 78 B.C.[110]

More interesting is what is known of Chonouphis' daughter Thauēs, also known as Asklepias. Sometime before 87 B.C. a marriage settlement

---

[105] UPZ 109, introduction.

[106] Compare the Hermias process in Thebes from the late second century B.C., UPZ 160–69. Greek documents also occur in the Embalmers' Archive from Hawara, Reymond (1973), nos. 22-25. Also see Peremans (1985).

[107] UPZ 125, as Konouphis; the spelling varies, cf. 117.3, Chenouphis.

[108] Pestman (1971), 26, suspects the interest was somewhere hidden within the loan. (For regular interest-free loans among Jewish merchants and craftsmen in medieval Cairo, see Goitein 1967, 262, cf. 190.)

[109] UPZ 125.8-9 (89 B.C.); see 117.7-8 (86-83 B.C.) for orchards he owns near the temple of Asklepios (this and UPZ 114 may also originate in legal proceedings).

[110] P. Leid. 374.i.5-6 (App. B:17); other recipients are cousins from Chonouphis' generation and the assumption must be that Chonouphis is no longer alive.

had been drawn up by her husband Psintaēs in favor of his wife, whose portion had been 500 drachmas (25 deben), a contract in which the inheritance rights of their son Zmanrēs were also specified. We may assume that this contract, probably written in demotic, had been duly docketed in Greek and registered officially, perhaps in the Anoubieion, since when Psintaēs failed to meet his obligations to his wife in January 83 B.C., her father Chonouphis took the case to the Greek *chrēmatistai*, seeking redress, Greek-style, on behalf of his daughter. He won his case and, ten days after the judgment, an order was forwarded for action to the *praktōr xenikōn*, the "bailiff with responsibility in alien affairs," as the official who dealt with matters Egyptian was so significantly named by the immigrant Greek administration.[111] The final outcome of the affair is unknown, but the Greek ruling joined the family papers on the necropolis.[112]

The double name of Chonouphis' daughter, Thauēs/Asklepias, is equally significant. It is the first example in this community of the adoption of a Greek name. The theophoric name Asklepias is highly suitable for one whose family lived close by the temple of Imouthēs/Asklepios, and the phenomenon typifies a tendency towards integration which may be paralleled among the undertakers of the Theban necropolis of the same period.[113] Integration here, as at Thebes, takes the form of Egyptians Hellenizing both in nomenclature and in the use of Greek courts. There is no sign whatsoever of those of non-Egyptian origin entering this exclusive community of embalmers and mummifiers.

Zmanrēs, the son of Thauēs/Asklepias and of her unreliable husband Psintaēs, is from the last recorded generation of the Undertakers' Archive. The Hellenizing tendencies (linked to their physical relocation) which seem limited to this particular branch of the family date only from the early years of the first century B.C. In Memphis, as at Thebes, the Greek language and ways were, not surprisingly, slow to penetrate the tightknit, traditional communities of the embalmers and "men of Anoubis," whose normal sphere was the necropolis of the Egyptian desert.

[111] See Préaux (1955).
[112] *UPZ* 118 (25 January 83 B.C.).
[113] *UPZ* 190.4 (98 B.C.), Asklepias/Senimouthes.

6

APIS AND OTHER CULTS

The aspect of Egyptian religion which above all startled and intrigued outsiders, then as now, was the worship accorded to animals. The ubiquity of animal cults was both shocking and hard to understand. The Greeks were amazed; the Romans laughed. For those, however, who came to live in Egypt these peculiar practices seem soon to have lost their strangeness, and immigrants joined with the Egyptians in rendering cult to the animals, including birds, fish, and reptiles, of their adopted homeland.

Each area had its particular deity—Souchos, for instance, the crocodile of the Arsinoite nome, or the snub-nosed fish, the *oxyrhynchos*, of the neighboring Oxyrhynchite nome—and all members of the species shared in the divinity of the god. These animals, sometimes even bred for the cult, were cared for during life as gods; in death they became Osiris, preserved in mummified form. Memphis, as we have seen, both in its valley city and in the Sacred Animal Necropolis, was the home for many different animal cults. Along the dykes ibis were extensively farmed; the larger species with a single representation—the baboon of Thoth, for instance, or the Apis bull—were looked after while alive within the great temple of Ptah. In death, recognized as Osiris, the lesser gods might become an object of commerce for individual pilgrims. Just as at Tebtunis the mummies of small crocodiles were available for sale to pilgrims, so in Memphis were the ibis and hawks. The rites of preservation for the larger animals were on a grander scale; participation in these ceremonies belonged to priest and public alike.

Whatever the meaning to the participants of this form of worship, it was widely practiced, and whatever its appeal, it had many devotees. Much of the significance of these cults escapes the modern observer, and while it is possible to offer explanations based on cross-cultural comparisons[1]—the probable connections with fertility, with men's desire for powers and strengths found in the animal world, with forces to be placated or subsumed—such interpretations by association may well lie

[1] E.g., Willis (1975).

far removed from the thought world of ancient Egypt, a world in which religion pervaded all culture, forming the frame even of the country's history. The terms in which contemporaries described these animal gods were as emanations or souls of other gods. Thus Apis was the emanation or embodiment of Ptah, and in some respects subordinate to him. Their cults were closely related both in location and personnel. Others were different aspects of the same god, without subordination. So Thoth might be found in his (single) baboon or his (many) ibis, or Horos in his hawk, and at the same time the collective Hawk or Ibis had some form of reality of their own.[2] How this was envisaged and understood by the ancient Egyptians can only be a matter for conjecture.

What is undisputed is the proliferation and growing importance of these cults in what is called the Late Period of Egyptian history (664–323 B.C.), at a time when the power of Thebes had been eclipsed and the country was increasingly subjected to invasion from outside. It was a time, too, when pharaohs are known to have given financial support to the more important of these cults. The integrity of Egypt might thus appear to have been defined by the peculiar cults of the country; Egyptian society was characterized as different through the gods that were worshipped there. Whether or not, either consciously or unconsciously, such a process of cultural self-definition was involved in the expansion of animal worship, the expansion itself took place. And the ordinary Egyptian may have acted out the rituals of his religion unaware of any wider significance. In concentrating here on a description of these Memphite cults, I hope at least to convey some sense of their scale and importance.

THE APIS CULT

Without a doubt the most important of these Memphite cults was that of Apis. For the necropolis here belonged to Apis, and the House of Osiris-Apis was the most prominent of the many temple establishments on the bluff of North Saqqara. The burial vaults of the Apis bulls, explored by Mariette in A.D. 1850-53, have yielded approximately 7,000 stone dedicatory stelae, inscribed in both hieroglypic and demotic.[3] These, together with the demotic inscriptions copied from the doors and walls of the vaults and a variety of other supplementary sources, provide for the Apis

---

[2] See the helpful discussion of Hornung (1982), 109–38.
[3] Malinine, Posener, and Vercoutter (1968), vii–xvi, with details of their present whereabouts and condition.

cult of Ptolemaic Memphis a rare fund of information which has yet to be fully exploited.[4] Indeed, until the complete publication of this extensive material, any account can only be provisional.[5]

At Memphis the Apis burials excavated by Mariette started in the thirteenth century B.C., in the reign of Ramses II, but the cult of Apis itself and the connection of pharaoh with this cult go back to the earliest records of Egyptian history.[6] The burial among the bulls of the son of Ramses II, Prince Kha-em-wase, the governor of Memphis and high priest of Ptah,[7] serves to emphasize this link between Apis, with his connotations of strength and fertility, and the pharoah and his family.

The Apis cult, however, was not just a royal cult and, in the Late Period especially, like other animal cults in Egypt it grew in general popularity. At Memphis on the necropolis, the underground galleries for the mummified Apis bulls were started under Psammetichos I in the mid-seventh century B.C., while the court within Ptah's valley temple was built during the same reign for Apis during his life.[8] From the sixth century B.C., from the reign of Amasis, come both the first of the monumental black granite sarcophagi in which the later bulls were buried in their vaults,[9] and the earliest recorded burial of an Isis cow, the mother-of-Apis, in the Sacred Animal Necropolis of Hepnēbes.[10] The fine Isis temple in Memphis, described by Herodotus as erected by Amasis, was probably connected with this particular cult, in which the goddess was regularly portrayed in human form with a cow's head.[11] The tradition that the Persian king Darius provided 100 talents in gold as a reward in the search for a new Apis serves as further testimony to the growing importance of these two cults

[4] Malinine, Posener, and Vercoutter (1968) publish the Louvre stelae only to the reign of Psammetichos I; publication of the later material is still awaited. The early transcriptions of de Rougé (1885) and (1888), Brugsch (1884), (1886), and (1891), Revillout (1891a) and (1891b), and Spiegelberg (1904) are used here, as in Crawford (1980), 1-42; see Appendix D. Maspero (1882), 114-202, Appendix G, remains a basic study; see also Bresciani (1967); and Vercoutter (1958) and (1962) for the pre-Ptolemaic cult.

[5] The excellent discussion of E. Otto (1938) already makes some use of this evidence; cf. Bonnet (1952), 46-51, sv Apis and 751-53 sv Stier.

[6] E. Otto (1938), 11-15; Simpson (1957).

[7] Mariette (1857), 15-16; Gomaà (1973). For a human burial in the galleries of the mother-of-Apis, see Smith (1972), 178.

[8] Lauer (1976), 25; Hdt. 2.153, the court. For Psammetichos' connection with the hawk galleries, see Emery (1971), plate vi.2.

[9] Vercoutter (1962), 26, from Year 23.

[10] Smith (1972), 180, table 1.

[11] Hdt. 2.176; Emery (1970), 6 with plate ix.1, for the human form; Griffiths (1975), 219-21, for Isis as bos in Apuleius.

in a country he tried to control.[12] Other Persian kings were not so favorably inclined.[13]

It was in the fourth century B.C., in the last period of native independence, that along with other associated cults Apis received a further royal boost. The grand pylon of the Memphite Sarapieion guarded by two surviving lions was erected under Nectanebo I (379/8–362/1 B.C.) while under Nectanebo II (359/8–342/1 B.C.) were built both the small temple for the Sarapieion at the turn of the dromos and a somewhat smaller shrine for the Isis cow at Hepnēbes.[14] Modifications, too, were made within the Apis catacombs, and a special chamber was constructed at the entrance to the galleries where all later stelae were now placed. The separation of the dedications from the bulls they commemorate may make more difficult the actual identification of these bulls, yet the very number of these dedications bears witness to the growing popularity of the cult.[15] There are two major types among the dedications found erected here and those inscribed on the doors to the vaults, and in form they are similar to those from other animal catacombs. First, there are the official hieroglyphic stelae for the individual bulls which record their place and date of birth, the dates of their installation and of their death, and the main events of their "reigns." Second, there are the unofficial private dedications, prayers for blessing or records of work undertaken, set up by priests, masons, and private individuals. Of this second category, priestly records, normally in hieroglyphs or in hieratic script, were set up by those responsible for the burial of the bulls; normally on the blocking to the vaults (and hence lost), some were inscribed on separate stelae. Records of the masons and the ordinary Apis workers, normally in demotic with some in hieroglyphic, might be placed on separate stelae set up in niches in the galleries; occasionally they left graffiti too. Finally came the brief records of private individuals, mainly graffiti in both hieroglyphic and demotic, scrawled on the walls when the vaults were open.[16]

The growth of popularity in the Apis cult is comparable to that found

[12] Polyaenus 7.11.7.
[13] Both Kambyses and Artaxerxes Ochus were credited with murdering Apis; see chapter 4 n. 3.
[14] Lauer (1976), 24, pylon guarded by lions; 18, with E. Otto (1938); 21, temple (and gifts) at the Sarapieion; Emery (1969), 34-35; (1970), 5-6, temple in Hepnēbes.
[15] Malinine, Posener, and Vercoutter (1968), xiii.
[16] E. Otto (1938), 20, for stele types; Smith in Emery (1970), 8, on baboon stelae; Emery (1971), plate xii.4, with Smith (1972), cow stelae; Emery (1971), 5-6 with plate v.4, Imhotep stele connected with ibises and falcons.

for the Buchis bull at Armant in Upper Egypt. There the first granite sarcophagus burial in the Bucheum comes from the reign of Nectanebo II, and the funeral chamber and furnishings for this particular bull were on a lavish and magnificent scale not later matched. The earliest evidence for the cult of the Buchis mother similarly belongs to this same period.[17] Altogether it was a period when the growth of cult organization, with regular mummification rites and the burial of cows and bulls on the human pattern, with all the ceremonies and celebrations this involved, opened the cult for wider participation and more general popularity.[18] But royal patronage continued.

By the time Alexander visited Memphis as conqueror and sacrificed to Apis, the Apis cult had long been established as the central cult of the Saqqara necropolis. There it was joined by the cult of the mother-of-Apis, in death the Isis cow, and the lesser cult of the Apis calves for whom three priests are known from early in the second century B.C.,[19] in addition to the numerous other animal cults of the necropolis. Primarily an Egyptian cult, from an early date it caught the imagination of the Greeks (as later of the Romans) who visited Egypt and wrote of this unusual animal, describing his peculiar markings and the cult and customs connected with his worship.[20] Whereas the Hathor cow of Aphroditopolis was all white, Apis, according to Herodotus, was basically black in color, with double hairs to his tail, a white square on his brow, an eagle on his flank, and a scarab under his tongue. Neither the scarab nor the hairs in the tail may now be verified, but representations of the bull show an inverted white triangle on the forehead, the Horos falcon stretched over its flanks, and a vulture across the shoulders; judicious touching-up with paint might help on special occasions. From Herodotus on, the Apis bull took its place beside the sources of the Nile as a standard ingredient of classical accounts of the land of Egypt. Already in the early fifth century B.C. a Dorian Greek in Egypt had dedicated a bronze bull statuette

[17] Mond and Myers (1934), 1.20; E. Otto (1938), 18.

[18] Mond and Myers (1934), 1.7-8, speak of the democratization of the cult; cf. E. Otto (1938), 11-34.

[19] Pestman, *Rec.* 1-3 (201-181 B.C.), cf. *UPZ* 12-13 (158 B.C.). The three priests Pauouthes, Horos II, and Teebesis, who divide the office and revenues between them, probably shared a great-grandfather from whom the inheritance came; all were *w'b* (pure) priests, and Teebesis was also priest of the hill cult of Isis-in-*Hnt*.

[20] Hdt. 3.28.3; cf. Diod. Sic. 1.84.4-85.5; Strabo 7.1.22, 27, 31, with an untenable distinction between gods and sacred animals; Pomponius Mela 1.9.58; Pliny *HN* 8.184-86; Plutarch *DIO* 43; *Quaest.Conv.* 8.1.3(=*Mor.* 718b); Ael. *NA* 11.10, all with slightly different versions; Lucian, *deorum concilium*, 10-11, on problems of interpretation.

to Lord Apis,[21] while in the late third century B.C. the Cretan dream interpreter who practiced on the Memphite necropolis portrayed on his trade sign, in a primitive Greek style, an Apis bull standing between caryatid columns at a horned altar (plate vii).[22] The cult was so strong that in the mid-second century B.C. Ptolemaios son of Glaukias, in residence in the Sarapieion, dreamed, as we shall see, in the imagery of cows and bulls.[23] Yet, while Greek travelers, residents, or pilgrims in Egypt eagerly adopted Apis and while, as Sarapis, the deified bull was transplanted to the Greek milieu of Alexandria and exported overseas, in Memphis itself those involved in the full cycle of the bull cult, both in life and death, remained exclusively Egyptian.

APIS IN LIFE

Apis might appear anywhere in Egypt, and the death of Apis led to frantic searching up and down the country until his successor could be found. Who undertook the search is not recorded (perhaps the priests of Ptah), but the offering of royal rewards may have been regular, though rarely noted.[24] Once found, all bulls were known as Apis but distinguished individually by the name of the mother of Apis. Of the Ptolemaic bulls for whom a provenance survives (see Appendix D) two came from the Saite nome, a recent residence of kings (the bulls of Ta-Renenutet I and II from Damanhur), one from Tentyra in the Thebaid (the bull of Ta-nt-Amun), one from Oxyrhynchos (the bull of Ta-nt-Amun/Ta-Igesh), one perhaps from Athribis (the bull of Gerg(et) I), and one from Pagereghor in the Athribite nome[25] (the bull of Ta-nt-Hor). The bull of Ta-nt-Bastet may have come from the Boubastite nome, the bull of Gerg(et) Mut-iyti was from Sehetep in the Heliopolite nome, and the bull of Gerg(et) II in the reign of Ptolemy VIII Euergetes II was conveniently born in the temple of Memphis itself. All areas of Egypt are here represented and all temples participated in what had become a national cult.[26]

Once found, Apis was brought to Memphis, though not perhaps at

---

[21] Spiegelberg (1926); Jeffery (1961), 355, no. 52; Masson (1977), 61-63.

[22] Grimm (1975), plate 13, no. 12; see Quaegebeur (1971a), 196, for the altar. The columns may be based on those of the Apis shrine built by Psammetichos, Hdt. 2.153.

[23] *UPZ* 77.22-32; see chapter 7 below.

[24] Polyaenus 7.11.7 for Darius; Amm. Marc. 22.14.6, Julian, who may have put up a reward, is informed of the discovery of Apis.

[25] See Bresciani (1967), 31, on Vienna stele 6.2-3.

[26] Evidence both predates and postdates the Ptolemies: Vercoutter (1962), 127; *SB* 9346 (A.D. 156-70); *W. Chrest* 85.15-20 (A.D. 170), *byssos* for use in mummification.

once.[27] Diodorus Siculus preserves the information that the bull first
spent forty days in Nilopolis; here the potential of the young Apis as a
symbol of fertility was openly acknowledged as women raised their skirts
before the bull.[28] (Similar rites were performed spontaneously by the local women when Mariette unearthed a full-size limestone Apis bull,
painted with its characteristic markings from the dromos of the Sarapieion [plate i].)[29] Nilopolis in this account is clearly the city on the east
bank of the Nile close to Old Cairo.[30] The official hieroglyphic stele of
the bull of Gerg(et) II records the bull's voyage and a somewhat shorter
visit to the Nile temple at Heliopolis close by before its installation in the
Ptah temple at Memphis.[31] The close connection between the Heliopolite
Mnevis bull and Apis of Memphis is well documented from all periods;
under the Ptolemies they might share an embalmer-in-chief, and the
same police officer (Chaiapis under Ptolemy II) carried responsibility for
law and order during their festivals.[32] The bull's link with the Nile, that
other source of fertility for the country, may be found in Pliny's story of
precious gold and silver goblets being thrown into the river on Apis'
birthday; the crocodiles then kept away for seven days.[33] But while
through most of Egypt the Nile was also the source of water, at Memphis
the Apis bull was apparently watered from a separate source; Plutarch
somewhat surprisingly speaks of the need to avoid the fattening effects of
Nile water.[34] On the river voyaging bulls (and cows) were a regular feature of traffic, but special sacred barges were prepared to take these animals on their travels.[35]

The installation and coronation ceremony of the Apis bull took place

[27] Ael. NA 11.10, after a four-month milk diet and special care; departure would coincide
with a full moon.
[28] 1.85.2.
[29] Maspero (1882), 30.
[30] See A. Burton (1972), 246, on the problem.
[31] Louvre stele 4246, de Rougé (1885), 118, and Brugsch (1886), 26, with somewhat different timetables; see Appendix D. Revillout's translation, (1891b), 141, of Louvre stele 191
has the bull of Ta-nt-merwer mummified in the Heliopolite nome (in March 279 B.C.); cf.
Brugsch (1886), 39, for name and date.
[32] See chapter 5 n. 103, and chapter 3 n. 46 with plate v; chapter 4 n. 82, for Mnevis
visiting Memphis in 182 B.C.
[33] Pliny HN 8.186; Aristides 36.124 for Apis as synonymous with Nile. Mond and Myers
(1934), 1.15, draw attention to Nilometers attached to the temples at both Memphis and
Armant.
[34] DIO 5; Ael. NA 11.10.
[35] Ael. NA 11.10; Diod. Sic. 1.85.2, a thalamēgos with gilded cabin; Daressy (1911) 5, for
Apis voyaging (from his birth place) in 186/5 B.C.; Mond and Myers (1934), I.12–14, for
peripatetic Buchis, cf. III, plate cix, for an illustration.

within the temple of Ptah. Priests gathered from all Egypt; Roman writers record one hundred of them in attendance.[36] As in royal coronations, the high priest of Ptah officiated at this ceremony, which was similarly timed for the full moon.[37] Sometimes the ruler might be present, recalling thus the central role that Apis played when he in turn was crowned.[38] So, when later Vespasian's son Titus attended such a ceremony adorned with diadem, his presence there was justifiably regarded with suspicion.[39] As for a king, the years of Apis were used by his subjects as a means of dating, and the Ptah/Apis/Ptolemy network was inextricably interwoven.

Apis spent a pampered life within his quarters in the southern court of the central valley temple of Ptah. The cult of Apis calves supports both the testimony of classical writers and common-sense expectations that the bull was used for breeding.[40] Visited by pilgrims and by regular tourists in his stall close to that of the mother-of-Apis,[41] according to later classical writers he was well known also for the oracles and fortune-telling which became connected with the cult.[42] When he left his quarters, all adorned, it was for processions, travels, royal coronations, and the like. On ceremonial occasions, besides a crown adorned with gold and lapis lazuli, the Buchis bull might wear a face net against the flies.[43] Apis may have done the same. The various crowns, however, and the *menat* (a peculiar Hathor necklace which also served as a musical instrument of percussion)[44] perhaps belong to its traditional portraiture rather than representing actual adornments of the bull. Just as on the necropolis Osiris-Apis had his special keeper called his *boukolos*,[45] so in his lifetime Apis had his keepers coming under the general supervision of the temple of Ptah. Three of the high priests of this temple are named as *s3-st* of the living

<hr/>

[36] Sethe (1904–16), 2.198 no. 37.4; Pliny *HN* 8.184; Amm. Marc. 22.14.8.

[37] Chassinat (1900), 10-11, no. 39 = Malinine, Posener, and Vercoutter (1968), 21-22, no. 22. E. Otto (1938), 16; Griffiths (1970), 511, for full moon.

[38] See chapter 4.

[39] Suet. *Tit.* 5.

[40] Diod. Sic. 1.84.6; cf. Pliny, *HN* 8.186, with chapter 1 n. 118.

[41] Strabo 17.1.31; this also formed a window of appearances, Smith (1972), 177 n. 3. Some cows, however, never made the transfer to Memphis in life, and Ta-Renenutet I and Ta-nt-Amun died where Apis was born; see Smith (1972), 177, and table 6. Also see Appendix D below.

[42] Courcelle (1951), with evidence imperial in date; the stele of the Cretan dream interpreter (n. 22 above) is evidence for this connection earlier.

[43] Mond and Myers (1934), 1.16.

[44] Quaegebeur (1983b).

[45] *UPZ* 57.7 (161 B.C.); cf. Diod. Sic. 1.84.8.

Apis, as is Chaiapis, father of the high priest Psenamounis I.[46] Others too
may have held this post. Surviving Buchis accounts suggest a staff of
around twenty officials actively involved with the needs of that bull in his
lifetime,[47] and Apis perhaps had more. The diet of these sacred bulls was
also more than adequate, with grain and greenstuffs supplemented by the
gifts of pilgrims.[48]

The Ptolemaic period saw fourteen rulers, thirteen high priests, and
thirteen Apis bulls.[49] The care and attention lavished on these bulls resulted in long lives, though none attained the advanced age of twenty-five
when, according to one dubious tradition, mercy killing was practiced
and the bulls were drowned.[50] The average age to which Ptolemaic bulls
lived was twenty-two.[51]

APIS IN DEATH

When Apis died the country mourned, and in Memphis the seventy-day-
long preparations for burial commenced at once. The ritual, with detailed
instructions on how to mummify, survives in part in a bilingual papyrus
text, in both hieratic and demotic, preserved perhaps among the papers
of the family of undertakers discussed above.[52] The surviving copy of this
ritual belongs to the last century of Ptolemaic rule; perhaps it was copied
for the archentaphiast Petesis, son of Chonouphis, who probably presided over the funeral of the bull of Gerg(et) II, which died in September

[46] Petobastis III, Psenptais III, Imouthes/Petobastis IV; see figure 5. The demotic equivalence of the post is "scribe in the House of Life of the living Apis."
[47] Mond and Myers (1934), 1.21.
[48] Compare Mond and Myers (1934), 1.14, 158, for Buchis fodder accounts.
[49] Skeat (1954); reckoning from Alexander's death, I exclude the brief reigns of Ptolemy
VII Neos Philopator (145 B.C.) and Ptolemy XI Alexander II (80 B.C.). For high priests, see
figure 5. It remains unclear, however, whether the appointment of Esisout I/Anemhor I
dates from the very beginning of the period, while the last high priest, Psenamounis II, was
probably a Roman appointment. For bulls, see Appendix D. The earliest and last bulls are
known only from the mother-of-Apis stelae; see Smith (1972) with some modifications
(Crawford 1980, 12 n. 2).
[50] Plut. DIO 56, comparing twenty-five letters in the alphabet, with Griffiths (1970), 509-
11; Pliny HN 8.184, "non est fas eum certos vitae excedere annos," with Griffiths (1970),
273.
[51] This calculation is based on bulls nos. 2–12; see Appendix D. The average life of Buchis
was twenty years; see Mond and Myers (1934), 1.18. Vercoutter (1958), 340, reckons an
average life of eighteen years for all Apis bulls from the reign of Ramses II; later bulls may
have been better cared for.
[52] P. Vindob. 3837; Spiegelberg (1920), with English translation of some parts in Mond
and Myers (1934), 1.18-20, 60-64; Vos' dissertation (1984), which is the basis for this account, will be published in the series Etudes préliminaires aux religions orientales.

119 B.C.[53] The ritual itself is of a much earlier date, recording modifications made under Amasis before the Persians came. The Egyptian priesthood formed a literate group, and the long life of the bulls made necessary this written form of guide which preserves both the ritual and the techniques of mummification.

Immediately on the bull's death, structures necessary to the ritual were prepared. One canopy, with linen stretched over poles, was erected down on the shore of the Lake of Pharaoh to the northwest of the temple of Ptah; a second tent was set up closer to the Apis stall, from where the mummified bull would start his final journey to his vault in the desert above. The process of mummification was to take place in the Embalming House close by the Apis stall,[54] while outside public mourning and participation was carefully orchestrated to coincide with ceremonies within.

First came the cleansing and preparation of the carcass, a procedure lasting fifty-two days. Laid on one of the great alabaster tables surrounded with drainage channels, the body was drained of blood and liquids and the brain removed, either by aid of a spike though the nose, or else perhaps dissolved with liquefying agents.[55] The implements (enema, douche, and two anal retractors) and the substances found in the excavation of the Bucheum at Armant fit well the details of the papyrus guide; such we may assume were the implements used for Apis too. Natron, myrrh, incense, and different oils were employed in the mummification process.[56] A cut on the left side of the bull allowed the clearing of the stomach and the chest. The intestines were placed in two jars, each within its shrine, whereas the heart was replaced in the bull after careful removal and treatment. A priest with special responsibility for cleaning out the carcass (the *wr-irj*) used a resinous oil (perhaps *kedria*) for this purpose, before filling the bull with bags of natron and sawdust to preserve its skin and form. The first four days appear to have been spent over this preliminary preparation, and in the heat it will have been necessary to act with speed. During this period those in high places might abstain from

[53] Vos dates this copy, which was purchased from a Cairo dealer in A.D. 1822, to 125–75 B.C. Petesis, son of Chonouphis, married in 131 B.C., *P. Leid.* 373a = App. B:8; if he married at the age of twenty-five and survived into his seventies he might also have presided over the much delayed burial of the bull of Gerg(et) Mut-iyti in 87/6 B.C.

[54] See figure 3 and chapter 1 n. 49.

[55] Compare Hdt. 2.87, for human mummification.

[56] Mond and Myers (1934), 1.20, 148–51; *PSI* 328 = *Pap. Lugd. Bat* 20.50 with commentary; Préaux (1939a), 369, for the supply.

all food and drink; a limited fast with nourishment confined to bread, water, and vegetables was normal for the entire seventy days.[57] Next would come the pickling, with the body packed in dry natron until it was cured and dry. And now, as the bull was bound, the process of rebirth began.

The binding of the bull during the following sixteen days, until day 68, was the responsibility of various priests presided over by the Overseer of the Mystery, the *ḥrj-sštȝ* or *stolistēs* in Greek, whose role was that of Anoubis presiding over the mystery of resurrection. His particular task was the preservation of the head, while four lector-priests, *ḥrj-ḥb.w*, bound the rest of the corpse. Seated one to a limb, the two in front would also look after the chest, while the two behind would deal with the anus and tail. Two further *smr*-priests would aid the Overseer of the Mystery with opening the mouth and other *wꜥb*-priests would watch the boat shrines in which the embalming material was stored. Before all this could start, the chamber was prepared, the linen strips and squares placed in readiness on a mat, and a heap of sand made ready for the bull. The bull was dragged into the chamber, on tree trunks used as rollers, and placed on its bed of sand. Ritually cleansed, the priests who would bind the bull could now begin their task.

The papyrus instructions record the process of binding—a mixture of rituals and techniques to be applied as the bull was brought back to life. The mouth was washed with terebinth resin and two of the teeth were removed; as artificial teeth were put in their place, the bull received new milk teeth and so became young again. In the place of eyes, great wads of linen filled out the sockets, to be covered with the bindings. For the recovery of sight a magical instrument might be used, or rolled papyrus spells were bound within the eyes. The four legs of the bull were bound, stretched out before and behind; gilded hooves replaced the unclean originals, which by now were falling off. Two versions survive for the anus. The recto of the papyrus describes how, all under a sheet, the anal canal was emptied, washed out with water and then filled with linen swabs. The more elaborate, and more costly, version of the verso describes the use of small packages of natron and myrrh within a larger parcel made to pack out the anus, to desiccate and so prevent decay. The binding finished, a further rite took place outside. In full view of the massed worshippers, the priests rent a sheet of linen; all set up a wail and mourned

---

[57] For humans, see the stele of Anemhor, Spiegelberg (1904), no. 31099.7 (73 B.C.); Lichtheim (1980), 132, in the story of Setne I; a royal fast, Vercoutter (1962), 38-39, text E.

the bull. The inner coffin for the bull was now prepared with its message of resurrection, a sheaf of corn and djed pillars, sacred symbols of Osiris. With care, the bull, bound to a board with rings attached, was lifted with a tackle and lowered within the coffin. It was day 68 of the ritual, and the masses were gathered as the final stages began.

Next morning, to the weeping and wailing of all participants, the coffin was hauled out of the Embalming House, placed within a shrine and then upon a boat. The boat rested on a wheeled base, as it moved along in procession westwards to the Lake of Pharaoh (plate ii).[58] In this great procession the gods took part; in its drama was reenacted the sending of the spirit of divine life. With Apis on his float were the divine sisters, the twins Isis and Nephthys, a part which, as we shall see, was played by local girls. Before went the standards of the two wolf gods who "opened the ways," Wepwawet, the gods of the north and the south; they were followed by Horos and Thoth, with Apis in the rear. All the priests were there in their robes, and the populace looked on. On arrival at the shore Apis was placed again on a bed of sand, his face turned towards the south. And now representatives of the priests embarked in a papyrus boat, the sacred bark of Osiris and Ra, to make the crossing over. Here on the lake, to the reading of the nine holy books which are listed in the ritual, were reenacted in this voyage the battles waged in mythical times, of Horos and Seth, of Ra, and of Apophis, the serpent of the deep. The sacred texts were recited, the crowds watched the show, and Apis faced southwards in witness; the victory that was gained was that of resurrection.

To mark this resurrection, Apis was now taken under the canopy which had stood erected on the shore of the lake from the very start of the ceremonies. Entering from the west, he left it from the east, and so symbolized rebirth. Within the tent took place that vital ceremony, the Opening of the Mouth, when new life might enter the bull. And now Apis was returned to the House of Embalming, through the Gate of the Horizon where the sun rose. This was a cosmic resurrection, and again to symbolize and secure rebirth the priests threw down in front of him the mud-brick of birth, the $mshn.t$-brick. It had been a long, full day, and Apis, magically reborn, was now returned to the second tent, close by his stall, where he spent his final night before burial the next day. And here the papyrus breaks off.

[58] For illustrations, Mariette (1872), plate 35; Petrie (1911a), plate 31 (in a boat on wheels), now in the Fitzwilliam Museum, Cambridge (plate ii, this volume); El-Amir (1948), plate xvii.4.

Throughout this ritual, recorded for those who took part, each individual role is carefully defined. At the center of the ceremony is the bull, the god to be reborn through the meticulous craft of the different priests and servants. It was not only the regular Ptah priests who were required for the ceremonies, but there were tasks too for private individuals, the twins hired to play the parts of Isis and Nephthys and all the regular mourners whose participation was, it seems, essential to the successful completion of the rites. As in human mummification, concentration on religious ritual and the ceremonies for the immortal soul overlay the physical nastiness of the process of preserving the body. Readings from sacred texts might accompany the counting of jars and clamps, and the winding of the linen bandages which went around the carcass. Popular participation gave grandeur to the spectacle, for the crowd also took part in the action of this greatest show of all, the mystery of Osiris.

In death Apis had become Osiris, and on the seventieth day he went to join the other Osiris cults of the Memphite necropolis. This day the bull was ferried over the lake and, on its sled,[59] dragged up the hillside and over the desert headland to its final place of rest. The crowds gathered by the thousands, and a special police officer was charged with control during the whole of this period of seventy days.[60] The men of Anoubis wore their ritual dress, the chantresses of Boubastis will have sung, and all the inhabitants and priests came out as the procession mounted the sphinx-lined way and appeared over the top of the bluff. The bull's coffin had already been put in place, and the ceremony culminating in the entombment of the bull was four days long. On the day of burial a further fast might be observed.[61] The necropolis community was now involved in the major ritual of its ceremonial life. The inhabitants of Memphis, with many visitors and pilgrims, joined in the celebrations.

The Hellenomemphites of the city had long taken part in this essentially Egyptian festival,[62] and with the great influx of Greeks following the conquest of Alexander, attempts were made to interpret these Memphite rituals in terms of Dionysiac mysteries, with Memphis now located

---

[59] Plut. *DIO* 35, *schedia*; Emery (1971), 9, remains of a wooden sledge in the burial area of the mothers-of-Apis; Farag (1975), 165-67; Martin (1979), 53, no. 173. For ruts on the avenue (not necessarily caused by the bull), see Smith and Jeffreys (1979), 24; Smith (1981), figure 1, opposite p. 334.

[60] The Phoenician Chaiapis, son of Paneith (plate v), *PP* 2139/5856, probably presided over the funeral of the bull of Ta-Renenutet I.

[61] Vos (1978), 264, for Buchis; Vercoutter (1962), 18, text B; Smith (1972), 178.

[62] Portrayed, for instance, in procession with a cow and bull, R. V. Nicholls in Martin (1979), 74-78, no. 284, with frontispiece.

within the traditional Greek topography of Hades. The Lake of Pharaoh which the Apis crossed was that of Acherousia. The staffs and scepters of the priests become Dionysiac *thyrsoi*, while the dress the men of Anoubis wore were *nebrides*, the fawn skins, of the Bacchic revelers. The great gates of the Sarapieion were those of Lethe and of Kokytos, bound in bronze and found within the temple of Hekate. The Greek Dionysiac statuary of the avenue to the Sarapieion stood as a forerunner to the syncretic accounts of later writers.[63]

The Apis Vaults

The lowering of the black granite lid of the massive sarcophagus of the Apis bull terminated the celebration for which preparations had started many years before. While Apis lived down in the valley temple of Ptah, up on the necropolis already his masons served their master at their task of hewing out the rock and building in the burial vaults. A fresh vault off the main corridor within the Sarapieion was prepared for each bull in advance. The sarcophagus was then obtained and brought downstream to Memphis from the south. Brought around by ship, this coffin was dragged up into the Sarapieion (probably from the west), then down the vaults and into place. The records left by the workers on their stelae at the entrance to the vaults illustrate these operations and their scale. Their labors, deep within the hillside, were seen to form in part a religious service for the god.

Employment as an Apis worker, a *by* or *mnḥ* of Osiris–Apis, was a low-grade priestly office performed in shifts,[64] and as with other priestly offices this labor force would normally change each month.[65] In this way the income and the divine blessing which accompanied this employment were spread more widely within the community. Men worked in smallish gangs of family groups. Twelve seems an average size for a group, made up of two or three families, with father, son, and sometimes grandson working on the job together, under the supervision of one or two

[63] Diod. Sic. 1.96.7-9; Plut. *DIO* 29 and 35 with Griffiths (1970), 403-4 and 431-32. The nebris might alternatively refer to the panther's skin worn by the high priest of Ptah.

[64] Apis-Osiris and Osiris-Apis are used indiscriminately. Bresciani (1967), 24, discusses the terms; despite her definition of *mnḥ* as the "dresser," the man concerned with preparing the bandages, men with this title are found working on the vaults. The Greek equivalents were perhaps *laaxos* and *hieroglyphos*.

[65] E.g., Brugsch (1884), 111, no. 2, for Mesore; 117, no. 5, for Phamenoth. For monthly office, cf. Pestman, *Rec.* 2.6 (201 B.C.), the priests of the Apis calves.

priest-supervisors.[66] When recorded, larger groups would have more priests in charge, and the different groups came under the general control of a priest-architect or clerk of works whose authority continued through the year and probably stretched widely over the Sarapieion and the Sacred Animal Necropolis to the north. Like the job of mason, this post too was a family preserve; one family of priest-architects is recorded stretching over what are probably four generations, from 229 to 97 B.C.[67]

The records put up by the masons, both to preserve the historical record of their existence and to bring themselves to the favorable attention of the god(s), give some indications of the nature of the group of those involved in this service for the Apis bull. The same names frequently recur and the same families certainly worked also for the Isis cow, the mother of Apis, for the two cults were closely linked with prophets shared by both.[68] In Phamenoth (March/April) 229 B.C. one Apis mason, Horenpe, the son of Totoes, traced his family back over 280 years for twelve generations, recording the results on a stele which marked the start of work on the burial vault for the bull of Gerg(et) I, then in its third year.[69] If Revillout is right, the source of his information lay close at hand, in records still existing which preserve the names he copied out, some of them incorrectly. Yet, as it stands, the family tree is easily reconstructed, and even if the first family working group has mistakenly been backdated some twenty years, or several of his direct ancestors upgraded in their posts, nevertheless the stele of Horenpe provides lively testimony to the sense of his place in history of an ordinary Apis mason.[70] It was this sense of continuity over time which so impressed Herodotus when he visited Egypt.

Work on the vaults of the Apis bulls may be charted in Appendix D, and the mothers-of-Apis now provide comparative information;[71] the

[66] Generally described as divine fathers and agents (*rḏ*); in chronological order: Revillout (1891b), 141, Louvre stelae 40 (2247) and 191; Brugsch (1884), 110, no. 2; 117-20, no. 4 = Revillout (1891b), 133-35, Louvre stele 114; Bresciani (1967), 29-30, stele 2.4; Revillout (1891b), 131, Louvre stele 107 (3367); 133, Louvre stele 39; 146, Louvre stele 112; Bresciani (1967), 35-36, stele no. 4.4; Revillout (1891b), 146, Louvre stele 113; 133, Louvre stele 24.

[67] Called *mr-kȝw.t*; in descending order: Onnophris, his sons Onnōphris and Nepherprēs, his son Kemnouphis, Revillout (1891b), 133-35, Louvre stele 114; Bresciani (1967), 27-28, stele no. 1(b).5; 32-34, stele no. 3.2; Revillout (1891b), 131, Louvre stele 107 (3367); 133, Louvre stele 39; Bresciani (1967), 34-38, stele no. 4.4; 38-40, stele no. 5.6.

[68] See Onnōphris I (*PP* 5657) and Herieus II (*PP* 5359), figure 6.

[69] Brugsch (1884), 117-20, no. 4 = Revillout (1891b), 133-35, Louvre stele 114.

[70] Cf. Smith (1972), 178 n. 10, a workman failing to find his ancestor's memorial; Crawford (1980), 10 n. 3, a family of Ptah priests recorded over sixty generations.

[71] Smith (1972); Vercoutter (1962), 125-30, at an earlier date.

fullest details that survive are for the bulls of Ta-Renenutet I and II. Build-ing might start as early as the bull's third year (the case for the bulls of Ta-Renenutet I and Gerg(et) I). Foundations were prepared, the walls were hewn and lined with stone, and efforts were made to tidy off the vault. Next the sarcophagus could be brought around through the wadi, dragged up the slope to the Sarapieion and down into the vault. This was a lengthy procedure; the sarcophagus for the bull of Ta-Renenutet I took thirty-five days, from 26 September to 31 October 248 B.C., before it finally rested in place. The great black granite sarcophagi were of course far heavier than the bulls, and extra rations were paid to the weary work-men who hauled them over the sand.[72] Complete, the vault was wreathed and decorated before being closed, to await the actual burial of the bull for whom it was prepared.

Normally it was only when work was in progress in the vaults or dur-ing the actual funeral that the great doors down into the Sarapieion vaults were opened, enabling the priests and workmen to go in. Surviving ded-ications all date from such periods of opening and, in their survival, they help to fill out the record. Occasionally the doors were open on other special days and, whereas among the earlier stelae from the vaults Mar-iette remarked on the numbers dedicated to mark a New Year's Day,[73] from the Ptolemaic period it is the festival of Imhotep which is twice named as the particular occasion of a dedication.[74] The opening of the vaults upon this feast day suggests the importance at this period of the cult of Imhotep/Asklepios, and of his link with the Apis bull, lord of the necropolis.

Some day it should be possible to comment from this record on the costs, in terms of men and rations, of all these operations, but such an enterprise requires the full publication of the stelae which survive. In the meantime, however, one stele, the record of an unnamed architect, per-mits two preliminary observations. In a record of the construction of the vault for the bull of the cow of Ta-Renenutet I, the dedicant lists the pe-riods spent on this work over the five years and five months from 11

[72] Maspero (1882), 113; Vercoutter (1962), xiii, an empty sarcophagus weighed 70 tons. Smith (1981), 338, for the route; (1972), 178, for the rations.

[73] Mariette (1857), 29; of the stelae for the first Apis of Dynasty XXVI, the majority are from 1 Thoth of Year 21.

[74] Brugsch (1886), 20, no. 24, Louvre stele 4157 (11 March 158 B.C.), 11, Mecheir; no. 31 (18 February 131 B.C.), 27, Tybi. The latter date does not appear as a major festival in Wildung (1977a), 75, no. 47.

August 253 B.C. to 8 January 247 B.C.[75] Within these periods were recorded the number of days during that period which were not worked, the implication being that only days actually worked were paid. So, the excavation of the vault lasted 105 days, of which 17 days were not worked; the building of the vault 185 days, with 33 idle; the entry of the sarcophagus lasted 35 days, with 7 idle; while the completion of the vault took 69 days, with 12 days idle. Of the total period of five years and five months, only one year and one month was actually spent on the job and, of these 394 days, the workforce was idle on 69. Whereas this shows a fairly consistent pattern of one day off for every five to six days worked, it also illustrates the uneven availability of the work. No Apis mason could expect to make a living on one job alone, especially when the work was further divided into monthly shifts. And while gangs of workmen seem likely to have moved around the necropolis and worked on different projects, the intermittent availability of this work made alternative sources of income desirable. It therefore comes as no surprise to find in the surviving masons' records a second function for these men; they are servants also of the living Apis in his stall.[76] Cults of the bull in life and death were always closely linked, and those who dug his vaults might also serve the living bull.

In Egyptian society a single priestly function would seldom provide a sufficient livelihood. The more successful an individual priest proved at accumulating functions, the more important he appeared to be within the hierarchy; many of the more lowly priests looked to work outside their cults to supplement their priestly income.[77] The masons for Osiris-Apis, who might also serve the living Apis, were not important men. And yet, through their corporate dedications, remembered not singly but with their families and those who shared their work, their record has survived, and with it details of the cult in which they served.

Burial was not the end, and, as with human burial places, the Apis vaults with the temple above served as the site for continuing cult. Sacrifices were made, libations poured, and dedications brought by pilgrims to the scene. As elsewhere in the other shrines of the Memphite necrop-

---

[75] Brugsch (1884), 112, no. 3; Revillout (1891b), 129, Louvre stele 82. I follow the timetable of Brugsch.

[76] Spiegelberg (1901b), 197-98; Bresciani (1967) contains many examples. In the Ptolemaic period there is no record of Ptah priests in this cult, cf. earlier Vercoutter (1962), 127-28.

[77] Crawford (1971), 176-81, priests as crown farmers; on accumulated functions, see chapter 4 above.

olis, the Sarapieion and its personnel supported an active cult life. The activities of these various cults are partially illustrated in the papers of the two sons of Glaukias and the ostraka of their contempoary Hor.[78]

OTHER MEMPHITE CULTS

Like Apis or the Isis cow, the ibis of Thoth and the hawk of Horos (at times combined as Harthoth) had their own priesthoods, chapels, and catacombs. And, as with the bull, both the production and the aftercare of the birds were the daily concern of a vast array of working priests. A chapel of birth and an ibis-rearing center are recorded down on the lake in the valley below, while up on the necropolis ibis eggs were also found in a courtyard excavated at the entrance to the ibis vaults.[79] The nightmare experienced by the priest Hor in Memphis gives some suggestion of the scale of ibises bred: "He said to me, Bring your clover, this food (for) the 60,000 ibises. I said to him, it is (in) Pi(?)-Thoth together with my fenugreek."[80] How long the birds were allowed to live is a matter for speculation. On death they were mummified, wrapped in linen, and placed in jars for dedication. With perhaps 10,000 ibis mummified and buried every year, the large-scale production of these birds produced a livelihood for numerous servants of the god. Thoth the ibis or Horos the hawk was present in each of these dedications and the god was honored with his image. Similar too, we may assume, was the pattern of organization for the many other animal cults of the necropolis, the cat of Bastet, the dog of Anoubis, the baboons, the rams, and the lionesses.[81]

The participation of the wider public was crucial to the continuation of these cults.[82] Whereas royal subsidy might meet the costs of basic upkeep, the contributions of pilgrims and visitors to the shrines were essential to their continuing success. Pilgrims came for many reasons, and the small bronze and faience figurines found over the slope of North Saqqara are witness to their piety. They purchased potted birds to dedicate or made

---

[78] See chapter 7.

[79] This section is based largely on Ray (1976), 130-6 (dreams and oracles), 136-44 (the ibis cult). See futher *P. Louvre* E 3266.6.C–D (197 B.C.) = App. B:2; Emery (1971), 4-9.

[80] *Hor* 8 recto.18-19.

[81] Ray (1972). The baboon stelae are to be published by J. D. Ray and H. S. Smith and the Isis-cow stelae by C.A.R. Andrews and H. S. Smith; see Smith (1974), 41-43, with preliminary observations.

[82] See *UPZ* 122 (157 B.C.) for a crown farmer from the neighboring Herakleopolite nome who visited the necropolis each year "to sacrifice."

offerings at the many shrines connected with the burial vaults that honeycomb the hillside.

Oracles and dreams formed part of the spiritual life connected with these cults, and their interpretation was practiced both by specialized priests and by others in the area.[83] Medical help might also be provided by these gods, and a large deposit of anatomical casts of Ptolemaic date, found in the area behind the temple terrace of the Sacred Animal Necropolis, is witness to the gratitude of pilgrim-patients. Similar dedications came from within the Upper Baboon Galleries, and it seems that Imhotep's healing power, which will be discussed below, was shared by other deities of the necropolis.[84] The fragments, however, of a Greek medical text from among the debris of the area may suggest that, serving as the god's interpreters, priests did not rely on the power of dreams and oracles alone.[85]

The reputed powers of the different gods drew individual pilgrims to the area, and the organized festivals of the gods attracted many more. Apis burials might take place only four times in a century, but the processions of the Ibis and the Hawk and the opening of their galleries for the mass burials underground of dedicated mummies formed an annual event on the necropolis, an occasion for celebration and popular participation. For, with entry to the actual shrines and temples restricted to priests, such public occasions played an important part in allowing more general participation in the cult.

The proper upkeep and administration of the various cults of the Sacred Animal Necropolis were essential for the goodwill of the gods, and that was the concern of rulers and their representatives alike. The priests, however, did not always play their part, and human weakness led to racketeering on the site. Gullible pilgrims wishing to dedicate a mummified bird in a pot, or perhaps an anatomical cast, might find themselves the victim of sharp practice from the priests. The temples each had their own deliberative council of priestly representatives to which appeal could be made, but, when matters got completely out of hand, the temple of Ptah might intervene. As seen above,[86] Hor's account of the abuses alleged in the ibis cult in the early second century B.C., and of the repeated attempts

[83] Sauneron (1959), 40-53; Posener (1960), 85-86, on the Egyptian tradition; Ray (1976), 130-36.

[84] Emery (1971), 3-4.

[85] Turner (1975a), 250, of the fourth or third century B.C. For temples as the center of medical knowledge, at a later date, see Reymond (1976).

[86] See chapter 4, n. 93, for the ruling: "one bird, one pot."

made to bring them under control, suggests that the consumer-pilgrims must have continued to suffer. However, in spite of this, these animal cults remained popular throughout the Ptolemaic period.

Animal cults were not the only cults of Memphis and its necropolis. Down in the valley it was the great temple of Ptah which dominated, and Ptah was worshipped here in many forms and with many consorts. The main Memphite Triad was that of Ptah, the craftsman mummiform god; Sachmet, his lioness consort; and their son, Nefertem/Nephthimis, the god of the lotus-flower.[87] But, as we have already seen, in the divine family Sachmet might be replaced by Astarte, while both Imhotep/Imouthes and Anoubis are also named as sons of Ptah. It is easier to list the cults of Memphis[88] than it is to know what they each involved or how they were organized. One of these cults stands out in importance, and that is the cult of Imhotep, architect of the great step-pyramid at Saqqara of the Third Dynasty pharaoh Zoser (c. 2600 B.C.). For the Greeks this somewhat unusual Egyptian deity, Imhotep/Imouthes, became identified with Asklepios, the god of healing.[89]

IMOUTHES/ASKLEPIOS

The process of deification of the priest-architect Imhotep, which may be partially traced, was complete by the time the Ptolemies arrived. The traditional site of his tomb, probably down on the desert edge somewhere north of the Temple of the Peak, had by this time become the great Asklepieion.[90] Judging both from the nomenclature of the area, where Imouthes and Peteimouthes, Asklepiades and Asklepias are regular Memphite names, and from the large number of bronze statues of the god discovered here, the cult of Imouthes/Asklepios was a major Memphite cult. A further measure of the god's importance, in at least one of his roles, is the tale already related of the birth of Imouthes/Petobastis, the last high priest of Ptah to hold office under the Ptolemies (see fig. 5). The hieroglyphic funeral stele of this high priest's mother, Taimouthes, records her birth and her marriage to Psenptais III, the high priest of Ptah, to whom she proceeded to bear three daughters.[91] Time passed and still they had no son.

[87] Quaegebeur, Clarysse, and Van Maele (1985).
[88] Kiessling (1953); Quaegebeur (1971b), 245.
[89] Wildung (1977a), 1-197; (1977b), 31-81.
[90] *UPZ* 125.8-9 (89 B.C.), with the discussion of topography in chapter 1 above.
[91] B.M. 147; Reymond (1981), 165-77, no. 20; Lichtheim (1980), 59-65.

I prayed together with the high priest to the majesty of the god great in wonders, effective in deeds, who gives a son to him who has none: Imhotep son of Ptah.

He heard our pleas, he hearkened to his prayers. The majesty of this god came to the head of the high priest in a revelation. He said: "Let a great work be done in the holy of holies of ʿAnchtawy, the place where my body is hidden. As reward for it I shall give you a male child."[92]

The high priest did what was asked of him. He built in the god's innermost shrine, he performed the relevant rituals (both sacrifices and the Opening of the Mouth for the god), and he richly rewarded the sculptors who worked on the shrine. His wife then conceived a male child, who was born on 15 Epeiph Year 6, 15 July 46 B.C., a feast day of Imouthes, son of Ptah.[93] As we have seen, they named the child Imouthes/Petobastis, in honor of the god.

It was not only the high ranks of the clergy but others, too, who addressed the god in hopes of a son, or a cure. The prayers and expectations of the Egyptian stelae with the tales of miracles the god performs are indeed similar in tone and content to contemporary Greek inscriptions from the shrine of the god Asklepios at Epidaurus. The god works wonders and, both in advance and in return, his worshippers make offerings at his shrine, so recording the works he performs. The sick might come to his shrine, and sometimes they were healed;[94] "throughout the two lands" it was Imhotep, son of Ptah, to whom they called "because of his magic-making."[95]

Besides his role as a god of healing, Imouthes was a scribal god of learning. Statuettes of the god portray him as a young man seated with a papyrus scroll on his knees, and in this guise he was also portrayed in small private shrines.[96] It seems probable too that, on a regular pattern, the stone bowls into which the Sarapieion twins poured daily libations when they mourned the Apis bull were fashioned like those of a scribe.[97] As a god of learning and script, he had an international following, as may be seen in a fine small bronze of the god, a papyrus on his knee, with a Phoenician inscription below. The statuette, which is from Memphis,

[92] Translated by Lichtheim (1980), 62.
[93] 16 Epeiph is given as the god's birthday in B.M. 512; see Wildung (1977a), 73-78, no. 47.
[94] *P. Petrie* I 30.(1).4-5 = III 42.H.(4) (third century B.C.); cf. Ray (1975), 185, with a statue made. On healing, see further chapter 7 n. 310 below.
[95] *Hor* 16 recto. 6-7 with notes.
[96] Wildung (1977a), 82-83, 86; (1977b), 39-43.
[97] Wildung (1977b), 47; on the twins, see chapter 7 below.

dates from the early Ptolemaic period, or shortly before.[98] The scribal image continued through the ages. The papyrus turned into a tablet, and for Arab scholars of the tenth century A.D. Imouthes/Asklepios became both physician and alchemist.[99]

Egyptian cults were never exclusive, and the attributes of one deity were often shared by others, especially when their shrines were close. We have already noted the anatomical dedications made along the temple terrace on the western side of the Saqqara bluff; for Thoth shared Imouthes' powers to heal and cure. Imouthes was not the only god to read and write; Thoth too was known for his learning. And so in a Memphite setting, with such overlapping functions and identifications, the increasing syncretism of later Egyptian religion flourished, and might provide what both pilgrims and local worshippers would look for from their gods.

[98] Lipiński (1986), 160, no. 134.
[99] Wildung (1977b), 76-78; he was also identified with Joseph, another who dealt in dreams.

7

BETWEEN TWO WORLDS: THE SARAPIEION

The visitor to the Sarapieion who followed Strabo's route, as described in chapter 1, up the long sphinx-lined avenue over the Saqqara bluff, eventually came out in the Sarapieion complex (see fig. 4). To the left was the temple of Nectanebo II, important as the last of the native kings and the object locally of cult as a falcon-god. Opposite, slightly to the left, the unwary visitor was faced by a semicircle of eleven marble statues, Greek sages and poets, seated or standing in formal pose.[1] The sight is startling in the desert landscape, and whether these learned men, sculpted in limestone probably in the early second century B.C., decorated a small portico—a place for shelter against the stinging storms of sand, for refreshment among the desert dunes—or guarded a shrine of some importance—the site once perhaps of Alexander's tomb[2]—in their classical severity they form a bold statement of the new mastership of what before had been an Egyptian world.

Glancing right down the paved avenue to the Sarapieion and the entrance to the Apis vaults, on either side the visitor would find an interesting assortment of limestone statues, Greek and Egyptian deities, and symbols. Here on the northern side lay two chapels side by side, first a small one-chambered Greek building, with steps and four Corinthian columns, which served as home to those who tended the sacred lamps, and beyond a small Egyptian chapel which housed a brightly painted limestone statue of the Apis bull, which now stands in the Louvre.[3] Together and yet separate, the buildings and statues were there for the Greeks and Egyptians who worked and worshipped in Memphis. Here Apis was Osor-Hapi, the deified Apis bull, yet as Sarapis to the immigrants his chthonic aspect was that of Dionysos. The strange jumble of Dionysiac symbols—with peacocks and panther, a singing Siren and Ker-

[1] Maspero (1882), 16, the retaining wall was added later in antiquity; on the statues, see chapter 4 n. 60 above.
[2] The statues of course would postdate the removal of the actual body to Alexandria.
[3] Maspero (1882), 29; Lauer and Picard (1955), 13, figure 8.

beros mounted by a child—standing beside the bull, lion, and sphinxes of Egypt may serve to introduce the complex, bifocal world of the Sarapieion.[4]

The cult of Sarapis, that Greek masterpiece of adaptation of an old Egyptian cult, is known from literary sources,[5] but it is the collected papers of one man, his family and his friends, from the midyears of the second century B.C. which, for a brief twenty years or so, illuminate the community of the Memphite Sarapieion, the original Egyptian home of the new Hellenistic god.[6] Recently supplemented by the demotic ostraka of the Egyptian priest Hor/Harthoth, who came from the Delta to serve in the neighboring ibis cult of Thoth,[7] the Sarapieion archive sheds light on both the religious and day-to-day lives of many of those associated with the shrine.

At the center of the Sarapieion archive is Ptolemaios, son of Glaukias. His father was a soldier, a Macedonian, settled in the neighboring Herakleopolite nome where he owned a house in the village of Psichis.[8] His mother is unknown, but in spite of the Greek names of her sons (Ptolemaios, Hippalos, Sarapiōn, and the youngster Apollonios), she may have been Egyptian; such mixed marriages were not uncommon among the army communities settled on the land, and in this case is suggested by the degree of Egyptianization found particularly in Apollonios. An army career like his father's would have been the normal expectation for Ptolemaios, but events which followed the death in 180 B.C. of Ptolemy V Epiphanes caused major confusion and disruption in the life of many inhabitants of Egypt. The times in which these boys grew up were troubled times. On the throne was (again) a child, Ptolemy VI Philometor, while, until her death in 176 B.C., power lay in the hands of the queen mother with the courtiers Eulaios and Lenaios.[9] The earlier loss, in 200 B.C., of Koile Syria and of Ptolemaic possessions in the Aegean and Asia Minor had deprived Egypt of overseas income and a source of silver. Egypt was constantly under arms. The break in cleruchic settlement records for one

---

[4] Maspero (1882), 29-30; Lauer and Picard (1955), 173-260.
[5] Surveyed by Fraser (1972), 1.246-59; see Préaux (1978), 649-55.
[6] Wilcken (1927), with pp. 104-16; the archive must have been discovered around A.D. 1820.
[7] Ray (1976), with pp. 117-54.
[8] *UPZ* 9-11 (160 B.C.); see now N. Lewis (1986), 69-87.
[9] Mørkholm (1961); Fraser (1972), 2.211 n. 212; Walbank (1979), 355.

nearby Fayum village for the first thirty years of Philometor's reign [10] is but one sign of the same troubles, while the victory near Pelusium in 169 B.C. of the Syrian king Antiochus IV Epiphanes brought a brief interruption to Ptolemaic rule in Egypt.[11]

When therefore in 172 B.C. Ptolemaios, son of Glaukias, came to the Sarapieion and was "held" there by the god,[12] whatever its origins his detention, or *katochē* (which will be discussed below), should be seen against this background of troubles and confusion. About the same time Hor of Sebennytos also joined the community of North Saqqara and, though he is nowhere labeled *enkatochos*, a detainee, the safety of the temples here may have exercised a similar attraction for this Egyptian priest.[13] It is simply from the chance survival of the Sarapieion archive that so much is known of Ptolemaios, of Apollonios his younger brother who was also briefly "held" from February until September 158 B.C., and of other detainees; and yet this chance survival of the Sarapieion papers of Ptolemaios and of the ostraka of Hor, supplemented as they can be by the evidence of the excavations of the Sacred Animal Necropolis, does allow an investigation of the position of such detainees, of the cults of the necropolis, and of the social and economic life of its inhabitants. And throughout the evidence—often very personal evidence—in the record of dreams and the daytime preoccupations of those who wrote, in their official reports and in the copies they made of current or classical literature, are reflected some of the concerns and tensions, the hopes and the fears both of the recent immigrants and of the old Egyptian inhabitants who together formed the newly mixed society of the Sarapieion.

In this study of the Sarapieion two areas of investigation are of particular concern. First, the small-scale interests and daily activities of the protagonists of the archive must be set in the wider context of the political events and economic developments of the times. The one illuminates the other, and within the society of the Sarapieion stand reflected events of both national and international importance. Second, however, and with greater emphasis here, is the attempt to portray and analyze the nature of the society and culture which had evolved in this place after a century and a half of Ptolemaic rule. Separate in many respects, the two nations who

---

[10] Crawford (1971), 61.
[11] Walbank (1979), 321-25, surveys the evidence.
[12] *UPZ* 15.5
[13] Ray (1976), 119.

together formed the major part of the population of Egypt sometimes met on common ground.

THE SONS OF GLAUKIAS AND THEIR CIRCLE

In October 163 B.C. the royal couple, Ptolemy VI Philometor and Kleopatra II, were in residence in the royal palace in Memphis. The flood had subsided; the pharoah was permitted again to travel by river, and the city of Memphis was a suitable place to celebrate the new Egyptian year which started 1 Thoth, 3 October 163 B.C.[14] For his subjects, the king was now available to receive local appeals and petitions, and they may well have taken advantage of his presence.[15] For the authorities, such visits presented security problems, and, with unrest in the countryside, the fear of terrorism exercised those with responsibility for the safety of the king. On 16 Thoth, 18 October 163 B.C., a tip-off resulted in a search for arms in the Sarapieion. Ptolemaios, son of Glaukias, reported after the event:

To king Ptolemy and queen Kleopatra his sister, the Theoi Philometores, greetings from Ptolemaios son of Glaukias, Macedonian. I have spent ten years in detention in the Astartieion in the Sarapieion and have not left the pastophorion where I am shut in up to the present time. On 16 Thoth, Ptolemaios, the representative of the chief of police in the Anoubieion, and Amōsis, the chief priest's deputy, bringing guards with them entered the Astartieion in the great Sarapieion where I am detained, as already stated, up to the present time. Claiming there were arms there, they searched the place from top to bottom but found nothing. They left having done nothing irregular. Late in the evening, carrying a torch, Amōsis, the chief priest's deputy, returned with Imouthes who is in charge of the pastophoroi, Harendōtēs son of Katytis, Harendōtēs son of Nikchthnibis, Herbellēs son of Harimouthēs and Psenchōsis, the servant of Amōsis; they laid hands on me with force and stripped the shrine, carrying off everything on deposit there; they put a seal on everything else.

On the 17th of the same month they returned early in the morning and removed the remaining objects they had sealed; in addition they plundered the deposits of other detainees. And one Harmais, recognizing his own personal storage jar, which held his savings, laid hold of it; Amōsis put a seal on this too, and handed it over to a certain Theōn, son of Paēs. Adding insult to

[14] Wilcken (1927), 250. The twins celebrated the New Year Egyptian style with the purchase of goose flesh for sacrifice, *UPZ* 84.57-58, 73 (163 B.C.), and the day is recorded as a festival in the temple calendars at Edfu, Dendera and Esna, *UPZ* 89, introduction.
[15] E.g., *UPZ* 42.3, the twins.

injury he entered the innermost sanctuary of the goddess and stripped it, destroying the shrine.

Harimouthes, deputy of the epistates, came back on another occasion and, entering, found a bronze dish belonging to the goddess which he [grabbed] and removed. Further, Pabelphis son of Peteharendōtēs and Nikchthnibis son of Imouthes entered the place with evil intent and searched it; finding nothing of value, when they found some lead drinking cups they did not even leave these for us. When we inquired the reason for this intrusion the reply was that they had come to seize the pledged property and were sent by Psoulis who is in charge of the pastophoroi; but they handed the cups over to Kephalas who guards the door.

This, O sovereign, is the reason I beg you not to ignore me since, on each of these occasions, I am set upon by those named above in such a cruel manner, since I am insulted and used lawlessly. And, if it meets your approval, require Demetrios son of Sōsos the Cretan, to appear before you to put the case on my behalf, since on account of my detention I may not do this. Those named above should also appear so that, under your guidance, they may make me just amends. In this way shall I be granted your aid and succor. Farewell.[16]

Besides addressing the royal couple, Ptolemaios made a similar appeal to Diodotos, the strategos.[17] An Egyptian, who shared a pastophorion (a priest's chamber) with Ptolemaios, filed a demotic report on his loss on the same occasion.[18] Whatever the facts of the case—and legitimate arms searching would seem to have led on to illegitimate looting, while the seizure of pledged property[19] on another, later occasion was perhaps unrelated but provided a valid reason for entry—this incident may be used to introduce some of the problems connected with the protagonists of our archive.

Both Ptolemaios and Harmais, the probable author of the demotic complaint just mentioned (UPZ 6a),[20] are detainees subject to katoche.

[16] UPZ 6. My translation is at times free, but I hope correct. (On the meaning of line 11 see Préaux 1942, 152). The spelling of the Egyptian names is interesting from the point of view of Ptolemaios' local accent.

[17] UPZ 5. On whether both petitions were sent, see Clarysse (1986), 49.

[18] UPZ 6a (cf. Revillout 1893, xvii) with the important re-edition by Clarysse (1986) which renders invalid earlier discussions of the text; see especially Delekat (1964), 22-25, 77.

[19] Pledges occur in later accounts of Ptolemaios, SB 7616.65 margin, 83; UPZ 112 verso; cf. 99.33 (158 B.C.).

[20] The natural assumption is that the author of this text is the Harmais of UPZ 6.19 and (p. 648) 7.25-26 (November 163 B.C.), but his claim is to have been [attached to] the shrine for eight years, UPZ 6a.2, appears at variance with UPZ 2.2 (163 B.C.), "in the fifth year of detention," of the same year. It could be that the figure was changed in the translation into Greek, that Harmais was unsure of the time involved, or that he had spent three years in the shrine before becoming an enkatochos.

Astarte's shrine is where these individuals lived, while the great Sarapieion is the more general scene of action. The economic status of the detainees is mentioned here—their savings, deposits, and personal possessions.[21] The question is also raised of relations between the temple and
state authorities. Both join in the arms search of the pastophorion, but
later complaints are made to secular offices concerning the subsequent
activities of the temple representatives. Law and order in this community
was a difficult matter.

The institution of katoche has been a subject of continuing discussion
since the Sarapieion archive was first published. Discussions have quite
naturally concentrated on the reasons for detention, on the personal restrictions under which the detainees lived, their role within the life of the
temple, and on the possibility of release from the condition. Almost all
the Greek and some of the demotic evidence on which such discussions
are based is contained in Wilcken's edition of the collected Sarapieion papyri, *Urkunden der Ptolemäerzeit* I. Combined with the reedition of several
crucial documents, Delekat has questioned earlier interpretations of some
of these difficult texts,[22] and recently Clarysse has reexamined *UPZ* 6a, a
key demotic text which, as he shows, tells more of the presuppositions
of earlier editors than of katoche itself.[23] That some of the evidence is
contained in a dream text is a complicating factor,[24] and the few recorded
cases of such detention from outside Egypt add nothing of substance to
the Memphite material.[25]

The limited nature of the surviving evidence has resulted in a series of
alternative explanations based on different interpretations of the same
pieces of evidence. The interpretations given to katoche range from detention with a legal origin, arising from debt or misdemeanor,[26] to a primarily religious detention by the god, which followed an omen or sign
and involved some form of self-dedication of the detainee.[27] The enkato-

[21] A contemporary bronze savings box from the Memphite Sarapieion, with an interesting mixture of Greek and Egyptian motifs, is described by Vermeule (1962).
[22] Delekat (1964), 22-25 (*UPZ* 6a), 48-55 (*UPZ* 3), 51-55 (*UPZ* 4), 141-44 (*UPZ* 78).
[23] Clarysse (1986).
[24] *UPZ* 79,13-14 (159 B.C.), the only evidence for katoche applying to the twins, central
to the argument of Delekat.
[25] At Priene, Hiller von Gaertringen (1906), no. 195.29 (*c.* 200 B.C.), in the cult of the
Egyptian gods; *OGIS* 262.25, of Ouranios Zeus (Baal) of Baitokaikē in Syria; *CIG* 2.3163
(A.D. 212), of Sarapis in Smyrna. See Wilcken (1927), 70-75, for the literary evidence.
[26] Sethe (1913); von Woess (1923); with further literature in Delekat (1964), 1-10. Frenkian (1967) tends to the "secular" interpretation.
[27] Wilcken (1927), 55-62, with earlier references. Delekat (1964), 176-81, takes elements
from the two approaches with reference to Canaanite precedents; Ray (1976), 162, surveys

choi have been variously interpreted as petty criminals, benefiting from temple asylum, or as religious recluses, with lives dedicated to the service of either Sarapis or Astarte. The legal basis of their position has been subjected to thorough scrutiny with reference to the laws of asylum, manumission, and adoption.[28]

Here my aim is to present the limits of what is known of Memphite katoche and to locate the institution within the social and religious context of the mixed society of the Sarapieion. First, the physical setting of detention in Memphis was the great Sarapieion, where in 161 B.C. a certain Diphilos is described as "one of those servants detained by Sarapis."[29] It was, however, as noted above, the Astarte temple where at least some of these detainees actually passed their time. Ptolemaios, son of Glaukias,[30] like his Egyptian companion Harmais or, briefly in 158 B.C., his younger brother Apollonios,[31] spent his days in the service of Astarte. He was lodged in a pastophorion, in some sort of storeroom or cell, within the Astartieion, and Astarte is the goddess in whose cult these enkatochoi were involved. Indeed, Sarapis appears secondary in this respect—a later, Egyptian connection, perhaps, to an earlier Phoenician institution,[32] which may indeed have arisen from the position of the Astarte temple within the Memphite Sarapieion.[33] Second, we may consider the detainees themselves. What is particularly striking here is the variety of backgrounds from which these men might come. This was no exclusive status, and Harmais the Egyptian shared accommodation with Ptolemaios, a Macedonian (though born in Egypt). If Ptolemaios appears to have made a greater success of his position, that is probably because it is his archive which survives.

The status itself brought with it certain material benefits, for the enkatochoi were housed and Ptolemaios at least was on the temple payroll, coming under the supervision of the pastophoroi. Normally low-level employees, belonging to the "forecourt" of the temple and involved in cult activities without enjoying priestly status,[34] the pastophoroi func-

---

the question with reference to the demotic evidence; Préaux (1978), 653-55, argues for a form of novitiate.

[28] Especially by German scholars: von Woess (1923); Delekat (1964).

[29] *UPZ* 8.18-19, *tōn parakatechomenōn hypo tou Sarapios therapeutōn.*

[30] *UPZ* 7.9-11; 8.9-10.

[31] From February to September, *UPZ* 12.36-37; 13.18; 97.13-14, 17. Other detainees: Hephaistion, *UPZ* 59; 60 (168 B.C.); perhaps Harendōtēs, *UPZ* 98.98; 99.6-7 (158 B.C.).

[32] Cumont (1929), 260-61 no. 68; see Delekat (1964), Canaanite.

[33] *UPZ* 52.6; 53.6.

[34] Ray (1976), 136; Schönborn (1976). The demotic is *wn-pr.*

tioned as part of the temple community in their relations with the enkatochoi. The man in charge of the pastophoroi, Imouthes,[35] was among
those who invaded Ptolemaios' pastophorion on the evening of 18 October 163 B.C., and it was a pastophoros (in 158 B.C. Aonchis,[36] replaced
in 156 B.C. by Patos)[37] who disbursed the temple grant to Ptolemaios.
Ptolemaios himself was closely associated with the pastophoroi, though
he is never called by that title. Of his monthly allowance from the temple,
40 drachmas was designated for the pastophoroi;[38] it would grant him
participation in their processions, and probably also in their communal
feasts.

Besides benefits, however, there were limits to personal freedom. Once
accepted as an enkatochos, an individual seems to have been confined
within limits. Normally, these limits were those of the enclosure of the
Sarapieion,[39] though in the case of Ptolemaios it appears they were those
of his pastophorion.[40] While it provided some form of protection from
the outside world, this also meant that dealings with that world were
mainly secondhand. Only when others visited the temple might firsthand
contacts be made. There were therefore constraints on freedom of movement for a detainee but, as we shall see, in the political and economic
turbulence of the second century B.C., this condition might nonetheless
be sought and voluntarily entered into. Release too from katoche, as in
the case of Apollonios, seems to have been straightforward, though the
psychological effects of long-term confinement might result in a personal
reluctance to leave the protection of the sanctuary.

Once a man was accepted into this status, within the overall framework
of constraints opportunities existed for him to better his condition in both
official and unofficial capacities. The daily responsibilities and concerns
of men like Ptolemaios are nowhere conveniently listed or summarized.
But some sense of the varied activities with which they filled the day, of
their involvement in a wide variety of enterprises, and of their strategies

[35] UPZ 5.14; 6.12-13. In 5.42-43 and 6.31 Psoulis is given this title; Wilcken is probably
right to insert ho para making Imouthes subordinate to Psoulis.
[36] UPZ 97.1, 4; 98.56; 99.2, 34-35 (158 B.C.). 200 drachmas are still owed him in 156 B.C.,
UPZ 101.10; cf. 103.1 for 154/3 B.C.
[37] UPZ 101.1; 102.5.
[38] UPZ 98.139; 99.8-10; SB 7617.44.
[39] So Wilcken (1927), 62-77.
[40] Prepared, like Delekat (1964), 20-21, to take UPZ 6.3-5, 8-9 (163 B.C.), at face value, I
differ here from Wilcken (1927), 62-63, 358-59. Of the texts he adduces, UPZ 78 is a dream
text and 6a now removed from the debate. The reference in UPZ 53.6 (162/1 B.C.) to "in
the presence of Sarapis" need not exclude the Astarte shrine within the Sarapieion.

for survival within the temple community may perhaps be gained from a close perusal of their documents. Among the scrap papers of Ptolemaios there survive records of the "account of Astarte"[41] in which expenditure is listed for cult purposes from 158 and 156 B.C.[42] Here, in drafts full of arithmetical blunders, duplicate entries, and general obscurity, together with his monthly allowance of 100 drachmas, are listed the sums regularly owed to Ptolemaios by the temple for incense (140 drachmas a month), wood for sacrificial fuel (60 drachmas a month), for temple lighting,[43] and other occasional cult expenses.[44] For in some obscure way Ptolemaios seems to have carried responsibility for the acquisition of these cult ingredients. The temple, however, was rarely prompt in its reimbursements and the accounts become more often the record of sums owed than of repayment.[45]

Within the temple community existed a multiplicity of ways of making good such losses, and over the years these detainees became expert both in spotting and in exploiting any opportunity. One of the ways in which Ptolemaios might recoup the money owed him by the temple was through his organization of the sale of porridge within the temple community. *Athēra*, a porridge made of olyra flour mixed with either milk or (as here) with water, was, it seems, a regular Egyptian form of sustenance and was prepared for sale to two groups of temple workers called taplaeitai and atastitai.[46] Cooked in an oven fired by rushes, it was sold in units reckoned by the bronze pot or vat, *chalkion*, in which it was cooked. One chalkion was the equivalent of a metretes containing 80 hin or 36.48 liters. It provided either a month's supply for an individual or, more probably, a daily supply for the group and, at the cost of 150 drachmas, was purchased by a different individual or pair of individuals each day.[47] The price assumes a higher level of syntaxis for most temple employees than that of the monthly 100 drachmas which Ptolemaios received in cash. It also illustrates well the way in which state subsidies to the temple benefited the temple community at large.

---

[41] *SB* 7617.52, 79 (158 B.C.).

[42] *SB* 7617 (158 B.C.); *UPZ* 99; 101 (156 B.C.).

[43] *UPZ* 99.6-7, 40 drachmas for *lychnia* in Phamenoth, in the form of a pledge from Harotōtēs; *SB* 7617.54, 82 with *UPZ* 99.33, a further pledge for four times the amount in Pachons. In Pauni, *ellychnia* accounted for 150 drachmas, *SB* 7617.62

[44] Water for use in festivals, 24 drachmas recorded for Pachons (June) 158 B.C., *SB* 7617.55, cf. 88, under Pauni.

[45] E.g., *UPZ* 99.2.

[46] Hellanikos, *FGrH* 323a, F.192; Pliny, *HN* 22.121; Hesych. *s.v.* with milk; Ps.-Callisthenes 1.32.12, fed to the *agathoi daimones* in Alexandria.

[47] *UPZ* 98 and 99 for the operation; 98.10, 94, for the chalkion as metrētēs; Viedebantt (1913), 1644-49, for the hin. The entries for Harmais in 98.35, 58, and 114 remain obscure.

In the spring of 158 B.C. the quantities of water, flour, and rushes used for the cooking were recorded by Ptolemaios, and, through the pasto-phoros Aonchis, the costs were assumed by the temple.[48] Over the twenty-one days recorded in the account, 316 *keramia* (jars) of water at 7.5 drachmas each were supplied by the water carrier Petosor( ); 7,600 bundles of reeds were bought from Teebēsis at a cost of 1,900 drachmas, and the *hypokaustēs* who stoked the oven was paid 405 drachmas for his labor.[49] The flour used for the porridge, 34½ measures in all, is recorded without a price under the names of those who provided it: the taplaeitai, Ptolemaios himself, his roommate Harmais, and Harendotes;[50] as with the loaves supplied to the Sarapieion twins, this flour seems to have been issued as part of the syntaxis. Assuming all this evidence is relevant to the one operation, 4,675 drachmas were spent on the preparation of 32½ chalkia of porridge which would sell for 4,875 drachmas. The profit, which is not great, would presumably in theory go to the temple author-ities who purchased the ingredients, but Ptolemaios (and maybe others) was able to set this income against the money owed him by the temple.[51] Many interests were therefore served by such an arrangement—those of Ptolemaios, of the temple, and of those whose sustenance came from the preparation.

Athera was, it seems, a specifically Egyptian food but the names of Astarte's servants, listed in two groups of atastitai and taplaeitai,[52] suggest that the language of the cult, in the organization of which the Macedonian Ptolemaios was so closely involved, was neither Greek nor Egyptian, but rather that of the Phoenician homeland of the goddess. Here, within the confines of the Sarapieion, people from the mixed backgrounds of the Ptolemaic city lived, fed, worked, and worshipped together.

Besides illustrating his involvement in cult supplies and the provision of porridge for groups within the temple, separate accounts record, for short periods, allowances made by the temple for Ptolemaios' basic needs. A water account for July/August of an unknown year lists sixty-three keramia at 5 drachmas each provided over a period of forty-one days.[53] One or two keramia are the order of most days, but in mid-August, not

<hr/>

[48] *UPZ* 98.56; 99.1-5 (158 B.C.).
[49] *UPZ* 98.60-61, 81 (water), 11-19, 49 (reeds), 94-98 (flour), 128 (total); 98.50, cf. 95.5, 45 drachmas (hypokaustes).
[50] *UPZ* 98.94-98.
[51] *UPZ* 99.22-27.
[52] *UPZ* 98.2, 44, 86, 99; see chapter 3 above.
[53] *UPZ* 105; cf. 82 (163–161 B.C.), two jars a day; 98.131-47 (April 158 B.C.), one jar a day (and not therefore connected with the porridge supply); 99.1-25 with *SB* 7617.1-30 (158 B.C.), two-plus jars a day.

surprisingly, consumption goes up, and two keramia are standard, with three on one day. With no source of water on the necropolis, the daily journeys of the water carrier,[54] back and forth from the valley below, will have been as regular a feature of life on the western escarpment as it still is today. In this particular account Ptolemaios records 315 drachmas as owed him by the temple for the cost of his water; 200 drachmas were paid immediately, 50 drachmas sometime later, and 65 drachmas were still outstanding at the time the account was drawn up in its present form. The scale of arrears is regular.[55] With a monthly water consumption standing at approximately 230 drachmas, the irregularity of receipt was such that Ptolemaios would need to fall back on other resources to meet the cost of this essential requirement.

In addition to water, oil was an essential daily requirement. Kiki oil (castor oil) was issued to those in the temple's employ at the rate of one *lekythos* of 15 kotylai every ten days;[56] the lekythos was not always full, with 14.5 kotylai often recorded instead.[57] With 144 kotylai to the metretes, the allowance, a generous one, would seem to stand at 3 ½ metretai a year.[58] Castor oil, however, was suited primarily for lighting and may not be used in cooking. Perhaps, therefore, this generous allowance was made to cover some of the temple lighting. Or perhaps, more likely, the allowance included an element of substitution for edible sesame oil; a reverse substitution (sesame for kiki oil) is certainly documented for the twins (see below). As with water, the cost of oil came to Ptolemaios from the temple, and as with water it was often overdue.[59] At the foot of the account recording the outlay on temple cult from June to August in 158 B.C., Ptolemaios listed 1,320 drachmas as owed him for 2½ measures of kiki oil; 400 drachmas were paid him by Teuthratis (otherwise unknown), and the remaining 920 drachmas came in later.[60] The price therefore envisaged here for castor oil is 55 drachmas a lekythos.

A grain allowance also came to Ptolemaios from the temple. Probably

[54] Water was transported in skins: *UPZ* 8.34, 36 (161 B.C.), a *sakkophoros* and an *asillophoros*.

[55] *UPZ* 21-25; cf. 98.28 and *SB* 7617.30, 522.5 drachmas owed for sixty-eight jars (i.e., at 7.5 drachmas a jar).

[56] *UPZ* 104.

[57] *UPZ* 94.21-45 (February–August 158 B.C.).

[58] See the discussion in chapter 5, nn. 96-97, and this chapter, n. 161.

[59] *UPZ* 99.46 (158 B.C.), 920 drachmas owed up to the end of Epeiph (August).

[60] *UPZ* 99.50-52 (158 B.C.). For *cho(es)* instead of *me(trētai)*, see 98.94 (158 B.C.). *SB* 7617.76 prints 1,380 drachmas, perhaps a mistake.

standing at one artaba (of olyra) a month,[61] in practice it was issued in small quantities of different grains, in spelt, emmer (olyra called *palaios sitos*), or as kyllestis loaves.[62] Twelve artabas of olyra, the equivalent of only 122.6 kilograms of unmilled wheat a year, is below a subsistence minimum. This basic allowance must have been supplemented, either by purchase with his cash allowance or from his involvement in activities on the side. For with such temple allowances both minimal in rate and uncertain in arrival, supplementation from outside the temple was not only desirable but also necessary.

Any who sought asylum within the safety of the Sarapieion needed a protector to provide them with food.[63] So too Ptolemaios depended on outside subventions to support him. When in October 164 B.C. his father died during the troubles in the kingdom, Ptolemaios was already in the Sarapieion, with three younger brothers, Hippalos, Sarapiōn, and Apollonios, in the family home at Psichis in the Herakleopolite nome. Without their elder brother to protect them, the brothers found themselves harassed by the local headmen and also by the neighbors.[64] Ptolemaios responded in his usual way, took up his pen, and drafted an appeal to Philometor and his queen Kleopatra, whom, with an eye to obtaining their help, he addresses as "savior and beneficent gods."[65] The reasons he gives for his appeal are both personal and economic: the intervention of the strategos is requested since his brothers provide his bread supply and so support him, and in the present circumstances they were hindered from providing this support.[66] The theme recurs when, on 3 October 158 B.C., after a short period during which his youngest brother Apollonios joined Ptolemaios in detention, Ptolemaios petitioned the royal couple, asking them for help in getting Apollonios enrolled in the army. He was without children and, once in the army, Apollonios could help his elder

---

[61] *SB* 7617.91-103 (158 B.C.), 1½ artabas in Pharmouthi and 1 artaba in Pachons, Pauni, and Epeiph (the figure 4½ in line 98 represents artabas [corrected] rather than drachmas); *UPZ* 98.58-59.

[62] *UPZ* 94.11-20 (159/8 B.C.), the white loaves are specifically for the Isis festival.

[63] Cf. Hdt. 3.48, the Corcyrean youths sent to Sardis by Periander are fed by the Samians after taking asylum in the Hera temple; *P. Cair. Zen.* 59620.13-15 (late second century B.C.), Arsinoe supplies Eutychos. Ptolemaios perhaps played this role earlier for the twins and Herakleia; see below.

[64] *UPZ* 9 (161/60 B.C.), the *archontes*; 10; 11 (160 B.C.), the neighbors.

[65] *UPZ* 9.9-10 (161/60 B.C.); cf. 3.10-11 (164 B.C.). On the connotations, see Nock (1972), 720-35.

[66] *UPZ* 9.14 (161/60 B.C.); 24.9-10, 22 (162 B.C.), "my younger brother who provides my *trophē*."

brother. "I shall have the chance," he writes,[67] "of a decent standard of living and of his help." Such outside help, it seems, in the form of food was needed to guarantee Ptolemaios a reasonable existence within the confines of the Astarte temple. Enkatochoi were, it is clear, very marginal characters within the life and structure of the temple community.

For Ptolemaios, Apollonios was never a reliable source of support and, during a period of extreme economic difficulty outside the Sarapieion, this added to the many problems which troubled him. From his papers Ptolemaios appears a self-absorbed and troubled individual who on occasion might even absentmindedly sign himself Ptolemaios, son of Ptolemaios.[68] His troubled personality may be seen in the strange episode in 164 B.C. of the young girl Herakleia. Herakleia was a teenager (a *korasion*) who had taken refuge in the temple where, perhaps in return for her keep, she worked for Ptolemaios. When she was seized by Zoilos, a *rhabdouchos* or magistrate's attendant, and handed over to the military authorities down in Memphis, Ptolemaios complained, again to the king and queen, that she had been forcibly removed from the protection of the temple. The background to this one-sided report is obscure, and the two papyri which treat the episode are particularly fragmentary, with the result that modern editors have presented very different interpretations of the episode.[69] One word, however, is clear—*teknopoēsasthai*, "to become a father,"[70] and this perhaps was Ptolemaios' aim in trying to hold on to Herakleia. With the death of his father it was a bad year for Ptolemaios, and his own childlessness, in a society where children provided support for their parents, continued to trouble him.[71] Concern for the future combined with sexual frustration comes clearly through his dreams.[72] Herakleia perhaps filled a hole in the life of a lonely enkatochos; what we shall never know is whether Zoilos' intervention relieved her from unwanted attention. She is not heard of again.

The Herakleia incident was a brief one and, in the record of Ptolemaios'

[67] *UPZ* 14.13-14; cf. 15.20-22, protection; 16.7 (156 B.C.), food supply. See below on the rate of pay.
[68] *UPZ* 9.2 (161/60 B.C.).
[69] *UPZ* 3, cf. Delekat (1964), 46-50; 4 (164 B.C.), cf. Delekat (1964), 51-55 and 56-71, where he gives full rein to his imagination. Discussion has mainly concentrated on the legal aspects of the relationship on the (to me unlikely) assumption that Herakleia was adopted by Ptolemaios.
[70] *UPZ* 3.5 (164 B.C.). Wilcken's translation as "adoptierte ich sie" is unsupported.
[71] *UPZ* 14.13 (158 B.C.).
[72] *UPZ* 77-78; 80, discussed with some new readings by Delekat (1964), 139-55. *UPZ* 78 seems particularly relevant; might *aphesis* also signify "release from temptation"?

dreams, it is the twin daughters of Nephoris who constantly recur.[73] The visual expression in dreams of the subconscious is likely to be molded by the experience of the dreamer's own society. Demotic literature like the Setne Romance and the animal cults of the necropolis perhaps form a framework for the dreams of Ptolemaios and his friends; childbirth, for instance, is seen in bovine imagery, and the Dream of Nectanebo was a favorite text which influenced the imagery and (misquoted) the language of the dreams he dreamed himself.[74] Tempted to follow the trade of the Cretan dream interpreter whose attractive billboard (plate vii) designated his practice on the necropolis in iambic trimeters, the modern reader of these dream texts interprets them in a contemporary idiom. Taous is a sexual tease;[75] there is the danger that her twin Thauēs may be pregnant.[76] Among his papers Ptolemaios preserved the dreams his friend Nektembes dreamed on Ptolemaios' problems and his plight;[77] he lists his own dreams, which concern his family and his friends (especially Thauēs), ending with the enigmatic "Ptolemaios consumed."[78] Although such dreams may tell more of fantasy than of real life, in recording them Ptolemaios shows the same troubled psychology as is revealed elsewhere—in his obsession with his accounts which were worked and reworked with a neurotic application unmatched by accuracy.

The accounts of Ptolemaios belong to a more mundane context. Besides his profitable involvement in the production of porridge, in an attempt to improve his economic situation Ptolemaios also dealt in cloth and clothes. On the necropolis existed a constant demand for linen, for lengths of cloth as winding sheets, for padding and bandages for the mummies, and for clothes which were often secondhand.[79] It was this demand that Ptolemaios sought to meet, exploiting his home connections with the Herakleopolite nome. In a series of deals in lengths of cloth and clothes, his brother Apollonios and the twins worked for Ptolemaios, but it was the detainee who masterminded and controlled this operation from within the confines of the Sarapieion.

From between October 163 and the summer of 159 B.C. there survive

---

[73] *UPZ* 77.i.14-29, ii.11-12; 78.8-46.
[74] *UPZ* 77.ii.26-30; 81.17-18, with Clarysse (1983a), 60.
[75] *UPZ* 77.i.18-20, 23-40, cf. 79.21-22.
[76] *UPZ* 77.i.1-13, ii.7-9; 78.13-14, 17-20, cf. Delekat (1964), 141, for a new text. At 136-55 Delekat stretches this material to its limit, if not beyond.
[77] *UPZ* 79 (159 B.C.).
[78] *UPZ* 80 (158 B.C.).
[79] Bataille (1952), 211-20, presents the Theban evidence.

detailed accounts kept by Apollonios and Ptolemaios which illustrate these deals. Though not recorded, the operation probably continued even after this date since on 17 June 156 B.C. Ptolemaios had three lengths of cloth (two othonia or winding sheets, and one *sindōn* or shroud) which he pawned, together with a girl's garment and two silver drachmas, in order to raise 4,500 drachmas from Teebēsis, the seller of rushes.[80] There are two points of particular interest in this transaction. First, it appears that the rush shop with which Ptolemaios and Apollonios had regular dealings in the purchase of fuel[81] was a source of ready cash. Second, it throws light on the status of silver drachmas, which were bought or sold as objects of value on a par with shrouds or winding sheets. Though expressed in bronze drachmas,[82] the value of these silver coins was that of bullion, not of currency. And in general terms, these dealings of Ptolemaios and his close associates, while providing evidence for the production and retail of cloth and clothing in the record of credits and debits, also illustrate the economic interaction of Greek capital and Egyptian labor.

Documents of the Cairo Geniza show flax in Egypt to have been a product of great importance in the eleventh century A.D.; the Fayum and the area of Abousir are both named as important centers of production.[83] Already in the third century B.C. the Zenon archive, as we have seen, shows Memphis as an urban center of cloth production with small workshops and slave establishments like that of the dioiketes Apollonios. Much of the flax used here was grown in the Herakleopolite nome, the source too, according to the Sarapieion archive, of much of the cloth in which Ptolemaios dealt. Through his agents lengths of cloth were purchased from independent weavers and then resold for use. They may have been stored safely together with his papers, for puzzling traces were found of linen cloth and scarlet threads attached to a papyrus from the archive.[84]

The items most regularly purchased in this way were lengths of linen used for winding sheets and shrouds, napkins or towels (*ekmageia*), dyed lengths of cloth (*bapta*), and tunics (*kithōnes* in the Ionic dialect of the city). Not all lengths of linen cloth served for burial purposes. Othonia

---

[80] *UPZ* 101.18-21.

[81] *UPZ* 98.11-19, 130; 99.4; *SB* 7617.34 (158 B.C.). On Apollonios' problems with Teebēsis' sons, see below.

[82] *UPZ* 88.13 (161/60 B.C.), 8 silver drachmas worth 4,100 drachmas; 93.3 (159 B.C.), probably the same 8 silver drachmas now worth 4,260 drachmas in bronze.

[83] Goitein (1967), 224-28, cf. 105.

[84] Wilcken (1927), 2, on *UPZ* 40.

might be used as bedcovers[85] as well as daytime wraps.[86] Prices of course varied according to both quality and quantity, and there was a wide range of them. The finest length came at 4,200 drachmas while an Arsinoite length, bought by the twins in 160 B.C., was priced at 520 drachmas.[87] Sindones were possibly of finer linen, but the term is often used interchangeably with othonion, with both words used to designate the same length of cloth[88] and with the range of prices much the same.[89] Overall for shrouds and lengths of cloth, the mean price was 1,332 drachmas while the median stood at 1,050 drachmas of bronze. Dyed cloth came in smaller lengths with a mean price of 625 drachmas and a median of 475 drachmas.[90] Napkins, the use for which is obscure,[91] varied greatly in price and presumably in size; 330 drachmas was a mean price and 165 drachmas the median.[92] Of ready-made clothes, tunics were priced at 740, 350, and 250 drachmas, and a small tunic came at 240 drachmas.[93] The cloak, *himation*, which Apollonios sold for 380 drachmas,[94] was perhaps made up from a length of cloth he bought; payments to a fuller, dye shop, and seamstress are recorded from Apollonios and the twins, and in May 159 B.C. 120 drachmas were spent on purple dye.[95] Other garments are listed in these accounts, such as the *parthenē*, which must have been a woman's garment, perhaps a girdle.[96] Wool too was bought by Apollonios,[97] and it may be that woolen cloth, although forbidden to priests, was also handled by his elder brother.

[85] *UPZ* 85.8 (162 B.C.).

[86] E.g., *PSI* 418.20-22, a temporary alternative to a himation.

[87] *UPZ* 84.83, 4,200 drachmas (x 1 item); 85.42, 2,500 drachmas (x 2); 88.10-11, 2,000 drachmas (x 1); 84.80, 1,350 drachmas (x 1); 84.41, 82, and 85.44-45, 1,200 drachmas (x 3); 84.78, 1,150 drachmas (x 1); 83.5, 1,100 drachmas (x 2); 84.37, 59, 74; 84.66-67; 85.8, 1,000 drachmas (x 3); 84.63, 700 drachmas (x 2); 84.45, 68, 600 drachmas (x 1); 84.82-83, 520 drachmas (x 1); 92.4 and 93.4, 500 drachmas (x 1).

[88] *UPZ* 84.45, 68, *othonia*, cf. 85.13, *sindōn*; 84.7-8, *sindones*, cf. 84.63 and 85.8, *othonia*. Bartina (1965), 28, *othonion*, the generic term which may include *sindōn*.

[89] *UPZ* 85.43, 3,000 drachmas (x 1); 88.12, 2,100 drachmas (x 1); 84.4, 1,000 drachmas (x 2); 84.7, 700 drachmas (x 2); 85.13, cf. 84.45, 68, 600 drachmas (x 1).

[90] *UPZ* 84.76, 800 drachmas (x 2); 83.8, 10, 750 drachmas (x 2); 84.5, 500 drachmas (x 2); 84.38, 60, 450 drachmas (x 2).

[91] Perhaps they were used for padding out the mummies (cf. Bataille 1952, 211), or as sanitary towels.

[92] *UPZ* 85.43-44, 1,000 drachmas (x 1); 84.84, 750 drachmas (x 2); 84.77, 480 drachmas (x 2); 83.7, 350 drachmas (x 2); 84.81, 165 drachmas (x 2); 84.9, 39, 61, 74; 84.74, 80 drachmas (x 6).

[93] *UPZ* 84.15, 48, 71, 740 drachmas; 83.6, 350 drachmas; 84.12, 43, 66, 250 drachmas (linen specified); 85.45, 240 drachmas.

[94] *UPZ* 93.4 (159 B.C.).

[95] *UPZ* 93.10 (159 B.C.), fuller; 84.10; 85.9 (163–160 B.C.), dye shop; 93.10 (159 B.C.), seamstress; 91.17 (159 B.C.), dye.

[96] *UPZ* 101.21 (156 B.C.).

[97] *UPZ* 91.12; 93.8 (159 B.C.).

Their major supplier appears to have been the linen weaver Psenobastis, son of Horos, who probably worked in Memphis. Purchases from him were secured by payment in advance.[98] There existed other sources too, men who perhaps were also producers: Nektheraus,[99] Nikeratos,[100] Arēs,[101] Sōsis,[102] Phathrēs,[103] Konnas and Hakebēsis,[104] Asgēs, son of Tothēs,[105] and Amonamois and Amphias.[106] Konnas and Hakebēsis seem to have worked in partnership, and Egyptian names outnumber Greek. On 8 June 160 B.C., however, a large purchase was made from a certain Demetrios of two othonia, one sindon, one napkin, and two othonia for the twins, together with a small tunic.[107] The twins bought clothes from both Herakleopolis and the Arsinoite nome, and on one occasion purchased what was probably a secondhand othonion from a dream interpreter.[108]

As already noted, some of these clothes are described as bought for the twins,[109] but most will have been for resale, either as shrouds and mummy wrappings or tunics and cloaks to wear. The details and accounting of the transactions are difficult to follow. Whereas some lengths of cloth were sold by Ptolemaios on behalf of his brother Apollonios,[110] and the twins too paid in to the brothers the sums that they made,[111] in general the accounts which survive are insufficiently complete to allow either the reconstruction of the turnover or calculation of the profits made. Unexplained, too, are the large sums credited to Ptolemaios from Aphrodeisios, Horos and indeed Sarapis.[112] If, as seems possible, these

[98] *UPZ* 83.1-2; 84.3, 14, 36, 47, 58, 70-71, 75; 85.3, 14, 30?.
[99] *UPZ* 84.11, 23, 43, 65; 85.10. Associated payments to Kollouthēs seem to be for goosemeat.
[100] *UPZ* 84.18, 44, 67-68; 85.12-13.
[101] *UPZ* 84.17; cf. 86.4, 6-12.
[102] *UPZ* 84.66.
[103] *UPZ* 88.12.
[104] *UPZ* 84.6, 40-41, 62-63, 67-68; 85.6.
[105] *UPZ* 88.10-11.
[106] *UPZ* 84.77-78.
[107] *UPZ* 85.41-46; cf. 102.2 (156 B.C.).
[108] *UPZ* 84.79-83. On the importance of the secondhand clothes trade in medieval Egypt, see Goitein (1967), 150 (dealers with their own bazaar in Cairo).
[109] *UPZ* 85.44-45 (160 B.C.).
[110] *UPZ* 91.4; 93.4 (159 B.C.). Apollonios kept careful accounts of both income and expenditure.
[111] *UPZ* 85.24, 5,000 drachmas in July 160 B.C..
[112] From Aphrodeisios: *UPZ* 84.88-89; 88.4, 2,000 drachmas, October 164 B.C.; 84.50-55; 86.4-5, 1,500 drachmas, October 162 B.C.; 84.90-92; 88.4, 2,000 drachmas, March–April 160 B.C.; 85.22, 4,000 drachmas total, July 160 B.C. From Horos: *UPZ* 85.17-18; 88.3, 4,000 drachmas, March 160 B.C.; 85.22, 6,000 drachmas, July 160 B.C. From Sarapis: *UPZ* 85.19-20; cf. 88.3, 4,000 drachmas, in 163-62 B.C.

are not loans [113] but rather the price paid him for clothes supplied, though not recorded in detail, this will be further evidence for the nature of these transactions. For generally the picture is of small-scale Egyptian supply from men like those named above, and large-scale purchase by both Greeks and Egyptians in which, from the Sarapieion, Ptolemaios, through his brother and the twins, exploits his home connections [114] to act both as coordinator and middleman. This active business role and grasp of any chance to make a profit typify the sort of man Ptolemaios represents. Like Zenon of Philadelphia before him, Ptolemaios exemplifies the Hellenistic man of affairs. The type is unlikely to be new, but it is only in the Hellenistic world that its existence is so well documented.

Clothes dealing for Ptolemaios was but one of the many activities which served to supplement his minimal allowance from the temple. From the confines of the Astarte temple, the extent of his worldly involvement on occasion caused offense. His problems in October 163 B.C. have already been related, and the background of general unrest in the country is likely to be relevant. [115] On 12 November of the same year an assault on Ptolemaios was mounted by a motley collection of individuals. In his deposition to the strategos made soon after the event, Ptolemaios identified his assailants as the temple cleaners of the great Sarapieion, the breadmakers who lived in the Anoubieion but spent time in the temple on a daily basis, the doctor Harchēbis, Mys the seller of cloaks, and others unknown to him. When set upon, Ptolemaios managed to shut himself up in his pastophorion, leaving Harmais to bear the brunt of the attack. The reason Ptolemaios gave for this attack, as for the earlier ones, was that "I am Greek." [116]

Two years later, in the same month, a similar incident occurred and Ptolemaios was set upon, attacked with sticks and stones. Like most temple workers, the temple cleaners probably served on a monthly basis, and when on this occasion they are identified in his petition to the strategos, Ptolemaios probably also names his earlier assailants. With these cleaners once again were the native doctor Harchēbis, Imouthes the baker, and Mys the seller of winding sheets, together with Psosnaus the yoke carrier,

[113] So Wilcken (1927), 109. A loan made by Ptolemaios to Asges, son of Harmais, is recorded in *UPZ* 84.26-31 (April 162 B.C.).

[114] Especially Lysimachos, *UPZ* 61.1; 84.87; 85.3, cf. 80-81 (161 B.C.). See Wilcken's commentary on 85.23-37 and his reconstruction of Apollonios' movements, 91.1-5n, questioned by Delekat (1964), 28.

[115] *UPZ* 7.19-21 (163 B.C.) explicitly mentions these.

[116] *UPZ* 7 (163 B.C.), reedited on page 648, *para to Hellēna me einai.*

Harembasnis the grain merchant, a carpet weaver whose name is illegible, Stotoetis the water carrier, and others specified later.[117] Once again Ptolemaios alleges his Greek nationality as the reason for the attack. It is of course true that in this Egyptian temple community Ptolemaios as a Greek was the exception; such a reason might also be thought likely to move the strategos, Dionysios. Of equal significance, however, would seem to be the assailants' occupations, with clothes dealer, baker, and grain merchant among them. It is not improbable that Ptolemaios' extra-cultic activities, his dealings in clothes and textiles, together with his organization of the cooked cracked emmer wheat supply, to some extent interfered with the normal life of the Egyptian necropolis and thereby caused offense. This is not to deny that Ptolemaios' nationality was probably a contributory factor in this series of attacks against him, but it is unlikely to have been the only reason for his unpopularity. As so often, it is difficult to disentangle ethnic origin and economic activity as reasons for hostility and discrimination.

Whereas some of the Sarapieion workers appear to have disliked Ptolemaios and what he stood for, his life as a detainee in the Astarte temple was in fact lived mainly among Egyptians. On more than one occasion he took up his pen to write to the authorities on behalf of Harmais, his Egyptian roommate, and the temple personnel with whom he dealt were all Egyptian.[118] Though Ptolemaios served a Phoenician goddess in an Egyptian setting, his concerns were generally economic, his problems personal ones. Yet the state of the country in a period of upheaval, with troubles both external and on the home front, is reflected in the surviving record of those who dwelled in the comparatively secure environment of the Sarapieion.

Indeed, for many in these troubled times the Sarapieion had a strong appeal. Preserved among the papers of the sons of Glaukias are two letters addressed to a certain Hephaistion, from his brother Dionysios and from his wife Isias. Hephaistion had probably moved on before receiving them, or else he left them when he went. Perhaps a soldier, he had, it appears, been involved in the wars against Antiochus, but instead of returning home when the way was clear he had stopped off, detained in the Sarapieion. At home the news was received with mixed feelings, and the

---

[117] *UPZ* 8 (161 B.C.).

[118] While recognizing the problems associated with the use of nomenclature as an indication of nationality, I am prepared to use it when there is no variation within a closed social group; see, however, Clarysse (1985).

two letters testify to the difficulties and economic hardship suffered by Greeks and Egyptians alike in a time of invasion. The letter from his wife is dated 29 August 168 B.C., a month after Antiochus had left the country:

> When I received your letter from Horos in which you explained you were detained in the Sarapieion in Memphis, I immediately thanked the gods that you were safe and sound. But since all those who were cut off with you[119] have turned up back home I am most upset at your nonreturn. For as a result of the scale of the crisis your small boy and I went under; we were stretched to our very limit with the high price of corn. And now at least on your return I hoped to get respite.[120]

Hephaistion's brother is equally direct—indeed, the wording indicates collaboration—but he also suggests, and rejects, a reason for the delay of his brother's return.

> I hoped you too would return home to the city, like Konon and all the others who were cut off, so that Isias also, who has kept safe your small son when he was *in extremis* and has patiently suffered through times like the present, might now, with you back on the scene, enjoy some respite. For in whatever financial difficulties you find yourself you really should not delay until you provide yourself with something to bring back home; having survived danger one always tries to get home with all speed, to greet one's wife, one's children, and one's friends.[121]

For Hephaistion's brother, detention was envisaged as a possible means of improving low personal finances.[122] His family is glad that Hephaistion is safe but disapprove of the delay: "Unless something more pressing prevents you, you should do your best to get back home"[123] is his brother's advice. Detention is not seen as an insuperable condition, and Hephaistion may have felt the pull of home even before the letters arrived. Without similar ties Ptolemaios stayed on, detained in his pastophorion, "to provide himself with something." He may have dreamed of release[124] but there is no evidence that he ever obtained it.[125]

---

[119] Hepahistion is *en katochēi* (line 8) but there seems no reason to understand lines 11–12, *[p]a[nt]ōn tōn ekei apeilēmmenōn*, as referring to the same phenomenon, cf. Delekat (1964), 74–79. Interception from base or home is a regular occurrence in civil war, cf. Cic. *Att.* 8.11.4; see *P. Köln* 4.186.4 (second century B.C.) for a contemporary use of the term.

[120] *UPZ* 59.6–23.

[121] *UPZ* 60.9–20.

[122] So later Vettius Valens 5.1 (Kroll p. 210), on *katochē* arising from necessity, *anagkē*.

[123] *UPZ* 60.20–23.

[124] *UPZ* 78.39–46 (159 B.C.).

[125] Delekat (1964), 135–36, suggests he was finally ejected.

CHAPTER 7

HARMAIS AND TATHĒMIS

Sharing the pastophorion of Ptolemaios was the Egyptian, Harmais. Less successful than Ptolemaios at avoiding trouble, on 12 November 163 B.C. he suffered a beating with bronze scrapers at the hands of the temple cleaners; the month before, on 19 October 163 B.C., his savings had been forcibly removed from their room.[126] Ptolemaios constantly bewailed his lot but it was Harmais who generally suffered. Described by his room-mate as "one of the beggars," Harmais lived from mendicancy[127] and, for safety's sake, like others kept his savings in a jar (*stamnos*) within the temple confines. In later times, begging was a recognized feature of the followers of the Syrian goddess,[128] and it may be that detention in the Astartieion was the equivalent of a license to beg, something denied to ordinary refugees seeking asylum in the Sarapieion.

Like Ptolemaios, Harmais too shared his life with a female companion in the temple. The girl was Tathēmis, the young daughter of Nephoris and in all likelihood the sister of the twins, Taous and Thaūes, who played so large a part in the lives of Ptolemaios and his brother Apollonios; she also lived from tourists' gifts, which she entrusted to Harmais for safe keeping. Tathēmis is introduced to the reader of this archive on the occasion when her mother tricked Harmais out of 1,300 drachmas collected by Tathēmis. Claiming the time had come for her daughter's marriage which, Egyptian-style, was preceded by circumcision, Nephoris required the money for a dowry.[129] This was the purpose for which the money was needed, and its proper use was guaranteed Harmais. In the event, none of the mother's promises were fulfilled and, cheated of her savings, Tathēmis was understandably aggrieved. She turned against her companion, who was prevented by his detention from going down to Memphis to sort the problem out.[130] Instead, with the help of his friends the sons of Glaukias, in 163 B.C. he told his story and detailed his complaint to the strategos Dionysios.

[126] *UPZ* 7.25-29 on p. 648; 5.19-24; 6.19-21; 6a.12-13.
[127] *UPZ* 5.22; 6.18-19; 2.4 (163 B.C.).
[128] Apul. *Met.* 8.24.
[129] *UPZ* 2 (163 B.C.). Wilcken's doubts over Harmais' identity seem unnecessary; see no. 20 above. For a different interpretation of the incident, in which Harmais serves as pimp for the girl, see Delekat (1964), 70-71. In this archive there is certain evidence neither for sacred prostitution nor for eunuchs in connection with the Astarte cult, but see *P. Tebt.* 6.29 (140/39 B.C.), income from *aphrodisia*, and Strabo 17.1.46, suggesting the first was regular Egyptian practice.
[130] Delekat (1964), 28-30, argues (to my mind unconvincingly) that it was these very events that temporarily limited his movement.

This is Egyptian society and, although this stands as an isolated reference, the lack of comment from Harmais suggests that among the Egyptian population of the country female circumcision was a regular preliminary to marriage.[131] Tathēmis' father had been a friend of Ptolemaios and, following the death of her father, it was perhaps this connection which had brought her to the Sarapieion to collect together a dowry for herself either through begging or possibly prostitution.[132] Nowhere called a detainee, she lived and worked in the temple of Astarte. The special protection extended by Harmais may have suited both parties while it lasted; it was ended by the trickery of her mother.

THE TWINS AND THE BULL

Tathēmis relied on gifts to put together her dowry. Her twin sisters were more fortunate, and from April 164 B.C. they were chosen to play the parts of Isis and Nephthys during the official, seventy-day mourning period for the bull, the Apis of the cow Ta-Renenutet II. Even after the bull was buried in its granite sarcophagus, deep in the vaults of the Sarapieion, religious ceremonies continued and the twins remained on the temple books. As so often in these papyri, the evidence for their cultic role, their leitourgia, comes from a series of complaints made on their behalf, composed by their patron Ptolemaios and addressed both to Sarapiōn, the deputy financial official (the hypodioiketes), and to Philometor and his queen. The problems of the twins are twofold: they have been cheated of their oil allowance by their mother and stepbrother Pachrates, who have been drawing it fraudulently on their behalf,[133] and their rations from the temple authorities stand regularly in arrears.[134] The dossier which covers the years 164–160 B.C. illustrates both the personal story of the twins and the costs to temple and crown of one aspect of the major cult of the necropolis, that of Osorapis, the deified Apis bull.

The personal story is contained in two preliminary drafts together with the final version of the appeal made by the twins to Philometor and his queen when the royal couple visited the Sarapieion in October 163 B.C.[135]

[131] Aetius of Amida 16.115 (ed. Zervos), an Egyptian practice; cf. Xanthos of Lydia, *FGrH* 765, F.4.
[132] See *UPZ* 19 (163 B.C.) for the background.
[133] *UPZ* 17-41.
[134] *UPZ* 42-54.
[135] *UPZ* 18; 19, drafts; 20, appeal. See 41.4-6; 42.3-4 for the royal couple in residence in Memphis after Philometor's return from Rome. For the date of the appeal, see Wilcken (1927), 187, 197.

The girls came from an Egyptian family; their father was perhaps Argunoutis (the reading is unsure) and their mother was Nephoris, who already had a son, Pachrates, by a previous marriage. Nephoris, the villain also of Tathēmis' tale, had more recently taken up with a Greek soldier, Philippos, son of Sōgenēs, who was stationed in the area; for him she left her husband. Taking advantage of the troubles of the times, the aftermath of the revolt of Dionysios Petosarapis and the general unrest in the country which followed the withdrawal of Antiochus IV, this unscrupulous soldier had lain in wait for the supplanted husband, who, they recount, escaped with his life only by jumping into the river and swimming to a nearby island. From there he took a boat to the neighboring Herakleopolite nome where, soon after, he died of grief. Though his brothers fetched his corpse back home to the embalming establishments in Memphis, at the present time his wife had still not had him buried.

This crisis in their family life had occurred before 164 B.C. when the twins, with their elder sister Tathēmis, took refuge in the Sarapieion. Here they came under the protection of their father's friend Ptolemaios, son of Glaukias.[136] Although perhaps attending school on the necropolis,[137] there is no evidence to suggest the twins were either literate or spoke Greek, for they were clearly aided by their protector in the preparation of their reports. It was probably Ptolemaios who was responsible for the toned-down final version of their royal appeal; the family background, the role of Philippos, the dramatic escape of their father, and his wretched death have all disappeared from this version, which concentrates instead on the villainy of Nephoris and her son. It is she who has cheated them of the rent of two houses in which they should share,[138] so forcing them to flee to the Sarapieion. Her son has further tricked them out of their authorization for oil, which he collects on their behalf but fails to deliver. They have been badly advised in trusting him and now ask that Demetrios, son of Sōsos, Ptolemaios' friend, should take on this responsibility for collecting their allowance. They report on their good fortune in finding Ptolemaios, son of Glaukias, whose concern that they should lack no necessity is, in this version, ascribed to the god's command; indeed, the general view of those who did not know the facts or the rea-

[136] *UPZ* 19.22-23 (163 B.C.).
[137] *UPZ* 78.9-12 (159 B.C.), the school of Tothēs, in a dream text.
[138] *UPZ* 18.16-18; 19.18-20; 20.19-21, which as the final version records the rent as 1,200 drachmas, not 1,400 drachmas.

son for the protection he offers would call him their father.[139] Thus emerged the final version, penned by their protector, in which he clearly hopes that the ten years of his detention and his attention to the command of Sarapis may add strength to their case. The draft, as already seen, described him rather as a friend of the father, while the reader of Ptolemaios' dreams[140] might suspect other grounds for the attention shown to these young girls.

Whatever the reason, Ptolemaios helped them, and it is through the requests and complaints that he wrote that their service to Osorapis is known. The bull died early in April 164 B.C. and, still children,[141] the girls were now engaged for the mourning ceremonies and taken down to Memphis where mummification took place close to the temple of Ptah. As the two sister-goddesses, Isis and Nephthys, played their part in bringing Osiris back to life, so their human counterparts had a central role in ceremonies concerned with the afterlife of the bull. These ceremonies completed and the bull buried after seventy days, they continued to perform their cult responsibilities up in the Sarapieion. Here they poured libations for Osorapis on behalf of the king, the queen, and their children.[142] The direct connection made here in draft between cult duties for the bull and the royal cult is again omitted in the final version, where, instead, in more conventional form they pray that Sarapis and Isis together may grant their king victory and sovereign power over all the world.[143]

Closely connected to the cult of the Apis bull was that of Mnevis, the bull of Heliopolis. The two appear portrayed together on the dedications of devotees from an earlier date, and the Ptolemaic connections have already been noted.[144] So too with the twins who played some part in the mourning for the Mnevis bull.[145] There is no suggestion that the Mnevis was buried at Memphis nor indeed that the twins moved to work in Heliopolis; whatever ceremonies there were, took place, it seems, in the Memphite Sarapieion, with the citizens of Memphis gladly taking part. Such celebrations were integral to life in Egypt and, in arrogating

---

[139] *UPZ* 20.25-28; 18.30 (163 B.C.).
[140] See n. 73.
[141] *UPZ* 18.20-21; 20.22 (163 B.C.).
[142] *UPZ* 19.2-4; 17.5-6, 16-17 (163 B.C.).
[143] *UPZ* 20.63-64 (163 B.C.), cf. 42.48-52 (162 B.C.); 41.22-25 (161/60 B.C.).
[144] Malinine, Posener, and Vercoutter (1968), 1.3-5, no. 4 (Ramses II, Year 30); see chapter 6 n. 32 above.
[145] *UPZ* 96.2 (159/8 B.C.).

Mnevis, the Sarapieion would gain in importance while adding to the ceremonial life of the city. Occasions for music, procession, and feasting were always welcome amid the grim reality of daily life. At festival time, the twins, like others, would purchase goose meat for sacrifice Egyptian-style;[146] the gooseherds of the area were thus ensured a steady market for their products.[147]

Added to their duties for the bulls, the twins took over a daily libation for Asklepios/Imhotep at his stone vessels, which were placed up in the Sarapieion. This had earlier been the responsibility of their predecessors, but the priest called the herdsman, boukolos, of Osorapis had taken over the duty when these earlier twins had neglected their role.[148] The new twins performed the libation but had difficulty in acquiring the bread ration (three or four small loaves daily; see below) which went with the job.[149] The herdsman was still drawing these rations, and Ptolemaios and the twins of course complained.

The twins are once described as "in detention," like Ptolemaios and Harmais.[150] The source is a dream text, and how far the girls were free to move around has been the subject of debate.[151] When first they fled their unhappy home situation and sought protection in the Sarapieion, they were without cult connections. After their engagement as twins for the mourning and mummification ceremonies down in Memphis, from 7 April to 15 June 164 B.C.,[152] they were back in the Sarapieion. As we have seen, their sister Tathēmis probably lived from begging in the Astarte temple, but the cult connections of the twins are rather with Osorapis, the Greek Sarapis.[153] Accounts made out in their names for the years 163–159 B.C. suggest extensive contacts with weavers, dyers, and clothes mer-

---

[146] *UPZ* 84.13, 46, 69; 85.12, 500 drachmas in 162 B.C.; 84.73, 400 drachmas on 1 Thoth 162 B.C.; 89.10, 300 drachmas on 15 Phaophi 160 B.C. Geese came at 2,000 drachmas apiece, 83.14 (162 B.C.); 100.4 (157 B.C.).

[147] *UPZ* 100.3-4 (157 B.C.), Harontōtēs; 83.13; 84.11, 23-24, 42, 64; 85.10 (162 B.C.), Kollouthēs. For gooseherds singled out in royal decrees, see *C. Ord. Ptol.* 83.23, 27 (221–205 B.C.); 53.172 (118 B.C.).

[148] *UPZ* 57. I see no reason, with the editor, to connect *BGU* 2427.11 (third century B.C.) with this priest.

[149] *UPZ* 45.18-20; 46.22; 47.20-21, 4 loaves; 50.22-23, 31-34 (162/1 B.C.), 3 loaves; 51.12-14; 53.27-29 (161 B.C.), 4 loaves; 57.2, 3 loaves.

[150] *UPZ* 79.13-19 (159 B.C.), the dream of Nektembēs, possibly another katochos.

[151] Wilcken, *UPZ* 56.15 n., considers they had complete freedom, Delekat, (1964), 30-47, that this was confined to the Sarapieion.

[152] *UPZ* 54.22 gives the date of burial; the hieroglyphic evidence (see Appendix D) needs republication.

[153] It is fair to note that katoche connected to Sarapis is found outside Egypt; see n. 25.

chants, including some in the Herakleopolite nome.[154] A bank receipt dated 26 December 162 B.C. for the cost of oil is made out to the twins alone;[155] as Egyptian girls they probably enjoyed more freedom of legal action than would a Greek woman. And on 6 June 160 B.C. an account of bread rations paid actually records the fact that Taous went down (to Memphis understood).[156] Given this evidence for the freedom of movement and relative independence of the twins, the restrictions mentioned in that dream text should probably be discounted.

In their clothes dealings, however, it is difficult to disentangle the activities of the twins from those of Ptolemaios, who kept a close account of both. In these as in their dealings with officialdom,[157] it is possible that the young Apollonios acted as their messenger and agent. Others also worked for them when their duties kept them tied, and on 26 December 162 B.C., the same date as the bank receipt just mentioned, the allowance of oil paid for by the twins was actually issued to Demetrios, son of Sosos, who now with royal approval acted for them.[158] (On Demetrios' return to the Sarapieion, it was their patron Ptolemaios who actually took charge of the oil.)[159] The visit of Taous to Memphis to purchase bread on 6 June 160 B.C. probably arose from an unexplained innovation whereby in May–June of that year the twins received, instead of loaves, a cash allowance to purchase their own.[160] It seems sufficiently unusual an event for Ptolemaios to record it. But on the whole it appears to have been cult duties rather than institutional katoche which tied the twins to the temple precinct.

Once on the temple books, the twins were due regular allowances of bread and oil. Their annual oil allowance was one metretes (of twelve *chous*) each of edible sesame oil and one of kiki oil, to be used for lighting. Kiki oil had only half the value and on occasion two metretai of kiki might be replaced by one of sesame oil.[161] Reckoned in artabas their olyra allowance normally came in native bread—the kyllestis loaves already

---

[154] Details are contained in *UPZ* 84-85 (163–160 B.C.); cf. 85.25-37 (September 161 B.C.) for the Herakleopolite nome. Clothes accounts end and food accounts begin in 160 B.C. We are at the mercy of our evidence.

[155] *UPZ* 30.

[156] *UPZ* 56.15. Delekat (1964), 34, argues that Taous went down only as far as the bakery at the desert edge; but this too would be outside the great Sarapieion.

[157] *UPZ* 22.11-16; 24.8-10, 21-23 (162 B.C.); 51.18-19; 52.7-8 (161 B.C.).

[158] *UPZ* 29; cf. 20.31-36, dealing for them outside the temple.

[159] *UPZ* 31 (162 B.C.), receipt from Ptolemaios to Demetrios.

[160] *UPZ* 56.13 (160 B.C.) with Pauni perhaps mistakenly used for Pachons.

[161] *UPZ* 25.23; 26.15 (162 B.C.).

noted by Herodotus, which are also called "cooked bread," artoi peptoi.[162] The bread allowance came at different rates. While they were down in Memphis for the mummification of the Apis bull, the twins, like their predecessors, received six loaves each a day for seventy days. Loaves came in pairs with fifteen pairs (thirty loaves) to the artaba; expressed in terms of regular wheat, six kyllestis loaves were the equivalent of approximately 2 kilograms a day. On coming up again to the Sarapieion, the rate dropped from six to four loaves each day, from 73 to 48⅔ artabas of olyra a year.[163] Compared with the 12 artabas of olyra a year which Ptolemaios received, even the lower rate is very high. And in addition, their libation duties for the god Asklepios/Imhotep in the Sarapieion carried an extra daily allowance of three to four loaves between them issued from the Asklepieion.[164] Whereas in the payment of these allowances, theory and practice were often far apart, the details they give for subsistence are worth consideration. As already noted, olyra wheat was far less nutritious than the pyros (durum wheat) brought in by the Greeks; in Ptolemaic accounts it stood at the rate of 5:2. The twins' allowances therefore expressed in artabas of pyros were 29.2 artabas or 746 kilograms a year, when in receipt of six loaves each a day, and 19.46 artabas or 497 kilograms a year, when their rate dropped to four; if ever paid, the extra allowance from the Asklepieion might restore the loss. In theory the allowances were generous[165] and their cultic duties well rewarded.

These allowances came from the syntaxis, the block grant made to the temples by the crown,[166] and different systems were used in the issue of the two products. Oil, a product closely controlled by the crown, was released by a crown official down in Memphis[167] at the nominal price of 21 drachmas, 2 obols a metretes.[168] The twins received a *symbolon* or token which entitled them to oil; it was this token which their stepbrother

---

[162] Hdt. 2.77.3; *UPZ* 20.12 (163 B.C.); 46.15 (162/1 B.C.). On the arrangement and detailed interpretation of these rations I follow Wilcken (1927), 288–95.

[163] *UPZ* 54 (161 B.C.). An artaba of 40 *choinikes* is used, and the five *epagomenoi* days at the end of Mesore are included.

[164] See n. 148.

[165] See chapter 5 n. 94.

[166] *UPZ* 20.10–15, 49–50 (163 B.C.); 42.6–7, 19–22 (162 B.C.); 46.15; 47.15–17, 19; 50.20–21 (162/1 B.C.); 52.9–10, 20–21; 53.10–11, 20–21 (161 B.C.). On syntaxis see chapter 4 n. 19.

[167] Theon was probably the man in charge, *UPZ* 25.1; 26.1; 27.1, 3; 28.10, 12 (162 B.C.), but above him was the *epimelētēs* Mennides.

[168] *UPZ* 29.11–12; 30.6–7 (162 B.C.), the official receipt; cf. 21.6 (162 B.C.), where 24 drachmas 2 obols is the figure given.

had acquired when he cheated them of their allowance.[169] Loaves, however, were issued directly through the temple, and the supply was administered by Psintaes, the epistates of the temple, with his deputies, and paid out by the oikonomoi.[170] When therefore the allowances were not paid on time, the twins were faced with a twofold problem. In both cases the top ranks of authority were ultimately the same—the king, dioiketes, hypodioiketes, and *epimeletai*;[171] below this level, however, came, for oil, the crown officials in the city and, for their bread ration, the temple administration. All were part of the central bureaucracy though the contrast in nomenclature is striking: city officials have Greek names, while in the temples the epistatai and their deputies without exception bear Egyptian names. In such a case, as already argued, a correlation between name and nationality seems likely (though it might be purely tactical), with native Egyptians holding administrative posts in the temples. An understanding of the intricacies of the Ptolemaic bureaucracy was probably one way in which Ptolemaios guided his protégées through their problems.

The complaints of the twins and the many drafts which preceded them form a lively introduction to the bureaucracy at work in its different aspects. Between October 163 and 160 B.C. the two girls and their protector Ptolemaios deluged the relevant authorities with complaints, reports and appeals. Only a selection of these have survived in the dossier as it stands, but internal references make it clear that many other approaches were made during this time, including even one on the subject of their bread allowance to the pheritob, an official rarely recorded who was perhaps responsible in Alexandria for the syntaxis grant and the royal administration of the temples.[172] The use at this date of an Egyptian term for a high official in the central administration has already been noted; it forms an interesting reflection of the adaptations and concessions made to the native ways of Egypt.

When in doubt, aim for the top. Ptolemaios was experienced in the art of complaint, and under his guidance petitions were sent to the king and queen about these problems—two on the subject of the oil allowance (one in 163 B.C. when other complaints were added,[173] and one again in 161/0

[169] *UPZ* 18.21-28; 19.24-30 (163 B.C.).
[170] *UPZ* 20.55-57 (163 B.C.); 42.19-25 (162 B.C.). *Hoi pros tois cheirismois* are probably the same as the oikonomoi, 56.7-10 (160 B.C.).
[171] *UPZ* 25-26 (162 B.C.) for the officials involved.
[172] *UPZ* 51.18 (161 B.C.); see chapter 4 n. 25.
[173] *UPZ* 20 with 18 and 19 as drafts, accepting Wilcken's correction of the date.

B.C.)[174] and in October 162 B.C. one on the subject of the bread ration of the twins.[175] On the subject of bread rations, earlier approaches had already been made to the epimeletai and, in person, to temple officials. Achomarres, the crown appointee in the Sarapieion, had proved "the hardest man on earth," and a more successful appeal to the son of Psintaes (the general epistates of the temples) had been brought to nothing when the epistates left the area.[176]

Reference to the crown, however, was not sufficient, and Ptolemaios and the twins followed this up with approaches to various officials, in particular to Sarapiōn, the hypodioiketes, who traveled the country representing his superior, the dioiketes. On the subject of the bread ration, four separate approaches are recorded: one from Ptolemaios and the twins in 162/1 B.C.,[177] one from the twins alone in the same year,[178] one in 161 B.C. from Ptolemaios and the twins,[179] and finally, in 161 B.C., one from Ptolemaios by himself.[180] At the same time, they were also petitioning Sarapiōn about the oil allowance, but in different reports since the subsequent course of action was down a different line of command. On the subject of the oil allowance, five separate approaches are recorded: from the twins in 163 B.C.,[181] from Ptolemaios and the twins in December 162 B.C.,[182] from Ptolemaios alone in the same year on their oil allowance up to and including Year 19 (163/2 B.C.),[183] in the following year from Ptolemaios on arrears including Year 20,[184] and finally in 161 B.C. from the twins alone detailing the whole history of the problem.[185] Including the royal petitions therefore, together with many drafts, there survive seven attempts to deal with the oil allowance and five with the ration of loaves. Yet in spite of orders and counterorders and numerous internal reports within the bureaucracy,[186] the draft accounts kept by Ptolemaios

---

[174] *UPZ* 41.
[175] *UPZ* 42; the same question had been raised the year before, 20.55-57, but not pursued.
[176] *UPZ* 42.16-31 (162 B.C.).
[177] *UPZ* 43-45 (162/1 B.C.).
[178] *UPZ* 46-50 (162/1 B.C.).
[179] *UPZ* 51 (161 B.C.).
[180] *UPZ* 52 (161 B.C.). Wilcken's arrangement of these documents and discussion is masterful throughout.
[181] *UPZ* 17 (163 B.C.).
[182] *UPZ* 22 (162 B.C.).
[183] *UPZ* 24 (162 B.C.).
[184] *UPZ* 33-36 (161 B.C.).
[185] *UPZ* 39-40 (161 B.C.); it is unclear where 58 verso belongs.
[186] E.g., *UPZ* 21 (162 B.C.); 37 (161 B.C.), Dorion, *antigrapheus*; 25-26 (162 B.C.); 38 (161 B.C.), Mennides, *epimeletēs*; 27 (162 B.C.), Theon; 23 (162 B.C.); 37 (161 B.C.), scribal reports.

(which continue until July 160 B.C.)[187] suggest that they met with little success. It might be argued, however, that there existed some positive correlation between number of appeals and the rate of success, since by the end the issue of oil is slightly less in arrears than is the ration of loaves.

The reasons why the problem was never satisfactorily sorted out are of course various, the most obvious being the very nature of the bureaucracy and of the society in which it functioned. This was after all only one of many problems in particularly troubled times. Further, the sphere of the hypodioiketes was a wide one and he was often not available. On one occasion Apollonios, in his familiar role as messenger boy, finally tracked Sarapiōn down in Ptolemais in the Arsinoite nome,[188] and in January 161 B.C. Ptolemaios and the twins express the fear that he may go off up-country before he deals with their problem.[189] Lower officials, it is clear, often lacked either the ability or the inclination to make decisions; with their skill in always passing on responsibility, little was achieved apart from paperwork.

In the case of the bread ration, the twins suggest that the crown representatives in the temples are taking advantage of the scarcity and high price of corn (again a result of troubled times) and, instead of providing loaves, have sold off the olyra allowance for 300 drachmas an artaba.[190] While 300 drachmas an artaba was a regular price in these years,[191] there is no way in which the accusation can be checked. The temple authorities, and in particular Psintaes' deputy Amosis, had clashed with Ptolemaios on other occasions,[192] so personal animosity may be what is involved here; but it may also be the case that what would seem a sensible policy on the part of the Ptolemies—the appointment of Egyptians to administer the temples—might in fact result in collusion and racketeering. This after all was nothing new in Egypt.

The delay in the oil supply was only partly the fault of Theon, the official with responsibility for oil in Memphis,[193] since, as we have already seen, the twins had early on surrendered their token to the unreliable Pachrates. A further reason for the nonissue of oil may be seen in the copy, preserved in the dossier, of the following clarification, full of jar-

[187] *UPZ* 54-55 (161 B.C.); 56 (160 B.C.).
[188] *UPZ* 22.13-16 (162 B.C.); cf. 21.27.
[189] *UPZ* 33.12-13; 34.8; 35.17-18; 36.15-16 (161 B.C.).
[190] *UPZ* 52.16-19; 53.18-20 (161 B.C.). The text of *UPZ* 52 is puzzling.
[191] See Wilcken (1927), 409, prices ranging between 250 and 360 drachmas.
[192] *UPZ* 5-6 (163 B.C.); see n. 16 above.
[193] *UPZ* 25.1; 26.1; 27.1, 13; 28.10, 12 (162 B.C.).

gon, issued from within the scribal office of Mennides, the epimeletes, and made on 14 December 162 B.C.:

> (Report of) Apoll(onios)
> The above report presented to Sarapiōn, hypodioiketes with the rank of *diadochos*, from Ptolemaios who is patron to the twins in the great Sarapieion, on the subject of the annual allowance of sesame and kiki oil due to them from the royal treasury, came with the instruction: "To Mennides. Look into the question of how much is due them." You then countersigned it: "To the scribes. Look into the matter and report." The report contained the information that an appeal had been made to the king. We took the copy of this appeal, together with the decision made on it, and attached it to the dossier. Dorion, the copying clerk [*antigrapheus*], taking this over, sent a copy of the report of what had been done to Sarapiōn, in which it is stated:
> "Year 6. From Phamenoth, the month of mourning, up to Mesore, there has been issued from the oil allowance due for six months: 6 chous of sesame oil and 6 of kiki oil.
> Year 18. The allowance due of one metretes (sesame) oil and one metretes kiki oil, as the relevant instructions directed, was delayed over into Year 19 and not issued since calculations are done on an annual basis.
> Considering the situation for Year 19, we find that the allowance has not been issued."
> The dioiketes has given instructions: "Issue half of that allocated the temples." But the king, in response to the appeal made to him, has ruled: "If they received it before, give it them now." And Sarapiōn, the hypodioiketes, gave us instructions through the above memorandum: "Look into it, issue what is due." This is our report. [Year 20], Hathyr 13.
> He subscribed: "Full agreement to issue (the oil)."[194]

Here it seems was a clash of authorities contributing to the delay. The twins had been wise in addressing their complaint to the king himself since his financial minister, the dioiketes, presumably as an emergency measure, had issued an instruction requiring a 50 percent saving in the temple allocations. The results of this requirement may be seen also in the record of the twins' bread ration;[195] the temple authorities were perhaps not as unscrupulous as they suspected. These were hard times, and harsh government measures may have been necessary, but it is interesting that the temples were the sector chosen to suffer, especially at a time when many were taking refuge there to escape economic hardship.[196] It seems likely that these punitive measures were taken against centers of Egyptian sentiment following the revolt of Dionysios Petosarapis and the associ-

[194] *UPZ* 23 (162 B.C.).
[195] *UPZ* 54.6-8, 11 (161 B.C.).
[196] *UPZ* 59-60 (168 B.C.), Hephaistion; see above.

ated unrest in the countryside.[197] Sarapiōn, however, if his is the decision that Apollonios, son of Glaukias, recorded at the foot of the report,[198] had no doubt that the royal instruction was overriding. In the event, the sesame oil rations for Years 18 and 19 were finally issued to Demetrios, son of Sōsos, acting for the twins, twelve days later on 26 December 162 B.C.[199]

In attempting to deal with their problems, the twins were in contact with two separate systems. For their bread supply, responsibility lay with the temple authorities whom they accused of underhand disposal of temple assets. The only effective means of approach to these was a personal one, working through family contacts.[200] Their oil supply, on the other hand, came under the authorities of Memphis working through a system of scribal offices, with reports and yet further reports. Of the two, the latter system appears less inefficient. So to some very limited extent, Egyptian subjects might have confidence in the administration of their Macedonian king.

The composition of appeals and reports to officials was one problem, and delivering them another; and hand-to-hand delivery was always the safest. Up on the Sarapieion, an audience window facilitated the control of access when the king visited, and petitions were timed to coincide with royal visits or residence in the city.[201] The evidence of this dossier makes it clear that, wherever he went, even to sacrifice, a king or crown official was incessantly showered with written appeals.[202] The later ways of the Roman Empire would come as no surprise to Egyptian subjects.[203]

One final aspect of these appeals, the presentation of their arguments, may be considered further. While it is above all the personalities of the individuals involved—of Ptolemaios and the twins—which are seen portrayed in these appeals, so too the values and ideals of the Ptolemaic bureaucracy come through reflected in the lines of argument used. The twins forever stress the human side of their suffering: they are weak, worn down, in danger of death from starvation, and hard-pressed by

---

[197] Diod. Sic. 31.15a; W. Otto (1934), 91-96; Übel (1962).
[198] *UPZ* 23.26 (162 B.C.), with Wilcken's note.
[199] *UPZ* 29-31 (162 B.C.).
[200] *UPZ* 42.24-26 (162 B.C.), the son of Psintaes.
[201] *UPZ* 53.5n. (161 B.C.); Wilcken (1927), 63-65.
[202] *UPZ* 24.4 (162 B.C.); 41.4-5; 42.3-4 (161/60 B.C.); 52.6; 53.6 (161 B.C.), "in the presence of (the god) Sarapis."
[203] Millar (1977), 1-2, 537-49.

need.[204] Their final resort is to threaten to leave the temple[205]—scarcely a real threat when there was little prospect of alternative employment. And yet they must have hoped the religious implications of their threat would carry weight with a Greek official.

Ptolemaios is somewhat more subtle in expression, though his tone changes as the months go by. Using a favorite expression, he flatters Sarapiōn, suggesting it will be his "inherited inclination" which guides him in his dealings with the twins;[206] but he is also prepared to act the suppliant, begging the official to come to their aid.[207] He invokes the prospect of both royal and divine approval: "may you always enjoy success before the king,"[208] "may Sarapis and Isis bring you grace and beauty before the king and queen for the piety you show in the face of the divine."[209] The twins are servants of the god, and Sarapiōn is encouraged to act with piety, receiving in return charm, grace, beauty, success, and good fortune in all matters from the servants of the god and all connected with the temples.[210] The expression here of Ptolemaios' appeal is Egyptian,[211] and Sarapiōn was promised god-given qualities, of high value in the society in which he functioned. But when flattery fails, Ptolemios became impatient, trying in his despair to jog the memory of the hypodioiketes.[212] "Don't you remember," he declares, "I presented you with an appeal stamped with the king's signet about the twins, and in the presence of Sarapis you asked me, 'What business is it of yours, you who are in detention?' I nominated for you Apollonios, my younger brother, as my representative. We have no help apart from you and Sarapis." In his dealings with the bureaucracy, Ptolemaios thus relies on a combination of human appeal, the promise of official success, and the approval of the native gods of Egypt.

The final fate of the twins is not known. Their bread rations cannot have been properly reinstated since accounts from October 160 B.C. re-

[204] *UPZ* 17.22-23; 19.20-21 (163 B.C.); 42.8-9 (162 B.C.); 45.14-15 (162/1 B.C.); 52.18-19; 53.19-20 (161 B.C.).
[205] *UPZ* 46.9-10; 47.13-14; 48.12-13; 50.13-15 (162/1 B.C.); cf. 24.27-28 (162 B.C.).
[206] *Progonikē hairesis*, *UPZ* 43.5-8; 44.3 (162/1 B.C.), with Delekat (1964), 38-39; 20.26 (163 B.C.), for the phrase.
[207] *UPZ* 46.16-18; 47.22-24; 50.24-26 (162/1 B.C.); with Sarapis, 52.8-9; 53.8-9 (161 B.C.).
[208] *UPZ* 24.29-30 (162 B.C.); 52.25-27; 53.29-30 (161 B.C.).
[209] *UPZ* 33.8-11; 34.6-7; 35.12-15; 36.10-13 (161 B.C.); cf. 45.13-14.
[210] *UPZ* 34.12-14; 35.25-29; 36.21-25 (161 B.C.). For the twins as *hierodouloi*, see Delekat (1964), 89-90, 99-106.
[211] Crawford (1980), 18 n.1.
[212] *UPZ* 52.4-9; 53.4-9 (161 B.C.).

cord their purchase of both grain and bread.[213] The source of their cash is not recorded, but maybe they too somehow gained profit from those textiles deals. The same accounts do suggest a varied diet for the girls when working in the Sarapieion. Papyrus roots, bread, and salt were the basis, supplemented by a wide range of sticky cakes, vegetables, fruit, and nuts, with honey and beer as well. Even their most basic bread allowance, of 4 artabas each a month from the temple, represented approximately twice what may be considered an adequate level of subsistence.[214] In receipt of only half the syntaxis due, the twins seem likely to have enjoyed a better livelihood than that, for instance, of their beggar-sister Tathēmis. The picture of the girls reconciled with their mother,[215] of Thauēs pregnant by Apollonios and dismissed from her job,[216] based as it is on the evidence of dreams alone, may never be checked and is best dismissed as fanciful. For us the interest of the twins is as an introduction both to the workings of the Ptolemaic bureaucracy and to the Egyptian world of the temples which, adapted to new circumstances, still functioned under Ptolemaic rule.

APOLLONIOS, THE YOUNGEST SON

The final character of the Sarapieion archive is Apollonios, the youngest son of Glaukias. As with the twins, so too Apollonios may be seen both as an individual—the study of a fatherless, youngest son, strongly influenced by his eldest brother from whom he finally broke free—and as a means of investigating the mixed society of the period.[217]

Born perhaps on 14 December 175 B.C.,[218] Apollonios was still a child when Antiochus invaded Egypt. After his father's death in the following troubles, while frequently visiting Ptolemaios in detention in the Sarapieion, he continued to live with his other brothers Hippalos and Sarapiōn, in the family home at Psichis in the Herakleopolite nome. In the Sarapieion he perhaps spent some time in school; an early exercise in his

[213] *UPZ* 89.1-18 (October 160–January 159 B.C.); 96.1-50 (December 159–March 158 B.C.).

[214] See chapter 5 n. 94.

[215] Leningrad ostrakon no. 1129 (Wilcken 1927, 351).

[216] Delekat (1964), 144-55.

[217] If *UPZ* 144.44-45 (164/3 B.C.) refers to his mother, he was not an orphan; his father died in 164 B.C.

[218] His birthday was 10 Hathyr, *UPZ* 20.68, and I am assuming he was eighteen when Ptolemaios started his attempt to get him enrolled in the army. For a later date of birth, see Wilcken (1927), 114.

hand is preserved among the papers, and he became a better scribe than Ptolemaios.[219] While still a youngster, for the six years from 164 to 158 B.C. he led a busy life under his brother's protection, running errands for Ptolemaios and the twins.[220] He was general messenger and go-between, bringing Ptolemaios sustenance from home[221] and learning the ways of officialdom as he sought to track down the hypodioiketes in distant parts and deliver yet another memo from his brother. By the autumn of 163 B.C. he was copying out his brother's appeals,[222] and it was Apollonios who acted for Ptolemaios when trouble with the neighbors endangered their property and livelihood in Psichis.[223] In a rudimentary way he learned to keep accounts and used home contacts in the purchase of cloth and clothing on behalf of his brother and the twins.[224] Down in Memphis he formed a relationship with the strategos Dionysios, hoping, it seems to use the copying services of some of his staff.[225] At this time Apollonios depends greatly on his brother, whom he sometimes addressed as "father,"[226] and in their differing ways it is clear their dependence was mutual.

In 158 B.C., briefly, Apollonios too joined his brother as detainee in the temple of Astarte. In March of that year he received a sum for cult expenses—for incense and for fuel—and he was now confined to the Sarapieion.[227] The circumstances behind this change in role go unrecorded, but temperamentally Apollonios appears unsuited for a constricted life. His hotheadedness was shown on 23 June 158 B.C. when, still working for his brother who needed rushes to fuel the fire for cooking porridge, the teenager Apollonios found himself at odds with the sons of Teebēsis who kept shop for their father while he was absent on cult duty for the Apis calves.[228] As priest for the Apis calves, Teebēsis had cult duties (and

---

[219] *UPZ* 147; Wilcken (1927), 110-11, on their handwriting.

[220] *Paidarion: UPZ* 24.26 (162 B.C.); 39.19; 40.14; 51.19; 62.30 (161 B.C.). I follow Wilcken's reconstruction; Delekat (1964), 12-18, on the basis of 13.16, considers Apollonios to have been in detention since a very young age.

[221] *UPZ* 24.22 (162 B.C.).

[222] Wilcken (1927), 115, for a list of the documents in his hand. The demotic reference to him as Ptolemaios' agent, *P. B.M.* 10231 (159 B.C.) described by Sethe (1913), 87 (cf. Revillout 1888, 47) is not repeated in Sethe (1920), 432-35, Urk 17. It awaits republication.

[223] *UPZ* 9 (161/60 B.C.); 10-11 (160 B.C.). Apollonios also kept in regular touch with his brothers, 73-74; *SB* 7618.

[224] *UPZ* 90.1-17; 91.1-20; 93.1-12 (159 B.C.).

[225] *UPZ* 62; see below.

[226] *UPZ* 93.1 (159 B.C.); 101.24 (156 B.C.); 65.3 (154 B.C.); 68 verso (152 B.C.); 70.2 (152/I B.C.).

[227] *UPZ* 97.10-22 (158 B.C.), 10 Mecheir.

[228] Pestman, *Rec.* 2.6 (201 B.C.).

revenues) on specified occasions, which included Pauni 25 (June 23) as one of the thirteen special feast days of the year; this was the day of the affray, and their father's absence may explain the incident with his sons. Apollonios visited Teebēsis' shop within the temple to purchase rushes, and disagreed with his sons over the quality he was to buy.[229] Two versions of the incident survive, and the differences between the account of the earlier version and the later draft of the report that Apollonios prepared for the strategos suggest strongly that he was as much at fault as were the sons of Teebēsis. The sons were donkey drivers by trade and they chased Apollonios back to his pastophorion where, in an attempt to recover their due by self-help, they beat him soundly with their donkey goads. So goes the earlier version. In the later draft, which breaks off before the end, Apollonios omits the earlier part of the story: the three sons of Teebēsis made an unprovoked attack upon him as he sat quietly in his pastophorion. Apollonios follows his brother's example in appealing to the Greek authorities, to the strategos under whose control even temples came, but unlike his brother he did not employ the racial argument. Good relations with the family of Teebēsis were, however, soon restored, and two years later, in June 156 B.C., as already noted, Ptolemaios borrowed a sizeable sum (4,500 drachmas) from the same shopkeeper.[230] Teebēsis perhaps also acted as pawnbroker for the community of the Sarapieion. Multiple occupations were regular within this community, with secular and religious functions often shared. Brought up from a young age in this mainly Egyptian society, Apollonios was equally familiar with Egyptian language and culture.[231] His Greek has a strong Egyptian flavor, and if the demotic record betrays the language of his dreams, he dreamed in Egyptian too.[232]

His dreams were troubled, but so were his daytime thoughts, as he tried the life of a detainee enclosed in the world of the Sarapieion. The presence of the twins added to this adolescent's problems: "I'm faint with worry over my detention and over Thauēs—how may we survive?" he wrote in Greek on a demotic papyrus, going on to record an order that

[229] *UPZ* 12-13 (158 B.C.). *UPZ* 13 appears to be the second version; see the spirited interpretation of Reich (1933b), 147-77.

[230] *UPZ* 101.18-24 (156 B.C.).

[231] Wilcken (1927), 115; Reich (1933b), 163, for his spelling mistakes, perhaps suggesting Egyptian pronunciation; *UPZ* 13.28-29 (158 B.C.) with Reich (1933b), 168, for an Egyptian expression ("hope in Harchonesis").

[232] *P. Bologna dem.* 3173; 3171 with Wilcken (1927), 350-51, and Reich (1933b), 156-62. Wilcken doubts whether Apollonios could write demotic, and Bresciani, Bedini, Paolini, and Silvano (1978), 95-104, even doubt the dreams are his; this seems unduly cautious.

the bread ration must now be bought for cash.[233] In these circumstances Ptolemaios thought it best for all concerned that Apollonios join the army.

In October 158 B.C., when Ptolemy VI Philometor and Kleopatra his queen were visiting Memphis, Ptolemaios took the occasion to appeal for their help in the enlistment of his youngest brother.[234] In the absence of children he stresses his own reliance for support on Apollonios; with an improvement in his own conditions he would, he reminds them, be better placed to fulfill his sacrifices on behalf of the royal couple and their children. The language of his appeal is one we have met before. Apollonios himself, with much experience in such matters, was responsible for delivering the request through the royal audience window in the Sarapieion. The account of the subsequent fortunes of this appeal provides one of the most complete illustrations to survive of the Ptolemaic bureaucracy at work.

The original request was made during the royal visit on 3 October 158 B.C., and it was only on 23 February 157 B.C., nearly five months later, that steps were finally taken to enroll Apollonios into Dexilaos' local division on full and regular pay. In the intervening period Apollonios made at least thirty-two separate trips in connection with the matter, carrying letters back and forth both between and within departments, through a jungle of different offices of men involved with the appointment.

The original request was succinctly and speedily dispatched: "Take action, but report on the cost" was how Ptolemaios' appeal was countersigned by the king. Apollonios then referred this document to Demetrios who, as chief bodyguard and forces' scribe, seems to have held a key position in overseeing military affairs in the area. Within Demetrios' department inquiries were made on the rates of pay for the division in question. As messenger boy, Apollonios went from Demetrios to Ariston, from him to Dioskourides in the pay office, from Dioskourides to Chairemon, and from him to Apollodoros. It was 25 January 157 B.C. before Demetrios reported back to the court on the current monthly rate of pay: 150 drachmas and 3 artabas of wheat, of which one came in kind (the equivalent of approximately 307 kilograms of unmilled wheat a year) and the other two in cash at the (excessively low) equivalent of 100 drachmas

---

[233] *UPZ* 63 (158 B.C.?).
[234] *UPZ* 14 (158 B.C.). My interpretation of the dossier owes much to Wilcken. See now N. Lewis (1986), 77-79.

an artaba.[235] Apollonios took this report to the court, returning with reasonable speed from Alexandria on 4 February 157 B.C., with written orders for both Demetrios and the dioiketes Dioskourides. Each of these men headed a further line of command, and in expediting further progress Apollonios hurried from office to office, carrying instructions and memoranda in an attempt to secure his enlistment.

On 7 February 157 B.C. Demetrios sent orders to Sostratos who, as his second-in-command, three days later instructed his own office to put the matter in hand. On 12 February Demetrios wrote to Dioskourides the dioiketes, enclosing a copy of his letter to Sostratos. Apollonios also carried letters from Demetrios to the strategos Poseidonios, to the chief paymaster Ammonios, and to the scribe Kallistratos. The letters were actually delivered on 17 February and Demetrios' responsibility had now been fulfilled.

In the meantime, in the office of the dioiketes, two documents had been received, the royal order which was filed away for Ptolemaios, the recorder of memoranda (hypomnēmatographos), and the letter from Demetrios filed in the department of correspondence (epistolographeion) with Epimenes. Apollonios brought these documents to the attention of Dioskourides, the dioiketes, and presumably found him favorably disposed to follow the instructions. From the dioiketes Apollonios consulted Isidoros, who as autotelēs may have been an independent advisor instructing the layman on the intricacies of government offices. The end result was two letters sent by the dioiketes on 23 February 157 B.C., one to Dorion, the epimeletes, and one to Poseidonios, the strategos, to authorize the enlistment and army pay of Apollonios.

The procedure leading up to these two letters was a complex one, and it appears that different departments had responsibility for different types of letters.[236] To obtain the letter for Dorion, Apollonios, on the advice of Isidoros, went first to Philoxenos, then to Artemon and on to Lykos, who drafted out the relevant letter; he then took the draft back to Sarapiōn, the assistant of Epimenes in the central office. For the second letter he was directed to Eubios and on to Dorion, who made a draft which was likewise returned to Sarapiōn. Forwarded by Sarapiōn, the two drafts

---

[235] *UPZ* 14.48-9, 71-78 (158/7 B.C.). Since olyra was currently priced somewhat over 300 drachmas an artaba (Wilcken 1927, 409) and stood to wheat at a ratio of 5:2, the rate of *adaeratio* here appears ludicrously low. For the kilogram equivalent, see chapter 5 n. 93, above.

[236] On the dioiketes' office, see further *P. Corn.* 1 with p. 452.

were now shown to the dioiketes. Dioskourides checked the drafts and gave his authorization. Back to Epimenes they went, on to his assistant Sarapiōn, and finally from Sarapiōn to Nikanor, the official scribe who copied the two letters out for Dorion and Poseidonios. These must then have been returned to the dioiketes for his signature before Apollonios could eventually deliver them on 23 February 157 B.C. The paperwork was finally complete, all had been officially informed, and the enrollment could proceed.

Apollonios nowhere records his financial outlay in recovering documents filed away and in steering papers from desk to desk, but we may assume that it was not insignificant, for Isidoros at least, and probably others, would require remuneration for their services. The time, however, and the nervous energy necessarily involved in this bureaucratic process, with almost five months devoted to the one appointment, may be fully appreciated only by those with personal experience of a comparable administrative structure.

It further comes as no surprise that, in the event, the appointment failed his brother's expectations. Apollonios was not in receipt of regular pay, and his postings out of town removed the service and the help Ptolemaios hoped for. A year later Ptolemaios once more complained to the crown, painting a grim picture of his own besieged position. Specific complaints were two. Through nonprovision by the army he was deprived of the rations his brother would have passed on, and the young man's absence encouraged the worse elements of society in the Sarapieion to mount attacks against him.[237] He had hoped that, once a soldier, Apollonios might have been posted to the Astarte temple where he could protect Ptolemaios from harassment, seizure, and attack at the hands of priests, pastophoroi, and the like. Now, in the absence of aid and protection, he is stoned through his window and set upon because he is a Greek. He has already approached the strategos Poseidonios and now appeals to the Sun King in the hopes of changing the situation. Himself a religious devotee in the temple of Astarte, Ptolemaios scorns the priests and pastophoroi, the Egyptians who mount attacks in the Sarapieion. Ptolemy's intervention is looked for as Ptolemaios prays that Isis and Sarapis, greatest of the gods, may establish, for time everlasting, rule for the royal couple and their children over the earth which Helios surveys.[238] In his recourse to

[237] *UPZ* 15-16 (156 B.C.).
[238] *UPZ* 15.42-48; in 16.30-34 the twelve gods of Herakleopolis, home of Ptolemaios, are added.

Isis, Sarapis, and especially Helios-Ra, Ptolemaios belies the Hellenism he claims, illustrating rather the bifocal culture of which he was a part.

As a result perhaps of Ptolemaios' request, from the summer of 156 B.C. Apollonios was back in service on the necropolis, answerable now to the *archiphylakitēs*, the chief of police, in the Anoubieion. Here he kept an eye on the changing population of the temple enclosures, noting those who took asylum in the Sarapieion and reporting back to his superior. He knew the area and its people well and could be of service to the chief of police, who on occasion praised him,[239] entrusting him with the police files which have survived among his personal papers. Such documents might aid him in his identifications; this use perhaps explains the origin of the reports on lost slaves and the dossier on the murderous kiki workers both from August 156 B.C., of the complaint of the crown peasant and pilgrim Harmais from the Herakleopolite nome (who was beaten up and lamed by the strategos' men searching for robbers in what he claimed was a case of mistaken identity), and possibly other reports made to the strategos which survive in the Sarapieion archive.[240]

As a center of asylum the Sarapieion contained a rough assortment of inhabitants, and Apollonios' job as police informer was not a pleasant one. Eventually the work began to trouble him and his worries took over. On 3 August 152 B.C., when writing to his brother about business deals in Herakleopolis and asking for instruction on the cash for the purchase of a goose, he ended his letter recounting his nightmares.[241] He was worried, very worried, about his brother and about the Apollonios who was epistates of the Anoubieion; and in his dreams he saw a certain Menedemos chasing him. On the same day he wrote to the epistates on matters of mutual concern with the promise of a speedy return; again he ended with his bad dreams of the runaway Menedemos.[242] In this letter to his namesake the epistates, Apollonios claimed that "without the gods there is nothing," yet his next letter to his brother Ptolemaios, whom he still addresses as father, contains a violent denunciation of his god Sarapis and of his whole religion.[243] Addressed ironically to "those who speak the

---

[239] *UPZ* 64 (156 B.C.).

[240] *UPZ* 121, slaves, cf. *P. Cair. Zen.* 59620 (mid-second century B.C.); 119–20, kiki workers; 122, Harmais; posibly also 123. It is unclear whether the four demotic papyri (*P. B.M.* 10405-6; 10242; 10231 [159 B.C.], Salt papyri) from the office of the archiphylakites in the Anoubieion, belong to the main Sarapieion archive; see Revillout (1888), 45–49; Sethe (1913), 86–96; Thissen (1980).

[241] *UPZ* 68 (152 B.C.).

[242] *UPZ* 69 (152 B.C.).

[243] *UPZ* 70 (152 B.C.).

truth," the letter blames the gods in whom Ptolemaios had put his faith. It is they who are responsible for his fine of fifteen talents (of this no more is known), and the runaway will not permit Apollonios and his brother to continue alive. The shame is intolerable, and the sons of Glaukias have been misled by the gods, trusting as they have in dreams. On this note of despair, fear, and final rejection Apollonios disappears. On 20 September 152 B.C. the epistates wrote to Ptolemaios complaining that in appalling circumstances with brigands at his door he had been left abandoned by Apollonios.[244] And here the dossier ends, with the forces of violence and disorder in ascendance and no help from the gods.

In September 152 B.C. Ptolemaios is still confined to his pastophorion "following the truth,"[245] but the end of the archive is likely to mean the end of his residence in the Sarapieion if not of his life. We do not know the circumstances of such a change, but the papers left there form a rich source for this mixed community of priests, pilgrims, criminals, and detainees in the mid-second century B.C. Before attempting to evaluate the nature of this community, and the tensions and forces for change within it, there is one set of papers still to be considered. These are the literary texts found amid the documents of the Sarapieion archive. Too often the scholar's interest is perforce confined to the content of a literary papyrus, with no account taken of the social context in which it was copied or preserved. In the case of the sons of Glaukias, the use and reuse of papyrus for both literary and nonliterary ends provides a glimpse of the literary interests and the cultural concerns of two known individuals within a particular setting. To make sense of this evidence is not easy, but the opportunity to attempt this may not be ignored.[246]

THE CULTURE OF THE SONS OF GLAUKIAS

The survival of an astronomical work, the *Art of Eudoxos*, among the papers of the sons of Glaukias raises a host of interesting problems. The name of the piece, the earliest illustrated scientific work to have survived from antiquity,[247] is given to it from an acrostic on the verso,[248] and the

[244] *UPZ* 71 (152 B.C.); 72 (152 B.C.); a letter from Myroullas and Chalbas to Dakoutis was perhaps penned by Apollonios on the same day.
[245] *UPZ* 71.19-20.
[246] See now the excellent introductory discussion by Clarysse (1983a), 57–61; see D. J. Thompson (1987) for more detailed discussion.
[247] Fraser (1972), 2.849 n. 346. Text in Blass (1887), with translation in Tannery (1893), 283–94; Laserre (1966) does not recognize Eudoxos' authorship.
[248] Page (1941), no. 112. The acrostic reads downwards *Eudoxou Techne* and consists of

didactic work on the recto of the papyrus actually takes the form of a
treatise on the nature of the universe presented to the Ptolemies by a certain Leptines.[249] The contents of the treatise, which is certainly not the
original work of Eudoxos of Knidos, nevertheless reflect his doctrine of
concentric spheres in which are charted the complex courses of the sun,
moon, and planets. Reckonings of the lunar and the solar calendars and
of the rise and setting of key constellations and stars are given, and the
different calculations of Eudoxos, Demokritos, Euktemon, and Kalip-
pos are recorded for the intervals of the solstice and the equinox.[250] Full
of interesting observations—the moon which is smaller, it is claimed, reflects the light of the sun[251]—the treatise displays a knowledge of the astronomy of Egypt consistent with the tradition of Eudoxos' sojourn
there.[252] In columns 7–8 the author observes the disagreement between the
calculations of astrologers and the Greek calendar; the lunar reckoning is
used by astrologers and *hierogrammateis* alike for fixing popular feast days
according to the Egyptian calendar, which neither adds nor intercalates.
Such an explanation of different Greek and Egyptian practices is a feature
of this period, a regular concern found in both popular and scientific
works. Ptolemaios himself kept a careful account of his birthday and
those of his brothers,[253] and also preserved in the archive is a list of Athe-
nian and Macedonian months showing a similar chronological concern.[254]

The colored illustrations to the treatise are carefully placed within the
text, thus forming an integral whole (plate viii).[255] Diagrams of the sun
and moon are there, the signs of the zodiac and what appear to be Egyptian vignettes—Thoth both as mummified ibis and as baboon, a scarab in
a circle. Towards the end of the treatise, both within and following a
circle, which contains the names of the zodiacal signs, are found added
the words "oracles (*chrēsmoi*) of Sarapis" and "oracles of Hermes." Such a

---

eleven lines (months) of thirty letters (days) and one of thirty-five, representing the Egyptian year.
[249] xxiv.2-4, *didaskalea ouranios*.
[250] The dates of the solstice and equinox, xxii.21-xxiii.14, may give a date for composition of 193–190 B.C., but the text is in the same hand as *UPZ* 110, suggesting a date for the
copy shortly before 164 B.C.; see Wilcken, *UPZ* 110 introduction.
[251] xviii-xx.16.
[252] Strabo 17.1.29; Diog. Laert. 8.86; Sen. QNat. 7.3.
[253] *UPZ* 77 ii.32; 20.67-69 The observation is that of Clarysse (1983a), 58.
[254] *P. Par.* 4 = Pack (1965), no. 2332.
[255] Weitzmann (1959), 6 and figure 2; (1970), 49-50 and plate XIII.37. More work is needed
on the interrelation of this text and its illustrations.

description may be seen to suggest one of the uses to which such astro-nomical calculations might be applied. The oracular roles of both Apis and of Thoth, found here in Greek form, enjoyed a popular vogue; they were further connected with the interpretation of dreams.[256] This com-bination of oracle and astronomy verging on astrology, which later be-came so popular in the Roman world, with the rise of Hermes Trisme-gistos and works like the *Tetrabiblos*, finds its roots here firmly fixed in Egypt of the second century B.C.[257]

The identification of this work as from the Sarapieion papers is based on marginal additions made to the verso in the hand of Ptolemaios, son of Glaukias. Besides the acrostic, four separate documents are transcribed on the back of the treatise, and the scribe of the treatise also wrote the first of these. In a space in column 1 are added the words: "Within, con-cerns of Hermes."[258] Such a label, made for easy reference, seems to imply that the long papyrus was preserved in a roll, but the problem remains of the circumstances which brought such a work into the hands of Ptole-maios, who was certainly not its copyist. The contents of the verso may begin to give an answer. Here are found both official instructions and private letters, copied, composed, and corrected in such a manner as to suggest the influence of some form of literary instruction for officials.[259] Whatever their purpose here, the genuineness of the contents of the doc-uments has never been challenged. The decrees recorded are clearly real decrees, the instructions appear genuine instructions, which were once sent out, and the letters, though perhaps linguistically based on *exempla*, probably arise from real situations.

The first of the documents on the verso, *UPZ* 110, contains instruc-tions dating from 164 B.C. which arise from a decree promulgated by the brothers Ptolemy VI Philometor and Ptolemy VIII Euergetes, with Kleo-patra II, to deal with the major crisis caused both by the revolt of Dion-ysios Petosarapis and by the severe economic difficulties of a country suf-fering from the effects of a foreign invasion followed by civil war. The noncultivation of land was a serious problem, and agricultural involve-

---

[256] See Wilcken (1927), 33.

[257] Cumont (1937); Gardiner (1938); Quaegebeur (1980/81), 233-34, the connection of Hermes/Thoth and priestly learning in the House of Life; Strabo 17.1.29, 46, priests as philosophers and astronomers and the connection of such learning with Hermes.

[258] Wilcken (1927), 475. Hermes/Thoth was of course the god of writing, and the label might simply signify "literature."

[259] On the use of both sides of the papyrus, see the masterful analysis of Wilcken, *UPZ* 110.

ment had been imposed by the authorities on the population, with compulsory leases often at a reduced rent.[260] The decree, however, had been put into effect indiscriminately and the necessary exceptions had not been made. *UPZ* 110 records instructions to his deputy made by Herodes, the dioiketes, which he now forwards to further officials, making exceptions in the case of officials, the military, tax collectors, and the poverty-stricken. Indeed the whole dossier may be interpreted as an official climb-down from a decree which had proved unworkable, while at the same time it bears witness to the difficulties experienced in the resumption of normal agriculture. As a result of pressure, almost all are now excluded from the effect of the decree; it is hard to imagine who was left to undertake the compulsory leases. The exemptions are dressed up in an intolerably dense, pompous, and ponderous language, with long periodic and moralizing sentences, one of which runs for sixty lines.[261] This feature, perhaps purposely, serves to obscure the meaning of the dioiketes. But while rebuking his subordinates for their childish irresponsibility in interpreting the ruling (lines 85–86), he shows a clear awareness of the real hardship of the countryside, of the dire state of the peasantry suffering shortage of the things they need to survive (100–103).

At the end of this set of letters comes a date (23 October 164 B.C.) in the same hand as writes the private letter (*UPZ* 144) that follows immediately after. If *UPZ* 110 stands as an extreme example of the obscurity of official jargon, the two private letters which follow may be read with profit as examples of the art of saying nothing, at great length. The style is complex, the vocabulary elaborate, and the sense obscure. The reader, struggling through a mass of subordinate clauses and self-righteous sentiments, longs for the forthright bluntness of the complaints penned by the sons of Glaukias. In *UPZ* 144 the writer complains of the ill will now shown him by an earlier friend of his family. He seems involved in a lawsuit on the subject (45–46), and he calls down the ire and wrath of the gods (47–51) on the man who, in spite of his upbringing, has acted so disgracefully towards him (17–23). He has always considered just and pure behavior to be a guiding principle and the greatest good, and he urges his adversary to act in the same spirit (28–31). For now, suffering in the provision of his livelihood, he is deprived of all he needs, even indeed of his house (32–35). The complaint perhaps sounds familiar, or

[260] Kaplony-Heckel and Kramer (1985), 44-47; the rate in 116 B.C. from Krokodilopolis (Pathyrite) of 8¹/₁₆ artabas to the aroura (p. 52) seems unusually high.
[261] *UPZ* 110.34-64.

so I shall suggest, but the language and its sentiments come straight from the Greek bureaucratic tradition, tempered somewhat by a religiosity and touching faith in the power of the deity.

Next, but written earlier, follows the acrostic and a further private letter, *UPZ* 145, which is even more obscure in content. The recipient perhaps was an official since the writer hopes for the benevolence of the king towards him. He is, he writes, unable to sail downstream to greet him since he may not leave without special orders.[262] The text is fragmentary and the meaning uncertain, but in times of trouble the writer would seem to offer thanks and good wishes to a patron. After this, at the end of the papyrus, comes a copy of a royal letter to Dionysios, strategos of the Memphite nome, in which Ptolemy (VI Philometor) urges the immediate implementation of a recent amnesty decree.[263] The letter is dated, in both Egyptian and Macedonian reckoning, 22 September 163 B.C.

The close connection here between the official and private letters on the verso of this long papyrus, both in actual hands and in the bureaucratic language of their content, suggests perhaps a common origin in some form of official context. However, although the astronomical treatise of the recto was recognized and read by Ptolemaios, this use of the verso seems to imply that the scientific text, so carefully copied, was later ignored by its copyist when he reused the same sheet simply as a large piece of almost blank papyrus on which the later texts are penned. And what is still not explained is how this complex papyrus came into the hands of Ptolemaios, son of Glaukias, who, in his own way, registered the contents of the scientific treatise on the recto.

A possible explanation for this phenomenon is perhaps to be found in *UPZ* 62, an undated letter to Ptolemaios from one Dionysios, an official who was in the habit of visiting the Sarapieion.[264] Here again we meet the somewhat formal style of a Greek bureaucratic letter; the practice of punctuation found here is paralleled in *UPZ* 144-45, perhaps the product of the same office.[265] But here the tone is somewhat different, the cry rather of a tortured heart. Dionysios had always used the freedom that his office brought him to the high purpose of helping all, and especially aiding Ptolemaios and his brother (Apollonios). Recently Apollonios had approached him, asking that, in return for some consideration, Diony-

---

[262] *UPZ* 145.6-7. Could this be a reference to katoche?
[263] *UPZ* 111 (163 B.C.).
[264] *UPZ* 62.33-34.
[265] See Wilcken's introduction to the various documents.

sios' scribes should undertake his work. Dionysios was not agreeable to this proposal though he made alternative suggestions. He had also urged Apollonios to attend on him early the next day to separate out some oil seed in Memphis that he wished sent to Alexandria. The boy had not appeared and Dionysios, it seems, was most upset. If it is a question of shame, he hopes Ptolemaios may sort the matter out and send his brother to him. He himself is busy, lacking time to come up to the Sarapieion, but he is suffering real agony, fearing lest the boy be ill. When next he comes to pray to the god he will not impose himself on Ptolemaios, but will stay instead in the lodging house of Protarchos.[266] All he seeks is reassurance about the boy.

Dionysios is a man of importance with scribes at his disposal; his feelings for Apollonios are clearly deep. Perhaps, as the first editor suggested,[267] he is the strategos of the Memphite nome, the recipient also of that royal letter[268] on the back of the *Art of Eudoxos*. On this occasion his hard line had led to a break in relations with Apollonios, but it seems not unlikely that on earlier occasions he had offered favors to the boy, and that his office had undertaken correspondence on behalf of the sons of Glaukias. No names are recorded in the two private letters *UPZ* 144-45 which might support this view, but the contents of the first are, at the very least, suggestive. The period from 164 B.C. was a hard one generally, and especially for Ptolemaios and his brothers. Their father had been killed in October 164 B.C., and the sons were victims of the same troubles which official policy sought to remedy.[269] Ptolemaios lived in the Sarapieion; his brothers lived at home, at Psichis in another nome. Here there were problems with the neighbors and Ptolemaios feared for his livelihood.

It is indeed tempting to interpret *UPZ* 144 as a bureaucratic draft[270] for a letter Ptolemaios might send, addressed to the neighbor who troubled his brothers the most. The inroads made by the neighbors, Hesperos, Ataios, and Polemon, against his father's home are more clearly described in a somewhat later appeal to the crown, made by Ptolemaios

[266] See *UPZ* 120.11 (156 B.C.?) for the same katalyma used by runaway kiki workers; the alternatives to staying with friends would seem to be few.

[267] Brunet de Presle, cf. Wilcken (1927), 306.

[268] *UPZ* 111.

[269] *UPZ* 14.8-9 (158 B.C.).

[270] See *UPZ* 144.46 where the scribe gives up: *meta ta loipa. P. Erasm.* 6 (mid-second century B.C.) is comparable in its use of literary vocabulary.

himself in 160 B.C.;[271] the neighborhood would seem from the names to be that of the Greek cleruchs settled in the area. In the end Sarapiōn, one of the other sons of Glaukias, married a daughter of Hesperos and the problem was solved, but that was not until September 153 B.C.[272] If ever sent, this earlier formal letter (if such it is) composed for Ptolemaios by the office of Dionysios had no effect. For argument it relies on high-minded principles, tempered by fear of the gods. Good behavior makes a man, and education serves this aim. The vocabulary and sentiments here are Greek, untouched by things Egyptian found elsewhere. And whether or not these formal letters were ever used for the purpose for which they were composed, they were clearly studied by the sons of Glaukias on whose otherwise more blunt and forthright style may occasionally be seen the influence of their formal, pompous tone.[273] In this respect, as in his brother's use of friendly Greek officials and their offices, Ptolemaios provides good evidence to uphold his claim to be a Greek.

If, as suggested, *UPZ* 144 and possibly 145 were composed for the sons of Glaukias, the copy which follows on the papyrus of the letter of Phi-lometor dated 22 September 163 B.C.[274] will also have interested Ptole-maios; the papyrus may have come into his hands around this time. In this royal letter the king announced an early visit to the city. As we have already seen, Ptolemaios helped the twins to exploit the occasion in deliv-ering directly their congratulations on the king's safe return from Rome, coupled with complaints on the subject of their ration of bread. Fore-knowledge of the royal itinerary was thus put to good use by Ptolemaios.

It may then be that the astronomical treatise was originally copied by a scribe in a Memphite office. Reused, the papyrus came later into the hands of the sons of Glaukias—a happy bonus from an office where a clean sheet of papyrus was valued more highly than science. But Ptole-maios read the treatise, and placed it among his papers. Here among the documents, with other works of literature, it provides some evidence both for the breadth of cultural interest of the official milieu and for the literary diet available to Ptolemaios and his brother, boys from a Mace-donian military family in the Egyptian *chōra* of the mid–Ptolemaic period.

[271] *UPZ* 10 (160 B.C.); cf. 9 (161/60 B.C.), complaining of the local officials.

[272] *UPZ* 66 (153 B.C.), he informs his brothers in the Sarapieion and asks for oil. The Berenike of *UPZ* 74.4 may be Sarapion's wife.

[273] E.g., *UPZ* 144.11-12, picked up by Apollonios in 12.44-47; so in 42.10 (162 B.C.) *philautia* is unlikely to be a word in everyday use. Similar influences on Ptolemaios' style may be seen in his description of his father's death, 4.8; 14.8-9; 9.4 with Kornemann (1901), 61 n. 1.

[274] *UPZ* 111.

It was not only science but philosophy, too, to which they had access—more writing, "the stuff of Hermes" as Apollonios labeled it on the verso.[275] We cannot know if the brothers read the text as well as labeled it before reuse, nor from where it came. What remains, fragmented, are fifteen columns of a treatise on negatives, the work, it seems, of an author unknown.[276] In attacking a logical system with, in his view, overly precise rules about negation, the author illustrates his points from a wide range of Greek poets. As often, Euripides is quoted most but there are others too: Timotheos and Thespis, Sappho and Ibykos, Alkman and Anakreon.[277] Even if the logic of the argument was not easily accessible, the recognition of the Greek poetry quoted may have provided some pleasure to the sons of Glaukias. Papyrus was in short supply outside government offices, and big sheets with one side blank formed a precious commodity. On the back of one in 159 B.C. Ptolemaios wrote down the dreams of his friend Nektembes, copied out an account for his brother Apollonios covering April to May, and the two brothers used the rest for other accounts from the same year.[278] Such was the fate of a treatise of logic in this quarter of the Sarapieion.

Science and philosophy were the affairs of Hermes, but literature was a thing for men. On occasion the brothers took respite from complaints and from accounts and turned their hands, in stilted Greek, to works of literature. For that we must be grateful. In Alexandria a library stood in the Sarapieion.[279] So too perhaps in Memphis, or perhaps the works they copied here were brought by visitors. One papyrus in particular preserves the brothers' fascination with Greek literature; it is a long papyrus, full of interest.[280] On the one side, misleadingly ascribed to Euripides, was copied a forty-four-line extract which, it seems, was rather from Menander or another comic poet.[281] But how were they to know? The original hand is not otherwise known, but later, on the other side, Ptolemaios repeats

[275] *UPZ* 101.17 (159 B.C.), crosswise; see n. 258 above.
[276] Von Arnim (1923), frag. 180; illustrated by Norsa (1939), Tav. 36; ascribed to Chrysippos by Bergk (1886), 137, who also, 131-33, commented on mistakes in the Greek text; Cavini (1985), 85-121, convincingly rejects this authorship.
[277] Euripides scores 7, the others 1 each. Bergk also identifies Pindar, Choirilos, and the *Kypria*; these are not named.
[278] *UPZ* 79; 90; 101.
[279] Fraser (1972), 1.28.
[280] *P. Louvre* 7172 = *P. Didot*; see Pack (1965), nos. 31, 401, 1319-20, 1435. The only study of the papyrus as a unity is Weil (1879), with the important observations and identification of the hands by Wilcken (1927), 112, 115.
[281] Sandbach (1972), 328-30, *P. Didot* 1; Austin (1973), no. 287; Gomme and Sandbach (1973), 723-26.

the piece he may by then have learned by heart. The poetry of the extract is undistinguished, the play unknown. The speaker chides her father, who plans a wealthy wedding for his daughter, prepared to take her from the man she loves. Below the original version the young Apollonios, not more than fifeen years old,[282] pens eight lines from Euripides' *Medea*, a longer extract from Aeschylus' *Carians*, otherwise known as *Europa*,[283] and finally fifteen lines from a prologue of Menander.[284] All these are described at the end as the "lessons of Ariston, the philosopher." Perhaps Ariston was simply a wise man, Apollonios' teacher, or just a learned friend; the range of his reading was wide, from an impressive selection of literary texts.[285]

The choice of extracts is, I think, a personal one, which seems to reflect the daily concerns, the worries and hopes of the two sons of Glaukias, as known from other papyri in the archive—their letters, their petitions, and the records of their dreams. The first long extract, with the family tensions it outlines, may be read as a Greek record of some of the Egyptian sentiments known from the *Potter's Oracle*, a description of times that were out of joint. For Medea, in the passage quoted here, a problem has been that of adjustment to a foreign land, while the note of the Aeschylus extract is one of gloom and foreboding. In the Menander prologue that follows the speaker has undergone a conversion in his life. From earlier dark times he now had been saved, as though through incubation in a temple of Asklepios. The setting is Greece, probably the city of Athens, with Asklepios, the god of Epidauros. The Greek detainees of the Memphite Sarapieion, close to the shrine of Imhotep/Asklepios where incubation also occurred, might well identify. They too knew bad times, darkness, and gloom; perhaps one day they too might live a life untroubled in the sun. The selection of extracts may have expressed the choice of the copyist as much as the availability of the texts.[286]

However, the problems of real life intervened in the literary pastimes of these scribes, and the bread account for the twins which follows, from the summer of 160 B.C., is in Ptolemaios' hand. This same hand covers the back. First Ptolemaios repeats the daughter's lament of the recto,

---

[282] The date *ante quem* is given by the account.

[283] Fraenkel (1942), 238.

[284] Sandbach (1972), 330, *P. Didot* 2; Austin (1973), no. 288; Gomme and Sandbach (1973), 726-29; perhaps from the *Hypobolimaios*, see Zuntz (1956).

[285] See, however, Gaiser (1968), 205-6, for the suggestion that *ariston philosopho[i]s mathēmata*, "for lovers of wisdom the best thing is learning," may have been what Apollonios meant.

[286] Thompson (1987), 112-17, elaborates this theme.

omitting a line and misremembering others. Then follows the pick of the papyrus, two epigrams of Poseidippos, otherwise unknown. Both written to commemorate acts of dedication, their scene is Alexandria: the Pharos lighthouse set up to Zeus Soter by Sostratos of Knidos, and the temple to Aphrodite Zephyritis set up by Kallikrates of Samos.[287] The pious acts of earlier crown officials perhaps appealed to Ptolemaios, or maybe rather it was the landmarks of Alexandria that caught his attention, as reminders of time spent in the first city of the country.[288]

A final extract of Greek literature, part of the prologue of Euripides' *Telephos*,[289] the back of which was once again used for a letter and accounts, may provide further evidence for the personal choice of the brothers in the extracts they collected. Originating from Arcadia, Telephos finds himself among the Mysians and bewails his fate there as a Hellene among barbarians. The piece is in Apollonios' hand and at the end he has added the lines: "Apollonios the Macedonian . . . a Macedonian I say." A comparison with the brothers' situation is unavoidable.

It was a strange cultural life up on the desert edge of Memphis. At one extreme came the plays of Menander and Euripides, the epigrams of Poseidippos, at the other works in demotic, moral maxims and religious handbooks straight from the traditions of Egypt. At least three extracts of moral tracts have survived among the Sarapieion papyri; others still may lie unedited in European museums. The most substantial collection of moral maxims, in the form of advice of an older man to his junior, follows on the demotic complaint probably of Harmais, *UPZ* 6a, on the subject of confiscations made by the temple authorities in October 163 B.C.;[290] the Greek accounts of *UPZ* 92 (159 B.C.) are on the back. The world of these maxims and hortatory *sententiae* is that of 'Onchsheshonqy or the Insinger papyrus.[291] The strength of the city lies in the strength of the gods, and good, upright, and peaceable conduct in public and private

---

[287] Gow and Page (1965), lines 3099-3119, nos. xi and xii; see Fraser (1972), 2.810-11 nn. 129, 139; Chamoux (1975), on the Pharos.

[288] *UPZ* 78.28-39, for Ptolemaios' knowledge of the city seen in dreams; he sits on a great tower there, perhaps indeed the Pharos (though impossibly there is a crowd to the north and east). *P. Ryl.* 552 may be a further literary text from the archive.

[289] *P. Med.* 1.15, especially lines 14-16; illustrated by Norsa (1939), Tav. 4; Handley and Rea (1957), for the plot; *SB* 7617; 7618 (158 B.C.), for the verso; Clarysse (1983a), 58, already makes this connection.

[290] *P. Louvre* 2414, Revillout (1893); Volten (1955), 271-80; Hughes (1982). I see no reason to accept the suggestion of Revillout (1893), xx, that Harmais, as Ptolemaios' student, is the recipient of these instructions. For the other shorter extracts on the verso of *UPZ* 84 and 85, see Williams (1976), 264-69.

[291] Glanville (1955); Lichtheim (1980), 159-84, cf. 184-217, the Insinger papyrus. For the literary type, see Leclant (1963); Lichtheim (1983), 93-100 and (1984).

affairs alike should be the aim of the individual. Here, as in other tracts, are everyday rules for social life, as there are for personal relations; the family is of prime importance, with respect required for all its members.

Such was the moral framework of Egyptian society and, through Harmais and their Egyptian friends, the sons of Glaukias learned the ways of the world in which they lived. From the twins perhaps they collected the demotic instructions for the mummification of the Apis bull, the record of wrappings and ointments used for the job, the careful description of cult objects, of ritual required. (These may, however, as suggested above, come rather from the Undertakers' Archive.) Such detailed technical literature will have been a regular part of temple libraries concerned with the preservation of the wisdom of the cult. Much of the demotic material from Saqqara remains to be deciphered, and the more recent finds of papyri from the Sacred Animal Necropolis, with their demotic tales and popular literature, have added to our picture of culture on the Egyptian side.[292] The stories of the high priests of Memphis delighted a wide readership,[293] and the list of alphabetical birds perched on alphabetical bushes[294] makes it clear that Egyptian schooling encouraged a wide awareness of the natural world. Egyptian culture here was strong and could not be ignored.

In the mixed society of the times, these cultures had to meet. The different points of contact made may serve to chart the relative strengths both of the people and the art involved. The Egyptian language was difficult, at least to read and write, but the tales of Egypt had long exercised a wide appeal. Herodotus was not alone in appreciating the popular literature of the country, and the emergence of tales in translation made native literature more accessible to the new immigrant population.[295]

Such is the Dream of Nectanebo penned by Apollonios, with a boyish illustration at the end of a head which looks much the same whichever way up it is put.[296] Nectanebo, of course, is well known from the Alexander Romance as a famous magician as well as a king. This Greek version of an essentially Egyptian tale is described at its start as that of Pe-

[292] Smith and Tait (1983); there is more to follow.
[293] Lichtheim (1980), 125-51; Spiegelberg (1906), 91-94, on Sethon in Herodotus 2.141; Smith (1974), 19, for stories among more recent finds.
[294] Smith and Tait (1983), 198-213, no. 27.
[295] Spiegelberg (1906), on Herodotus.
[296] *UPZ* 81; Boswinkel and Sijpesteijn (1968), 6a-b; Wilcken (1905); Lavagnini (1922), 37-42; Perry (1966), 327-33; Clarysse (1983a), 60 and (1983b); and, most recently, Koenen (1985).

tesis, a carver of hieroglyphs, who addressed his tale or report to the king Nectanebo. (In this address we find again the same desire to ascribe knowledge as in the Leptines address of the astronomical *Technē* of Eudoxos, or in the "lessons of Ariston the philosopher" copied out by Apollonios.) Set in Memphis, this tale of Nectanebo, that pious last pharaoh of Egypt who, like the god Onouris, came from the capital Sebennytos, tells of the king's dream, of a vision of gods with Isis at its center, and of unfinished work on a shrine. It also contains the adventures of Petesis sent to complete the unfinished work. True to form, the papyrus breaks off just as the beautiful Hathursepses makes her entrance, but not before the introduction of the themes of drink and love, themes long part of the traditional folk tales of Egypt.[297] But here the storyteller is also well aware of his new audience, and the Egyptian features and gods of the story are translated into Greek, as is the tale itself.[298] In Apollonios' version, the Dream of Nectanebo forms a striking example of part of the culture of old Egypt now made accessible to the new inhabitants of the country.

An Egyptian folk tale is thus translated with explanatory notes for the Greek-speakers of the country, and the archive of the sons of Glaukias contained both Greek and demotic, often together on the same sheet of papyrus.[299] When Apollonios dreams his dream in which a singer sings "Apollonios speaks Greek, Peteharenpi speaks Egyptian,"[300] in presenting the dual aspect of his own life, his subconscious reflects also a bifocality in the society in which he lived.

There was the primarily Greek sphere—of officials, soldiers, and settlers—and there was the primarily Egyptian sphere—of priests, peasants, and workers—but these were not exclusive. The two worlds overlapped and a large part of the population belonged to both. Such were the sons of Glaukias. Their friends and associates come from both nationalities and from many parts of society, soldiers like the Cretan Demetrios, son of Sosos; officials like Dionysios down in Memphis; but also Harmais, Nektembēs, and the twins in the temple. Back home in the Herakleopolite nome their family and friends were from among the Greek military settlers of the area, while up on the Sarapieion the purchases they made

[297] Cf. Hdt. 2.174, Amasis.
[298] *UPZ* 81.ii.7 (a papyrus boat is *rôps* in Egyptian), 15-16 (Onouris is Ares in Greek).
[299] See Clarysse (1983a), 58-59.
[300] *P. Bologna dem.* 3173.9-12, in Bresciani, Bedini, Paolini, and Silvano (1978), 95-98. The translation is that of J. D. Ray, who suggests that Peteharenpi may be the Egyptian name by which Apollonios was also known.

were from Egyptians: Talous and Petēsis, grain merchants;[301] Simminis, the bread seller;[302] Harontotes, Kollouthēs, and Petenēth, the gooseherds;[303] or Konnas, Akebēsis, and Horos, son of Psenobastis, who sold them winding sheets.[304] This was a mixed society and it was a bilingual society. Literacy, on the other hand, when it occurred, was likely to be single; so the bilingual dream of Nektembēs, recorded for him by Ptolemaios, is transcribed only in Greek.[305]

The future, on the whole, lay with the Greeks and those who spoke their language. When Harmais, the detainee, suffered at the hands of a fellow Egyptian on the temple staff, the complaint he drafted was in his native language.[306] Yet, like the twins, in other dealings with the authorities of the city he recognized the advantage of friends who wrote in Greek (however poor that Greek might be).[307] It is through this system of appeals, as through the courts, that the Greek administration slowly came to be both accepted and exploited by Egyptians of town and countryside alike. When Nephoris, the mother of the twins, left their father for Philippos, she had fallen victim to a soldier's glamor.[308] But this soldier was a Greek, and the added prestige she might now gain from such a liaison perhaps compounded his appeal. Her husband fled the city. So too in literature. Egyptian stories might find translators into Greek, but if the plays of Euripides and of Menander found an Egyptian audience it was still in Greek that they were known. The picture was a complex one, with different factors carrying more weight in the different cultural, economic, and social spheres. Nephoris may have chosen a Greek soldier, but in mid-second-century B.C. Memphis the Egyptian side of life was strong. With the temples of Ptah and Apis, Memphis was widely recognized as a religious center; this was a native world with the temples of the city largely staffed with Egyptian priests and personnel. Here incubation occurred as those in search of a cure slept in the temple, hoping for guidance, and dreams were interpreted and medicine was practiced, mainly

---

[301] *UPZ* 91.8, 12, 17-18; 92 ii.9, iii.16; 93.7 (159 B.C.).

[302] *UPZ* 96.44 (159/8 B.C.).

[303] Harontotes: *UPZ* 100.3. Kollouthēs: 83.13; 84.11, 23-24, 42, 64; 85.10. Petenēth: 68.4.

[304] Konnas and Akebēsis: *UPZ* 84.6, 40-41, 62-63; 85.[6] (163-160 B.C.). Horos, son of Psenobastis: 83.1-2; 84.3, 14, 36, 47, 58, 70, 75; 85.3, 14; 88.3, 9 (163-160 B.C.).

[305] *UPZ* 79.4-5 (159 B.C.). In contrast, the author of *P. Cair. Goodsp.* 3 = Witkowski (1911), no. 30.7-9 (third century B.C.) proposes, in Greek, to record his dream in Egyptian; the demotic follows, perhaps suggesting literacy in both languages.

[306] *UPZ* 6a with Revillout (1893), xvii–xix; Clarysse (1986), with important modifications; perhaps this version was prepared for translation into Greek.

[307] *UPZ* 2 (163 B.C.).

[308] *UPZ* 18-19 (163 B.C.).

Egyptian-style.[309] Indeed, the one sure example of a Greek who studied the Egyptian script did so to make a living with a native doctor specializing in the use of douches as a cure.[310]

Astarte was an exceptional goddess for taking in servants from an immigrant background, for in the Sarapieion the native hold was strong. Though it was Sarapis and Isis, not Apis and the mother-of-Apis, to whom Ptolemaios prayed, the terms of the prayers he made for crown officials and for his sovereign and his queen were regularly those of his Egyptian friends. And in his daily dealings there, it sometimes did not help to be a Greek. Truly for the sons of Glaukias, life in the Sarapieion was life between two worlds.

[309] The Cretan dream interpreter (plate vii) shows that this was not only an Egyptian activity.

[310] UPZ 148 (second century B.C.), not necessarily from Memphis; see the ingenious discussion of Rémondon (1964). For an *iatroklystēs* from Memphis, see UPZ 8.34, Harchēbis, cf. 7-8 (163/1 B.C.). On medicine in temples see Sauneron (1957), 166-67; P. Cair. Zen. 59426, the god's remedy (including honey) for disease of the eyes; P. Tebt. 44.8-9 (114 B.C.), incubation at an Isis shrine.

8

ROMAN MEMPHIS: AN EPILOGUE

Alexandria fell to Octavian Caesar on 3 August 30 B.C. In Memphis the high priest Imouthes/Petobastis IV had perished two days before, though how is unrecorded. The new conqueror visited the body of his Macedonian predecessor (breaking off part of Alexander's nose in the process) but was uninterested in the remains of the Ptolemies. Further, "accustomed to worship gods, not cattle," he declined to visit the Apis bull at Memphis.[1] The break with the past was made and the tone of the new nononsense rule of the Romans was clearly set. And whereas under the Ptolemies the international city of Memphis with its mixed population enjoyed an influential, if secondary, role in the social, economic, and, particularly, the religious life of the country, the Roman city in contrast shows few distinctive features.[2] Some elements of Roman Memphis may be seen as marking continuity, but in the main change and control were the keynotes of the new regime, as Memphis, like other cities, was absorbed into the administration of the new Roman province. For the Ptolemies, however harsh their rule, Egypt was their own kingdom where they lived; for the Romans it was simply a province to be exploited.[3] It was, however, an exceptional province under the direct control of the emperor governing through an equestrian prefect.

In appearance, perhaps, the city changed little, but the replacement by numbered *amphoda*, at least fifteen, of the individually named ethnic quarters of the Ptolemaic city bears the hallmark of Roman rule.[4] Local administration was standardized while district officers kept the lists and tax records for each district.[5] Extending to the south on Kom Sabakha, the remains of mud-brick buildings with the occasional stone constructions suggest a population undiminished in size during the first two cen-

---

[1] Dio. Cass. 51.16.5, cf. 17.4–5; Suet. *Aug.* 93.

[2] The distinctive Memphite dress is a welcome exception, Philostr. *VA* 6.5.

[3] Nock (1972), vol. 1, 215.

[4] 1: *P. Lond.* 3.915 (p. 27).9, 18 (A.D. 160); 2: *BGU* 833 (A.D. 174); *P. Stras.* 195.3–4 (A.D. 174); 3: *BGU* 434.3 (A.D. 169); *P. Cair. Goodsp.* 10.6 (A.D. 180); *P. Bour.* 26.21 (third century A.D.); 4: *BGU* 777.3–4 (A.D. 145/6); 5: *P. Vindob. Sijp.* 24.9 (A.D. 131/2); 15: *P. Cair. Goodsp.* 10.6 (A.D. 180).

[5] *P. Stras.* 195.3–4 (A.D. 174); *P. Cair. Goodsp.* 10.5 (A.D. 180), *praktores argyrikōn.*

turies at least.[6] Some lived in opulence, with bronze fitments to the doors of their dwellings,[7] and it is only from Memphis that professional landlords, *argoi*, are recorded.[8] Though undocumented, renting was probably an important source of income already in the Ptolemaic period. Of the earlier foreign communities in the city little trace remains. On the whole the adoption of Greek or Greco-Egyptian names by now masks earlier immigrants,[9] though the evidence of nomenclature may identify the more recent arrival of Nubian families to the city.[10] Several Roman potteries lying south of the Ptah temple enclosure form some indication of continued economic activity in the city.[11]

There are others too. As earlier, the Nile and agriculture were the mainstays of the city's economic life. Still an important port, Memphis served the northern villages of the Arsinoite nome, the Fayum, where a new Roman tax sheds some light on the cargoes transported overland and shipped through the city. Paid at the Fayum customs houses of Dionysias, Soknopaiou Nesos, Karanis, Bakchias, Philopator (also called Theogonis), Philadelphia, and possibly elsewhere,[12] the tax of Memphis harbor was levied both on livestock (generally imported camels) and on what these camels and donkeys carried through these posts; the rate of tax is only rarely given.[13] The chief Fayum import, both through Bakchias and Soknopaiou Nesos, was wine, transported in jars by camel and donkey. Oil, on the other hand (together with green olives), was a regular export out through Soknopaiou Nesos; so too were dates. Wheat crossed the frontiers in both directions, out from Soknopaiou Nesos, Karanis, and probably Dionysias, and in to Philadelphia. Vetch, *orobos*, was a standard export from the area, and pulses, *osprea*, are regularly recorded out of Philadelphia. Other exports known from the harbor tax were vegetables and vegetable seeds, black beans, lentils, mustard, wild chickling (arakos), and garlic; as earlier, reed baskets were imported into the Fayum. Other taxes were of course levied on these same loads at the Fayum cus-

---

[6] Jeffreys (1985), 17-18.

[7] Petrie, Mackay, and Wainwright (1910), 44.

[8] Montevecchi (1973), 178.

[9] *BGU* 712.13 (second century A.D.), Abaros, a Semitic name in a wine account, is an exception. The undated Karikos from an inscription, Letronne (1848), no. 333, might be a Carian.

[10] *P. Oslo* 24 (A.D. 131); *BGU* 777 (A.D. 168/9) with 833 (A.D. 174); *SB* 9022 (13) (third century A.D.) with Bingen (1968).

[11] Petrie (1909a), 14; Abdulla el-Sayed Mahmud (1978), 4.

[12] See Appendix E and figure 1.

[13] Only in *P. Alex. Giss.* 11 (second or third century A.D.), 6 chalkoi on 6 artabas of *orobos*; *P. Stras.* 250e (A.D. 159), 1½ obols on 3 artabas of wheat.

toms houses.[14] The payment here of the Memphite harbor tax, a payment eventually made to its own grammateus,[15] suggests an origin or destination along the Nile beyond the city itself—Alexandria often, and other cities of the Delta. In Memphis, too, further tolls were levied on freight passing through the city,[16] and Memphis remained a center both of shipping and of shipbuilding.[17] In volume, grain probably still formed the largest cargoes, and the remains of a sample sack of barley records a Memphite *gubernator*, Chairemon, son of Anoubion.[18] The tax receipts of the Arsinoite toll stations, sealed with the Apis bull,[19] thus serve to illustrate both the cargoes shipped through Memphis and the wide variety of Arsinoite produce. Evidence for agriculture in the Memphite area itself is more circumscribed. Vines and oil crops are known from their produce[20] and, as today, date palms grew amid the other crops.[21] Sheep in the area might be reared for wool[22] and the long-established textile production of the city went on.[23] Metal working too continued.[24] Still known as a market center,[25] under the Romans the city boasted more than one private bank.[26] Whereas Alexandrians might lend money in Memphis,[27] Memphites in turn exploited land outside the immediate area.[28] Around the city itself there is some evidence for reasonably large estates in the second and third centuries A.D.[29] That of Lucius Antonius Minor had its own in-

[14] Eitrem (1932); Borkowski (1971); *BGU* 2304 (A.D. 114) with editor's note; see Sijpesteijn's forthcoming study.

[15] *P. Coll. Youtie* 54 (late second century A.D.); see *P. Mert.* 15.5 (A.D. 114) with *P. Wisc.* 16 introduction, for earlier.

[16] *P. Oxy.* 919 (A.D. 182); 1650 and 1650a (first to second centuries A.D.); *P. Ross. Georg.* 2.18.126 (A.D. 140); a text of A.D. 241 or 242 to be published by C. Hoogendÿk and P. Van Minnen records (ll. 14–15) the posting of toll rates on a stele in Memphis.

[17] *W Chrest.* 31 (A.D. 156), a barge for dung; *P. Vindob. Bosw.* 14.3 (third century A.D.), aging barges; *M. Chrest.* 342.4–5 (A.D. 326); *SB* 6.9148 (third to fourth centuries A.D.).

[18] Guéraud (1933), 63, in black ink on the leather sack.

[19] E.g., *BGU* 3.764 (A.D. 166); Boak (1935), 25.

[20] *BGU* 712; *P. Ross. Georg.* 2.46.18–19, 35, 55, 68, 90, festival accounts; *SB* 4425 (all second century A.D.); *BGU* 14.v.5, 20 (A.D. 255); *PSI* 820 (A.D. 314); *P. Oxy.* 3142 (A.D. 424).

[21] *BGU* 2127 (A.D. 156).

[22] *P. Hamb.* 89 (second to third centuries A.D.); *SB* 9912 (A.D. 270).

[23] *P. Ross. Georg.* 2.16 (A.D. 121), payment to a *himatiopōlēs; P. Athen.* 63.14 (second century A.D.), chitons; *BGU* 93.22 (second to third centuries A.D.), cloaks and a *delmatikē.*

[24] *BGU* 434.4 (A.D. 169); 2530.4 (A.D. 161–69 or 176–80), goldsmiths pay poll tax; Reinsberg (1980), 282.

[25] *P. Ross. Georg.* 3.9.14 (fourth century A.D.); *SB* 5614 (A.D. 324), a large bakery.

[26] *P. Ross. Georg.* 2.16.4–5 (A.D. 121), of Herakleides, son of Anoubion; *P. Lond.* 2.317.3, 11 (p. 209) (A.D. 156), of Sarapion, son of Areios, and of Apollonios, son of Asklepiades; 3.1164 b.8 (p. 157)(A.D. 212), of Bernikianos Methodion.

[27] *P. Ross. Georg.* 2.18 (A.D. 140), introduction.

[28] *P. Ross. Georg.* 2.21 (A.D. 154/5); 3.32.2–3 (A.D. 504).

[29] *P. Mich.* 8.503 (late second century A.D.) with Geremek (1969), 62; *BGU* 14 (A.D. 255) with Johnson (1936), 215–19.

town base, a *katagōgion* for employees.[30] Roman landownership comes as no surprise.

A further important export of Roman Memphis was men, both skilled and unskilled, who left in search of work. The Roman writer Pliny was once treated by a Memphite doctor,[31] and under the emperor Domitian the *princeps equitum*, pilloried in Rome as a salt-fish seller, probably came from the city.[32] Under Roman rule opportunities abroad existed on a scale unknown before.

The prosperity of Memphis and the Memphite nome compared to other parts of Egypt might perhaps be measured through the local rate of poll tax, which was significantly lower than in neighboring nomes. Introduced by Augustus as a capitation tax (it was translated into demotic as "head tax"), *laographia* was charged at different rates in different areas. In the fertile Arsinoite nome to the south, the tax stood at 40 drachmas a year with a preferential rate for metropolitans and some others of 20 drachmas; in the Oxyrhynchite nome the preferential rate was 12 drachmas (with perhaps 16 drachmas as the full rate), while in Hermoupolis Magna metropolitans paid 8 drachmas, with the full rate in the nome perhaps standing at 12 drachmas a year.[33] In Memphis, however, and in the Memphite nome, the standard rate for all seems to have stood at only 8 drachmas a year.[34] Such variation between different areas was contrary to normal Roman practice, but since the basis for the calculation of this tax remains unknown it would be unwise to draw any economic conclusions from its rate. (Lower rates might, for instance, be linked with the need to maintain a garrison.)

The military annexation of Egypt was, however, marked by a change of army base for the area.[35] Babylon downstream now became the main legionary post of Middle Egypt, though soldiers still visited Memphis and some were posted there. Indeed, a complex built of raw brick to a regular gridded plan on Kom Sabakha south of the city may have served as a barracks.[36] A stele from the Sacred Animal Necropolis records the dedication of a Roman veteran, once a *decurio* of the *ala Apriana*,[37] and during the Jewish revolt of A.D. 115–17 Roman troops were centered in

---

[30] *P. Mich.* 8.503.3.
[31] Pliny *Ep.* 10.5-7, 10-11.
[32] Juv. 1.26-30; 4.1-33; 108-9; Mart. 7.99.1-2; 8.48.
[33] Wallace (1938), 116-34.
[34] Nelson (1984), collecting the evidence.
[35] Speidel (1977), 511-15, for these changes.
[36] Jeffreys (1985), 17.
[37] J. J. Wilkes in Martin (1979), 121-23, no. 459.

the area.[38] Two Judaean coins from Saqqara contemporary with the Jewish war of A.D. 67–72 raise the possibility that persecuted Jews from the homeland had on this earlier occasion sought refuge in the city.[39] Like the connection of houses burned down in the eastern area of the city with earlier anti-Semitic riots, this remains a hypothesis only.[40] In A.D. 117 the fighting was bitter and the devastation widespread, but eventually the Roman soldiers came out on top. A garrison force may have remained in the city which, as we have seen, earlier had a Jewish element to its mixed population.[41] Following the reforms of Diocletian, garrison troops were certainly back in the city, where they are known from the record of their supplies. Officials were charged with the provision of chaff (for heating the baths), wine, and meat,[42] and on one occasion, in A.D. 311, 4,850 pounds of meat (presumably salted) was supplied for the soldiers in the city.[43] Sufficient as a day's supply for 2,425 legionaries or 4,850 other ranks,[44] for ten days such a shipment might feed a garrison of about 400. Unfortunately there is no hint of the length of time these provisions were to last, so the only indication that survives for the scale of the Memphite garrison is seriously incomplete. By the later fourth century, the fifth Macedonian legion formed the garrison and was recorded as stationed here in *Notitia dignitatum*; some form of garrison probably remained in the city until the Arab conquest.[45]

The effects of Rome on her provinces were perhaps most felt through the two institutions of the Roman army and Roman law. Both came to Memphis. In a colorful tale of earlier times preserved by Aelian, it was when he was sitting in judgment in Memphis that the pharaoh Psammetichos had dropped into his lap a sandal of Rhodopis, the most attractive of courtesans.[46] The event was unique, the occasion, however, often repeated. And once the Romans arrived, bringing with them the system of regular provincial *conventus*,[47] it was the prefect who presided. The legal

[38] *C. Pap. Jud.* 438 (A.D. 116/17); 439 (A.D. 117).

[39] From Year 2 of the revolt, they will be numbered 647.5848 in the Anoubieion publication. (Information from M. J. Price.)

[40] Petrie, Mackay, and Wainwright (1910), 45, with Lesquier (1918), 18 n. 3, for the date of A.D. 44 rather than 55.

[41] *P. Flor.* 278 iii.15, 21 (third century A.D.).

[42] *O. Mich.* 186 (A.D. 303); *P. Mich.* 8.1012 (A.D. 305); *PSI* 820 (A.D. 314); cf. *SB* 9131.9 (A.D. 300/301), dates. For Roman bathhouses, see *P. Stras.* 195 (A.D. 174).

[43] *P. Oxy.* 2668.11-13 (A.D. 311).

[44] See A.H.M. Jones (1964), 1261-62 n. 44.

[45] *W. Chrest.* 380.1-2 (A.D. 381); *BGU* 3.899.1-3 (fourth century A.D.); *Notitia dignitatum* (ed. Seeck) Or. 28.4.14; *PSI* 1424.4 (fourth to fifth centuries A.D.); *BGU* 255.7 (A.D. 599).

[46] Ael. *VH* 13.33.

[47] G. P. Burton (1975), 99-100.

system now was changed and Roman law prevailed;[48] Egyptian courts had disappeared. And in Memphis annual assizes were held from late January to early April to serve both Upper and Middle Egypt.[49]

With the temples and clergy of Egypt, as we have seen, the Ptolemies had on the whole developed a working relationship which served for mutual reinforcement.[50] In some respects there was continuity, and under the high empire Ptah and Apis still dominated the religious life of the city. The temple of Ptah/Hephaistos was known to the medical writer Galen,[51] and in the third century A.D. it still boasted a native clergy with expertise in financial affairs.[52] However, the fate of the high priesthood of Ptah forms a measure of the extent of Roman interference in this traditional center of native influence; indeed, the contrast between Ptolemaic and Roman rule is nowhere more explicit than in Octavian's attitude towards Memphis and its gods. Following his sudden death on 1 August 30 B.C.,[53] the high priest Imouthes/Petobastis IV lay unburied, his mummy in store. It was only two and one-half years later, in 27 B.C. (probably only after the events in Rome of 13 January), that a successor was appointed, and the new high priest, Psenamounis II, was cousin to Imouthes/Petobastis IV.[54] The appointment, made thus within the family, was traditional and, like his predecessor, the new high priest of Ptah had duties in the ruler cult. The title of "prophet of pharaoh" was modified to that of "prophet of Caesar," but the office now held by Psenamounis was in essence the same. Elsewhere in the provinces, imperial cult may have owed more to the earlier cults of Roman magistrates than to that of Hellenistic kings,[55] but in Egypt the cult of Augustus followed directly from that of the Ptolemies. The new emperor was speedily integrated into Egyptian cult; his birthday was recognized and celebrated on the same day each month.[56]

The apparent reconciliation of the Memphite clergy with the new Ro-

[48] Modrzejewski (1970), 322-26.
[49] Foti Talamanca (1974) with N. Lewis (1976), 5-14; Parsons (1980), 236-37, and Thomas (1984), 111-12. The following may now be added: *P. IFAO* 37 (A.D. 77 or 90); *C. Pap. Jud.* 446.26-27 (A.D. 118); *BGU* 2492.8-9 (second century A.D.); *SB* 10967 (A.D. c. 165-75); *P. Alex. Giss.* 54 = *SB* 10651 M.5 (second century A.D.).
[50] Johnson (1984), 115-16; see chapter 4 above.
[51] Bergman (1968), 43.
[52] Quaegebeur (1980a), 74-76, on *P. Ross. Georg.* 3.26 (A.D. 233/4).
[53] See chapter 4 n. 222.
[54] B.M. stele 184 = Quaegebeur (1974), 66, no. 12 = Reymond (1981), no. 29.11.
[55] Bowersock (1965), 116-20; cf. Price (1984), 40-47, 73-74.
[56] Louvre stele 335, Brugsch (1891), 887-89, with Grzybek (1978), 156-58. For monthly celebrations, see *OGIS* 456 = *IGR* 4.39; Price (1984), 61-62, 105, 217-18.

man emperor was consolidated in 23 B.C. (another crucial year in Rome)
when on 9 April, after almost seven years of waiting in the House of
Embalming, Imouthes/Petobastis IV was finally laid to rest. The occasion was the funeral of his aunt Tnepherōs, prophetess of Caesar and
great wife of Ptah, and his cousin Psenamounis II performed the ceremony.[57] In a key province no expense was spared, and after initial suspi-
cions Augustus now, though briefly, played the part of pharaoh. The ceremony was magnificent but the reconciliation illusory, and this double
burial, with all its pomp and circumstance, proved a last gesture of the
old style. After Psenamounis II no more is heard of the family of high
priests of Memphis, and as the new regime settled in to control, so the
independent direction of the old cults of Egypt was effectively suppressed.

For with Rome much was changed. Although on a personal level the
arrival of the Romans probably had little effect on religious practices for
the majority of the population, on an organizational level there was
strong Roman interference. The economic power of the temples was significantly diminished as the state took over temple lands, and the power
of the clergy was curbed.[58] Priests now came under the secular administration headed, from the reign of Hadrian, by the chief priest of Alexandria and all Egypt. After that brief interlude under Augustus, the post of
chief priest in Memphis became an official appointment of limited tenure,
no longer the monopoly of only one family.[59] And if the title *orapeia* associated with the *archipropheteia* does have some reference to the earlier
title of the high priests of Memphis, that is the only resemblance to be
found—and even this has been questioned.[60] Chief priests had now become bureaucrats, issuing certificates, regulating the membership of the
priesthood through permission to circumcise, and even, with the prefect,
making legal rulings on religious affairs.[61] While some such bureaucrats
might become experts in sacred law,[62] the framework in which they now
functioned was that allowed and controlled by the state. So too the lesser

---

[57] B.M. stele 188 = Quaegebeur (1974), 66, no. 13 = Reymond (1981), no. 27.12-13.

[58] *W Grund.* 300-302 with Whitehorne (1980), 218-26; Stead (1981), 411-18. For the continuing wealth of some temples, however, see the fourth-century Panopolis archive, Willis,
P. Congr. 15.22, introduction.

[59] Parsons (1974), 142-45; Bülow-Jacobsen (1978), 124-31; Cockle (1984), 109.

[60] Parsons (1974), 143, doubted by Quaegebeur (1980a), 54; whatever its origin, the term
is likely to be Egyptian.

[61] E.g., *BGU* 347 = *W. Chrest.* 76 (A.D. 171).

[62] As was Apollonides in the first century A.D., Parsons (1974), 155-60; Quaegebeur
(1980/81), on Semenuthi.

priestly orders increasingly came under state control. Mummification of course was still practiced, but under the Romans the successors to the undertakers of the Ptolemaic period shared duties as state doctors in the certification of death.[63] Priests no longer met in synods to formulate their policy, and the earlier role of women in the priesthood has gone from the Roman record.[64] In the imposition of this new authority old ways were generally abandoned and local sensibilities ignored. The fate of the temples and of the Memphite priesthood is but one sign of the wholesale change the Romans introduced.

Apis fared somewhat better. The bull was well known throughout the Roman world,[65] and in Memphis its cult personnel was supported by the state.[66] Roman officials might now sit in session in religious matters within the temple of Apis.[67] Augustus' disdain for the cult [68] did not set an invariable pattern, and Apis' earlier connection with royal coronations was keenly remembered by later emperors fearful of competition. Visits to Memphis were always open to suspicion, and the limitation Augustus laid on senatorial and other distinguished visits to the country, in the case of Germanicus, was applied even to his family.[69] When later Titus attended the installation of an Apis, wearing a diadem "according to the custom and rite of the ancient religion," the significance of the occasion did not go unremarked in Rome,[70] while in Alexandria the event was perhaps recorded for posterity in the burial chambers of Kom el Chougafa.[71] Under Hadrian the *Historia Augusta* records that when, after a long interval, an Apis bull was located, a dispute could (and did) arise as to where the bull should be housed. Only imperial interference settled the matter.[72] It is unknown how long the search had actually continued but, whatever the historicity of the incident, coins and monuments suggest a

[63] P. Oxy. 3.476 (second century A.D.), post-mortem for official purposes performed by entaphiastai; cf. P. Oxy. 51.4 (A.D. 173); 52.6-7 (A.D. 325); 475.5 (A.D. 182), by public doctors.

[64] W. Otto (1905), 93.

[65] Kater-Sibbes and Vermaseren (1975a, b, 1977); Toutain (1916), on the Roman cult.

[66] P. Ross. Georg. 5.15; 16 (A.D. 209), sacred nurses, doctors and animal workers; SB 12143.8 (A.D. 41-54), a bull-burier.

[67] W. Chrest. 76 (A.D. 171).

[68] See n. 1.

[69] Tac. Ann. 2.59-61; Pliny HN 8.71.185.

[70] Suet. Tit. 5.3.

[71] Malaise (1972), 414, cf. Société archéologique d' Alexandrie, Les bas-reliefs de Kom el Chougafa (Munich), plates ii and ix. The emperor is shown here in full Egyptian dress with double crown without a diadem.

[72] S.H.A. Hadr. 12.1; Dio 69.8.1.

particular attachment of Hadrian to the Memphite cult.[73] And Memphis in return, like so many cities in the Greek East,[74] had its temple to Hadrian. (That the one recorded chief priest of the Hadrianeion[75] also owned a bank forms yet a further indication of a change in priestly status under the Romans.) Like that of Buchis, the Apis cult continued during the second century and "my lord Apis" was still a potent force for some of the inhabitants of Egypt.[76] The great vaults of the Sarapieion were closed after Kleopatra's bull, and the burial chambers of the Roman bulls have not yet been discovered.[77] But the burials continued, the cost now partly met by contributions from all the temples of Egypt. What earlier devotees might provide through traditional religious fervor was now laid down and codified in the rule book for use by a Roman official, the *Gnomon of the Idios Logos*.[78] The temples complied and senior officials received the byssos wrappings that they sent.[79]

The disappearance of significant demotic sources after the first century B.C. makes it difficult to trace the specifically Egyptian side of this cult, which certainly continued to flourish. Sacrifices were made for the bull[80] and it remained a tourist attraction. For overseas visitors it was the mantic and magical powers which especially caught the imagination. Although perhaps apocryphal, Pliny's tale of Apis refusing food proffered by Germanicus, so foretelling his early death,[81] well illustrates the reputation of the bull as correctly foreseeing the future. For others the prophecy came through children either playing or speaking aloud.[82] Apis oracles had a long and continuous tradition.[83] So too with the magical qualities of the bull. Lucian's sorceror's apprentice served in the vaults of Memphis, where his teacher Pankrates served as priestly scribe.[84] When under Julian

[73] Kater-Sibbes and Vermaseren (1975a), 25, no. 89, plate lx; (1977), 10-12 nos. 24-29, 16-17 nos. 47-48 and 51. The influence of Pankrates remains a matter of speculation; see von Fritz (1949), 618-19.

[74] Price (1984), 69.

[75] *P. Lond.* 2.317.11, 209 (A.D. 156), Sarapion, son of Areios.

[76] Mond and Myers (1934), 2.32-36; *SB* 9903.6 (A.D. 200).

[77] See Arnobius, *Adv.nat.* 6.6; penalties were laid down for anyone divulging information on the subject.

[78] *BGU* 5.89.203-4, *stolismata* for both Apis and Mnevis; the fiscus perhaps met the balance.

[79] *SB* 9346 (A.D. 156-70), Apis of Glameous; *P. Gen.* 36 = *W. Chrest.* 85 (A.D. 170), Apis of Tha[.]ois; cf. *P. Tebt.* 313 = *W. Chrest.* 86 (A.D. 210/11), for Mnevis.

[80] *P. Ross. Georg.* 5.19 (A.D. 236); I understand *tokades* as geese.

[81] Pliny, *HN* 8.71.185 with Weingärtner (1969), 140-46 and Malaise (1972), 393-94. Tac. *Ann.* 2.54 ascribes the story to the Apollo oracle at Claros, cf. 2.61.1.

[82] Courcelle (1951), 216-31.

[83] Smith (1974), 15; Lucian, *Astrol.* 7; *Theōn Ekklēsia* 10.

[84] Lucian, *Philopseudes* 34-36; see n. 73 above.

in A.D. 362 a new Apis was eventually found, this favorable omen was said to herald rich harvests and other successful events.[85] Maybe. But no more is heard of Apis and, along with all pagan sanctuaries, the cult was finally suppressed by the edict of Theodosius in 391 A.D.[86] The Christian monks of Apa Jeremias on the desert heights did much to destroy the monuments of this earlier Memphite cult, and in time Apis was relegated to the study of antiquarians.[87]

As the most influential, Apis is the best documented of the animal cults of Memphis. That the cult retained a popular following under the Romans may be shown through Memphite nomenclature. Names referring to the Egyptian form of the cult—Apion, Paapis, Taapis—are now less common than those with reference to its Hellenized form—Sarapion, Serapion, Sarapammon, and Sarapous. Together in number these Apis-names are equaled only by those with reference to Anoubis, with Anoubas, Anoubion, Asklanoupis, Buchanoupis, Iranoupis, and Tetanoupis all occurring in Memphite documents. Of the other key cults of Hellenistic Memphis, Ptah is now only fleetingly commemorated in nomenclature (Hephaistion, Psenpthas), while names with reference to both Imhotep (Imouthes, Asklepiades) and, more often, Amon (Ammonios, Heraklammon, Thamounis, Sarapammon, Psenamounis) are found in the Roman period. Harpokrates (Harpokration) seems more popular than Horos (Horos, Hierakion) in this respect, and Thoth has disappeared.[88] Proportionally, however, Egyptian names or names with reference to Egyptian gods are far fewer in number in the papyri which survive from the three centuries after Augustus than from the three before.

The temples too suggest the same decline, the success of Roman policy. The Mithraeum located close to the eastern edge of the city may have been rebuilt.[89] It survived at least into the second century A.D. and perhaps even longer, given the popularity of the cult with Roman troops. After considerable depredation, the temple complex of the Sacred Animal Necropolis was abandoned and built on by a Christian village.[90] Sometime, too, before the tenth century A.D., Imouthes/Asklepios became

---

[85] Amm. Marc. 22.14.6.

[86] A.H.M. Jones (1964), 168.

[87] Claud. *Cons. Hon.* 570-76.

[88] The names of *SB* 9997 (A.D. 222) exclude a Memphite provenance for this list of ephebes; Leontopolis seems much more likely.

[89] Smith, Jeffreys, and Málek (1983), 40; Jeffreys (1985), 43-44; cf. *BGU* 1936.1-2 (perhaps with *katoch[ē]*). Were the Roman baths, apparently cultic, on Kom Sabakha connected with a further Mithraeum? See Jeffreys (1985), 17–18 with n. 133.

[90] Smith (1974), 29-32; (1976), 16-17.

confused with Joseph; his temple was identified as Joseph's prison and the medical connotation of the cult was now transferred to alchemy.[91]

As the rulers had changed, so must have changed the form of imperial cult in the city. The temple of Hadrian has already been mentioned. Meanwhile in Egypt, as elsewhere, a new religion had entered the scene. Although animal worship was finally forbidden only in the late fourth century, the temples began to be replaced by Christian churches even earlier in Memphis. St. Pachomios, the founder of monasticism, was said to have visited Memphis in his youth;[92] Apollo, Anoup (Anoubis), and Phib (the ibis) became the names of holy men.[93] Both in the valley city and on the necropolis, with the rich monastery of St. Jeremias, the Coptic church prevailed.[94] But although the gods had changed, Memphis remained a religious center. Then in 641 A.D. came the capture of Babylon and with it the Arab conquest of Egypt. Yet even after the Arabs came, Memphis remained a bishopric, and up on the desert edge the monasteries struggled on. For Apa Jeremias, marble imports now ceased, but the community there continued, surviving into the ninth century.[95]

By the tenth century, however, Memphis had become a fable; "the city of Pharaoh with seventy gates and walls of iron and copper" is how Ibn al Fakîh described it;[96] and in A.D. 1315 the name of Memphis is missing from the cadastral survey.[97] The city which under the Ptolemies had been the second city of Egypt had decisively given way to Babylon, the modern Cairo. Memphis was never a medieval city, and of its earlier functions only its military role has survived to the present day.

[91] Stricker (1943); Jeffreys (1985), 55-56, discusses Joseph toponyms in the area.
[92] *Vita Pachomii* 2.
[93] Quibell (1908), 64, with plate xliv for Apollo and Phib; cf. 67, gravestone with Anoup.
[94] *P. Lond.* 6.1917.9 (A.D. 330–40), a community on the island of Memphis; Petrie (1911a), 23; in Engelbach (1915), 33; *EES. Report for the Year 1983/84*, 4, all in the valley; Quibell (1908), 63-69; (1909), 1-19; (1912), 1-30, for St. Jeremias; cf. (1909), iii, for St. Apollonios.
[95] Quibell (1909), i-vi; (1912), i-vii.
[96] Butler (1978), 221 n. 1.
[97] Butzer (1960), 35; cf. Jeffreys (1985), 11-12.

APPENDIXES

APPENDIX A
MEMPHITE PROFESSIONS ADDITIONAL TO THOSE RECORDED IN THE ZENON ARCHIVE

The following professions may be found in the indices to *UPZ* (Greek) and *Ḥor* together with the papyri listed in Appendix B (demotic).

Official and military professions: Greek

archiphylakitēs; eisagōgeus; epimeletēs; epistatēs tōn hierōn; epistatēs tōn phylakōn; grammateus tōn klērouchōn; grammateus tōn machimōn; ho epi tōn prosodōn; monographos; praktor xenikōn; prostatēs; syngraphophylax; timouchos; topogrammateus

Trades and occupations: Greek

artokopos; asillophoros; basilikos georgos; emporiophylax; enhypniokritēs; ēpētria; hiatroklystēs; himatiopolēs; kassēpētria; kikourgos; koproxystēs; linophantēs; othoniopōlēs; plagophylax; sakkophoros; sitokapēlos; tapidyphos

Trades and occupations: Demotic

beer seller; goldsmith; oil and wine seller; pigeon seller; resin seller; seller of mixed wine; silversmith

Priests and temple workers: Greek

archentaphiastēs; atastitēs; enkatochos; hieroglyphos; ho epi tōn pastophorōn; kallyntēs; pastophoros; taplaeitēs; taricheutēs

Priests and temple workers: Demotic

astrologer; dancers; gods' chancellors; gods' questioners; libation pourers; men of Anoubis; oracle givers; servants of the falcon; singers; supervisor of the necropolis

APPENDIX B
THE UNDERTAKERS' ARCHIVE[1]

Undertakers

1. *P. Leid.* 373 b–c (January 203 B.C.): E. Revillout, "Hypothèque légale de la femme et donations entre époux," *Revue égyptologique* 1 (1880), 128 n. 1; K. Sethe, *Demotische Urkunden zum ägyptischen Bürgschaftsrechte* (Leipzig, 1920), 724–26; E.A.E. Reymond, *Embalmers' Archives from Hawara* (Oxford, 1973), 37.

2. *P. Louvre* E 3266 (May–June 197 B.C.): F. de Cenival, "Un acte de renonciation consécutif à un partage de revenus liturgiques Memphites (*P. Louvre* E 3266)," *BIFAO* (1972), 11–65.

3. *P. Louvre* 2408 (197 B.C.): Sethe, *Demotische Urkunden*, 727–28; Reymond, *Embalmers' Archives*, 38.

4. *P. Louvre* 2409 (15 March 184 B.C.): E. Revillout, "Taricheutes et choachytes," *ZÄS* 18 (1880), 115–16 (not 2309; see P. W. Pestman, *Chronologie égyptienne* [Leiden, 1967], 127 n. 31).

5. *P. Vienna* 3874 (149/8 B.C.): E. Revillout, *La propriété*, 525; Reymond, *Embalmers' Archives*, 37.

6. *P. Hermitage* 1122 + *UPZ* 127 (6 August 135 B.C.): I. G. Livshitsa, *Shampol'on (Zh.-F.). O egipetskom ieroglificheskom alfabite* (in Russian) (Moscow, 1950), 156.

7. *P. B.M.* 10384 (11 November 132 B.C.) = Malcolm papyrus: Revillout, *Propriété*, 356–58; "Textes démotiques d'époque ptolémaique et romaine transcrits en hiéroglyphes," *Revue égyptologique* 14 (1914), 59–63. Texts for 6 and 7 provided by Cary J. Martin.

8. *P. Leid.* 373 a + *UPZ* 128 (30 October 131 B.C.): E. Revillout, "La question du divorce chez les égyptiens," *Revue égyptologique* 1 (1880), 91–93; *ZÄS* 18 (1882), 132 n. 2; E. Lüddeckens, *Ägyptische Eheverträge* (Wiesbaden, 1960), 93–95, Urk. 37; P. W. Pestman, *Marriage and Matrimonial Property in Ancient Egypt* (Leiden, 1961), B6.[2]

9. *P.B.M.* 10398 (120/19 B.C.): Revillout, *La propriété*, 526–27, 557; Reymond, *Embalmers' Archives*, 37.

10. *P. Louvre* 2419 + 3265 (13 February 102 B.C.): E. Revillout, "Un quasi-mariage après concubinat," *Revue égyptologique* 2 (1882), 94 n. 1; *Précis du droit égyptien* (Paris, 1903), 1008–9; Pestman, *Marriage*, C15.

11. *UPZ* 106–109 (99/8 B.C.).

12. *UPZ* 125 (89 B.C.).

---

[1] Studies of the archive have been promised both by Jelínková (Reymond) (1957), 51 n. 8, and Pestman (1963), 8; according to de Cenival (1972a), 12 n. 2, this would be "un travail intéressant." On the contents of the archive, see Revillout (1882a), 92–93; Pestman (1963), 9–23; Reymond (1973), 23–38.

[2] I do not accept Teos as a son of Heriobastis, which would make this a marriage between uncle and niece.

13. *UPZ* 114 (86 B.C.).
14. *UPZ* 117 (86/3 B.C.). For the date, which must be after *UPZ* 114 (86 B.C.), see E. Van 't Dack, *Aegyptus* 29 (1949), 10–11; *Aegyptus* 32 (1952), 448–49.
15. *UPZ* 118 (25 January 83 B.C.).
16. *P.B.M.* 10229 + *UPZ* 135 (15 January 78 B.C.): P. W. Pestman, "Les documents juridiques des 'chanceliers du dieu' de Memphis à l'époque ptolémaique," *OMRO* 44 (1963), 19–23; read Tybi 6 in *UPZ* 135.[3]
17. *P. Leid.* 374 i–ii (22 May 78 B.C.): Pestman, *OMRO* 44 (1963), 9–18.
18. *P. Innsbruck* + *UPZ* 136 (23 November 75 B.C.): W. Spiegelberg, "Ein demotischer Papyrus in Innsbruck," *RecTrav* 25 (1903), 103; Sethe, *Demotische Urkunden*, 737–40; Reymond, *Embalmers' Archives*, 29–30.
19. *P. Louvre* 3268 (27 February 73 B.C.): Revillout, *Revue égyptologique* 2 (1882), 91–92.
20. *P. Louvre* 3264 ter (27 February 73 B.C.): Revillout, *Revue égyptologique* 2 (1882), 92 n.
21. *P. Bibl. Nat.* 224–25 + *UPZ* 137–38 (2 September 68 B.C.): Lüddeckens, *Ägyptische Eheverträge*, 172–77, Urk. 10; Pestman, *Marriage*, 150, C17.
22. *P. Louvre* 3264 and 2411 + *UPZ* 139–40 (5 November 65 B.C.): Revillout, *Revue égyptologique* 2 (1882), 95; Sethe, *Demotische Urkunden*, 747, with incorrect date.

In addition to *P. Louvre* 2407 + 3267 (T. Devéria, *Catalogue des manuscrits égyptiens* [Paris, 1872], 221–22, xii.29 + 30, mentioned also by de Cenival, *BIFAO* 71 [1972], 54), the following papyri probably belong to the same archive:

23. *P. Leid.* 381 (October 226 B.C.): Lüddeckens, *Ägyptische Eheverträge*, 146–49, Urk. 3 Z; Pestman, *Marriage*, C5.
24. *P. Leid.* 378 (April 160 B.C.): E. Revillout, *Nouvelle chrestomathie démotique* (Paris, 1878), 113–20; *La propriété*, 527–28; S.R.K. Glanville, *Catalogue of demotic papyri in the British Museum*. I (London, 1939), 25.
25. *P.B.M.* Forshall 41 + *UPZ* 129 (13 October 124 B.C.).
26. *P. Pavese* 1120 (22 August 118 B.C.): G. Botti, "Il papiro demotico n. 1120 del museo civico di Pavia," *Bolletino Storico Pavese* 2 (1939), 17–36.[4]
27. *P. B.M.* Forshall 42 (?97/6 B.C.): E. Revillout, *Chrestomathie démotique* (Paris, 1880b), xx.
28. *P. Leid.* 380 a–b + *UPZ* 141 (2 August 64 B.C.): Sethe, *Demotische Urkunden*, 745–46.

Choachytai

29. *P. Louvre* 2412 (316–304 B.C.): K. Th. Zauzich, *Die ägyptische Schreibertradition* (Wiesbaden, 1968), 69–71, Urk. 94.[5]

[3] This papyrus belongs to the archive on the assumption that Teōs, father of the bride (line 3), is the son of Tauēs and Petēsis, whose marriage contract survives as *P. Leid.* 373a (131 B.C.), cf. *P. Leid.* 374.i.5 (78 B.C.).
[4] This is the least certain ascription.
[5] To make sense both of the family tree and the property division, the mother of Imouthes in line 2 should read Hedjenpaouni; Taous/Heriobastis gives Hedjenpaouni a receipt for her

30. *P. Leid.* 379 + *UPZ* 126 (2 March 256 B.C.): Revillout, *Revue égyptologique* 1 (1880a), 125 n. 1; *La propriété*, 5359; Sethe, *Demotische Urkunden*, 712–16.
31. *P. Bruss.* 3 (November–December 238 B.C.): W. Spiegelberg, *Die demotischen Papyrus der musées royaux du Cinquantenaire* (Brussels, 1909); Sethe, *Demotische Urkunden*, 720–21; J. Quaegebeur, "Les papyrus démotiques des musées royaux d'art et d'histoire à Bruxelles," *Enchoria* 8 (1978), 26, with an earlier date and inventory number E6033.

Choachytai from the family are also recorded in *P. Louvre* E 3266 (May–June 197 B.C.), *P. Louvre* 2409 (15 March 184 B.C.), and *P. B.M.* 10384 (3 Nov. 132 B.C.).

---

one-sixth of property from Imouthes, Imouthes' mother, and his wife (her mother) Nehoëris; her son Haryothes acts as witness and guarantor.

APPENDIX C
A PROPERTY SETTLEMENT IN 197 B.C.

Property from Tauēs' family of choachytai		*P. Louvre*
Tauēs to Imouthēs	Receipt	E 3266.1.M–N, 2.M–N, 3.E–F, K–M, O–P, 8.B–C, L–M, 10.C, M, R, 12.S–T
	Release	
Tauēs to Shemti	Receipt	
	Release	
Imouthēs to Shemti	Receipt	
	Release	= E 3266
Shemti to Imouthēs	Receipt	
	Release	

Property from Tauēs (T)		
Tauēs to Imouthēs	Receipt ½T	E 3266.12.R–S
	Release ½T	
Tauēs to Shemti	Receipt ½T	
	Release ½T	E 3266.12.L
Imouthēs to Tauēs	Receipt ½T of Shemti	2408
	Release ½T of Shemti	
Shemti to Tauēs	Receipt ½T of Imouthēs	2408
	Release ½T of Imouthēs	

Property from Tauēs (T), from Ptahmaacherou (P), grandfather of Ptahmaacherou her first husband, and from Samōus (S), her second husband		
Imouthēs to Shemti	Receipt ½S + ½T	
	Release ½S + ½T	= 2408; E 3266.12.I, M
Shemti to Imouthēs	Receipt P + ½T	
	Release P + ½T	2408; E 3266.12.H, P–R, 13.A–B

APPENDIX D

APIS BULLS OF THE PTOLEMAIC PERIOD[1]

1. Bull of the Cow Ta-nt-Aset II

Known only from the cow stelae, Smith (1972), tables 4–5. Ta-wry has now been (provisionally) reread.

2. Bull of the Cow Ta-nt-Merwer

Date	Apis Year	Activity	Reference
24 Mecheir Year 3 [of Ptolemy II] 24 April 282 B.C.	19	Sarapieion open	Brugsch (1886), 39, no. 58
21 Phamenoth Year 3 21 May 282 B.C.	19	Sarapieion open	Brugsch (1886), 39, no. 59, cf. Revillout (1891b), 141, Louvre stele 40 (2247), with slightly different dates and events
16 Phaophi Year 6 16 December 280 B.C.	22	Doors open for the purification of the bull	Revillout (1891b), 141, Louvre stele 191[2]
25 Tybi Year 6 25 March 279 B.C.	22	Bull mummified at Taub(ta)mai in the Heliopolite nome	
28 Tybi Year 6 28 March 279 B.C.	22	Bull taken into the vaults	

3. Bull of the Cow Wadjet-iyti

Known only from the cow stelae, Smith (1972), Table 5

[1] Pending the full publication of this material, this list should be regarded as provisional.
[2] The readings of Revillout here and elsewhere should be treated with caution; he here assumes the reign of Ptolemy I Soter.

APIS BULLS

4. *Bull of the Cow Ta-Renenutet I* (from the Saite nome)[3]

Date	Apis Year	Activity	Reference
17 Pauni Year 32 [of Ptolemy II Phila-delphos] 7 August 253 B.C.	3	Sarapieion open with work on vault	Brugsch (1884) 110, no.1, cf. de Rougé (1888), 7, Louvre stele 3740
21 Pauni Year 32–1 Phaophi Year 33 11 August–24 November 253 B.C. 4 Phaophi–[9 Pharmouthi] Year 33 27 November 253 B.C.–[31 May] 252 B.C.	3	Foundations built for burial place Walls built and building finished	Brugsch (1884), 112, 117, no. 3 (with Apis Year 2); Revillout (1891b), 129, Louvre stele 82
Tybi Year 33 February–March 252 B.C.	3	Work recorded for Pauni (July–August 253 B.C.)	Brugsch (1884), 110, no. 1 (with incorrect Apis Year)
Mecheir Year 33 March–April 252 B.C.	3	Work on burial place	Brugsch (1884), 110–11, no. 2, Berlin stele
8 Mesore Year 37 26 September 248 B.C.		Stone sarcophagus brought up, taking 35 days Interior work on the vault	Louvre stele 82 (see above) so Brugsch so Revillout
8 Thoth Year 37 31 October 248 B.C.		Sarcophagus in place	so Brugsch
8 Mesore Year 37–[17 Hathyr] Year 38 26 September 248 B.C.–[8 January] 247 B.C.		Building completed and closed	so Brugsch (Revillout has 7 Hathyr)

[3] For the original homes of the cows, see Bresciani (1967), 25–26.

5. Bull of the Cow Gerg(et) I (from Ḥa-ta-.., perhaps Athribis)

Date	Apis Year	Activity	Reference
21 Pharmouthi Year 16 (of Euergetes I) 7 June 231 B.C.		Bull appeared in Ḥa-ta-..	Brugsch (1884), 117, no. 5, perhaps reading Choiak (7 February)
Phamenoth Year 18 March–April 229 B.C.	3[4]	Building work	Revillout (1891b), 133–35, Louvre stele 114; Brugsch (1884), 117–25, no. 5
Phamenoth Year 20 April–May 227 B.C.		Building work	Brugsch (1884), 117–25, no. 5
1 Phamenoth Year 22 16 April 225 B.C.	8		de Rougé (1888), 5, Louvre stele

6. Bull of the Cow Ta-nt-Amun (from Tentyra)

Date	Apis Year	Activity	Reference
(195/4 B.C.?)	15		Revillout (1891a), 95–96, Louvre bilingual stele 59
Year 14 (of Ptolemy V Epiphanes) 192/1 B.C.	19	Work in the vaults	Brugsch (1884), 127, no.8, Louvre stele
Year 14, 192/1 B.C.	20		Brugsch (1884), 126, no. 7
Year 15, 191/0 B.C.	20	Work in the vaults	Brugsch (1884), 127, no. 9, Louvre stele
Year 16, 190/89 B.C.	20		Brugsch (1884), 127, no. 10, Louvre stele
9 Mecheir Year 16 16 March 189 B.C.	20	Building work	Brugsch (1884), 128, no. 11, from Sarapieion door

[4] Gauthier (1916), 251 n. 2, reads Apis Year 4.

Date	Apis Year	Activity	Reference
30 Phaophi Year 19 7 December 187 B.C.	24	Stele set up	Brugsch (1884), 128, no. 13, Mariette no. 3354
30 Phaophi Year 19 7 December 187 B.C.	24	Burial of Apis	Brugsch (1884), 128, no. 14, Louvre stele
30 Phaophi Year 19 7 December 187 B.C.	24	Stele set up	Brugsch (1884), 128, no. 15, Louvre stele
30 Phaophi Year 19 7 December 187 B.C.	24	Stele set up	Brugsch (1884), 128, no. 12, Louvre stele
14 Tybi Year 19 19 February 186 B.C.		Date added to this stele	

7. Bull of the Cow Ta-Renenutet II (from Damanhur in the Saite nome)

Date	Apis Year	Activity	Reference
13 Choiak Year 19 (of Ptolemy V Epiphanes) 19 January 186 B.C.		Birth at Damanhur in the Saite nome	Brugsch (1884), 125–26, no. 6, hieroglyphic stele, Louvre stele 2409
Year 20, 186/5 B.C.		Journey (to Memphis)	Daressy (1911), 5; (1916/17), 175–79
22 Thoth Year 21[5] 29 October 185 B.C.		Apis enthroned in Ptah temple	Brugsch (1884), 125–26, no. 6, hieroglyphic stele
Pachons Year 6 (of Ptolemy VI Philometor) June 185 B.C.	11	Building in the vaults	Brugsch (1884), 131, no. 18, from Sarapieion door (now in Paris)
Pachons Year 6 June 185 B.C.	11	Building in the vaults	Brugsch (1884), 131, no. 17, Mariette no. 5352

[5] The reading of the date is that of J. D. Ray. Brugsch (1884), 136, and (1886), 27, records 20 Thoth, while reading 2 Thoth in (1884), 126.

287

Date	Apis Year	Activity	Reference
2 Epeiph Year [7] 3 August [174] B.C.	12	Building in the vaults	Brugsch (1884), 131, no. 19, in Louvre[6]
2 Pharmouthi Year 8 4 May 173 B.C. 7 Pauni Year 8 8 July 173 B.C.	14[7]	Building in the vaults Stele set up	Brugsch (1884), 132, no. 21, in Louvre
4 Pharmouthi Year 8 6 May 173 B.C.	13	Sarcophagus brought in	Brugsch (1884), 131, no. 20, on Sara-pieion door
24 Pachons Year 8 25 June 173 B.C.	13	Stele set up	
30 Pharmouthi Year 8 1 June 173 B.C. 9 Pauni Year 8 10 July 173 B.C.	14[8]	Wreathing of the burial vault Stele set up	Brugsch (1884), 132, no. 22, on Sara-pieion door
[165/4 B.C.]	23	Work on the crypt	Bresciani (1967), 27–29, no. 1
7 Phamenoth Year 6 7 April 164 B.C.		Death of Apis	Brugsch (1884), 125–26, no. 6, hiero-glyphic stele [9]
7 Phamenoth Year 6 7 April 164 B.C. 4 Pachons Year 6 3 June 164 B.C. 9 Pachons Year 6 8 June 164 B.C.		Death of Apis Opening of the Sara-pieion Stele set up	Brugsch (1884), 131, no. 16; cf. UPZ 18.20–1; 19.23–5; 21.8–9, cf. p. 294

[6] Brugsch assumes Year 8 of Ptolemy VI Philometor.
[7] The Apis Year should probably be 13.
[8] The Apis Year should probably be 13.
[9] The date given here is 6 Phamenoth; for 7 Phamenoth, see p. 133. The bull had a life of 22 years, 2 months, and 23 days.

Date	Apis Year	Activity	Reference
16 Pachons Year 6 15 June 164 B.C.		Burial of the bull	*UPZ* 54.22

8. *Bull of the Cow* Ta-nt-Ḥor (from Pagereghor in the Athribite nome)

Date	Apis Year	Activity	Reference
Year 23 (of Ptolemy VI Philometor), 159/8 B.C.	7		de Rougé (1888), 6, Louvre stele 4157
11 Mecheir Year 23 11 March 158 B.C.	7	Stone foundations for the vault	Brugsch (1886), 20, no. 24, Mariette
26–30 Phamenoth Year 23 25–29 April 158 B.C.		Imhotep festival Work started	no. 4157[10]
1 Pharmouthi Year 23 30 April 158 B.C.		Bringing of ..	
24 Pharmouthi Year 23 23 May 158 B.C.		Opening of the Sara- pieion	
Year 24, 158/7 B.C.		Stele set up	
Year 24	8		de Rougé (1888), 6, Louvre stele 3352
2 Mecheir Year 24 1 March 157 B.C.	8	Building in the vault	Brugsch (1886), 21, no. 27, on Sara- pieion door
28 Phamenoth Year 24 24 April 157 B.C.		Opening of the crypt	Brugsch (1886), 20, no. 25, copied in Egypt
Year 25, 157/6 B.C.		Stele put up	Read as Apis Year 7
29 Phamenoth Year 24 27 April 157 B.C.	8	Building in the vaults	Bresciani (1967), 29– 32, no. 2, in Vi- enna

[10] Year 24 and Apis year 8, according to Bresciani (1967), 31. For further relevant inscriptions, see Brugsch (1891), 980, Louvre stelae 5362, 5371, 5369, and an inscription on a Sarapieion door.

Date	Apis Year	Activity	Reference
Pauni Year 24 July 157 B.C.	8	Building in the vaults	Brugsch (1886), 22, no. 28, on Sara-pieion door
1 Tybi (?) Year 25 29 January 156 B.C.	9		de Rougé (1888), 6, Louvre stele 3363
14 Mecheir Year 25 13 March 156 B.C.	9		de Rougé (1888), 6, Louvre stele 4166
1 Pauni Year 29 27 June 152 B.C.	13		de Rougé (1888), 6, Louvre stele 3348
8 Phamenoth Year 30 5 April 151 B.C.	14		de Rougé (1888), 6, Louvre stele 6072; Brugsch (1891), 993
18 Mesore Year 30 12 September 151 B.C.	14	Building in the vaults	Brugsch (1886), 22, no. 29, from Sara-pieion
20 Mecheir Year 35 17 March 146 B.C.	18		Brugsch (1886), 22, no. 30, Mariette no. 4142
26 Pauni Year 27 (of Ptolemy VIII Euergetes II) 20 July 143 B.C.		Death of Apis	Brugsch (1886), 20, no. 26, Mariette no. 4179

9. Bull of the Cow Gerg(et) II (from the Ptah temple in Memphis)

24 Tybi Year 28 (of Ptolemy VIII Euergetes II) 18 February 142 B.C.		Birth of Apis in the Ptah temple in Memphis	de Rougé (1885), 118; Brugsch (1886), 23, 26–27; Louvre hiero-glyphic stele 4264[11]
Until 1 Thoth Year 31 27 September 140 B.C.		In the temple at Memphis	

[11] I adopt the interpretation of Brugsch.

Date	Apis Year	Activity	Reference
20 Thoth Year 31 16 October 140 B.C. 21 Thoth Year 31 17 October 140 B.C. 23 Thoth Year 31 19 October 140 B.C.		Apis taken to An (Heliopolis) Start of coronation in Memphis End of coronation in Ptah temple	
21 Phaophi Year 38 14 November 133 B.C.	10	Stele set up	de Rougé (1888), 2, Louvre stele 3327
7 Hathyr Year 39 30 November 132 B.C.		Stele set up	Cairo demotic inscription no. 31110; Malinine (1943), 157–61
21 Tybi Year 39 12 February 131 B.C.	12	Stele set up	de Rougé (1888), 2–3, Louvre stele 3342
27 Tybi Year 39 18 February 131 B.C.	12	Building in the vaults; Imhotep festival	Brugsch (1886), 24, no. 31; Mariette no. 4155
28 Phamenoth Year 39 20 April 131 B.C.	12	Building work	Brugsch (1886), 25, no. 32; de Rougé (1888), 3, Louvre stele 3438
22 Pachons Year 39 13 June 131 B.C.	12		de Rougé (1888), 3, Louvre stele 4155
9 Mecheir Year 40 2 March 130 B.C.	13		de Rougé (1888), 3, Louvre stele 6102
22 Mecheir Year 47 13 March 123 B.C.		Building work	Brugsch (1886), 26, no. 35
28 Mecheir Year 47 19 March 123 B.C.		Building work	Brugsch (1886), 25–26, no. 33, in Louvre

Date	Apis Year	Activity	Reference
12 Pauni Year 47 1 July 123 B.C.	21		Brugsch (1886), 26, no. 34, Louvre stele 3381
24 Pauni Year 47 13 July 123 B.C.		Building work	Revillout (1891b), 131–41, Louvre stele 107 = 3367
13 Mecheir Year 48 4 March 122 B.C.	20		de Rougé (1888), 3, Louvre stele 3381
In period 143/2–120/ 19 B.C.		Stele set up	Bresciani (1967), 32–34, no. 3; compare names for date
22 Mesore Year 51 8 September 119 B.C.		Death of Apis	de Rougé (1885), 108–20, Louvre stele 4246; Brugsch (1886), 23
27 [Phaophi][12] Year 52 17 November 119 B.C.		Burial of Apis	

10. Bull of the Cow Gerg(et) Mut-iyti (from Sehetep in the Heliopolite nome)

Date	Apis Year	Activity	Reference
c. 107 B.C.		Stele set up	Bresciani (1967), 40–43, no. 6, in Vienna
Year 11 (of Kleopatra III and [Ptolemy X Alexander I]) 107/6 B.C.	13		Brugsch (1886), 29, no. 37, in Louvre
11 Tybi Year 13 = 10 26 January 104 B.C.	16		de Rougé (1888), 4, Louvre stele 4143
Year 14 = 11 104/3 B.C.	?		Brugsch (1886), 29, no. 38, reading Apis Year 15

[12] The stele reads 27 Thoth (19 October) which must be a mistake (so de Rougé); Brugsch reads 28 Thoth (20 October). The bull had a life of 23 years, 6 months, and 29 days.

Date	Apis Year	Activity	Reference
Year 14 = 11 104/3 B.C.	16		Brugsch (1886), 29, no. 39, in Louvre
Tybi Year [14 =] 11 Jan./Feb. 103 B.C.	17		Brugsch (1886), 38, no. 55
12 Tybi Year 14 = 11 27 January 103 B.C.	?	Building work	Brugsch (1886), 28, no. 36, reading Apis Year 15
22 Mecheir Year 15 = 12 8 March 102 B.C.	18		de Rougé (1888), 4, Louvre stele 3336
27 Mecheir Year [15 = 12][13] 13 March [102 B.C.]	18	Building work	Revillout (1891b), 133, Louvre stele 39
2 Pharmouthi Year 15 = 12 17 April 102 B.C.	18		de Rougé (1888), 4, Louvre stele 3713
Pharmouthi Year 12 April/May 102 B.C.	?		Brugsch (1886), 38, no. 56, reading Apis Year 17
2 Pauni Year 15 = 12 16 June 102 B.C.			Revillout (1896), 165–67, Louvre stele 110 = 3709
10(?) Mesore Year 15 = 12 23 Aug. 102 B.C.	?		Brugsch (1886), 29, no. 40, reading Apis Year 17
2 Epeiph Year 13 15 July 101 B.C.	19		de Rougé (1888), 5, Louvre stele 4160[14]

[13] Revillout reads the date as Year 18 = 21, which is not possible.
[14] This must be from Year 16 = 13. Brugsch, however (1886), 29, no. 41, reads the same stele as from Phamenoth Year 15; his Apis Year is 19.

Date	Apis Year	Activity	Reference
Year 17, Sept./Oct. 101 B.C.	19	Building work	Brugsch (1886), 30, no. 42, on Sarapieion door
26 Mesore Year [16][15] 7 September 101 B.C.	19	Building work	Brugsch (1886), 30, no. 43, on Sarapieion door
Mesore Year 15 (of Ptolemy X Alexander and Kleopatra Berenike) Aug.–Sept. 99 B.C.	20		Brugsch (1886), 30, no. 57
Year [17] c. 97 B.C.	22	Work on the crypt	Bresciani (1967), 38–40, no. 5
Epagomenoi Year [17] c. 11 Sept. [97 B.C.]	22	Work on the crypt	Bresciani (1967), 34–38, no. 4
Year [17] c. 97 B.C.		Work on the crypt	Revillout (1891b), 146, Louvre stele 112
20 Thoth Year 18 5 October 97 B.C.			Brugsch (1886), 30, no. 44
Year 18 97/6 B.C.	23		de Rougé (1888), 5, Louvre stele 3364
28 Tybi Year 18 10 February 96 B.C.	23		Brugsch (1886), 30, no. 30, in Louvre
28 Phamenoth Year 18 11 April 96 B.C.	23		de Rougé (1888), 5, Louvre stele 3378
18 Pharmouthi Year 18 1 May 96 B.C.	23		Brugsch (1886), 30, no. 46, Mariette no. 3391

[15] Brugsch reads regnal Year 17, but if the Apis year is correct this is impossible; I adopt Year 16 [= 13]. Alternatively the Apis year may be incorrect with the stele dating from 7 September 97 B.C.

Date	Apis Year	Activity	Reference
28 Pachons Year 18 10 June 96 B.C.	23		de Rougé (1888), 5, Louvre stele 3373
29 Pachons Year 18 11 June 96 B.C.	23		de Rougé (1888), 5, Louvre stele 4156
Year 31 (of Ptolemy IX Soter II re- stored) 87/6 B.C.	11[16]	Burial of Apis of Gerg(et)	Revillout (1891b), 146, Louvre stele 113; perhaps also Reymond (1981), 126, no. 17.25–26

11. *Bull of the Cow Ta-nt-Amun Ta-Igesh* (from Oxyrhynchos)

Date	Apis Year	Activity	Reference
Year 31 (of Ptolemy IX Soter II re- stored)	11	Burial of previous bull; work in crypt	Revillout (1891b), 146, Louvre stele 113
17 Mecheir Year 31 27 February 86 B.C.		? brought into the vaults	Brugsch (1886), 32, no. 47
12 Phamenoth Year 31 24 March 86 B.C.	11	Material brought in for building work; vaults open for second coronation	Brugsch (1886), 32– 33, no. 50 a,b,c, in Louvre; (1891), 871
2 Pharmouthi Year 31 13 April 86 B.C.	11		Brugsch (1886), 31, no. 48
4 Pauni Year 31 14 June 86 B.C.	11		Brugsch (1886), 32, no. 49
8 Pauni Year 31 18 June 86 B.C.	11		de Rougé (1888), 7– 8, Louvre stele 3349
29 Phaophi Year 36 10 November 82 B.C.		Building in vaults	Revillout (1891b), 146, Louvre stele 70

[16] This is the Apis Year of the next bull, of the cow of Ta-nt-Amun Ta-Igesh.

Date	Apis Year	Activity	Reference
22 Hathyr Year 37 2 December 81 B.C.	18	Building in vaults completed	Brugsch (1886), 33, no. 51; Revillout (1891b), 146, Louvre stele 111
Mecheir Year 2 (of Ptolemy XII Neos Dionysos) February 79 B.C.	16 sic		Brugsch (1886), 34, no. 52
17 Phaophi Year 7 (?) 27 October 75 B.C.(?)		Death of Apis; Anemhor served 70 days	Brugsch (1886), 36, no. 52 (for 53); Cairo dem. inscr. 31099.11, reading Year 8
27 [Choiak Year 7] 5 [January 74 B.C.]	21	Burial of Apis	Revillout (1891b), 146, Louvre stele 218, reading Tybi (Feb.)

12. Bull of the Cow Ta-nt-Bastet (from Gereghor, perhaps in the Boubastite nome)

Year 28 (Ptolemy XII Neos Dionysos restored) 54/3 B.C.	19	Stele set up	Brugsch (1886), 38, no. 53
Year 3 (of Kleopatra VII with Ptolemy XIII) 50/49 B.C.		Building work	Brugsch (1886), 38, no. 54; Mariette no. 3376
Year 3 50/49 B.C.		Mourning for bull; offerings made by queen	Revillout (1891b), 133, Louvre stele 24

13. Bull of the Cow Ta-nt-Leby

Known only from the cow stelae, Smith (1972), table 7. The new reading is from C.A.R. Andrews. This was perhaps the Apis whom Octavian refused to visit in 30 B.C., Diod. Sic. 51.16.5.

APPENDIX E
THE TAX OF MEMPHIS HARBOR

The Memphis harbor tax is recorded as paid at the following customs posts:

Dionysias
BGU 2029 (A.D. 161/9); SB 7822 (A.D. 208).

Soknopaiou Nesos
BGU 2307 (first cent. A.D.); P. Fuad Univ. 34 (A.D. 42); BGU 2305 (A.D. 51); 2306 (A.D. 52); P. Lond. 3.1265b (p. 36) (A.D. 83); BGU 2309 (A.D. 99/100); 2315 (late first cent. A.D.); 2105 (A.D. 114); 2324 (A.D. 130); P. Stras. 250b (A.D. 137); BGU 2106 (A.D. 142); 2310; 2314 (A.D. 145); SPP 22.153 (A.D. 146); 13 (A.D. 149); 149 (A.D. 150); P. Grenf. 250d (A.D. 176/80); BGU 2321 (A.D. 177); P. Aberd. 40a (A.D. 178/9); P. Grenf. 2.50e (A.D. 179); SB 11568 (A.D. 180 or 212); P. Aberd. 40b (A.D. 190); 40c (A.D. 192); SB 7828 (A.D. 198/9); P. Ryl. 2.370; P. Stras. 124; P. Ryl. 2.197c, d; P. Lond. 3.1266d (p. 39); P. Aberd. 40d (all second century A.D.); SB 7829 (A.D. 201); P. Gen. 2.112 (A.D. 207); SB 7818 (A.D. 215); 12189; P. Grenf. 2.50k; P. Ryl 2.368; P. Stras. 12; 250c; P. Alex. Giss. 11; P. Fay. 69; P. Aberd. 40e; BGU 3.768 (all second or third century A.D.).

Karanis
P. Lond. 2.469b (p. 86) (A.D. 164); BGU 2109 (A.D. 165); BGU 3.764; 765 (A.D. 166); P. Lond. 3.1266e (p. 39) (A.D. 171); 2.206c (p. 85) (A.D. 177); P. Amh. 116 (A.D. 178).

Bakchias
P. Fay. 174 (A.D. 106); P. Wisc. 2.80 (A.D. 114), report for Thoth from the *epiteretes*; P. Stras. 250a; P. Fay. 74.164–65 (second century A.D.); 72; P. Aberd. 40g; P. Fay. 173; 170; 171; 168; 72; 166; 169; 172; 188; P. Köln 2.93; SB (all second or third century A.D.); P. Fay. 167 (A.D. 211).

Philadelphia
P. Aberd. 42e (A.D. 106); P. Heid. 235 (A.D. 120); SPP 22.11 (A.D. 133); P. Stras. 250e (A.D. 157); P. Hamb. 77 (A.D. 176); P. Stras. 250f (A.D. 178?); BGU 1592 (A.D. 212); 2322 (A.D. 180 or 212); P. Aberd. 40f (A.D. 195?); BGU 3.763; SB 7566; P. Hamb. 78; P. Leeds Museum 11; P. Stras. 389; P. Princ. 2.51; P. Grenf. 2.50l; BGU 1594 (all third century, A.D.).

Philopator/Theogonis
P. Heid. 4.316 (A.D. 214).

The tax is further recorded in *P. Stras.* 630 (second century B.C.) and *P. Aberd.* 40h (A.D. 211?).

P. Lond. 3.1107 (p. 47) (third century A.D.) records the tax paid on goods originating in Apias, Arsinoe, Alexandrou Nesos, Hermoupolis, Theoxenis, Magais, and Philagris.

I am most grateful to P. J. Sijpesteijn for adding to this list. He will shortly publish a full collection of customs house receipts, which will supersede this appendix.

BIBLIOGRAPHY

Only works referred to in the course of this study are listed here. For abbreviations see the list in the front.

Abdulla el-Sayed Mahmud. 1978. *A New Temple for Hathor at Memphis*. Egyptology Today 1. Warminster, Eng.

Aimé-Giron, N. 1925. "Un ex-voto à Astarté." *BIFAO* 25, 191–211.

———. 1931. *Textes araméens d'Egypte*. Cairo.

Anthes, R. 1959. *Mit Rahineh 1955*. Museum Monographs. Philadelphia.

———. 1965. *Mit Rahineh 1956*. Museum Monographs. Philadelphia.

Austin, C. 1973. *Comicorum graecorum fragmenta in papyris reperta*. Berlin and New York.

Badawi, A. 1948. *Memphis als zweite Landeshauptstadt im neuen Reich*. Cairo.

Barguet, P. 1953. *La stèle de la famine à Séhel*. Institut français d'archéologie orientale. Bibliothèque d'étude 24. Cairo.

Bartina, S. 1965. "ΟΘΟΝΙΑ ex papyrorum testimoniis linteamina." *Studia Papyrologica* 4, 27–38.

Bataille, A. 1952. *Les Memnoneia. Recherches de papyrologie et d'épigraphie grecques sur la nécropole de la Thèbes d'Egypte aux époques hellénistique et romaine*. Institut français d'archéologie orientale. Recherches d'archéologie, de philologie et d'histoire 23. Cairo.

Beeston, A.F.L. 1937. "Two South-Arabian inscriptions: Some suggestions." *Journal of the Royal Asiatic Society of Great Britain and Ireland*, 59–78.

Bergk, Th. 1886. *Commentatio de Chrysippi libris περὶ ἀποφατικῶν*. Kleine philologische Schriften 2. Halle.

Bergman, J. 1968. *Ich bin Isis. Studien zum memphitischen Hintergrund der griechischen Isisaretalogien*. Acta Universitatis Upsaliensis. Historia religionum 3. Uppsala.

Bernard, A., and Masson, O. 1957. "Les inscriptions grecques d'Abou-Simbel." *REG* 70, 1–46.

Bevan, E. R. 1927. *A History of Egypt under the Ptolemaic Dynasty*. London (reprinted Chicago, 1968).

Bieżuńska-Małowist, I. 1974. *L'esclavage dans l'Egypte gréco-romaine*, I, *Période ptolémaïque*. Warsaw.

Bingen, J. 1946. "Les colonnes 60–72 du P. Revenue Laws et l'aspect fiscal du monopole des huiles." *CE* 21, 127–48.

———. 1967. Review of Bernard Boyaval, "21 documents inédits de la collection Despoina Michaelidès," *BIFAO* 64 (1966), 75–93. *CE* 42, 236–37.

———. 1968. "Mummy labels and ghost names." *BASP* 5, 35–36.

———. 1978. "Economie grecque et société égyptienne au IIIᵉ siècle," in *Das ptolemäische Ägypten*, ed. H. Maehler and V. M. Strocka, 211–19. Mainz-am-Rhein.

Bingen, J. 1984. "Les tensions structurelles de la société ptolémaïque," in *Atti del XVII congresso internazionale di papirologia*, III, 921–37. Naples.

Blass, Fr. 1887. *Eudoxi ars astronomica*. Kiel.

Bloedow, E. 1963. "Beiträge zur Geschichte des Ptolemaios XII." Inaugural-Dissertation. Würzburg, FRG.

Boak, A. E. 1935. *Soknopaiou Nesos: The University of Michigan Excavations at Dimê in 1931–32*. Ann Arbor, Mich.

Boardman, J. 1980. *The Greeks Overseas*. New and enlarged edition. London.

Boerner, E. 1939. "Der staatliche Korntransport im griechisch-römischen Aegypten." Dissertation. Hamburg.

Bonneau, D. 1961. "Le souverain d'Egypte voyageait-il sur le Nil en cru?" *CE* 36, 377–85.

———. 1971. *Le fisc et le Nil. Incidences des irregularités de la crue du Nil sur la fiscalité foncière dans l'Egypte grecque et romaine*. Paris.

Bonnet, H. 1952. *Reallexikon der ägyptischen Religionsgeschichte*. Berlin.

Borkowski, Z. 1971. "Toll receipts for ἑκατοστή, ὁ καὶ ν and ἐρημοφυλακία from Berlin." *JJP* 16/17, 131–39.

Boswinkel, E., and Sijpesteijn, P. J. 1968. *Greek Papyri, Ostraca and Mummy Labels*. Amsterdam.

Bosworth, A. B. 1980. *A Historical Commentary on Arrian's History of Alexander*, I, *Commentary on Books I–III*. Oxford.

Bothmer, B. V. 1960. *Egyptian Sculpture of the Late Period 700 B.C.–A.D.100*. New York.

Botti, G. 1939. "Il papiro demotico n. 1120 del museo civico di Pavia." *Bolletino Storico Pavese* 2, 9–36 + 2 tav.

———. 1941. *Testi demotici*, I. Pubblicazioni dell'Istituto di papirologia "G. Vitelli" della R. Università di Firenze. Florence.

Bowersock, G. W. 1965. *Augustus and the Greek World*. Oxford.

Bowman, R. A. 1941. "An Aramaic journal page." *American Journal of Semitic Languages and Literatures* 58, 302–13.

Boyaval, B. 1966. "21 documents inédits de la collection Despoina Michaelidès." *BIFAO* 64, 75–93.

Brady, T. A. 1935. *The Reception of the Egyptian Cults by the Greeks 330–30 B.C.* The University of Missouri Studies 10.1. Columbia, Mo.

Brandon, S.G.F. 1965. *History, Time and Deity: A Historical and Comparative Study of the Conception of Time in Religious Thought and Practice*. Manchester, Eng.

Braunert, H. 1964. *Die Binnenwanderung. Studien sur Sozialgeschichte Ägyptens in der Ptolemäer- und Kaiserzeit*. Bonner historische Forschungen 26. Bonn.

Breasted, H. J. 1906. *Ancient Records of Egypt*, IV. Chicago.

Breccia, E. 1911. *Iscrizioni greche e latine*. Catalogue général des antiquités égyptiennes du musée d'Alexandrie nos. 1–568. Cairo.

Bresciani, E. 1958. "La satrapia d'Egitto." *Studi classici e orientali* (Pisa) 7, 132–88.

———. 1967. "Stele demotiche dal Serapeo di Menfi nel Kunsthistorisches Museum di Vienna." *Oriens antiquus* 6, 23–45.

———. 1975. *L'archivio demotico del tempio di Soknopaiu Nesos nel Fayum (P.Ox.Griffith)*. Testi e documenti per lo studio dell'antichità 49. Milan.

————. 1983. "Note di toponomastica: I templi di *Mn-nfr, Wn-ḫm, Pr-ḥ ῾pj-mḫt.*" *EVO* 6, 67–73.

Bresciani, E., and Kamil, M. 1966. "Le lettere aramaiche di Hermopoli." *Atti della Accademia nazionale dei Lincei* 363, 357–428.

Bresciani, E., Bedini, E., Paolini, L., and Silvano, F. 1978. "Una rilettura dei Pap. Dem. Bologna 3173 e 3171." *EVO* 1, 95–101.

Brugsch, H. 1884. "Der Apis-Kreis aus den Zeiten der Ptolemäer nach den hieroglyphischen und demotischen Weihinschriften des Serapeums von Memphis." *ZÄS* 22, 110–36.

————. 1886. "Der Apis-Kreis aus den Zeiten der Ptolemäer nach den hieroglyphischen und demotischen Weihinschriften des Serapeums von Memphis." *ZÄS* 24, 19–40.

————. 1891. *Thesaurus inscriptionum aegyptiacarum.* Historisch-biographische Inschriften altaegyptischer Denkmaeler 5. Leipzig.

Bülow-Jacobsen, A. 1978. "The archiprophetes," in *Actes du* xvᵉ *congrès international de papyrologie*, Brussels, 1977. *Pap. Brux.* 19, 124–31. Brussels.

Burkhalter, F. 1981. Review of C. Reinsberg: *Studien zur hellenistischen Toreutik* (Gerstenberg, 1980). *Gnomon* 53, 690–93.

————. 1984. "Moulages en plâtre antiques et toreutique Alexandrine," in *Alessandria e il mondo ellenistico-romano. Studi in onore di Achille Adriani*, v, 334–47. Rome.

Burton, A. 1972. *Diodorus Siculus Book* i: *A Commentary*. Leiden.

Burton, G. P. 1975. "Proconsuls, assizes and the administration of justice under the empire." *JRS* 65, 92–106.

Butler, A. J. 1978. *The Arab Conquest of Egypt and the Last Thirty Years of the Roman Dominion.* 2d ed., rev. P. M. Fraser. Oxford.

Butzer, K. W. 1960. "Remarks on the geography of settlement in the Nile valley during Hellenistic times." *Bulletin de la société de géographie d'Egypte* 33, 5–36.

————. 1976. *Early Hydraulic Civilization in Egypt: A Study in Cultural Ecology.* Chicago.

Casson, L. 1971. *Ships and Seamanship in the Ancient World.* Princeton, N.J.

Cauville, S., and Devauchelle, D. 1984. "Le temple d'Edfou: Étapes de la construction; nouvelles données historiques," *Revue d'égyptologie* 35, 31–55.

Cavini, W. 1985. *Studi su papiri greci di logica e medicina.* Accademia toscana di scienze e lettere "La Columbaria," Studi 74. Florence.

Chamoux, Fr. 1975. "L'épigramme de Poseidippos sur le phare d'Alexandrie," in *Le monde grec. Hommages à Cl. Préaux*, ed. J. Bingen, G. Cambier, and G. Nachtergael, 214–22. Brussels.

Chassinat, E. 1899. "Textes provenant du Sérapéum de Memphis." *RecTrav* 21, 56–73.

————. 1900. "Textes provenant du Sérapéum de Memphis." *RecTrav* 22, 9–26 and 163–80.

Clark, C. and Haswell, M. 1970. *The Economics of Subsistence Agriculture.* 4th ed. London.

Clarysse, W. 1978. "Notes de prosopographie thébaine. 7. Hurganophor et Chaonnophris. Les derniers pharaons indigènes." *CE* 53, 243–53.

Clarysse, W. 1979. "Egyptian estate-holders in the Ptolemaic period," in *State and Temple Economy in the Ptolemaic Period*, II, ed. J. Quaegebeur (*OLA* 6), 737–43. Louvain.

———. 1980a. "A royal visit to Memphis and the end of the second Syrian war." *Studia Hellenistica* 24, 83–89.

———. 1980b. "Philadelpheia and the Memphites in the Zenon archive." *Studia Hellenistica* 24, 91–122.

———. 1981. "Aratomenes, brother of Komanos." *CE* 56, 347–49.

———. 1983a. "Literary papyri in documentary 'archives,' " in *Egypt and the Hellenistic World*. Proceedings of the International Colloquium, Leuven, 24–26 May 1982. *Studia Hellenistica* 27, 43–61.

———. 1983b. " 'De Droom van Koning Nektanebo' op een griekse papyrus (U.P.Z. 81)," in *Schrijvend Verleden*, ed. K. R. Veenhof, 367–71. Leiden.

———. 1985. "Greeks and Egyptians in the Ptolemaic army and administration." *Aegyptus* 65, 57–66.

———. 1986. "UPZ I 6a, a reconstruction by Revillout." *Enchoria* 14, 43–49.

———. 1987. "Greek loan-words in demotic," in *Aspects of Demotic Lexicography*. Acts of the Second International Conference for Demotic Studies, Leiden, 19–21 September 1984, ed. S. P. Vleeming, 9–33. Louvain.

Clarysse, W., and Hauben, H. 1976. "New remarks on the skippers in P. Petrie III 107." *APF* 24/5, 85–90.

Cockle, W.E.H. 1984. "State archives in Graeco-Roman Egypt from 30 B.C. to the reign of Septimius Severus." *JEA* 70, 106–22.

Courcelle, P. 1951. "L'oracle d'Apis et l'oracle ju jardin de Milan (Augustin, *Conf.* VIII 11, 29)." *Revue de l'histoire des religions* 139, 216–31.

Cowley, A. 1923. *Aramaic Papyri of the Fifth Century* B.C. Oxford.

Crawford, D. J. 1971. *Kerkeosiris: An Egyptian Village in the Ptolemaic Period*. Cambridge, Eng.

———. 1973. "The opium poppy: A Study in Ptolemaic agriculture," in *Problèmes de la terre en Grèce ancienne*, ed. M. I. Finley, 223–51. Paris and The Hague.

———. 1978. "The good official of Ptolemaic Egypt," in *Das ptolemäische Ägypten*, ed. H. Maehler and V. M. Strocka, 195–202. Mainz am Rhein, FRG.

———. 1979. "Food: Tradition and change in Hellenistic Egypt." *World Archaeology* 11, 135–45.

———. 1980. "Ptolemy, Ptah and Apis in Hellenistic Egypt." *Studia Hellenistica* 24, 1–42.

———. 1983. "Hellenistic Memphis: City and necropolis," in *Alessandria e il mondo ellenistico-romano. Studi in onore di Achille Adriani*, IV, 16–24. Rome.

Crowfoot, G. M. 1921. "Spinning and weaving in the Sudan." *Sudan Notes and Records* 4, 20–38.

Cumont, F. 1929. *Les religions orientales dans le paganisme romain*. 4th ed. Paris.

———. 1937. *L'Egypte des astrologues*. Brussels.

Darby, W. J., Ghalioungui, P., and Grivetti, L. 1977. *Food: The Gift of Osiris*. 2 vols. London, New York, and San Francisco.

Daressy, G. 1903. *Textes et dessins magiques*. Catalogue général des antiquités égyptiennes du musée du Caire, nos. 9401–49. Cairo.

————. 1911. "Un décret de l'an xxiii de Ptolémée Epiphane." *RecTrav* 33, 1–8.

————. 1914. "Sièges de prêtres." *BIFAO* 11, 234–40.

————. 1916–17. "Un second exemplaire du décret de l'an XXIII de Ptolémée Epiphane." *RecTrav* 38, 175–79.

Daumas, Fr. 1952. *Les moyens d'expression du grec et de l'égyptien comparés dans les décrets de Canope et de Memphis*. Cairo.

Dawson, W. R. 1949. "Anastasi, Sallier and Harris and their papyri." *JEA* 35, 158–66.

de Cenival, F. 1972a. "Un acte de renonciation consécutif à un partage de revenus liturgiques Memphites (*P. Louvre* E 3266)." *BIFAO* 71, 11–65.

————. 1972b. *Les associations religieuses en Egypte d'après les documents démotiques*. Cairo.

————. 1973. *Cautionnements démotiques du début de l'époque ptolémaïque*. Paris.

Delekat, L. 1964. *Katoche, Hierodulie und Adoptionsfreilassung*. Münchener Beiträge zur Papyrusforschung und antiken Rechtsgeschichte 47. Munich.

De Meulenaere, H. 1953. "Notes ptolémaïques." *BIFAO* 53, 103–11.

————. 1959a. "Prosopographica Ptolemaica." *CE* 34, 244–49.

————. 1959b. "Les stratèges indigènes du nome tentyrite à la fin de l'époque ptolémaique et au debut de l'occupation romaine." *Rivista degli studi orientali* 34, 1–25.

————. 1960. "Les monuments du culte des rois Nectanébo." *CE* 35, 92–107.

————. 1962. "Prosopographica Ptolemaica. Deuxième série." *CE* 37, 66–75.

————. 1963. "Trois monuments de basse époque." *OMRO* 44, 1–7.

————. 1967. "Prosopographica Ptolemaica. Troisième série." *CE* 42, 297–305.

————. 1974. "Le grand-prêtre Memphite Séhétepibrê-ankh," in *Festschrift zum 150jährigen Bestehen des Berliner ägyptischen Museums*. Staatliche Museen zu Berlin. Mitteilungen aus der ägyptischen Sammlung 8, 181–84. Berlin.

de Morgan, J. 1897. *Carte de la nécropole memphite*. Cairo.

de Rougé, E. 1885. "Mémoire sur quelques inscriptions trouvées dans la sépulture des Apis." *Revue égyptologique* 4, 106–20.

————. 1888. "Mémoire sur quelques inscriptions trouvées dans la sépulture des Apis." *Revue égyptologique* 5, 1–9.

Devauchelle, D. 1983. Review of E.A.E. Reymond, *From the Records of a Priestly Family from Memphis*, 1 (Wiesbaden, 1981). *CE* 58, 135–45.

Devéria, T. 1872. *Catalogue des manuscrits égyptiens écrits sur papyrus, toile, tablettes et ostraca en charactères hiéroglyphiques, hiératiques, démotiques, grecs, coptes, arabes et latins, qui sont au musée du Louvre*. Paris.

Donner, H., and Röllig, W. 1971. *Kanaanäische und aramäische Inschriften*. 3 vols. 3d ed. Wiesbaden, FRG.

Drioton, E. 1952. "A propos d'une statue naophore d'époque ptolémaique." *Bulletin de l'Institut d'Egypte* 33, 247–62.

Driver, G. R. 1957. *Aramaic Documents of the Fifth Century* B.C. Abridged and rev. ed. Oxford.

Dunand, F. 1985. "Les nécrotaphes de Kysis," in *Sociétés urbaines en Egypte et au Soudan*. Cahier de Recherches de l'Institut de Papyrologie et d'Egyptologie 7, 117–27. Lille, France.

Duncan-Jones, R. P. 1976. "The choinix, the artaba and the modius." *ZPE* 21, 43–52.

———. 1979. "Variation in Egyptian grain-measure." *Chiron* 9, 347–75.

———. 1982. *The Economy of the Roman Empire: Quantitative Studies.* 2d ed. Cambridge, Eng.

Dupont-Sommer, A. 1956. "Une stèle araméenne d'un prêtre de Ba'al trouvée en Egypte." *Syria* 33, 79–87.

Edgar, C. C. 1904. "An Ionian dedication to Isis." *JHS* 24, 337.

———. 1931. *Zenon Papyri in the University of Michigan Collection.* Ann Arbor.

Eitrem, S. 1932. "Two Greek papyri," in *Studies Presented to F. Ll. Griffith*, ed. S.R.K. Glanville, 214–17. London.

El-Amir, M. 1948. "The ΣΗΚΟΣ of Apis at Memphis." *JEA* 34, 51–56.

Emery, W. B. 1966. "Preliminary report on the excavations at North Saqqâra, 1965–66." *JEA* 52, 3–8.

———. 1967. "Preliminary report on the excavations at North Saqqâra, 1966–67." *JEA* 53, 141–45.

———. 1969. "Preliminary report on the excavations at North Saqqâra, 1967–68." *JEA* 55, 31–35.

———. 1970. "Preliminary report on the excavations at North Saqqâra, 1968–69." *JEA* 56, 5–11.

———. 1971. Preliminary report on the excavations at North Saqqâra, 1969–70." *JEA* 57, 3–13.

Engelbach, R. 1915. *Riqqeh and Memphis VI.* London.

Engelmann, H. 1975. *The Delian Aretalogy of Sarapis.* Leiden.

Erman, A. 1903. "Zur Erklärung des Papyrus Harris." *Sitzungsberichte der königlichen Preussischen Akademie der Wissenschaften* (Berlin), 456–74.

Estève, M.R.X. 1809. "Mémoire sur les finances de l'Egypte, depuis sa conquête par le sultan Selym Iᵉʳ, jusqu'à celle du général en chef Bonaparte." in *Description de l'Egypte. Etat moderne*, I, 299–398. Paris.

Evans, J.A.S. 1961. "A social and economic history of an Egyptian temple in the Greco-Roman period." *YClS* 17, 143–283.

Farag, S. 1975. "Two Serapeum stelae." *JEA* 61, 165–67.

Finley, M. I. 1985. *Ancient History: Evidence and Models.* London.

Forbes, R. J. 1956. *Studies in Ancient Technology*, IV. Leiden.

Forshall, J. 1893. *Description of the Greek Papyri in the British Museum*, Part I. London.

Foti Talamanca, F. 1974. *Ricerche sul processo nell' Egitto greco-romano.* I, *L'organizzazione del "conventus" del "Praefectus Aegypti."* Milan.

Fraenkel, E. 1942. "Aeschylus: New texts and old problems." *Proceedings of the British Academy* 28, 237–58.

Fraser, P. M. 1959/60. "Inscriptions from Ptolemaic Egypt." *Berytus* 13, 123–61.

———. 1972. *Ptolemaic Alexandria.* 3 vols. Oxford.

———. 1981. "Alexandria from Mohammed Ali to Gamal Abdal Nasser." *Aegyptiaca Treverensia* 1, 63–74.

Fraser, P. M., and Maas, P. 1955. "Three hellenistic epigrams from Egypt." *JEA* 41, 115–18.

Frenkian, A. M. 1967. " 'Deţinuţii' (ΕΓΚΑΤΟΧΟΙ) î templul lui Sarapis din Memfis." *Studii Classice* 9, 12–141.

Froidefond, C. 1971. *Le mirage égyptien dans la litterature grecque d'Homère à Aristote*. Aix-en-Provence, France.

Gaiser, K. 1968. "Ein Lob Athens in der Komödie." *Gymnasium* 75, 193–219.

Gara, A. 1984. "Limiti strutturali dell' economia monetaria nell' Egitto tardotolemaico," in *Studi ellenistici*, I, ed. B. Virgilio, 107–34. Pisa.

Gardiner, A. H. 1932. "The Astarte papyrus," in *Studies Presented to F. Ll. Griffith*, 74–85. London.

———. 1938. "The house of life." *JEA* 24, 157–79.

Gauthier, H. 1916. *Le livre des rois, IV, De la XXV dynastie à la fin des Ptolemées*. Cairo.

———. 1918. "Un nouveau monument du dieu Imhotep." *BIFAO* 14, 33–49.

———. 1919. "Les statues thébaines de la déesse Sakhmet." *ASAE* 19, 177–207.

Gauthier, H., and Sottas, H. 1925. *Un décret trilingue en l'honneur de Ptolémée IV*. Cairo.

Geertz, C. 1979. "Suq: The bazaar economy of Sefrou," in C. Geertz, H. Geertz, and L. Rosen, *Meaning and Order in Moroccan Society: Three Essays in Cultural Analysis*, 133–313. Cambridge and London.

Geremek, H. 1969. *Karanis: Un communauté rurale de l'Egypte romaine au II–III siècle de notre ère*. Warsaw.

Glanville, S.R.K. 1931. "Records of a royal dockyard of the time of Tuthmosis III: Papyrus British Museum 10056." *ZÄS* 66, 105–21.

———. 1932. "Records of a royal dockyard of the time of Tuthmosis III: Papyrus British Museum 10056." *ZÄS* 68, 7–41.

———. 1939. *Catalogue of Demotic Papyri in the British Museum, I, A Theban Archive of the Reign of Ptolemy I, Soter*. London.

———. 1955. *Catalogue of Demotic Papyri in the British Museum, II, The Instructions of Onchsheshonqy—British Museum Papyrus 105080*, Part I. London.

Goitein, S. D. 1967. *A Mediterranean Society: The Jewish Communities of the Arab World as Portrayed in the Documents of the Cairo Geniza, I, Economic Foundations*. Berkeley and Los Angeles.

Golb, N. 1965. "The topography of the Jews in Medieval Egypt. [Parts I–V]." *JNES* 24, 251–70.

———. 1974. "The topography of the Jews in Medieval Egypt. [Part VI]." *JNES* 33, 116–49.

Gomaà, F. 1973. *Chaemwese Sohn Ramses II und Hoherpriester von Memphis*. Ägyptologische Abhandlungen 27. Wiesbaden, FRG.

Gomme, A. W., and Sandbach, F. H. 1973. *Menander: A Commentary*. Oxford.

Goody, J. 1976. *Production and Reproduction: A Comparative Study of the Domestic Domain*. Cambridge, Eng.

Goossens, G. 1945. "Le temple de Ptah à Memphis." *CE* 39, 49–53.

Gordon, D. H. 1939. "The Buddhist origin of the 'Sumerian' heads from Memphis." *Iraq* 6, 35–38.

Gottleib, G. 1967. *Timuchen. Ein Beitrag zum griechischen Staatsrecht.* Sitzungsberichte der Heidelberger Akademie der Wissenschaften. Phil.-hist. Klasse, 1967, 3. Heidelberg.

Gow, A.S.F., and Page, D. L. 1965. *The Greek Anthology: Hellenistic Epigrams.* 2 vols. Cambridge, Eng.

Goyon, G. 1971. "Les ports des pyramides et le grand canal de Memphis." *Revue d'égyptologie* 23, 137–53.

Granger-Taylor, H. 1982. "Weaving clothes to shape in the ancient world: The tunic and toga of the Arringatore." *Textile History* 13, 3–25.

Grelot, P. 1972. *Documents araméens d'Egypte.* Paris.

Griffiths, J. G. 1970. *Plutarch's De Iside et Osiride.* Cambridge, Eng.

———. 1975. *Apuleius of Madaurus, the Isis-book (Metamorphoses, Book XI).* Leiden.

Grimm, G. 1975. *Kunst der Ptolemäer- und Römerzeit im Ägyptischen Museum Kairo.* Mainz am Rhein, FRG.

Grzybek, E. 1978. "Pharao Caesar in einer demotischen Grabinschrift aus Memphis." *Museum Helveticum* 35, 149–58.

Guéraud, O. 1933. "Deux documents relatifs au transport des céréales dans l'Egypte romaine." *ASAE* 33, 59–64.

Guidotti, M. C. 1984. "Nota su due modellini in fayence da Saqqara." *EVO* 7, 17–22.

Guilmot, M. 1962. "Le Sarapieion de Memphis. Etude topographique." *CE* 37, 359–81.

Hamdan, G. 1961. "Evolution of irrigation agriculture in Egypt," *Unesco, Arid zone research* 17, 119–42. Paris.

Handley, E. W., and Rea, J. 1957. *The Telephus of Euripides. BICS Supplement* 5. Institute of Classical Studies. London.

Hanson, A. E. 1972. "A Ptolemaic list of *aromata* and honey." *TAPhA* 103, 161–66.

Hauben, H. 1971a. "An annotated list of Ptolemaic naukleroi with a discussion of *BGU* x 1933." *ZPE* 8, 259–75.

Hauben, H. 1971b. "Quelques considérations au sujet du papyrus Petrie III 107." *Ancient Society* 2, 21–32.

———. 1979. "Le transport fluvial en Egypte ptolémaïque. Les bateaux du roi et de la reine," in *Actes du XV congrès international de papyrologie*, IV. Papyrologica Bruxellensia 19. Brussels.

———. 1985. "The guard posts of Memphis." *ZPE* 60, 183–87.

Heinen, H. 1966. "Rom und Ägypten von 51 bis 47 v.Chr. Untersuchungen zur Regierungszeit der 7. Kleopatra und des 13. Ptolemäers." Dissertation. Tübingen, FRG.

Hiller von Gaertringen, Fr. 1906. *Inshriften von Priene.* Berlin.

Himmelmann, N. 1981. "Realistic art in Alexandria." *Proceedings of the British Academy* 67, 193–207.

Holleaux, M. 1942. *Etudes d'épigraphie et d'histoire grecques,* III. Paris.

Holmberg, M. S. 1946. *The God Ptah.* Lund, Sweden.

Hopkins, K. 1978. "Economic growth and towns in classical antiquity," in *Towns in Societies*, ed. P. Abrams and E. A. Wrigley, 35–77. Cambridge, Eng.

———. 1983. "Introduction," in *Trade in the Ancient Economy*, ed. P. Garnsey, K. Hopkins, and C. R. Whittaker, ix–xxv. London.

Hornung, E. 1982. *Conceptions of God in Ancient Egypt: The One and the Many*, trans. John Baines. London, Melbourne, and Henley.

Hornung, E., and Staehlin, E. 1974. *Studien zum Sedfest*. Aegyptiaca Helvetica 1. Geneva.

Hughes, G. R. 1982. "The blunder of an inept scribe (Demotic papyrus Louvre 2414)," in *Studies in Philology in Honour of Ronald James Williams: A Festschrift*, 51–67. Toronto.

Huss, W. 1976. *Untersuchungen zur Aussenpolitik Ptolemaios' IV*. Münchener Beiträge zur Papyrusforschung und antiken Rechtsgeschichte 69. Munich.

Ibrahim, Mohiy E. A. 1975. *The Chapel of the Throne of Re of Edfu*. Bibliotheca Aegyptiaca 16. Brussels.

Jeffery, L. A. 1961. *The Local Scripts of Archaic Greece*. Oxford.

Jeffreys, D. G. 1985. *The Survey of Memphis*, I. Egypt Exploration Society Occasional Publications 3. London.

Jeffreys, D. G., Málek, J., and Smith, H. S. 1984. "The survey of Memphis, 1982." *JEA* 70, 23–32.

Jelínková, E.A.E. 1957. "Sale of inherited property in the first century B.C. (P. Brit. Mus. 10075, ex Salt coll. no. 418)." *JEA* 43, 45–55.

———. 1959. "Sale of inherited property in the first century B.C. (P. Brit. Mus. 10075, ex Salt coll. no. 418)." *JEA* 45, 61–74.

Johnson, A. C. 1936. *Roman Egypt to the Reign of Diocletian: An Economic Survey of Ancient Rome*, II, ed. T. Frank. Baltimore, Md.

Johnson, J. H. 1984. "Is the Demotic Chronicle an anti-Greek tract?" in *Festschrift für Erich Lüddeckens zum 15. Juni 1983*, ed. H.-J. Thissen and K.-Th. Zauzich, 107–24. Würzburg, FRG.

———. 1986. "The role of the Egyptian priesthood in Ptolemaic Egypt," in *Egyptological Studies Presented in Honor of Richard A. Parker*, ed. L. H. Lesko, 70–84. Hanover, N.H., and London.

Jomard, E. 1818. "Mémoire sur la population comparée de l'Egypte ancienne et moderne," in *Description de l'Egypte. Antiquités, mémoires*, II, 87–119. Paris.

———. 1836. *Coup d'oeil impartial sur l'état présent de l'Egypte*. Paris.

Jones, A.H.M. 1964. *The Later Roman Empire 284–602: A Social, Economic and Administrative Survey*. 2 vols. Oxford.

Jones, M., and Milward Jones, A. 1982. "The Apis house project at Mit Rahineh: First season, 1982." *JARCE* 19, 51–58.

———. 1983. "The Apis house project: Preliminary report of the second and third seasons, 1982–1983." *JARCE* 20, 33–39.

———. 1984. "The Apis house project in Mit Rahineh." *ARCE Newsletter* 125, 14–22.

Kaczmarczyk, A., and Hedges, R.E.M. 1983. *Ancient Egyptian Faience: An Analytical Survey of Egyptian Faience from Predynastic to Roman Times*. Warminster, Eng.

Kallerēs, I. 1950/51. "Hai prōtai hylai tēs hyphantourgias eis tēn Ptolemaikēn Aigypton." *Epetēris tou laographikou archeiou* 6, 78–230.

Kamal, Ahmed. 1904/5. *Stèles ptolémaiques et romaines.* 2 vols. Catalogue général des antiquités égyptiennes du musée du Caire. Cairo.

Kaplony, P. 1966. "Der Titel *wnr(w)* nach Spruch 820 der Sargtexte." *Mitteilungen des Instituts für Orientforschung* 11, 137–63.

Kaplony-Heckel, U., and Kramer, B. 1985. "Ein griechisch-demotisches Holstäfelchen mit Sitologenquittung und Privatabrechnung für Epigraphe aus Krokodilopolis." *ZPE* 61, 43–57.

Karkowski, J., and Winnicki, J. K. 1983. "Amenhotep, son of Hapu and Imhotep at Deir el-Bahari—some reconsiderations." *MDAIK* 39, 93–105.

Kater-Sibbes, G.J.K., and Vermaseren, M. J. 1975a. *Apis, I, The Monuments of the Hellenistic-Roman Period from Egypt.* Leiden.

———. 1975b. *Apis, II, Monuments from Outside Egypt.* Leiden.

———. 1977. *Apis, III, Inscriptions, Coins and Addenda.* Leiden.

Kees, H. 1931. "Memphis." *RE* xv.1, 660–88.

———. 1955. *Das alte Ägypten: Eine kleine Landeskunde.* Berlin.

———. 1961. *Ancient Egypt: A Cultural Topography,* ed. T.G.H. James. London.

Kemp, B. J. 1977. "The palace of Apries at Memphis." *MDAIK* 33, 101–8.

———. 1978. "A further note on the palace of Apries at Memphis." *GM* 29, 61.

Kiessling, E. 1953. "Die Götter von Memphis in griechisch-römischer Zeit." *APF* 15, 7–45.

Koenen, L. 1959. "ΘΕΟΙΣΙΝ ΕΧΘΡΟΣ. Ein einheimischer Gegenkönig in Ägypten (132/1ª)." *CE* 34, 103–19.

———. 1962. "Die 'demotische Zivilprozessordnung' und die Philanthropa vom 9 Okt. 186 vor Chr." *APF* 17, 11–16.

———. 1968. "Die Prophezeiungen des 'Töpfers.'" *ZPE* 2, 178–209.

———. 1970. "The prophecies of a potter: A prophecy of world renewal becomes an apocalypse," in *Proceedings of the Twelfth International Congress of Papyrology, Ann Arbor, 13–17 August 1968,* 249–54. American Studies in Papyrology 7. Toronto.

———. 1974. "Bemerkungen zum Text des Töpferorakels und zu dem Akaziensymbol." *ZPE* 13, 313–19.

———. 1984. "A supplementary note on the date of the oracle of the potter." *ZPE* 54, 9–13.

———. 1985. "The dream of Nektanebos." *ZPE* 22, 171–94.

Kornemann, E. 1901. "Zur Geschichte der antiken Herrscherkulte." *Klio* 1, 51–146.

Kraeling, E. G. 1953. *The Brooklyn Museum Aramaic Papyri: New Documents of the Fifth Century* B.C. *from the Jewish Colony at Elephantine.* New Haven, Conn.

Kyrieleis, H. 1975. *Bildnisse der Ptolemäer.* Deutsches Archäologisches Institut. Archäologische Forschungen 2. Berlin.

Lacau, P. 1921/2. "Les statues 'guérisseuses' dans l'ancienne Egypte." *Fondation Eugène Piot. Monuments et mémoires* 25, 189–209.

Lanciers, E. 1986. "Die ägyptischen Tempelbauten zur Zeit des Ptolemaios V. Epiphanes (204–180 v. Chr.)." *MDAIK* 42, 81–98.

———. 1987. "Die stele CG 22184: Ein Priesterdekret aus der Regierung des Pto-lemaïos VI Philometor." *GM* 95, 53–61.

Larson, B. K. 1982. "The structure and function of village markets in contem-porary Egypt." *JARCE* 19, 131–44.

Laserre, F. 1966. *Die Fragmente des Eudoxos von Knidos*. Berlin.

Lauer, J.-P. 1961. "Mariette à Saqqarah, du Sérapéum à la Direction des Antiqui-tées," in *Mélanges Mariette*, 3–69. Bibliothèque d'Etude de l'IFAO 32. Cairo.

———. 1976. *Saqqara, the Royal Cemetery of Memphis: Excavations and Discoveries since 1850*. London.

Lauer, J.-P. and Picard, Ch. 1955. *Les statues ptolémaïques du Sarapieion de Memphis*. Paris.

Launey, M. 1949/50. *Recherches sur les armées hellénistiques*. 2 vols. Bibliothèque des écoles françaises d'Athènes et de Rome 169. Paris.

Lavagnini, B. 1922. *Eroticorum scriptorum fragmenta papiracea*. Leipzig.

Lawrence, A. W. 1925. "Greek sculpture in Ptolemaic Egypt." *JEA* 11, 179–90.

Lefebvre, G. 1923/4. *Le tombeau de Petosiris*. 3 vols. Cairo.

Lepsius, R. 1897. *Denkmäler aus Aegypten und Aethiopien*, 1. Leipzig.

Lesquier, J. 1918. *L'armée romaine d'Egypte d'Auguste à Dioclétien*. Mémoires pu-bliés par les membres de l'Institut français d'archéologie orientale du Caire 41. Cairo.

Letronne, J.-A. 1848. *Recueil des inscriptions grecques et latines de l'Egypte*, II. Paris.

Lewis, D. M. 1977. *Sparta and Persia*. Cincinnati Classical Studies, N.S. 1. Leiden.

Lewis, N. 1976. "Notationes legentis." *BASP* 13, 5–14.

———. 1986. *Greeks in Ptolemaic Egypt: Case Studies in the Social History of the Hellenistic World*. Oxford.

Lichtheim, M. 1973. *Ancient Egyptian Literature*, 1, *The Old and Middle Kingdoms*. Berkeley, Los Angeles, and London.

———. 1980. *Ancient Egyptian Literature*, III, *The Late Period*. Berkeley, Los An-geles, and London.

———. 1983. *Late Egyptian Wisdom Literature in the International Context: A Study of Demotic Instructions*. Freiburg-Göttingen, FRG.

———. 1984. "Demotic proverbs," in *Grammata Demotika. Festschrift für Erich Lüddeckens zum 15. Juni 1983*, ed. H.-J. Thissen and K.-Th. Zauzich, 125–40. Würzburg, FRG.

Lidzbarski, M. 1902. *Ephemeris für semitische Epigraphik*, 1. Giessen.

Liebeschuetz, J.H.W.G. 1972. *Antioch: City and Imperial Administration in the Later Roman Empire*. Oxford.

Limme, L. 1972. "Deux stèles inédites du Sérapeum de Memphis." *CE* 47, 82–109.

Lipiński, E. 1986. *De Feniciërs en de Mediterrane Wereld*. Luxembourg.

Livshitsa, I. G. 1950. *Shampol'on (Zh.-F.). O egipetskom ieroglificheskom alfabite* (in Russian). Moscow.

Lloyd, A. B. 1975. *Herodotus Book II: Introduction*. Leiden.

———. 1976. *Herodotus Book II: Commentary 1–98*. Leiden.

———. 1978a. "Two figured ostraca from North Saqqâra." *JEA* 64, 107–12.

Lloyd, A. B. 1978b. "Strabo and the Memphite tauromachy," in *Hommages à Maarten J. Vermaseren*, II, 609–26. Leiden.

———. 1982. "Nationalist propaganda in Ptolemaic Egypt." *Historia* 31, 33–55.

Loebenstein, H. 1972. *Due Papyrussammlung der österreichischen Nationalbibliothek. Katalog der ständigen Ausstellung.* Biblos-Schriften 69. Vienna.

Lüddeckens, E. 1960. *Ägyptische Eheverträge.* Ägyptologische Abhandlungen 1. Wiesbaden, FRG.

Malaise, M. 1972. *Inventaire préliminaire des documents égyptiens découverts en Italie.* Leiden.

Malinine, M. 1943. "Le surnom 'Tryphon' de Ptolémée Euergète I." *Revue de Philologie* 17, 157–61.

Malinine, M., Posener, G., and Vercoutter, J. 1968. *Catalogue des stèles du Sérapéum de Memphis.* 2 vols. Paris.

Mariette, A. 1856a. *Mémoire sur la mère d'Apis.* Paris.

———. 1856b. "Fragment de sarcophage phénicien conservé au musée de Berlin." *Bulletin archéologique français (Athenaeum français)* 2.7, 49–50.

———. 1857. *Le Sérapéum de Memphis.* Paris.

———. 1872. *Monuments divers recueillis en Egypte et en Nubie.* Paris.

Martin, G. T. 1973. "Excavations in the sacred animal necropolis at North Saqqâra 1971–2: Preliminary report." *JEA* 59, 5–15.

———. 1979. *The Tomb of Hetepka.* Texts from Excavations 4, ed. T.G.H. James. London.

Maspero, G. 1879. *Etudes égyptiennes,* I. Paris.

———. 1882. *Le Sérapeum de Memphis par Auguste Mariette Pacha.* Paris.

Masson, O. 1977. "Quelques bronzes égyptiens à l'inscription grecque." *Revue d'égyptologie* 29, 53–67.

———. 1978. *Carian Inscriptions from North Saqqâra and Buhen.* Texts from excavations 5, ed. T.G.H. James. London.

Matz, F. 1957. Review of J.- Ph. Lauer and Ch. Picard, *Les statues ptolémaïques du Sarapieion de Memphis* (Paris: PUF, 1955). *Gnomon* 29, 84–93.

Meiggs, R. 1982. *Trees and Timber in the Ancient Mediterranean World.* Oxford.

Mellaart, J. 1975. "The origins and development of cities in the Near East," in *Janus: Essays in Ancient and Modern Studies,* ed. L. L. Orlin, 5–22. Ann Arbor, Mich.

Merkelbach, R. 1954. *Die Quellen des griechischen Alexanderromans.* Zetemata 9. Munich.

Milik, J. T. 1958. "Nouvelles inscriptions nabatéennes." *Syria* 35, 227–51.

———. 1960. "Notes d'épigraphie orientale." *Syria* 37, 94–98.

———. 1967. "Les papyrus araméens d'Hermoupolis et les cultes syro-phéniciens en Egypte perse." *Biblica* 48, 546–622.

Millar, F. 1977. *The Emperor in the Roman World (31 B.C.–A.D.337).* London.

Milne, J. G. 1905. *Greek Inscriptions.* Catalogue général des antiquités égyptiennes du musée du Caire. Oxford.

Modrzejewski. J. 1970. "La règle de droit dans l'Egypte romaine (Etat des questions et perspectives de recherches)," in *Proceedings of the Twelfth International*

Congress of Papyrology, Ann Arbor, 13–17 August 1968, 317–77. American Studies in Papyrology 7. Toronto.

Mond, R., and Myers, O. H. *The Bucheum*. 3 vols. London.

Montevecchi, O. 1973. *La papirologia*. Turin.

Mooren, L. 1975. *The aulic titulature in Ptolemaic Egypt. Introduction and Prosopography*. Brussels.

———. 1978. "Macht und Nationalität," in *Das ptolemäische Ägypten*, ed. H. Maehler and V. M. Strocka, 51–57. Mainz am Rhein, FRG.

Morenz, S. 1959. "Zur Vergöttlichung in Ägypten." *ZÄS* 84, 132–43.

Mørkholm, O. 1961. "Eulaios and Lenaios." *Classica et mediaevalia* 22, 32–43.

———. 1975. "Ptolemaic coins and chronology: The dated silver coinage of Alexandria." *ANS Museum Notes* 20, 7–24.

Morris, H. S. 1968. "Ethnic groups," *International Encyclopedia of the Social Sciences*, V, 167–72. Macmillan and Free Press, New York.

Munro, P. 1973. *Die spätägyptischen Totenstelen*. Ägyptologische Forschungen 25. Glückstadt, FRG.

Naveh, J. 1968. "Aramaica dubiosa." *JNES* 27, 318–25.

Nelson, C. A. 1984. "The Memphis poll tax receipts," in *Atti del XVII congresso internazionale di papirologia*, III, 1041–4. Naples.

Newberry, P. E. 1893. *El Bersheh. Part I*. Archaeological Survey of Egypt, ed. F. L. Griffith. London.

Nock, A. D. 1972. *Essays on Religion and the Ancient World*, ed. Z. Stewart. 2 vols. Cambridge, Mass.

Norsa, M. 1939. *La scrittura letteraria greca dal secolo IV a.c. all'VIII d.c.* Florence.

Onasch, C. 1976. "Zur Königsideologie der Ptolemäer in den Dekreten von Kanopus und Memphis (Rosettana)." *APF* 24/5, 137–55.

Orrieux, Cl. 1980. "Les archives d'Euclès et la fin de la *dôréa* du dioecète Apollonios." *CE* 55, 213–39.

———. 1981. "Les comptes privés de Zénon à Philadelphie." *CE* 56, 314–40.

———. 1983. *Les papyrus de Zénon: L'horizon d'un grec en Egypte au III siècle avant J.C.* Paris.

———. 1985. *Zénon de Caunos, parépidēmos, et le destin grec*. Paris.

Otto, E. 1938. *Beiträge zur Geschichte der Stierkulte in Aegypten*. Untersuchungen zur Geschichte und Altertumskunde Aegyptens 13. Leipzig.

———. 1954. *Die biographischen Inschriften der ägyptischen Spätzeit. Ihre geistesgeschichtliche und literarische Bedeutung*. Probleme der Ägyptologie 2. Leiden.

———. 1956. "Eine memphitische Priesterfamilie des 2 Jh. v.Chr." *ZÄS* 81, 109–29.

———. 1957. "Zwei Bemerkungen zum Königskult der Spätzeit." *MDAIK* 15, 193–207.

Otto, W. 1905. *Priester und Tempel im hellenistichen Ägypten. Ein Beitrag zur Kulturgeschichte des Hellenismus*, I. Leipzig and Berlin.

———. 1908. *Priester und Tempel im hellenistichen Ägypten. Ein Beitrag zur Kulturgeschichte des Hellenismus*, II. Leipzig and Berlin.

———. 1926. See Spiegelberg, W., and Otto, W.

Otto, W. 1934. *Zur Geschichte der Zeit des 6. Ptolemäers. Ein Beitrag zur Politik und zur Staatsrecht des Hellenismus.* ABAW, N.S. 11. Munich.

Otto, W., and Bengtson, H. 1938. *Zur Geschichte des Niederganges des Ptolemäerreiches: Ein Beitrag zur Regierungszeit des 8. und des 9. Ptolemäers.* ABAW 17. Munich.

Pack, R. A. 1965. *The Greek and Latin Literary Texts from Greco-Roman Egypt.* 2d rev. ed. Ann Arbor, Mich.

Page, D. L. 1941. *Greek Literary Papyri,* 1. London and Cambridge, Mass.

Parker, R. A. 1941. "Persian and Egyptian chronology." *The American Journal of Semitic Languages and Literature* 58, 285–301.

Parsons, P. J. 1974. "Ulpius Serenianus." *CE* 49, 135–57.

———. 1980. Review of G. Foti Talamanca, *Ricerche. JRS* 70, 236–37.

Peremans, W. 1975. "Ptolémée IV et les égyptiens," in *Le monde grec. Hommages à Claire Préaux,* ed. J. Bingen, G. Cambier, and G. Nachtergael, 393–402. Brussels.

———. 1985. "Notes sur les traductions de textes non littéraires sous les Lagides." *CE* 60, 248–62.

Perry, B. E. 1966. "The Egyptian legend of Nectanebus." *TAPhA* 97, 327–33.

Pestman, P. W. 1961. *Marriage and Matrimonial Property in Ancient Egypt: A Contribution to Establishing the Legal Position of Women.* Pap. Lugd. Bat. 9. Leiden.

———. 1963. "Les documents juridiques des 'chanceliers du dieu' de Memphis à l'époque ptolémaïque." *OMRO* 44, 8–23.

———. 1965. "Harmachis et Anchmachis, deux rois indigènes du temps des Ptolémées." *CE* 40, 157–70.

———. 1967. *Chronologie égyptienne d'après les textes démotiques, 332 av. J.C.–453 ap. J.C.* Pap. Lugd. Bat. 15. Leiden.

———. 1969. "The law of succession in ancient Egypt," in *Essays on Oriental Laws of Succession,* ed. M. David, F. R. Kraus, and P. W. Pestman, 58–77. Leiden.

———. 1971. "Loans bearing no interest?" *JJP* 16/17, 7–29.

Pestman, P. W., with the collaboration of J. Quaegebeur and R. L. Vos. 1977. *Receuil de textes démotiques et bilingues.* 3 vols. Leiden.

———. 1978. "L'agoranomie: un avant-poste de l'administration grecque enlevé par les égyptiens?" in *Das ptolemäische Ägypten,* ed. H. Maehler and V. M. Strocka, 203–10. Mainz am Rhein, FRG.

———. 1981. *L'archivio di Amenothes (P. Tor. Amenothes).* Milan.

———. 1983. "Some aspects of Egyptian law in Graeco-Roman Egypt." *Studia Hellenistica* 27, 281–302.

Petrie, W.M.F. 1909a. *Memphis I.* London.

———. 1909b. *The Palace of Apries (Memphis II).* London.

———. 1911a. *Roman portraits and Memphis (IV).* London.

———. 1911b. *Historical Studies.* British School of Archaeology in Egypt, Studies 2. London.

Petrie, W.M.F., Mackay, E., and Wainwright, G. 1910. *Meydum and Memphis III.* London.

Petrie, W.M.F., Wainwright, G. A., and Gardiner, A. H. 1913. *Tarkhan I and Memphis V.* London.

Porten, B. 1968. *Archives from Elephantine: The Life of an Ancient Jewish Military Colony*. Berkeley and Los Angeles.

Porter, B., and Moss, R.L.B. 1937. *Topographical Bibliography of Ancient Hieroglyphic Texts, Reliefs, and Paintings*, v, *Upper Egypt: Sites*. Oxford.

――――. 1939. *Topographical Bibliography of Ancient Hieroglyphic Texts, Reliefs, and Paintings*, vi, *Upper Egypt: Chief Temples (Excluding Thebes)*. Oxford.

――――. 1951. *Topographical Bibliography*, vii, *Nubia, the Deserts, and Outside Egypt*. Oxford.

Porter, the late Bertha, and Moss, R.L.B. 1972. *Topographical Bibliography of Ancient Hieroglyphic Texts, Reliefs, and Paintings*, ii, *Theban Temples*. 2d ed. Oxford.

――――. 1981. *Topographical Bibliography*: iii.2.fasc.3. Saqqâra to Dahshûr, 2d ed., rev. and aug. by J. Málek. Oxford.

Posener, G. 1936. *La première domination perse en Egypte. Recueil d'inscriptions hiéroglyphiques*. IFAO. Bibliothèque d'étude 11. Cairo.

――――. 1960. *De la divinité du pharaon*. Cahiers de la société asiatique 15. Paris.

――――. 1969. "Achoris." *Revue d'égyptologie* 21, 148–50.

Power, E. 1941. *The Wool Trade in English Medieval History*. Oxford.

Préaux, C. 1936. "Esquisse d'une histoire des révolutions égyptiennes sous les Lagides." *CE* 22, 522–52.

――――. 1939a. *L'économie royale des Lagides*. Brussels.

――――. 1939b. Review of A. S. Hunt, J. G. Smyly, and C. G. Edgar, *The Tebtunis Papyri III.2*. *CE* 28, 386–93.

――――. 1942. "Note de sémantique sur U.P.Z. 5 and 6." *CE* 17, 152.

――――. 1947. *Les grecs en Egypte d'après les archives de Zénon*. Brussels.

――――. 1948. "A propos des associations dans l'Egypte gréco-romaine." *RIDA* 1, 189–98.

――――. 1955. "Sur les fonctions du πράκτωρ ξενικῶν." *CE* 30, 107–11.

――――. 1965. "Polybe et Ptolémée Philopator." *CE* 40, 364–75.

――――. 1978. *Le monde héllenistique. La Grèce et l'Orient de la mort d'Alexandre à la conquête romaine de la Grèce (323–146 B.C.)*. 2 vols. Paris.

Price, S.R.F. 1984. *Rituals and Power*. Cambridge, Eng.

Quaegebeur, J. 1971a. "Ptolémée II en adoration devant Arsinoe II divinisée." *BIFAO* 69, 191–217.

――――. 1971b. "Documents concerning a cult of Arsinoe Philadelphos at Memphis." *JNES* 30, 239–70.

――――. 1972. "Contribution à la prosopographie des prêtres à l'époque ptolémaïque." *Ancient Society* 3, 77–109.

――――. 1974. "Inventaire des stèles funéraires memphites d'époque ptolémaïque." *CE* 49, 59–79.

――――. 1977. "Tithoes, dieu oraculaire." *Enchoria* 7, 103–8.

――――. 1978a. "Reines ptolémaïques et traditions égyptiennes," in *Das ptolemäische Ägypten*, ed. H. Maehler and V. M. Strocka, 245–62. Mainz am Rhein.

――――. 1978b. "Les papyrus démotiques des musées royaux d'art et d'histoire à Bruxelles." *Enchoria* 8, 25–28.

Quaegebeur, J. 1979. "Documents égyptiens et rôle économique du clergé en Egypte hellénistique," in *State and Temple Economy in the Ancient Near East*, II, ed. E. Lipiński, 707–29. OLA 6. Louvain.

———. 1980a. "The genealogy of the Memphite high priest family in the Hellenistic period." *Studia Hellenistica* 24, 43–82.

———. 1980b. "Une epithète méconnaisable de Ptah," in *Livre du Centenaire (1880–1980)*. Mémoires publiés par les membres de l'Institut français d'archéologie orientale du Caire 104, 61–71. Cairo.

———. 1980/81. "Sur la 'loi sacrée' dans l'Egypte gréco-romaine." *Ancient Society* 11/12. 227–40.

———. 1983a. "Twee laategyptische teksten rond dierenverering. Stèle Ny Carlsberg Glyptotheek 1681 en Papyrus BM 10845," in *Schrijvend Verleden*, ed. K. R. Veenhof, 263–75. Leiden.

———. 1983b. "Apis et la menat." *BSFE* 98, 17–39.

———. 1984. "Le terme *tnf(j)* 'danseur' en démotique," in *Grammata Demotika. Festschrift für Erich Lüddeckens zum 15. Juni 1983*, ed. H. -J. Thissen and K.-Th. Zauzich, 157–70. Würzburg, FRG.

———. 1985. "On the Egyptian equivalent of Biblical *ḥarṭummîm*," in *Pharaonic Egypt: The Bible and Christianity*, ed. S. Israelit-Groll, 162–72. Jerusalem.

———. 1986. "Osservazioni sul titolare di un libro dei morti conservato ad Assisi." *Oriens Antiquus* 25, 69–80.

Quaegebeur, J., and Rammant-Peeters, A. 1982. "Le pyramidion d'un 'danseur en chef' de Bastet," in *Studia Paulo Naster oblata*, II, ed. J. Quaegebeur, 179–205. OLA 13. Louvain.

Quaegebeur, J., Clarysse, W., and Van Maele, B. 1985. "The Memphite Triad." *GM* 88, 25–37.

Quibell, J. E. 1907. *Excavations at Saqqâra 1905–1906*. Cairo.

———. 1908. *Excavations at Saqqâra 1906–1907*. Cairo.

———. 1909. *Excavations at Saqqâra 1907–1908*. Cairo.

———. 1912. *Excavations at Saqqâra 1908–1909*. Cairo.

Ranke, H. 1932. "Istar als Heilgöttin in Ägypten," in *Studies presented to F. Ll. Griffith*, 412–18. London.

Rapaport, U. 1969. "Les Iduméens en Egypte." *RPh* 43, 73–82.

Ray, J. D. 1972. "The house of Osorapis," in *Man, Settlement and Urbanism*, ed. P. J. Ucko, R. Tringham, and G. W. Dimbleby, 699–704. London.

———. 1975. "Papyrus Carlsberg 67: A healing prayer from the Fayûm." *JEA* 61, 181–88.

———. 1976. *The Archive of Ḥor*. London.

———. 1978a. "Observations on the archive of Ḥor." *JEA* 64, 113–20.

———. 1978b. "The world of North Saqqâra." *World Archaeology* 10, 149–57.

———. 1978c. "The non-literary material from North Saqqâra: A short progress report." *Enchoria* 8, 29–30.

———. 1981. "An approach to the Carian script." *Kadmos* 20, 150–62.

———. 1982a. "The Carian inscriptions from Egypt." *JEA* 68, 181–98.

———. 1982b. "The Carian script." *PCPhS* 208, 77–90.

Reich, N. J. 1933a. "New documents from the Serapeum of Memphis." *Mizraim* 1, 9–129.

————. 1933b. "The Τεεβήσιος υἱοί and their quarrel with Apollonios (Papyrus Louvre n. 2364 = UPZ, 12 and 13)." *Mizraim* 1, 147–77.

Reinsberg, C. 1980. *Studien zur hellenistischen Toreutik.* Hildesheimer Ägyptologische Beiträge 9. Hildesheim, FRG.

Rémondon, R. 1960. "Les antisémites de Memphis (P.IFAO inv. 104 = CPJ 141)." *CE* 35, 244–61.

————. 1964. "Problèmes du bilinguisme dans l'Egypte lagide (UPZ I, 148)." *CE* 39, 126–46.

Revillout, E. 1878. *Nouvelle chrestomathie démotique.* Paris.

————. 1880a. "La question du divorce chez les égyptiens." *Revue égyptologique* 1, 87–98.

————. 1880b. "Hypothèque légale de la femme et donations entre époux." *Revue égyptologique* 1, 122–38.

————. 1880c. *Chrestomathie démotique.* Paris.

————. 1880d. "Taricheutes et choachytes." *ZÄS* 18, 70–80, 103–20, 136–48.

————. 1882a. "Un quasi-mariage après concubinat." *Revue égyptologique* 2, 89–95.

————. 1882b. "L'antigraphe des luminaires." *Revue égyptologique* 2, 78–83.

————. 1882c. "Le papyrus grec 13 de Turin." *Revue égyptologique* 2, 124–41.

————. 1885. "Les prêts de blé." *Revue égyptologique* 3, 25–27.

————. 1888. "Les papiers administratifs du Sérapeum et l'organisation sacerdotale en Egypte." *Revue égyptologique* 5, 31–62.

————. 1891a. "Stèles bilingues." *Revue égyptologique* 6, 95–100.

————. 1891b. "Leçon d'ouverture prononcée à l'école du Louvre, le lundi, 19 Décembre 1887." *Revue égyptologique* 6, 113–49.

————. 1893. "Deux papyrus moraux du Louvre," *Quelques textes traduits à mes cours.* 1st series. xii–xciii. Paris.

————. 1897. *La propriété, ses démembrements, la possession et leurs transmissions, en droit égyptien comparé aux autres droits de l'antiquité.* Paris.

————. 1903. *Précis du droit égyptien comparé aux autres droits de l'antiquité.* 2 vols. Paris.

————. 1914. "Textes démotiques d'époque ptolémaique et romaine transcrits en hiéroglyphes." *Revue égyptologique* 14, 39–69.

Revillout, V., and Revillout, E. 1896. "Textes égyptiens et chaldéens relatifs à l'intercession des vivants en faveur des morts." *Revue égyptologique* 7, 164–82.

Reymond, E.A.E. 1973. *Embalmers' Archives from Hawara: Catalogue of Demotic Papyri in the Ashmolean Museum,* 1. Oxford.

————. 1974. "Fragment of a temple account roll, P. Fitzhugh D.3 and D.4." *JEA* 60, 189–99.

————. 1976. *From the Contents of the Libraries of the Suchos Temples in the Fayyum,* Part I, *A Medical Book from Crocodilopolis, P.Vindob.D 6257.* MPER 10. Vienna.

————. 1977. "Alexandria and Memphis: Some historical observations." *Orientalia* 46, 1–24.

————. 1981. *From the Records of a Priestly Family from Memphis,* I. Ägyptologische Abhandlungen 38. Wiesbaden, FRG.

Rhodokanakis, N. 1924. "Die Sarkophaginschrift von Gizeh." *Zeitschrift für Semitistik und verwandte Gebiet* 2, 113–33.

Rice, E. E. 1983. *The Grand Procession of Ptolemy Philadelphus*. Oxford.

Rink, H. 1924. "Strassen- und Viertelnamen von Oxyrhynchus." Dissertation. Giessen.

Robert, L. 1935. "Sur des inscriptions de Theangela." *L'antiquité classique* 4, 157–73.

————. 1937. *Etudes anatoliennes; recherches sur les inscriptions grecques de l'Asie Mineure*. Etudes orientales 5. Paris.

————. 1966. "Sur un décret d'Ilion et sur un papyrus concernant des cultes royaux," in *Essays in Honor of C. Bradford Welles*, 175–211. American Studies in Papyrology 1. New Haven, Conn.

Rosati, G. 1986. "Antichità egizie ad Assisi II." *Oriens Antiquus* 25 (1986), 59–67.

Rostovtzeff, M. 1922. *A Large Estate in Egypt in the Third Century B.C.: A Study in Economic History*. University of Wisconsin Studies in the Social Sciences and History 6. Madison, Wisc.

————. 1941. *The Social and Economic History of the Hellenistic World*. 3 vols. Oxford.

Rubensohn, O. 1911. *Hellenistisches Silbergerät in antiken Gipsabgüssen aus dem Pelizaeus-Museum zu Hildesheim*. Berlin.

Ryckmans, G. 1935. *Répertoire d'épigraphie sémitique*, VI. Paris.

Sala, S.M.R. 1974. *Lexicon nominum semiticorum quae in papyris graecis in Aegypto repertis ab anno 323 a.Ch.n. usque ad annum 70 p.Ch.n. laudata reperiuntur*. Milan.

Samuel, A. E. 1965. "Year 27 = 30 and 88 B.C.." *CE* 40, 376–400.

————. 1970. "The Greek element in the Ptolemaic bureaucracy," in *Proceedings of the Twelfth International Congress of Papyrology*, Ann Arbor, 13–17 August, 1968, 443–53. American Studies in Papyrology 7. Toronto.

Sandbach, F. H. 1972. *Menandri reliquiae selectae*. Oxford Classical Text. Oxford.

Sauneron, S. 1950. "La ville de S3ḫbw." *Kêmi* 11, 63–72.

————. 1952. "Le 'chancelier du dieu' dans son double rôle d'embaumeur et de prêtre d'Abydos." *BIFAO* 51, 137–71.

————. 1954. "La manufacture d'armes de Memphis." *BIFAO* 54, 7–12.

————. 1957. *Les prêtres de l'ancienne Egypte*. Bourges, France.

————. 1959. *Les songes et leur interprétation*. Paris.

————. 1960. "Un document égyptien relatif à la divinisation de la reine Arsinoe II." *BIFAO* 60, 83–109.

Sauneron, S., and Yoyotte, J. 1952. "La campagne nubienne de Psammétique II et sa signification historique." *BIFAO* 50, 157–207.

Schäfer, H. 1902/3. "Ein Phönizier auf einem ägyptischen Grabstein der Ptolemäerzeit." *ZÄS* 40, 31–34.

Scheurleer, R.A.L. 1974. "Quelques terres cuites memphites." *Revue d'égyptologie* 26, 83–99.

————. 1978. "Ptolemies," in *Das ptolemäische Ägypten*, ed. H. Maehler and V. M. Strocka, 1–7. Mainz am Rhein, FRG.

Schnebel, M. 1925. *Die Landwirtschaft im hellenistischen Ägypten*. Münchener Beiträge zur Papyrusforschung und antiken Rechtsgeschichte 7. Munich.

Scholl, R. 1983. *Sklaverei in den Zenonpapyri. Eine Untersuchung zu den Sklaventer-mini, zum Sklavenerwerb und zur Sklavenflucht.* Trierer historische For-schungen 4. Trier, FRG.

————. 1985. "ΙΕΡΟΔΟΥΛΟΙ im griechisch-römischen Agypten." *Historia* 34, 466–92.

Schönborn, H.-B. 1976. *Die Pastophoren im Kult der ägyptischen Götter.* Beiträge zur klassischen Philologie 80. Meisenheim am Glan, FRG.

Segal, J. B. 1983. *Aramaic Texts from North Saqqâra.* Egypt Exploration Society. Texts from excavations 6, ed. T.G.H. James. London.

Segall, B. 1966. *Tradition und Neuschöpfung in der frühalexandrinischen Kleinkunst.* Winckelmannsprogramm der archäologischen Gesellschaft zu Berlin 119/120. Berlin.

Seidl, E. 1962. *Ptolemäische Rechtsgeschichte.* 2d ed. Ägyptologische Forschungen 22. Hamburg and New York.

————. 1965. "La preminente provisione succesoria del figlio maggiore nel diritto del papiri." *Rendiconti dell' Istituto Lombardo. Accademia di scienze e lettere* 99, 185–92.

Sethe, K. 1904–16. *Hieroglyphische Unkunden der griechisch-römischen Zeit*, II, *His-torisch-biographische Urkunden aus der Zeit der makedonischen Könige und Urkun-den des ägyptischen Altertums*, ed. G. Steindorff. Leipzig.

————. 1913. *Sarapis und die sogenannten "katochoi" des Sarapis.* Abhandlungen der königlichen Gesellschaft der Wissenschaften zu Göttingen. Phil.-hist. Klasse, N.S. 14.6. Berlin.

————. 1916. *Zur Geschichte und Erklärung der Rosettana.* Nachrichten von der königlichen Gesellschaft der Wissenschaften zu Göttingen. Phil.-hist. Klasse. Berlin.

————. 1920. *Demotische Urkunden zum ägyptischen Bürgschaftsrechte vorzüglich der Ptolemäerzeit*, mit einer rechtsgeschichtlichen Untersuchung von J. Partsch. Abhandlungen der phil.-hist. Klasse der sächsischen Akademie der Wissen-schaften 32. Leipzig.

Shore, A. F. 1979. "Votive objects from Dendera in the Graeco-Roman period," in *Orbis Aegytiorum speculum: Glimpses of Ancient Egypt. Studies in Honour of H. W. Fairman*, ed. J. Ruffle, G. A. Gaballa, and K. A. Kitchen, 138–60. Warminster, Eng.

Shore, A. F., and Smith, H. S. 1960. "A demotic embalmer's agreement: Pap. dem. B. M. 10561." *Acta Orientalia* 25, 277–94.

Simpson, W. K. 1957. "A running of the Apis in the reign of ʿAḥa and passages in Manetho and Aelian." *Orientalia* 26, 139–42.

Skeat, T. C. 1953. "The last days of Cleopatra." *JRS* 43, 98–100.

————. 1954. *The Reigns of the Ptolemies.* Münchener Beiträge zur Papyrusfor-schung und antiken Rechtsgeschichte 39. Munich.

————. 1974. *Greek Papyri in the British Museum (Now in the British Library)*, VII. *The Zenon Archive.* London.

Skeat, T. C., and Turner, E. G. 1968. "An oracle of Hermes Trismegistos at Saqqâra." *JEA* 54, 199–208.

Smelik, K.A.D., and Hemelrijk, E. A. 1984. " 'Who knows not what monsters demented Egypt worships?' Opinions on Egyptian animal worship in Antiquity as part of the ancient conception of Egypt," in *Aufstieg und Niedergang der römischen Welt*, ed. H. Temporini and W. Haase, II.17, 1852–2357. Berlin and New York.

Smith, H. S. 1968. "A note on amnesty." *JEA* 54, 209–14.

———. 1972. "Dates of the obsequies of the mothers of Apis." *Revue d'égyptologie* 24, 176–87.

———. 1974. *A Visit to Ancient Egypt: Life at Memphis and Saqqara (c.500-30 B.C.)*. Warminster, Eng.

———. 1976. "Preliminary report on excavations in the Sacred Animal Necropolis: Season 1974–1975." *JEA* 62, 14–17.

———. 1979. "Varia Ptolemaica," in *Orbis Aegyptiorum speculum: Glimpses of Ancient Egypt. Studies in Honour of H. W. Fairman*, ed. J. Ruffle, G. A. Gaballa, and K. A. Kitchen, 161–66. Warminster, Eng.

———. 1981. "A l'ombre d'Auguste Mariette." *Bulletin de Centenaire*. Supplement to *BIFAO* 81, 331–39.

Smith, H. S., and Jeffreys, D. G. 1977. "The Sacred Animal Necropolis, North Saqqâra 1975–76." *JEA* 63, 20–28.

———. 1978. "The North Saqqâra temple town survey: Preliminary report 1976–77." *JEA* 64, 10–21.

———. 1979. "The Anubieion, North Saqqâra: Preliminary report 1977–78." *JEA* 65, 17–29.

———. 1980. "The Anubieion, North Saqqâra: Preliminary report 1978–79." *JEA* 66, 17–27.

———. 1981. "The Anubieion, North Saqqâra: Preliminary report 1979–80." *JEA* 67, 21–23.

Smith, H. S., Jeffreys, D. G., and Málek, J. 1983. "The survey of Memphis, 1981." *JEA* 69, 30–42.

Smith, H. S., and Tait, W. J. 1983. *Saqqâra Demotic Papyri*, I. Egypt Exploration Society, Texts from excavations 7, ed. T.G.H. James. London.

Snodgrass, A. M. 1967. *Arms and Armour of the Greeks*. London.

Société archéologique d'Alexandrie. N.d. *Les bas-reliefs de Kom el Chougafa*. Munich.

Sottas, H. 1927. "Notes complémentaires sur le décret en l'honneur de Ptolémée IV." *Revue de l'Egypte ancienne* 1, 230–42.

Soukiassian, G. 1983. "Les autels 'à cornes' ou 'à acrotères' en Egypte." *BIFAO* 83, 317–33.

Speidel, M. 1977. *Studien zu den Militärgrenzen Romes*, II. Bonn.

Spiegelberg, W. 1896. *Rechnungen aus der Zeit Setis I (circa 1350 v.Chr.)*. 2 vols. Strassburg.

———. 1901a. "Buchis, der heilige Stier von Hermonthis." *APF* 1, 339–42.

———. 1901b. "Über einem Titel des Apisstieres." *RecTrav* 23, 197–98.

———. 1903. "Ein demotischer Papyrus in Innsbruck." *RecTrav* 25, 4–6.

———. 1904. *Die demotischen Denkmäler*. Catalogue général des antiquités égyptiennes du musée du Caire. Leipzig.

———. 1906. "Ägyptologische Randglossen zu Herodot." *ZÄS* 43, 84–96.

———. 1908. *Die demotischen Inschriften*. Catalogue général des antiquités égyptiennes du musée du Caire. Strassburg.

————. 1909. *Die demotischen Papyrus der musées royaux du Cinquantenaire.* Brussels.

————. 1915. *Die sogenannte demotische Chronik des pap. 215 der Bibliothèque nationale zu Paris.* Leipzig.

————. 1920. "Ein Bruchstück des Bestattungsritual der Apisstiere." *ZÄS* 56, 1–33.

————. 1925. *Beiträge zur Erklärung des neuen dreisprachigen Priesterdekretes zu Ehren des Ptolemaios Philopator.* SBAW (1925) 4. Munich.

————. 1926. "The god Panepi." *JEA* 12, 34–37.

————. 1928. *Neue Urkunden zum ägyptischen Tierkultus.* Sitzungsberichte der bayerischen Akademie der Wissenschaften. Philos.-philol. und hist. Klasse 1928, 3. Munich.

————. 1929a. "Die stele 119C des Louvre und das *Tyrion stratopedon.*" *Kêmi* 2, 107–12.

————. 1929b. *Aus einer ägyptischen Zivilprozessordnung der Ptolemäerzeit.* ABAW (1929), N.S. 1. Munich.

————. 1932. *Demotische Inschriften und Papyri.* Catalogue général des antiquités égyptiennes du musée du Caire. Berlin.

Spiegelberg, W., and Otto, W. 1926. *Eine neue Urkunde zu der Siegesfeier des Ptolemaios IV. und die Frage der ägyptischen Priestersynoden.* SBAW (1926) 2. Munich.

Stead, M. 1981. "The high priest of Alexandria and all Egypt," in *Proceedings of the XVI International Congress of Papyrology,* ed. R. S. Bagnall, G. M. Browne, A. E. Hanson, and L. Koenen, 411–18. American Studies in Papyrology 23. Chico, Calif.

————. 1984. "A model to facilitate the study of temple administration in Graeco-Roman Egypt," in *Atti del XVII congresso internazionale di papirologia,* III, 1045–52. Naples.

Stern, L. 1884. "Die biligue Stele des Châhap." *ZÄS* 22, 101–109.

Stricker, B. H. 1943. "La prison de Joseph." *Acta Orientalia* 19, 101–37.

Świderek, A. 1961. "Hellénion de Memphis—la recontre de deux mondes." *Eos* 51, 55–63.

————. 1975. "Sarapis et les Hellénomemphites," in *Le monde grec. Hommages à Claire Préaux,* ed. J. Bingen, G. Cambier, and G. Nachtergael, 670–75. Brussels.

Tannery, P. 1893. *Recherches sur l'histoire de l'astronomie ancienne.* Paris.

Tarn, W. W. 1936. "The Bucheum stele: A note." *JRS* 26, 187–89.

Teixidor, J. 1972. "Bulletin d'épigraphie sémitique." *Syria* 49, 413–49.

————. 1977. *The Pagan God: Popular Religion in the Greco-Roman Near East.* Princeton, N.J.

Thissen, H.-J. 1966. *Studien zum Raphiadekret.* Beiträge zur klassischen Philologie 23. Meisenheim am Glan, FRG.

Thissen, H.-J. 1980. "Ein demotischer Brief aus dem Anoubieion." *Serapis. The American Journal of Egyptology* 6, 165–69.

Thomas, J. D. 1984. "SB VI 9016 and the career of Iulius Lysimachus." *ZPE* 56, 107–12.

Thompson, D. B. 1964. "ΠΑΝΝΥΧΙΣ." *JEA* 50, 147–63.

Thompson, D. B. 1973. *Ptolemaic Oinochoai and Portraits in Faience: Aspects of the Ruler Cult*. Oxford.

Thompson (Crawford), D. J. 1983. "Nile grain transport under the Ptolemies," in *Trade in the Ancient Economy*, ed. P. Garnsey, K. Hopkins, and C. R. Whittaker, 64–75, 190–92. London.

Thompson-Crawford, D. J. 1984. "The Idumaeans of Memphis and the Ptolemaic politeumata," in *Atti del XVII congresso internazionale di papirologia*, 1069-75. Naples.

Thompson, D. J. 1987. "Ptolemaios and 'The Lighthouse': Greek culture in the Memphite Serapeum." *PCPhS* 213 (N.S. 33), 105–21.

———. 1988. "The high priests of Memphis under Ptolemaic rule." in *Pagan Priests*, ed. J. A. North and W. M. Beard. London.

Toomer, G. J. 1972. "The mathematician Zenodorus." *GRBS* 13, 170–92.

Toutain, J. 1916. "Le culte de taureau Apis à Memphis sous l'empire romain." *Muséon* 33, 193–202.

Traunecker, Cl. 1979. "Essai sur l'histoire de la xxixe dynastie." *BIFAO* 79, 395–436.

Turner, E. G. 1968. *Greek Papyri: An Introduction*. Oxford.

———. 1974. "A commander-in-chief's orders from Saqqâra." *JEA* 60, 239–42.

———. 1975a. "The Greek papyri," in *Proceedings of the XIV International Congress of Papyrologists, Oxford, 24–31 July 1974*, 250–51. London.

———. 1975b. "Four obols a day men at Saqqara," in *Le monde grec. Hommages à Claire Préaux*, ed. J. Bingen, G. Cambier, and G. Nachtergael, 573–77. Brussels.

Übel, F. 1962. "Ταραχὴ τῶν Αἰγυπτίων." *APF* 17, 147–62.

———. 1968. *Die Kleruchen Ägyptens unter den ersten sechs Ptolemäern*. Abhandlungen der deutschen Akademie der Wissenschaften zu Berlin. Klasse für Sprachen, Literatur und Kunst (1968) 3. Berlin.

van Groningen, B. A. 1933. *Aristoteles. Le second livre de l'Economique*. Leiden.

Van 't Dack, E. 1949. "Recherches sur l'administration du nome dans la Thébaide au temps des Lagides." *Aegyptus* 29, 1–44.

———. 1952. "Notes concernant l'épistratégie ptolémaique." *Aegyptus* 32, 437–50.

———. 1962. "Postes et télécommunications ptolémaïques." *CE* 37, 338–41.

———. 1980. *Reizen, expedities en emigratie uit Italië naar Ptolemaïsch Egypte*. Mededelingen van de koninklijke Academie voor Weteschappen, Letteren en schone Kunsten van België. Klasse der Letteren 42.4. Brussels.

Vélissaropoulos, J. 1980. *Les nauclères grecs. Recherches sur les institutions maritimes en Grèce et dans l'Orient hellénisé*. Geneva and Paris.

Vercoutter, J. 1958. "Une épitaphe royale inédite du Sérapéum. (Contribution à l'histoire des Apis et du Sérapéum de Memphis.)" *MDAIK* 16, 333–45.

———. 1962. *Textes biographiques du Sérapéum de Memphis: Contribution à l'étude des stèles votives du Sérapéum*. Bibliothèque de l'école des hautes études. 4th section. Paris.

Vergote, J. 1959. *Josèphe en Egypte. Genèse chap. 37–50 à la lumière des études égyptologiques récentes*. Orientalia et Biblica Lovaniensia 3. Louvain.

Vermeule, C. C. 1962. "A Ptolemaic contribution box in Boston." *ANS Museum Notes* 10, 77–80, plates xv–xvi.

Vernus, P. 1978. *Athribis. Textes et documents relatifs à la géographie, aux cultes, et à l'histoire d'une ville du Delta égyptien à l'époque pharaonique.* Bibliothèque d'étude 74. Cairo.

Vidal-Naquet, P. 1967. *Le bordereau d'ensemencement dans l'Egypte ptolémaique.* Papyrologica Bruxellensia 5. Brussels.

Viedebantt, O. 1913. "Hin," *RE* 8, 1644–49. Stuttgart.

Vleeming, S. P. 1983. "Een kleine demotische Wijsheidstekst (P. Louvre 2414)," in *Schrijvend Verleden,* ed. K. R. Veenhof, 382–86. Leiden.

Volten, A. 1955. "Die moralischen Lehren des demotischen Pap. Louvre 2414," in *Studi in memoria di I. Rosellini,* II, 271–80. Pisa.

von Arnim, J. 1923. *Stoicorum veterum fragmenta,* II, *Chrysippi fragmenta logica et physica.* Leipzig and Berlin.

von Bergmann, E. 1880. "Varia." *ZÄS* 18, 49–53.

von Fritz, K. 1949. "Pankrates." *RE* 8.3, 611–19. Stuttgart, FRG.

von Woess, F. 1923. *Das Asylwesen Ägyptens in der Ptolemäerzeit, und die spätere Entwicklung.* Münchener Beiträge zur Papyrusforschung und antiken Rechtsgeschichte 5. Munich.

Vos, R. L. 1978. "Demotic mummy labels containing permission to bury," *Pap. Lugd. Bat.* 18, Appendix G, 260–67. Leiden.

———. 1984. "Het Balsemingsritual van Apisstier (P. Vindob. 3873)." Dissertation. Amsterdam.

Wagner, G. 1971. "Inscriptions grecques du temple de Karnak (1)." *BIFAO* 70, 1–38.

Walbank, F. W. 1967. *A Historical Commentary on Polybius,* II. Oxford.

———. 1979. *A Historical Commentary on Polybius,* III. Oxford.

———. 1984a. Review of E. E. Rice, *The grand Procession of Ptolemy Philadelphus* (Oxford, 1983). *LCM* 9, 52–54.

———. 1984b. "Monarchies and monarchic ideas," in *Cambridge Ancient History,* VII.1, 2d ed., ed. F. W. Walbank, A. E. Astin, M. W. Frederiksen, and R. M. Ogilvie, 62–100. Cambridge, London, New York, New Rochelle, and Sydney.

———. 1985. *Selected Papers: Studies in Greek and Roman History and Historiography.* Cambridge, Eng.

Wallace, S. L. 1938. *Taxation in Egypt from Augustus to Diocletian.* Princeton, N.J.

Ware, C. F. 1931. "Ethnic communities," in *Encyclopedia of the Social Sciences,* V, 607–13. Macmillan and Free Press, New York.

Weil, H. 1879. *Un papyrus inédit de la bibliothèque de M. Ambroise Firmin-Didot. Nouveaux fragments d'Euripide et d'autres poètes grecs.* Paris.

Weingärtner, D. G. 1969. *Die Ägyptenreise des Germanicus.* Papyrologische Texte und Abhandlungen 11. Bonn.

Weitzmann, K. 1959. *Ancient Book Illustrations.* Martin Classical Lectures 16. Cambridge, Mass.

———. 1970. *Illustrations in Roll and Codex: A Study of the Origin and Method of Text Illustration.* Princeton, N.J.

Welles, C. Bradford. 1970. "The role of Egyptians under the first Ptolemies," in *Proceedings of the Twelfth International Congress of Papyrology, Ann Arbor, 13–17 August 1968*, 505–10. American Studies in Papyrology 7. Toronto.

Wheatley, P. 1969. *City as Symbol*. An inaugural lecture delivered at University College, London, 20 November 1967. London.

Whitehorne, J.E.G. 1980. "New light on temple and state in Roman Egypt." *Journal of Religious History* 11, 218–26.

Wilcken, U. 1903. "Referate und Besprechungen. Papyrus-Urkunden." *APF* 2, 116–47.

———. 1905. "Der Traum des Königs Nektanabos," in *Mélanges Nicole*, 579–96. Geneva.

———. 1917. "Die griechischen Denkmäler vom Dromos des Serapeums von Memphis." *JDAI* 32, 149–203.

———. 1927. *Urkunden der Ptolemäerzeit (ältere Funde)*, I, *Papyri aus Unterägypten*. Berlin and Leipzig.

———. 1957. *Urkunden der Ptolemäerzeit (ältere Funde)*, II, *Papyri aus Oberägypten*. Berlin.

Wildung, D, 1969. *Die Rolle ägyptischer Könige im Bewusstsein ihrer Nachwelt*, I, *Posthume Quellen über Könige ersten vier Dynastien*. Münchener Ägyptologische Studien 17. Berlin.

———. 1977a. *Imhotep und Amenhotep: Gottwerdung im alten Ägypten*. MAS 36. Munich and Berlin.

———. 1977b. *Egyptian Saints: Deification in Pharaonic Egypt*. New York.

Will, E. 1979. *Histoire politique du monde hellénistique (323–30 av.J.-C.)*, I. 2d ed. Nancy, France.

———. 1982. *Histoire politique du monde hellénistique (323–30 av.J.-C.)*, II. 2d ed. Nancy, France.

Willems, H. O. 1983. "A description of Egyptian kinship terminology in the Middle Kingdom c. 2000-1650 B.C." *Bijdragen tot de Taal-, Land- en Volkenkunde* 139, 152–68.

Williams, R. J. 1976. "Some fragmentary demotic wisdom texts," in *Studies in Honor of George R. Hughes*, 263–71. Studies in Ancient Oriental Civilization 39. Chicago.

Willis, R. 1975. *Man and Beast*. St. Albans, England.

Winter, E. 1978. "Die Herrscherkult in den ägyptischen Ptolemäertempeln," in *Das ptolemäische Ägypten*, ed. H. Maehler and V. M. Strocka, 147–58. Mainz am Rhein, FRG.

———. 1982. "Philensis-Dekrete." *Lexikon der Ägyptologie* 4, 1027–28. Wiesbaden, FRG.

Wipszycka, E. 1961. "The *Dorea* of Apollonios the dioeketes in the Memphite nome." *Klio* 39, 153–90.

———. 1965. *L'industrie textile dans l'Egypte romaine*. Wrokław, Warsaw, and Cracow.

Witkowski, S. 1911. *Epistulae privatae graecae quae in papyris aetatis Lagidarum servantur*. 2d ed. Leipzig.

Wörrle, M. 1977. "Epigraphische Forschungen zur Geschichte Lykiens, I." *Chiron* 7, 43–66.

Wuthnow, H. 1930. *Die semitischen Menschennamen in griechischen Inschriften und Papyri des vorderen Orients.* Leipzig.

Yoyotte, J. 1959a. "Les Bousiris et les Abousir d'Egypte (Toponymie de l'Egypte pharaonique I)." *GLECS* 8, 57–60.

———. 1959b. "Nectanébo II comme faucon divin." *Kêmi* 15, 70–74.

———. 1959c. "Encore Sakhebou." *Kêmi* 15, 75–79.

———. 1961. "Etudes géographiques." *Revue d'égyptologie* 13, 75–105.

———. 1962. "Etudes géographiques." *Revue d'égyptologie* 14, 75–111.

———. 1963. "Etudes géographiques." *Revue d'égyptologie* 15, 87–119.

———. 1967/68. "Religion de l'Egypte." *Annuaire de l'école pratique des hautes études,* Vᵉ section, *Résumés de conférences et travaux* 75, 101–11.

———. 1969. "Bakthis: Religion égyptienne et culture grecque à Edfou," in *Religions en Egypte hellénistique et romaine: Colloque de Strasbourg 16-18 mai 1967,* 127–41. Travaux du centre d'études supérieures spécialisé d'histoire des religions de Strasbourg. Paris.

———. 1972. "La localisation de Ouenkhem." *BIFAO* 71, 1–10.

———. 1973. "Reflexions sur la topographie et la toponymie de la région du Caire." *Bulletin de la société française d'égyptologie* 67, 27–35.

———. 1980/81. "Héra d'Héliopolis et le sacrifice humaine." *Annuaire de l'école pratique des hautes études,* Vᵉ section, *Résumés de conférences et travaux* 89, 31–102.

———. 1982/83. "L'Amon de Naukratis." *Revue d'égyptologie* 34, 129–36.

Zauzich, K.-Th. 1968. *Die ägyptische Schreibertradition in Aufbau, Sprache und Schrift der demotischen Kaufverträge aus ptolemäischer Zeit.* 2 vols. Ägyptologische Abhandlungen 19. Wiesbaden, FRG.

———. 1977. "Zwei übersehene Erwähnungen historischer Ereignisse der Ptolemäerzeit in demotischen Urkunden." *Enchoria* 7, 193.

———. 1978a. Review of J. D. Ray, *The Archive of Ḥor. Enchoria* 8, 95–100.

———. 1978b. "Neue Namen für die Könige Harmachis und Anchmachis." *GM* 29, 157–58.

———. 1980. "Lesonis," in *Lexicon der Ägyptologie 3,* 1008–1009. Wiesbaden, FRG.

Zgusta, L. 1970. *Neue Beiträge zur kleinasiatischen Anthroponymie.* Prague.

Zivie, A.-P. 1984. "La localisation de la tombe du grand-prêtre de Ptah Ptahemhat-ty." *Revue d'égyptologie* 35, 200–203.

Zucker, F. 1937. *Doppelinschrift spätptolemäischer Zeit aus der Garnison von Hermopolis Magna.* APAW (1937) 6. Berlin.

———. 1938. "Nachträge zur 'Doppelinschrift spätptolemäischer Zeit aus der Garnison von Hermopolis Magna.'" *Aegyptus* 18, 279–84.

Zuntz, G. 1956. "Interpretation of a Menander fragment." *Proceedings of the British Academy* 42, 209–46.

INDEX

INDEX

Apis (*cont.*)

203, 206; and Mnevis bull, 122, 123, 186,
196; mummification, 17n, 18, 123, 199–
200, 262; and Nile, 196; nomenclature,
195; Octavian and, 266, 273; Opening of
the Mouth, 201, 210; oracles, 254, 274;
priests, 17n, 142, 145, 191, 195, 202,
203–4, 206, 236; provenance, 195, 274–
75, 284–96 *passim*; Ptolemies and, 114,
115, 119, 121–22, 123, 124, 197; resurrection, 115, 201–2, 210, 235; in Roman
period, 271, 273–75; sacrifices to, 70n,
274; sarcophagi, 192, 202, 203, 205, 206,
285, 288; seal of, 268; shrine of, 28, 119,
212; sources on, 191–92, 284–96; stall (*sēkos*), 9, 10, 14, 18, 190, 192, 197, 199,
206; statue, 28, 196, 212, Plate i; stelae,
193, 284–96 *passim*; vaults, 27, 117, 150,
192, 193, 203–7, 274, 284–96 (dedications in, 191, 193, 205); workers, 193,
203–6. See also *archentaphiastēs*; Osiris–
Apis; Sarapis
Apis, mother-of- (Isis cow), 9, 10, 194;
burials, 22–23, 192, 193; double names,
144; feeding of, 17n; stall, 9, 18, 197;
temple of, 30–31, 193; vaults, 22–23, 30,
204–5; workers, 204
Apis calves, 29, 194, 197, 246–47
Apollo, 96n, 100, 104. See also Qos
Apollonieion, 101
Apollonios (*dioikētēs*), 36, 49, 52; and cults,
115, 147–48; Fayum estate, 36, 39, 44,
48, 49, 51 (*see also* Zenon Archive); influence, 63–64; livestock, 43, 44–45; Memphite estates, 36, 37n, 40, 41n, 51–52, 72;
orchards and gardens, 39–40; textile interests, 36, 47, 53–54, 58, 72, 226. See
also Zenon; Zenon Archive
Appollonios (son of Glaukias), 245–52;
army career, 223–24, 248–51; Dionysios
and, 246, 256–57, 263; dreams, 247, 263;
Egyptianization, 213, 247; *katochē*, 91,
214, 218, 219, 223, 246; literary interests,
259–61, 262–63; as messenger, 237, 241,
246, 248; personality, 246–47, 251–52,
261; as police informer, 251–52; and Ptolemaios, 223–24, 225, 246, 250; and
Thauēs, 245, 247
apomoira (tax), 77, 131, 137
Apries, palace of, 14, 16, 98

Arabia, imports from, 79, 83
Arabs, 44, 79, 86–87, 97, 211, 270, 276
arakos (chickling), 41, 267
Aramaic language, 44, 84, 98, 109; dockets
and seals, 16; papyri, 46, 73, 85; tombstones, 98
archentaphiastēs (embalmer-in-chief), 111,
156n, 186, 187, 196, 198, 279
archiereus, use of term, 111
architects, priest-, 204
archives. See Embalmers'; Hor, Archive of;
Sarapieion; Undertakers'; Zenon Archive
area of city, 32–33
Ariston (*stratēgos*), 187
Aristonikos (general), 120n, 121
[Aristotle], *Oikonomika*, 107
Armant. See Hermonthis
arms industry, 65–66, 72
army, 4, 276, 279; Apollonios in, 223, 248–
51; drill master, 73–74; immigrants in,
82, 85, 86, 88, 100, 104; pay, 248; priest
commanders, 113; Roman period, 269–
70; size, 37; soldiers, 234, 264; supply,
57, 57n, 72. See also bodyguard; garrison; mercenaries
Arrian, 106
Arsinoe II, 118; cult of, 63, 110, 126–27,
131–32, 136n, 137, 142; priests of, 131–
32, 142, 143
Arsinoe III, 118
Arsinoeia (festival), 63
Arsinoeia (temples), 126, 131
Arsinoite nome, 2, 87, 126n, 190, 227–28,
269. See also Fayum
Artaxerxes III (king of Persia), 106n, 193
arts and crafts, 65–70, 81, 93, 267, 268. See
also tradesmen
Ashmunein. See Hermoupolis
Asklepieion, 22–23, 24–25, 33, 39n, 40,
140, 209; undertakers in, 167, 186, 188
Asklepios, god of Epidauros, 210, 260. See
also Imhotep
Astarte, cult of, 26, 89–91, 116, 220; and
begging, 232; as consort of Ptah, 209;
Isis-, 88–89; Phoenician elements, 218,
221, 230, 265; shrine in Sarapieion, 22–
23, 29, 90, 91, 215, 217, 218, 229; syncretism, 104, 221, 265; temple relief, 90–
91, 92, Plate iv; valley temple of, 9, 10,
13, 14, 90, 98, 99

326

DATE DUE

NOV 2 6 1990		
JUL 2 8 1994		
JUN 0 9 2001		